Reading Made Easy

A Guide to Teach Your Child to Read

Valerie Bendt

Reading Made Easy: A Guide to Teach Your Child to Read

Revised Third Edition, ISBN: 1-882514-70-X

Text copyright 2000, 2001, 2004 by Valerie Bendt

Illustration Copyright 2000, 2001, 2004 by Valerie Bendt, lessons 3-96

Illustration Copyright 2000, 2001, 2004 by Michelle (Bendt) DeMicco, lessons 97-108

Cover Photography: Robin Hendershot

Front Cover Photo: Randall Bendt and his mommy (Valerie).

Back Cover Photo: Randall Bendt

Copy Editors: Bruce Bendt and Cathy Pierce

Acknowledgements: The author would like to thank the Washington County Free Library in Hagerstown, Maryland for use of the photograph of the first library book wagon in America. (See page 494.)

Originally Published by Bendt Family Ministries - Visit our website at **www.ValerieBendt.com**

This edition published by Greenleaf Press – Visit us on the web at www.GreenleafPress.com

Internet: www.greenleafpress.com
3761 Highway 109N, Unit D
Lebanon, Tennessee 37087
615-449-1617

I dedicate this book to my six children.
Teaching each of you to read has been one
of the most rewarding experiences in my life.
Thanks!

Table of Contents

Introduction

Learning to read encompasses a number of disciplines. If the child is overburdened with repetitious drills and boring primers, he will build animosity towards reading. It is desirous for the child to not only develop his reading skills but to cultivate a *love for reading*. This love for reading will carry him through his life-long educational endeavors.

Phonics is a device to be used when figuring out a difficult word or when combining sounds to form a word. Phonics is a tool for teaching reading. It should not become so complicated a study that it hinders the child from learning to read. Most children benefit from phonetic, sequential instruction; however, some children process information differently. Often these different types of learners benefit from alternate methods. Children tend to utilize a number of strategies when learning to read. Letter decoding is only one strategy that they employ. This is probably the most effective tool; however, it is not the only one at their disposal. We read so we may derive some meaning from the text. Therefore, children will often make use of the context of the printed material in order to decipher specific words. Their ability to predict the events in a story will confirm their phonetic choices. For instance, given the following sentence: *Bill jumped on his b____ and pedaled up the hill.* Given the first letter cue and the predictability of the sentence, a child could easily fill in the missing word. If the text is dull, boring, devoid of meaning, the child will be forced to rely on phonetic knowledge alone to decipher the material. The true essence of reading -- to derive meaning from the text, is missing.

When teaching my daughter, Mandy, to read, I used her keen interest in the *Little House on the Prairie* books to inspire her. Each day I would read to her from one of the *Little House* books, and then I would make up sentences pertaining to the day's reading for her to read aloud to me. These sentences were created with words and vocabulary Mandy was capable of reading. I would often introduce new words and phonetic combinations, which I would teach her in order that she may read the sentences I devised. Mandy was always eager to learn new words so she could read about Laura, Mary, and their bulldog, Jack. She was making excellent progress; however, I began to feel anxious about her reading, because we were not following a phonics manual. So, I continued with the sentences about Laura and Mary, but I also had her read phonetically controlled exercises from a phonics manual. One of the sentences she read was about a boy named Jack. It was obvious this was a sentence about a boy named Jack not a dog named Jack like in the Laura and Mary stories. After reading the sentence correctly, Mandy said, "This isn't *our* Jack. Is it?" I said, "No this is just a sentence about a boy named Jack." Then she looked at me with a puzzled expression and said, "Well, if this isn't about *our* Jack, then why are we reading it?" I responded with, "You are right. Why are we reading it?"

So we continued reading real sentences based on real stories. I realized the exercises in the phonics manual, although phonetically controlled and written at her level, did not *encourage* her to read. While the passages provided decoding practice, they did nothing to further enrich her life. Reading is not merely a skill to be learned. If it is to be conveyed as a meaningful event, it should have meaning right from the start. To a child, and anyone for that fact, the essence of what he reads is paramount. Don't expect boring primers to produce enthusiastic readers.

Once a child discovers the mystery of decoding words, he can almost learn to read by himself. Maturity as well as interest plays a large role in this significant advancement. How parents value reading determines a child's attraction for reading. Parental involvement and absorption in reading relates directly to the child's ability and desire to learn to read. It is obvious then that you, the parents, supply the key ingredients necessary for effective reading instruction. You provide the crucial elements of love, nurture, and example that can never be furnished by any reading manual.

Reading Made Easy is comprised of sequential lessons. The manual is based on seven points to assist you in beckoning your child into the world of reading.

Point 1

Reading Made Easy serves as both a parent/teacher guide and a student text.

Portions of the guide printed in this special font are to be read aloud by the parent to the child. Preparation time is minimal as the dialogue is fully scripted.

(The material contained in the parentheses offers the parent additional information about the lesson and should not be read aloud.)

Portions of the text to be read by the child are printed in this LucidaSansSchool font published by Portland State University. We highly recommend their Italic Handwriting Series. The Italic Handwriting Series workbooks can be ordered from:

Portland State University, Continuing Education Press, P.O. Box 1394, Portland, Oregon 97207

1-800-547-8887, ext. 4891

Point 2

It is not necessary for a child to know all of the letters of the alphabet and the sounds they make before beginning to read. Listening games are used to acquaint the child with the vowel and consonant sounds. The consonants include all of the letters of the alphabet excluding the vowels, which are a, e, i, o, and u. Mastery of individual words such as *hat, dig,* and *cup*, will be taught relatively early in the program. However, we do not want to dissuade the child from reading by having him recite such vacuous lines as:

Jan had a pan.

Jan had a tan pan.

Jan had a tan pan in the sand.

You will notice not only is the material above senseless and devoid of meaning; it is a tongue twister. This type of irrelevant composition is found in many beginning readers.

Several years ago when teaching my son Robert to read, he dutifully read the following passage from one of his readers:

Hop Fred, hop, hop, hop.

After successfully reading this line, Robert replied, "Mom, people don't really talk like that." Even this five year old found the book senseless, an insult to his intelligence. Robert had already developed an ear for good literature as many interesting and well-written stories were read to him daily. He knew this reader didn't contain real stories but only words pretending to be stories.

You may wonder how your child will successfully master beginning words without endless repetition as used in the majority of readers. This is easy. Games and activities provide a fun and effective means of developing beginning reading skills. Children joyfully participate in games and activities, whereas they find reading laborious and dull in the early stages.

You will find reproducible pages in the Appendix of this manual that will enable you to make effective, simple games and activities. Allowing you to make these games and activities serves at least two purposes. First, it keeps this manual at a reasonable cost. Second, if you make the items both you and your child will take greater pleasure in using them. I have found if we invest our time in an endeavor we value it more.

Point 3

We have employed the use of various print clues to aid the child in his recognition of the sounds made by specific letters or made by combinations of letters. For example, the short *a* sound as in *cat* is shown in a gray print thus representing a soft sound. The child will learn to recognize this as the short *a* sound each time he sees it depicted in this manner. This type of print clue is utilized for the short sounds made by all of the vowels.

a e i o u

a - cat   e - wet   i - pig   o – hop   u - cup

The long vowels are distinguished from the short vowels, and from the rest of the text, as they appear in a bold, black print thus representing a strong or hard sound. For example, the long *a* sound as in *cake* is shown in a bold, black print. The child will learn to recognize the long vowel sounds each time he sees them depicted in this manner.

a e i o u

a – cake   **e** - heat   **i** - bike   **o** – hope   **u** - cute

A dotted letter will represent silent letters such as *e* as in *cake*. Each time this print is used, the child learns the letter makes no sound.

c **a** k ⬚

The traditional method for marking short and long vowels and silent letters is as such:

cắt cākȩ cōạt

This tends to clutter the text and distract the child.

Often two or more letters combine to create a specific sound. For example, *ar* as in *car* or *or* as in *born*. As you teach these and other letter combinations, your child will readily recognize them within a given word as they are circled.

c(ar) b(or)n

Sight words such as *was*, *said*, and *they* will be underlined in black. We feel the print clues we have introduced will enable the child to quickly experience success in reading. The following sentence includes some of the print clues used in this manual.

Can you (fl)ap your wings and s(ing)?

As the child progresses through the lessons, these print clues are removed from the text.

Point 4

Our desire is to develop the child's reading abilities, so he can read independently. This is a gradual process that will take a significant step when the child is asked to read an entire sentence on his own. The sentence to be read by the child corresponds with a picture in the lesson. We will call this sentence and picture a *story*, although a very brief story. Discussion questions will follow which the child can answer as he looks at the picture. The picture offers additional material about the story, since the child's reading abilities allow him to read only a brief part of the story. Gradually these short stories will include several sentences.

In selected lessons, you will be asked to write a particular sentence from the story on index cards, one word per card. You will be instructed to use crayons to create print clues similar to those we have used in this manual. For example, the word *hid* can be written with a black crayon and a gray crayon as shown here. (You can substitute colored pencils or markers for crayons.)

The word *snake* can be represented as shown below with the letter *a* darkened and the letter *e* written in a dotted fashion. Sounds such as *sn* can be circled in gray. (We have actually put a very thin black circle around the *sn* sound. We suggest you use a gray crayon rather than a black crayon to draw the circles, as the lighter color does not break up the word as much. In the manual we will refer to our circles as *gray*.)

$$snake$$

You will then place the cards in proper sequence on the table to form the sentence. The child will read each word as you point to it. Then he will read the sentence again, more quickly, for better comprehension. Next, you will mix the cards, or allow the child to mix the cards, and then have him place them on the table in proper order and read the sentence again. At this point you will be instructed to discuss uppercase letters, specifically those used at the beginning of a sentence and at the beginning of a person's name. You will also explain a period is generally used at the end of a sentence. Later, we will discuss the use of question marks, exclamation points, quotation marks, and commas. The rules concerning uppercase letters and periods will help the child to place the cards in proper sequence to form the sentence. We have found children benefit from this hands-on interaction with the story.

We suggest you purchase a bag of thin rubber bands and several packages of blank index cards. Once you have finished with the index cards for a particular sentence, label the first card of the sentence with the appropriate lesson number, wrap a rubber band around the cards, and place the cards in a shoebox. The sentences can be used at any time for review. It is exciting for the child to look into a full shoebox and see all the sentences he has read.

Please us this index card activity in a manner that works best for your child. As your child progresses in the manual, you may want to alter this activity. After a time you may decide to write the cards without using the print clues, or you may choose to only use the index cards occasionally, especially for lessons the child finds more challenging. However, it is important that you go over the material in this portion of the lesson with the child, as much information about capitalization and punctuation is covered here.

Point 5

It is obvious the stories the child is capable of reading initially are rather brief. We want to foster a zeal for literature as well as an ability to read. For this reason, we are employing a unique technique to enable the child to both participate in the reading process and enjoy a longer story containing more detail. I have written a story called *Gideon's Gift*. This story is divided into twelve chapters. As you near the end of the reading manual, you will read the chapters aloud to your child. One chapter is included in each lesson. The story spans the last twelve lessons of the manual. After you have read a chapter from the story, the child will be asked to read a simplified version of that chapter. The sentences used in the simplified version are written on an appropriate reading level for the child and are printed with the print clues I mentioned previously.

Following this reading exercise, the child is given a picture depicting a scene from the chapter. He is then asked questions about the picture, which further strengthens his observation and thinking skills. As he listens to the chapter being read and then reads a simplified version of that chapter, he is able to participate in the story in a meaningful way. As the lessons progress, naturally the sentences become more difficult, and he is asked to read more sentences in each lesson.

As you continue teaching your child to read, you may want to develop simple reading exercises based on a book you are reading aloud. You can control the vocabulary by using words familiar to the child. (You will find a list of appropriate books and suggestions for developing further reading lessons from these books in the Appendix.) Read a passage or a chapter from the book you are reading aloud, compose a few simple sentences about the passage or chapter, and write them on index cards, one or two words per card. Lay the cards on the table in the proper order, and assist your child in reading the sentences. Mix the cards, and allow him to put them in proper order. Work on only one sentence at a time. As mentioned beforehand, you can use crayons to create print clues similar to those we have used in this manual. Wrap a rubber band around the cards for each sentence, and place them in a shoebox.

Point 6

The child will copy selected sentences from the lesson, which he has read aloud. He will copy them from your written model or the model provided in the manual.

To simplify this process, the child may write directly under your written model as shown below.

The snake hid in the grass.

It is necessary for you to write large enough and with sufficient spaces between letters and words to accommodate the child's immature abilities. We suggest you initially use unlined paper or paper with very large lines. Some children benefit from using marking pens, as they flow more easily than pencils. As stated previously, we highly recommend the *Italic Handwriting Series* from Portland State University.

If your child finds the writing exercises too laborious, disregard them until a future lesson when his motor skills are more fully developed. The child may wish to draw a picture to accompany his sentence. In most of the lessons we have provided a simple picture for the child to copy or trace that relates to the story he has read. These drawing exercises have been a highlight of the children who have tested this reading program. Before beginning the writing or drawing exercises, it is important to instruct the child in the proper way to hold a pencil. This information is covered in the *Italic Handwriting Series*. I cannot stress enough the importance of this seemingly small detail. We allowed one of our children to hold a pencil incorrectly when he was young, thinking he would soon outgrow this error. We were wrong. (Thankfully he types extremely well now!)

Point 7

Once the child has attained a certain degree of mastery with his reading, he can be encouraged to dictate his own sentences to you. These can be used for additional reading exercises. Some assistance will be needed for him to read certain words. You can use this opportunity to expose him to new words and new phonetic combinations. Later, the child can dictate entire stories to you and use them as his personal readers. He may also want to illustrate his stories. I was thrilled to see how each of my children's reading abilities skyrocketed as they used their own stories as readers.

I want to offer some additional ideas for making readers. Several parents using *Reading Made Easy* shared these wonderful ideas with me. These parents made simple little books from the patterns found in *Dinah Zike's Big Book of Books and Activities*. Then they wrote the sentences and stories their children dictated in these little books. The children then illustrated their readers. Another mom said she wrote the stories from the lessons in *Reading Made Easy* in the little books and allowed her daughter to add her own illustrations. She also wrote practice words from the lessons in the little books. These little books offer another fun way for the children to review material between lessons. Many homeschool catalog companies carry *Dinah Zike's Big Book of Books and Activities*. You will find easy-to-make projects in Dinah's book to enhance all subject areas.

More information can be found in the Appendix under the heading "Encouraging Your Child to Write His Own Readers."

Reading Made Easy is comprised of 108 lessons. A typical schedule is to have the child cover three lessons each week. Following this plan a child can complete the manual within a typical school year consisting of 36 weeks. <u>Material should be reviewed between lessons.</u> You may choose to have the child review a previous lesson in its entirety, review stories from previous lessons, or review some of the words and sentences you have written on index cards. This gives the child sufficient time to absorb the information you have taught before moving on to new material. It is necessary for the child to master the words from the previous lesson before advancing to the next lesson.

<u>It is important that you realize you are teaching the child, not the book.</u> Use the book in a manner as best serves the needs of the child. Take more time if necessary. Include lots of time for review. In a few years it will not matter if your child learned to read in 36 weeks or 72 weeks. The goal is to teach your child to read and to inspire him to *love* to read. If your child struggles with the beginning lessons, he is probably not ready to begin formal reading instruction. If your child is having difficulty at any point in the manual, it is best to put the manual aside for a few days or even weeks, and spend your time reading good books to him. Then later, take up the manual and review some of the earlier lessons. If this is successful, continue at a comfortable pace.

It is evident this manual fosters more than an ability to read. It helps the child to develop decoding skills, comprehension skills, thinking skills, composition skills, a love for literature and much more.

Have fun with your child and remember -- learning lasts a lifetime!

Pronunciation Key

Gray letters represent short vowel sounds. Bold black letters represent long vowel sounds. Dotted letters represent silent letters. Rings are drawn around letter combinations. When three letters appear together as in *aaa* or *mmm* this is to show that the sound can be drawn out.

letters	letter sounds	sample words
a	aaa	cat
p	p	cap ✓
m	mmm	Sam
t	t	bat
g	g	bag ✓
n	nnn	man
d	d	had
l	lll	ball
c	(c)	topic
r	rrr	fair
s	sss	glass
b	b	crib
f	fff	cliff
h	h	hush
a	a	cake
w	w	now
z	zzz	buzz
v	vvv	have
y	y	yes

j	j	jet
ck	c	back
k	k	bake
i	iii	pig
i	i	bike
nd	nnnd	land
o	ooo	hot
ng	nnng	bang
nk	nnnk	bank
ll	lll	hill
x	cks	fox
(sh)	sh	ship
o	o	hope
(st)	st	mist
e	e	heat
(qu)	kw	queen
(pl)	pl	play
(bl)	bl	black
e	eee	wet
(cl)	cl	clap
(sl)	sl	slap
(fl)	fl	flag

gl	gl	glad
dr	dr	dress
cr	cr	crab
fr	fr	frog
gr	gr	grass
pr	pr	prick
br	br	brass
tr	tr	trick
sc	sc	scat
sk	sk	skate
sm	sm	smoke
sp	sp	spill
sn	sn	snake
sw	sw	sweet
o	o	snow
ow	ow	cow
u	uuu	cub
oo	oo	cook
oo	oo	boot
ing	ing	sing
y	i	fly
or	or	corn

(all)	all	ball
(ink)	ink	drink
(oy)	oy	boy
(oi)	oi	boil
(ou)	ou	house
(ar)	ar	car
(ing)	ing	taking/hopping
(ph)	fff	phone
(ch)	ch	chip/patch
k n	nnn	knee
igh	i	night
(th)	th	thick/this
(aw)	aw	saw
(alk)	alk	talk
(er)	er	her
(ir)	ir	bird
(ur)	ur	turn
ed	d	played/looked
ed	eeed	landed
u	u	cute
y	e	baby
(c)	sss	face

Lessons at a Glance

Lesson 1: Informal introduction to the alphabet.

Lesson 2: Introduction to the *aaa* sound as in *cat*.

Lesson 3: Learn to distinguish between words containing the *aaa* sound as in *cat* and other sounds.

Lesson 4: Introduction to the sounds made by the letters *p* as in *cap* and *m* as in *Sam*.
Introduction *ap* and *am*.

Lesson 5: Introduction to the sounds made by the letters *t* as in *bat* and *g* as in *bag*.
Introduction to *at* and *ag*.

Lesson 6: Introduction to the sound made by the letters *n* as in *man* and *d* as in *had*.
Introduction to *an* and *ad*.

Lesson 7: The following letter combinations will be written on index cards: *ap, am, at, ag, an,* and *ad*.
Introduction to the sound made by the letters *l* as in *ball* and *c* as in *topic*.

Lesson 8: Introduction to the sound made by the letters *r* as in *fair* and *s* as in *glass*.

Lesson 9: Read words for the first time. Read the following words on index cards: *cap, lap, map, nap, rap, sap, gap,* and *tap*.

Lesson 10: Introduction to the sound made by the letters *b* as in *crib, f* as in *cliff,* and *h* as in *hush*.

Lesson 11: Introduction to the bold *a* sound as in *cake*.
Read a sentence for the first time: *a cat sat.*
Introduction to the use of periods.

Lesson 12: Introduction to the sound made by the letters *w* as in *now* and *z* as in *buzz*.
Introduction to the first sight word *has*.

Lesson 13: Introduction to the sound made by the letter *v* as in *have*.
Introduction to the sight word *the*.

Lesson 14: Introduction to the sound made by the letters *y* as in *yes* and *j* as in *jet*.

Lesson 15: Introduction to the use of uppercase and lowercase letters.
Introduction to the sight word *was*.
The sentence to be read is written on index cards for the first time.

Lesson 16: Review lesson

Lesson 17: Introduction to the *c* sound as in *back*. Read words on index cards such as *back, sack, rack,* etc.
Introduction to the use of silent letters. The letter *k* is silent in *back*.

Lesson 18: Review the bold *a* sound as in *cake* and read words with the bold *a* sound such as *tail, fail, hail,* etc.

Lesson 19: Introduction to the sight word *is*.
Read additional words with the bold *a* sound such as *cave, wave, pave,* etc.
Explain that names begin with an uppercase letter.

Lesson 20: Introduction to the sound made by the letter *k* as in *bake*.
Read additional bold *a* words such as *cake, bake, lake,* etc.

Lesson 21: Introduction to the sight word *to*.
Introduction to bold *a* words containing silent *y* such as *pay, say, way,* etc.

Lesson 22: Review lesson

Lesson 23: Introduction to the *iii* sound as in *pig*. Read words such as *dip, zip, sit,* etc.

Lesson 24: Introduction to the word *his*.
Review *iii* words.

Lesson 25: Introduction to the sight word *I*.
Introduction to the bold *i* sound as in *bike*.

Lesson 26: Introduction to the sight word *you*.
Introduction to the *nd* sound as in *land*.

Lesson 27: Introduction to the *ooo* sound as in *hot*.
Read words with the *ooo* sound such as *mop, top, hot,* etc.

Practice reading words written in conventional type for the first time in the copy work.

Lesson 28: Review lesson

Lesson 29: Read words with the *ang* sound such as *bang, sang, hang,* etc.
Introduction to the sight word *do.*
Introduction to the use of question marks.
Sentences take on a new aspect as they are now referred to as *stories* and they have a title.

Lesson 30: Read words with the *ong* sound such as *long, song, gong,* etc.
Read words with the *ank* sound such as *bank, Hank, rank,* etc.
Read *iii* words with *ll* sound such as *hill, fill, kill,* etc.

Lesson 31: Introduction to the *cks* sound made by the letter *x* as in *fox.*
Read words with *s* added to the end such as *dogs.*
Introduction to the sight word *what.*

Lesson 32: Read bold *i* words with *nd* sound such as *find, wind, mind,* etc.
Play *Sight Word Bingo* game.

Lesson 33: Introduction to the *sh* sound as in *ship.*
Introduction to the sight word *they.*

Lesson 34: Review lesson

Lesson 35: Make *Sight Word Worm.*
Introduction to the bold *o* sound as in *hope.*

Lesson 36: Play *Sight Word Memory* game.
Introduction to the sight word *are.*
Read part one of a four-part story.

Lesson 37: Introduction to the sight words *said* and *of.*
Introduction to the *st* sound as in *mist.*
Introduction to the use of quotation marks.
Read part two of a four-part story.

Lesson 38: Introduction to the sight word *put.*
Read part three of a four-part story.

Lesson 39: Play *Sight Word Bingo.*
Read part four of a four-part story.

Lesson 40: Review lesson

Lesson 41: Play *Sight Word Bingo*
Introduction to the bold *e* sound as in *heat.*

Lesson 42: Review lesson

Lesson 43: Introduction to the *kw* sound as in *queen.*
Introduction to the sight word *does.*

Lesson 44: Introduction to the *pl* sound as in *play.*

Lesson 45: Introduction to the *bl* sound as in *black.*
Introduction to the sight words *some* and *come.*

Lesson 46: Review lesson

Lesson 47: Introduction to the sight word *from.*
Introduction to the *eee* sound as in *wet.*

Lesson 48: Introduction to the *cl* sound as in *clap.*
Introduction to the *sl* sound as in *slap.*

Lesson 49: Introduction to the sight word *want.*
Introduction to the *fl* sound as in *flag.*
Introduction to the *gl* sound as in *glad.*

Lesson 50: Introduction to the *dr* sound as in *dress.*
Introduction to the *cr* sound as in *crab.*

Lesson 51: Introduction to the sight words *could, should,* and *would.*
Introduction to the *fr* sound as in *frog.*
Introduction to the *gr* sound as in *grass.*
Lesson 52: Review lesson
Lesson 53: Introduction to the *pr* sound as in *prick.*
Introduction to the *br* sound as in *brass.*
Introduction to the *tr* sound as in *trick.*
Lesson 54: Introduction to the sight words *there* and *where.*
Introduction to the *sc* sound as in *scat.*
Introduction to the *sk* sound as in *skate.*
Lesson 55: Introduction to the *sm* sound as in *smoke.*
Introduction to the *sp* sound as in *spill.*
Lesson 56: Introduction to the sight word *your.*
Introduction to the *sn* sound as in *snake.*
Introduction to the *sw* sound as in *sweet.*
Lesson 57: Introduction to the bold *o* sound as in *snow.*
Introduction to the *ow* sound as in *cow.*
Lesson 58: Introduction to the *uuu* sound as in *cub.*
Lesson 59: Introduction to the *oo* sound as in *cook.*
Introduction to the *oo* sound as in *boot.*
Lesson 60: Review lesson
Lesson 61: Introduction to the sight word *one.*
Introduction to the *ing* sound as in *sing.*
Lesson 62: Introduction to the bold *i* sound made by the letter *y* as in *fly.*
Lesson 63: Introduction to the *or* sound as in *corn.*
Lesson 64: Review lesson
Introduction to the use of exclamation points.
Lesson 65: Introduction to the sight word *many.*
Introduction to the *all* sound as in *ball.*
Lesson 66: Introduction to the *ink* sound as in *drink.*
Lesson 67: Introduction to the *oy* sound as in *boy.*
Introduction to the *oi* sound as in *boil.*
Lesson 68: Introduction to the sight word *who.*
Introduction to the *ou* sound as in *house.*
Lesson 69: Introduction to the sight words *Mama* and *Papa.*
Introduction to the *ar* sound as in *car.*
Lesson 70: Review lesson
Lesson 71: Introduction to the sight words *people* and *that.*
Introduction to the *ing* sound as in *sing* when added to a word such as *taking* and *hopping.*
Introduction to the *fff* sound made by the letters *ph* as in *phone.*
Introduction to the use of commas.
Lesson 72: Introduction to the *ch* sound as in *chip* and *patch.*
Lesson 73: Introduction to the *nnn* sound made by the letters *kn* as in *knee.*
Lesson 74: Introduction to the sight words *with* and *water.*
Introduction to the bold *i* sound as in *night.*
Lesson 75: Introduction to the *th* sound as in *thick* or *this.*
Lesson 76: Review lesson
Lesson 77: Introduction to the sight word *two.*

Introduction to the *aw* sound as in *saw*.

Lesson 78: Introduction to the *alk* sound as in *talk*

Lesson 79: Review lesson

Lesson 80: Introduction to the sight word *once*.

Introduction to the *er* sound as in *her*.

Introduction to the *er* sound as in *her* when it is added to the end of words such as *taller*.

Lesson 81: Introduction to the *ir* sound as in *bird*.

Lesson 82: Review lesson

Lesson 83: Introduction to the sight words *caught* and *taught*.

Introduction to the *ur* sound as in *turn*.

Lesson 84: Introduction to the sight word *new*.

Introduction to the *ed* ending as in *played* and *looked*.

Introduction to the *ed* ending as in *landed*.

Lesson 85: Introduction to the bold **u** sound as in *cute*.

Lesson 86: Introduction to the bold **e** sound made by the letter *y* as in *baby*.

Lesson 87: Introduction to the sight word *learn*.

Introduction to the *s* sound made by the letter *c* as in *face*.

Lesson 88: Review lesson

Lesson 89: Review lesson

Lesson 90: Review lesson

Lesson 91: Review lesson

Lesson 92: Review lesson

Lesson 93: Review lesson

Lesson 94: Review lesson

Lesson 95: Review lesson

Lesson 96: Review lesson

Lesson 97: Introduction to the sight words *Gideon*, *Hannah*, and *Sarah*.

Begin a twelve-part story called *Gideon's Gift*.

Gideon's Gift chapter one: "Gideon Wants to Read"

Lesson 98: Introduction to the sight words *brother* and *mother*.

Gideon's Gift chapter two: "Lessons for Gideon"

Lesson 99: Introduction to the sight words *Benjamin* and *Rachel*.

Gideon's Gift chapter three: "The First Lesson"

Lesson 100: Introduction to two-syllable words such as such as *wagon*, *dragon*, *button*, etc.

Gideon's Gift chapter four: "Going to Town"

Lesson 101: Practice reading words written in conventional type for the first time in the lesson itself.

Gideon's Gift chapter five: "News from Town"

Lesson 102: Introduction to the sight words *Anna*, *work*, and *cover*.

Gideon's Gift chapter six: "A Trip to the Book Wagon"

Lesson 103: Introduction to the sight word *four*.

Gideon's Gift chapter seven: "The Book Wagon at Last"

Lesson 104: Introduction to the sight word *money*.

Gideon's Gift chapter eight: "Mama's Story"

Lesson 105: Introduction to the sight words *aunt* and *about*.

Gideon's Gift chapter nine: "Going to see the Doctor"

Lesson 106: *Gideon's Gift* chapter ten: "Gideon Gives a Lesson"

Lesson 107: Introduction to the sight word *very*.

Gideon's Gift chapter eleven: "Gideon's Essay"

Lesson 108: Introduction to the sight word *shoe*. *Gideon's Gift* chapter twelve: "Gideon Gets a Letter"

Teaching Tips

In the beginning your child will be asked to read simple words. If he reads the words in a stilted or slow manner, have him read each word again more quickly so the words flow naturally. Eventually he will be asked to read sentences. Since this will probably be slow and stilted at first, have him read each sentence again for better flow and comprehension. In other words, each sentence should be read and then read again before moving on to a new sentence. Once the entire story has been read, you the parent should read the story aloud to the child. Often the child spends so much energy trying to read that he misses the meaning of the story. This method will allow the child to relax and enjoy the story. Afterwards, you will ask the child questions provided in the manual to help him with his reading comprehension skills.

If your child shows a strong interest in learning to read, but you feel he is too young, you might try limiting him to one or two lessons per week instead of the usual three lessons. I did this with my four-year-old son, Randall. I included lots of review between the lessons. If he became frustrated or disinterested, we postponed the lessons for a few days. I felt it was better to quit working before he became overwhelmed. Sometimes I divided the more difficult lessons in half. He enjoyed doing schoolwork like his older siblings, as long as it wasn't too much. In the beginning, I didn't require him to do any of the writing exercises. He did, however, enjoy drawing the pictures suggested for each lesson. This technique works well for young children who are ready to learn to read, or it can also be used with older children who need to take a slower approach for one reason or another. Remember, no matter what curriculum you are using, you should always tailor it to fit the child.

Some children are distracted if there is too much text on a page. To remedy this situation, fold a piece of 8 ½" x 11" blank paper in half lengthwise, and place it over the side of the page not being read. This works well for the pages where the text is printed in two columns. For the pages where the text runs all the way across the page, try placing the folded paper horizontally across the page, directly under the line being read.

As mentioned on page 10 under **Point 4**, you will write one or more sentences from each lesson on index cards, one word per card. You will lay these cards in sequential order, and then have the child read the sentences. Next, you will mix the cards from the sentences, or allow the child to mix the cards, and have him put them in the proper order to make the sentences again. (You will work with one sentence at a time.) As an additional exercise, my son Randall enjoyed making his own sentences from the words on the index cards. Sometimes he would rearrange the words so the sentence asked a question. For example, the sentence may have read: *I can buzz in my hive.* He would rearrange it to read: *Can I buzz in my hive?* Of course the punctuation would be incorrect, as we were missing the question mark, and the first word would not be capitalized. We discussed these things. It was exciting to me to see how he would make new sentences. His reading was strengthened and so were his thinking skills. He liked for me to close my eyes while he made new sentences. Then I would open my eyes, and he would read me the sentence he had made. He also enjoyed making nonsense sentences. He would read these and laugh. For example he would rearrange the sentence above to read: *I can hive in my buzz.* Additional exercises such as these offer the child extra practice with reading, while keeping things light and easy.

When teaching my daughter Mandy to read, I found it best to write all of her reading exercises on index cards. She had a vision problem, which made it difficult for her to focus on one word at a time when there were many words on a page. Writing her sentences on index cards, one word per card, enabled her to concentrate her efforts on just one word. She eventually progressed to reading sentences on a page, if I used a blank sheet of paper or an index card to underscore the sentence she was reading. If your child seems to have a similar problem, you may wish to write additional sentences from the lessons in this manual on index cards. One or more sentences will already be selected for use with this index card activity, but you may find it helpful to include more. This activity is also an excellent way for the child to review material between lessons.

Things to do Ahead of Time

✓ Purchase a box of crayons by lesson 7.

✓ Purchase a large package of 3" x 5" index cards by lesson 7. (Bulk packages are available at office supply stores.)

✓ Purchase a package of rubber bands to group index cards together by lesson 7.

✓ Make a copy of the *Sight Word Bingo* game boards found on pages 508 and 509 by lesson 32.

✓ Make a copy of the *Sight Word Worm* pattern found on page 510 by lesson 35

✓ Purchase colored construction paper. Cut 60 construction paper circles using the pattern for the *Sight Word Worm* body. (These are the small circles.) You may want to cut ten circles from six different colors. Cut four construction paper circles using the pattern for the *Sight Word Worm* head. (These are the large circles.) Do this by lesson 35. (You will not need all of the construction paper circles for lesson 35, but it is good to have them made in advance. You will probably make four *Sight Word Worms* during the course of the program. The sight words are written on the small circles. Each worm can be made up of approximately 14 small circles for the body and one large circle for the head. There are 56 sight words in all. Six of these are proper names. By cutting 60 circles, you will have four extra circles.)

✓ Purchase two sheets of poster board. You will glue each *Sight Word Worm* onto a half a sheet of poster board. Do this by lesson 35. (Here again, you will not need both sheets of poster board for this lesson. You will make only one *Sight Word Worm* in lesson 35. You will make additional *Sight Word Worms* in future lessons, but it is helpful to have the materials in advance.)

✓ Make a copy of the *Sight Word Bingo* game boards found on pages 511 and 512 by lesson 39.

Lesson 1

Materials: reading manual, large lined or unlined paper, marking pen or pencil, and a stack of your child's favorite books.

Instructions: In today's lesson, you will introduce the child to the letters of the alphabet in a very informal manner. The child is not expected to totally absorb this information. It is only a simple introduction.

In the first fourteen lessons, you will be teaching the letter sounds not the letter names. If your child already knows the letter names this is fine. However, it is not necessary to teach the letter names initially. This will be covered in a future lesson.

Please note the portions of the dialogue printed in this special font are to be read aloud to the child.

(The text contained in the parentheses offers you additional information about the lesson and should not be read aloud. You will find much of this information is repetitious. If you put the reading manual aside for a time, for one reason or another, you will find you may need this information when you resume with the lessons. After a while, you will automatically skip over the information you no longer need. Be careful, however, for occasionally we will add new information that is important for you to read. New information will follow the word *Note* in bold letters.)

Dialogue: Today we are going to begin an adventure. We are going to learn about letters and the sounds they make. You already know a lot about letters, because you see them all around. You see them on cereal boxes, you see them on signs, and you see them in the books we read.

Where else have you seen letters? Name some letters you know. Letters are used to make words, and words are used to make sentences. You know this

because we read sentences from our books everyday.

Can you find one of your favorite books? Let's look at the letters on the cover. Can you name the letters?

What are the letters in your name? Let's print these letters on paper. Now let's make a sentence about you. How about, "_____ is _____ years old." These are words and they are made up of letters. (Point to the individual words in the sentence as you read.)

This is a sentence. (Run your finger under the sentence.)

A sentence is usually made up of several words. Soon you will be able to read words all by yourself. After that you will be able to read sentences. Then you will be able to read stories and then an entire book.

Which book would you like for me to read to you now? Okay, that's a good book.

(After reading the book with the child, ask him what part he liked best. Encourage as much dialogue as possible about the story. Each day you should end the lesson by reading a book to the child. This reinforces that reading is important, enjoyable, and meaningful.)

Lesson 2

Materials: reading manual

Instructions: The letters we call vowels consist of *a, e, i, o,* and *u.* The consonants include all the other letters of the alphabet. In this lesson, you will help your child to hear the short vowel sound for the letter *a* within simple words. This letter makes the *aaa* sound as in *cat.* Slowly run your finger under the letters as you sound out each word. This will help your child to understand we read from left to right.

Emphasize the *aaa* sound in each word. Be careful not to add a vowel sound at the end of each consonant such as *uh.* For example, the word *bat* is pronounced *b aaa t.* Not *b(uh) aaa t(uh).* Try to blend the letters together as you say each word. Slowly pronounce each word without saying it in a choppy fashion. Remember, do not read aloud the text in the parentheses. This is for your information.

Dialogue: Today we are going to learn about the letter that makes the *aaa* sound (as in *cat*). (Point to the letter below.) This letter says *aaa* (as in *cat*). Did you notice the letter is gray?

a

Say *aaa* (as in *cat*) as I point to the letter.

Can you think of some words that begin with the *aaa* sound? (Allow the child time to respond.) Some more words that begin with the *aaa* sound are *apple, Adam, alligator,* and *attic.* (Emphasize the *aaa* sound in each word.)

There are lots of words that have the *aaa* sound. Sometimes the *aaa* sound comes in the middle of a word. Listen to these words that have an *aaa* sound in the middle. (Point to each letter as you sound out

the words. Emphasize the *aaa* sound, as in *cat*, in each word.)

m a t	b a g	t a p
b a t	c a b	c a p
	r a g	

Do you hear the *aaa* sound in each of these words? I will read them again.

Next, I want you to close your eyes and listen very carefully. I'm going to say some words that have the *aaa* sound, but I'm also going to say some words that have a different sound.

If you hear the *aaa* sound as I say a word, clap your hands. If you hear a different sound as I say a word, sit quietly. Remember, listen carefully for the *aaa* sound and clap if you hear it.

(Say the following words slowly then pause for a response. Emphasize the *aaa* sound in each word.)

b a g	r a p	m a d
p i g	j a c k	s a d
b o x	p a c k	r a t
d u c k	p a t	d e s k
t a g	b u g	f a t

24

Very good!

(If the child has difficulty with this exercise, go over each word again, telling him if it has the *aaa* sound or not. For example, "I hear an *aaa* sound in the word *mad*, but I do not hear an *aaa* sound in the word *pig.*")

Now we are going to play another listening game. You can keep your eyes open this time. (Do not show the child the words in the manual.)

I'm going to say two words. One word is an *aaa* word. That is, it has the *aaa* sound. The other word will have a different sound. Tell me which word has the *aaa* sound. (Be sure to emphasize the vowel sound as you say each word.)

I will do the first words for you. The words are *cap* and *cup*. (Repeat.) I hear an *aaa* sound in *cap*. I do not hear an *aaa* sound in *cup*.

(Say each pair of words twice. Remind the child periodically he is listening for the *aaa* sound.)

1. cap   cup

2. bat   bit

3. hit   hat

4. pin   pan

(Emphasize the *aaa* sound in *pan* even though it may seem a little awkward.)

5. back   buck

6. bed   bad

7. bath   Beth

8. fin   fan

(Emphasize the *aaa* sound in *fan* even though it may seem a little awkward.)

9. dish   dash

10. splash   splish

You did very well. Now let's read a book together. Try to listen for two or three words with the *aaa* sound as I read.

(Review the listening exercises before moving on to the next lesson. A typical schedule is to complete three lessons per week with review between lessons. If your child has trouble with this lesson even after review, move on to lesson 3. If your child still experiences difficulty with hearing the "*aaa*" sound within words after completing lesson 3, then move on to lesson 4. The material in lesson 4 is presented in a different manner, which may be easier for your child to understand.)

Lesson 3

Materials: reading manual

Instructions: First, you will review the *aaa* sound as in *cat* with the child. Next you will read the words in the list to the child while emphasizing the *aaa* sound. (See the list below.) This exercise will help the child distinguish between words that contain the *aaa* sound and words that do not. Remember, do not read aloud the text in the parentheses. This is for your information.

Dialogue: In the last lesson, we talked about words that have the *aaa* sound (as in *cat*). Today we are going to learn about some more words that have the *aaa* sound. Look at the letter below. Say *aaa* as I run my finger under the letter. Say *aaa* once more. Notice the letter is gray.

a

Good. Now I will say two words. One word will have the *aaa* sound, and the other word will have a different sound. Tell me which word has the *aaa* sound. (Emphasize the *aaa* sound and say each pair of words twice. Do not show the child the words in the manual.)

I will do the first words for you. The words are *mat* and *met*. (Repeat.) I hear an *aaa* sound in *mat*. I do not hear an *aaa* sound in *met*. (Periodically remind the child he is listening for the *aaa* sound.)

1. m a t   m e t

2. d a b   d u b

3. r u g   r a g

4. p o t   p a t

5. w a g   w i g

6. l a g   l o g

7. b a g   b e g

8. c u t   c a t

9. r a t   r u t

10. s p i t   s p a t

Now it's getting easier to hear the *aaa* sound isn't it? Look at the pictures below. I will tell you what each picture represents. As I name each picture, tell me if it has an *aaa* sound.

26

(Key for pictures)

cap	pig	map
frog	bed	gas
cat	duck	flag

Choose a book for us to read. Try to find at least one word with the *aaa* sound (as in *cat*) on each page. I will make a list of the words we find with the *aaa* sound.

(Review the listening exercises before moving on to the next lesson. A typical schedule is to complete three lessons per week with review between lessons. If your child experiences trouble with lesson 2 and lesson 3 even after review, try moving on to lesson 4. Some children have difficulty with hearing the "*aaa*" sound within a word. Often these children will pick up this concept later.)

Lesson 4

Materials: reading manual

Instructions: Today you will introduce the child to the sounds for the letters *p* and *m*. To isolate the sound for the letter *p*, say a word that ends in *p* such as *cap*. Say it again in a natural manner, listening carefully. Lift the *p* sound from the word *cap*. This is the way you should pronounce the letter *p* in isolation.

By utilizing this method, you do not add a vowel sound such an *uh* to the letter *p*. We do not want to say *puh*. To isolate the sound for the letter *m*, say the word S*am*. Lift the *mmm* sound from the word *Sam*.

At this point, we are teaching the letter sounds only, not the letter names. If your child already knows the letter names of course this is fine, but it is more important at this point for him to know the sounds the letters make than the names of the letters.

The child will review the *aaa* sound (as in *cat*). He will learn to combine the *aaa* sound with the letters *p* and *m* to make the *ap* and *am* sounds. Remember, do not read aloud the text in the parentheses. This is for your information.

Dialogue: Today you will learn two new letters and the sounds they make. Look at the letter below. The sound made by this letter is *p* (as in *cap*). (Say the letter sound, not the letter name. Run your finger under the letter as you say its sound, moving from left to right.)

p

Very good! Let's say *p* again. (Point to letter once more.)

The next letter you will learn makes the *mmm* sound (as in *Sam*). (Say the letter sound, not the letter name. Run your finger under the letter as you say its sound, moving from left to right.)

m

Sometimes we make this sound when we eat something that tastes good. Say *mmm* again. (Point to letter once more.)

Look at the letters below that you learned. I will say the sounds the letters make. As I say the sound, point to the correct letter.

p   m

Now let's try to put two letters together and see how they sound. You already learned this letter says *aaa* (as in *cat*). (Run your finger under the letter below.)

a

And this letter says *p* (as in *cap*). (Run your finger under the letter.)

p

If we put *aaa* with *p*, we have *aaap*. (Run your finger under each letter as you say the letter sounds.)

a p

Say *aaap* as I run my finger under the letters. Good, now try it again.

You also learned this letter says *mmm* (as in *Sam*).

m

If we put *aaa* with *mmm*, we have *aaammm*. (Run your finger under each letter as you say the letter sounds.)

a m

Repeat *aaammm* as I run my finger under the letters. Good, now try it again.

Look at the letters below. I will say the sounds the letters make. Point to the correct letters as I say them.

a m   a p

Now you say the sounds the letters make as I point to them. Good! Try it once more.

Let's read a book together. Try to listen for some words that have the *mmm* or *p* sounds.

(Review the letter sounds before moving on to the next lesson. A typical schedule is to complete three lessons per week with review between lessons.)

Lesson 5

Materials: reading manual

Instructions: Today you will introduce the child to the sounds for the letters *t* and *g*. The letter *t* makes the sound heard at the end of the word *bat*. To correctly pronounce the letter sound, lift the *t* sound from the word *bat*. Remember, do not add the vowel sound to the letter *t*. We do not want *tuh*.

Next, you will introduce the sound made by the letter *g* at the end of the word *bag*. To correctly pronounce the letter sound, lift the *g* sound from the word *bag*. Remember we are not looking for *guh*.

The child will review the *aaa* sound (as in *cat*). He will learn to combine the *aaa* sound with the letters *t* and *g* to make the *at* and *ag* sounds. He will also review the combinations *ap* and *ag*. Remember, do not read aloud the text in the parentheses. This is for your information.

Dialogue: Today you will learn two new letter sounds. Look at the letter below. This letter makes the *t* sound (as in *bat*). (Say the letter sound, not the letter name. Run your finger under the letter as you say the sound it makes.)

t

Repeat the *t* sound as I point to the letter. Very good!

The next letter you will learn today makes the *g* sound (as in *bag*). (Say the letter sound, not the letter name. Run your finger under the letter as you say the sound it makes.)

g

Repeat the *g* sound as I point to the letter. Very good!

Look at the letters below. Which letter says *t*? Which letter says *g*? (Say the letter sounds not the letter names.)

g   t

Look at the letters below. Which letter says *g*? Which letter says *mmm*? Which letter says *t*? Which letter says *p*? (Say the letter sounds not the letter names.)

m   g   p   t

Look at the letter below. What sound does this letter make? (*aaa* as in *cat*.)

a

Look at the letter below. You learned this letter today. What sound does this letter make? (*t* as in *bat*.)

t

We can put *aaa* with *t* to make the *aaat* sound. (Run your finger under each letter as you say the letter sounds.)

a t

Repeat the *aaat* sound as I point to the letters. Very good! Try it again.

Look at the letter below. You learned this letter today. What sound does this letter make? (*g* as in *bag*.)

g

We can put *aaa* with *g* to make the *aaag* sound. (Run your finger under each letter as you say the letter sounds.)

a g

Repeat the *aaag* sound as I point to the letters. Very good! Try it again

Look at the letters below. Which letters say *aaag*? Which letters say *aaat*?

a g   *a* t

Look at the letters below. Which letters say *aaag*? Which letters say *aaat*? Which letters say *aaap*? Which letters say *aaam*?

a p   *a* g   *a* m   *a* t

As I point to the letters, tell me what they say.

Let's read a book together now. You've worked hard today.

(Review the letter sounds before moving on to the next lesson. A typical schedule is to complete three lessons per week with review between lessons.)

Lesson 6

Materials: reading manual

Instructions: You will introduce the child to two new letters and the sounds they make. The letter *n* makes the sound as heard at the end of the word *man*. To correctly pronounce the letter sound, lift the *nnn* sound from the word *man*. Remember, do not add a vowel sound to the letter *n*. We do not want *nuh*.

Next, you will introduce the sound made by the letter *d* at the end of the word *had*. To correctly pronounce the letter sound, lift the *d* sound from the word *had*. Remember, we are not looking for *duh*.

The child will review the *aaa* sound (as in *cat*). He will learn to combine the *aaa* sound with the letters *n* and *d* to make the *an* and *ad* sounds. He will also review the following combinations: *ap, am, at,* and *ag*.

Dialogue: Today you will learn two new letters and the sounds they make. Look at the letter below. The letter makes the *nnn* sound (as in *man*). (Say the letter sound, not the letter name. Run your finger under the letter as you say the sound it makes.)

n

Repeat the *nnn* sound as I point to the letter. Good, say it again.

Look at the letter below. This letter makes the *d* sound (as in *had*). (Say the letter sound, not the letter name. Run your finger under the letter as you say the sound it makes.)

d

Repeat the *d* sound as I point to the letter. Good, say it again.

Look at the letters at the top of the next page. Which letter makes the *nnn* sound? Which letter makes the *d* sound?

d n

Look at the letter below. What sound does this letter make? (*aaa* as in *cat.*)

a

Look at the letters below. We can put *aaa* with *nnn* to make the *aaannn* sound. (Run your finger under the letters as you say the letter sounds.)

a n

Repeat the *aaannn* sound as I point to the letters. Very good! Try it again.

We can put *aaa* with *d* to make the *aaad* sound. (Run your finger under the letters as you say the letter sounds.)

a d

Repeat the *aaad* sound as I point to the letters. Very good! Try it again.

Look at the letters below. Point to the correct letter as I say the sound it makes. (Say letter sounds in random order.)

n m t d p g

Look at the letters again. Say the sound each letter makes as I point to it. Very good! You have remembered a lot of letter sounds.

Look at the next group of letters. Which letters say *aaag*? Which letters say *aaannn*? Which letters say *aaat?* Which

letters say *aaap*? Which letters say *aaammm*? Which letters say *aaad*?

a p a d a g

a n a m a t

As I point to the letters, tell me what sound they make.

You are doing very well! Let's take a break now and read a book. Can you find a book for us to read?

(Review the letter sounds before moving on to the next lesson. A typical schedule is to complete three lessons per week with review between lessons.)

Lesson 7

Materials: reading manual, blank index cards, gray crayon, and black crayon.

Instructions: In this lesson, you will review the material previously covered with the child. During the lesson, you will write the following letter combinations on blank index cards: *ad, ag, at, ap, an,* and *am.* Use a gray crayon to represent the *aaa* sound as in *cat,* as shown in the reading manual. Use a black crayon to write the consonants. Label the first card with the lesson number for future use. Place a rubber band around the cards when not in use.

You will also introduce the child to two new letters and the sounds they make. These letters are: *l* and *c.* To isolate the sound for the letter *l,* say the word *ball* and lift the *lll* sound from the word.

To isolate the sound for the letter *c,* say the word *topic* and lift the *c* sound from the word. This will prevent you from adding a vowel sound to the letter *c.* Remember, we want *c* not *cuh.* (We will teach the other sound for the letter *c,* where it makes an *sss* sound as in *face,* in a future lesson.)

Dialogue: You have learned lots of sounds so far. Today we are going to practice those sounds some more. Look at the letters as I point to them, and I will say the sounds the letters make.

d   g   t

p   n   m

This time, you say the sounds the letters make as I point to them. Very good! Look at the letter below. What sound does this letter make? (*aaa* as in *cat.*)

a

Great! Now look at the letters at the top of the page. Point to the correct

letters as I say the sounds the letters make. (Say the sounds in random order.)

ad   ag   at

ap   an   am

You are doing very well. I am going to write some letters on index cards. Tell me what sound I am writing on each card.

(Write the letter combinations listed below. Use gray for the letter *a* and black for the consonants. Have the child say the sound for each card as you write it.)

ad	ag	at
ap	an	am

Now I am going to mix the cards and put them face down on the table in a pile. Pick up the top card on the pile and read it. If you get the sound correct, you can keep it. If you do not get it correct, we will put it on the bottom of the pile.

(Continue with this game until the child has mastered all the cards.)

Next, you are going to learn the sound for a new letter. Look at the letter below. This letter makes the *lll* sound (as in *ball*). (Say the letter sound not the letter name. Point to the letter below as you say the sound.)

l

Say the /l/ sound as I point to the letter. Very good!

Look at the letter below. The next new sound you are going to learn is the c sound (as in *topic*). (Say the letter sound not the letter name. Point to the letter below as you say the sound.)

c

Say the c sound as I point to the letter. Great!

Now look at the letters below and tell me which one says c? Which letter says /l/?

c   l

Look at the four letters below. I will say the sound each letter makes. Point to the correct letter as I say the sound it makes. (Say the letter sounds, not the letter names, in random order.)

n   c   d   l

Tell me what sound each letter makes as I point to it.

That was very good! You learned a lot of new sounds today. Let's take a break and read a book.

(Review the letter sounds before moving on to the next lesson. Use the index cards for review. A typical schedule is to complete three lessons per week with review between lessons.)

Lesson 8

Materials: reading manual, index cards containing *ap, at, ag, an, am,* and *ad* from lesson 7.

Instructions: Retrieve index cards with *ap, at, ag, an, am,* and *ad*. Review these letter combinations with the child using the index cards. Today you will review the following letter sounds: *p, t, g, n, m, d, c,* and *l* by playing a listening game called, "I'm Thinking of..."

You will also introduce the child to two new letter sounds: *r* and *s*. To isolate the sound for the letter *r*, say the word *fair* and lift the *rrr* sound from the word. We do not want *ruh*. To isolate the sound for the letter *s*, say the word *glass* and lift the *sss* sound from the word.

Dialogue: Look at the letter below. What sound does this letter make? (*aaa* as in *cat*.)

a

Very good!

Let's review some letter sounds you have learned. (Retrieve index cards.) Say the letter sounds as I hold up each card.

a p	a t	a g
a n	a m	a d

Today we are going to play a listening game. This means you must listen very carefully. Look at the letter below.

t

I am thinking of an animal that starts with the t sound (as in *bat*). (Say the letter sound, not the letter name, as you point to the letter.)

This animal lives in the jungle and has stripes. Remember, it starts with the *t* sound. Can you tell me what animal it is?

(Pause for a response. If the child has trouble guessing the animal is a tiger, give him two animals to choose from. For example, say "Is it a leopard or a tiger? Which one starts with the *t* sound and has stripes? Use clues as needed throughout the guessing game.)

Great! You guessed it. The animal is a tiger. *Tiger* begins with the *t* sound. (Point to the letter *t* again.)

Look at the letter below.

p

I'm thinking of another jungle creature. This creature starts with the *p* sound (as in *cap*). (Say the letter sound, not the letter name. Point to the letter *p*.)

This creature is a bird and can sometimes sound like a person talking.

Remember, this creature starts with the *p* sound. (Point to the letter *p* again.) Can you tell me what it is? (Pause for a response. Parrot or parakeet is acceptable.)

That's very good! It is a parrot. *Parrot* starts with the *p* sound.

Look at the letter below.

g

I am thinking of a farm animal that starts with the *g* sound (as in *bag*). (Say the

letter sound, not the letter name. Point to the letter *g*.)

This farm animal gives milk. Be careful now. This animal starts with the *g* sound. Can you tell me what it is? (Pause for a response.)

Great! It's a goat. I didn't trick you. You guessed it. *Goat* begins with the *g* sound. (Point to the letter *g* again.)

Look at the letter below.

m

I'm thinking of another jungle animal. This animal starts with the *mmm* sound (as in *Sam*). (Point to the letter and say the letter sound, not the letter name.)

This animal has a long tail and can swing from tree to tree. Remember, it starts with the *mmm* sound. (Point to the letter and pause for a response.)

That's right! The animal is a monkey. *Monkey* starts with the *mmm* sound. (Point to the letter.)

Look at the letter below.

d

I'm thinking of animal that starts with the *d* sound (as in *had*). (Say the letter sound, not the letter name. Point to the letter.)

Many people have this kind of animal in their home. Remember, this animal starts with the *d* sound. (Point to the letter.) Can you guess what the animal is? (Pause for a response.)

Great! You guessed correctly. The animal is a dog. *Dog* begins with the *d* sound. (Point to the letter.)

Look at the letter below.

n

I'm thinking of a special animal home that starts with the *nnn* sound. Birds lay their eggs in this home. Remember, it starts with the *nnn* sound (as in *man*). (Say the letter sound, not the letter name. Point to the letter.)

Can you guess what this home is called? (Pause for a response.) Very good! This special home is called a nest. *Nest* starts with the *nnn* sound. (Point to the letter.)

Look at the letter below.

c

I'm thinking of another farm animal that gives milk. This animal starts with the *c* sound (as in *topic*). (Say the letter sound, not the letter name. Point to the letter.)

Can you guess what it is? (Pause for a response.) That's right! The animal is a cow. *Cow* starts with the *c* sound. (Point to the letter.)

Look at the letter below.

l

I'm thinking of a wild animal that starts with the *lll* sound (as in *ball*). (Say the letter sound, not the letter name. Point to the letter.)

This animal can roar very loudly. Remember, it starts with the *lll* sound. Can you guess what animal it is? (Pause for a response.)

Great! You are right. The animal is a lion. *Lion* starts with the *lll* sound.

You did very well with our listening game. Now you will learn two new letter sounds.

Look at the letter below. This letter makes the *rrr* sound (as in *fair*). (Say the letter sound, not the letter name. Point to the letter below as you say the sound.)

r

Say the *rrr* sound as I point to the letter. Good. Make the *rrr* sound again. (Point to the letter.)

Look at the next letter. This letter makes the *sss* sound (as in *glass*). It sounds like a snake. It even looks like a snake. (Say the letter sound, not the letter name. Point to the letter as you say the sound.)

s

Say the *sss* sound as I point to the letter. Good. Make the *sss* sound again. (Point to the letter.)

Now look at the letters below and tell me which one says *sss*. Which letter says *rrr*?

r   s

Look at the six letters at the top of the next page. I will say the sound for each letter. Point to the correct letter as

I say the sound it makes. (Say the letter sounds in random order.)

s   c   d

n   r   l

You have done a lot of hard work today. Would you like for me to read you a book?

(Review the letter sounds before moving on to the next lesson. Use the index cards for review. A typical schedule is to complete three lessons per week with review between lessons.)

Lesson 9

Materials: reading manual, blank index cards, gray crayon, and black crayon.

Instructions: Today you will review all the sounds for the letters learned so far. They are the sounds for: *a, p, t, g, n, m, d, c, l, r,* and *s.* You will also review the sounds for the following letter combinations: *ap, at, ag, an, am,* and *ad.*

In preparation for the lesson, write the following words on index cards: *cap, lap, map, nap, rap, sap, gap,* and *tap.* Use gray for the letter *a* and black for the consonants. Cut the index cards where indicated in the diagram. Label the first card with the lesson number for future use. Place a rubber band around the cards when not in use.

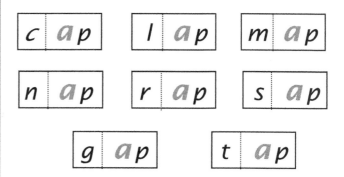

Dialogue: Look at the letters below. Which letter makes the c sound (as in *topic*)? Which letter makes the *lll* sound (as in *ball*)? Which letter makes the *rrr* sound (as in *fair*)? Which letter makes the sss sound (as in *glass*)?

l   s   c   r

Very good! Now look at the letters again and say the sound for each letter as I point to it.

Look at the letters at the top of the next page. Which letter makes the g sound (as in *bag*)? Which letter makes the *mmm* sound (as in *Sam*)? Which letter makes the *t* sound (as in *bat*)? Which letter makes the *nnn* sound (as in *man*)?

m   n   g   t

Very good! Now look at the letters again and say the sound for each letter as I point to it.

What sound does this letter make? (*aaa* as in *cat*.)

a

What sound does this letter make? (*p* as in *cap*.)

p

What sound do the letters make when we put them together?

a p

Great! The letters say *aaap*. (Point to the letter combination above.)

Today you are going to learn to read real words all by yourself. I have some cards with letters written on them that we will use to make words. I will place the stack of small cards face down in one pile and the stack of big cards face down in another pile.

Pick a small card from one pile and a big card from the other pile. Lay the cards on the table like this.

Example: | c | *a p* |

What sound does the small card make? What sound does the big card make? That's right, the small card says c, and the big card says *aaap*. If we put them together, we have c *aaa p*.

(Run your finger under the letters as you slowly sound out the word. Then say the word again, but more quickly.)

The word is *cap*.

Can you read the word to me now? Good. Now pick another small card and another big card.

Example: | l | *a p* |

The small card says *lll*. The big card says *aaap*, just like before. Can you sound out this word?

Great! The word is *lap*.

(Continue through all of the cards. Go through the set of cards once more.)

You are doing a great job. You are reading words all by yourself. Let's go over some sounds you learned before. What sound does this letter make? (*d* as in *had*.)

d

What sound do these letters make?

a d

Great! The letters say *aaad*. (Point to the letter combination above.)

Say the sound as I point to each group of letters.

37

at   ag   an   am

You have worked very hard today. Let's take a break and read a book together.

(Review the material before moving on to the next lesson. Use the index cards for review. Review the material from the previous lesson as well. A typical schedule is to complete three lessons per week with review between lessons.)

Lesson 10

Materials: reading manual, blank index cards, gray crayon, black crayon, and index cards from lesson 9.

Instructions: Today the child will review the sounds made by the following letters: *a, p, t, g, n, m, d, c, l, r,* and *s.* He will also review the sounds for the following letter combinations: *ap, at, ag, an, am,* and *ad.*

The following words will be reviewed as well: *cap, lap, map, nap, rap, sap, gap,* and *tap.* You will need to retrieve the word cards you made in the lesson 9.

Three new letter sounds will be introduced. They are: *b, f,* and *h.* To isolate the sound for the letter *b,* say the word *crib* and lift the *b* sound from the end of the word. Remember not to add a vowel sound when saying *b.* We do not want *buh.* To isolate the sound for the letter *f,* say the word *cliff* and lift the *fff* sound from the end of the word. Remember, we do not want *fuh.* To isolate the sound for the letter *h,* say the word *hush* and lift the *h* sound from the beginning of the word. This letter almost makes a whispering sound.

Dialogue: Look at the letters below, and say the sound each letter makes as I point to it.

m   n   g   t   p

l   s   c   r   d

Great! You are learning so much.

What sound does this letter make? (*aaa* as in *cat.*)

a

Look at the letters at the top of the next page. Which letters say *aaag*? Which letters say *aaammm*? Which letters say *aaap*? Which letters say *aaad*? Which letters say *aaat*? Which letters say *aaannn*?

*a*p   *a*t   *a*g

*a*n   *a*m   *a*d

You are doing very well. I think you are ready to learn some new sounds. Look at the letter below. This letter says *b* (as in *crib*). (Say the letter sound, not the letter name.)

b

Repeat the *b* sound as I point to the letter.

The next letter makes the *fff* sound (as in *cliff*). Repeat the *fff* sound as I point to the letter. (Say the letter sound, not the letter name.)

f

Look at the two letters and point to the letter that makes the *b* sound. Now point to the letter that makes the *fff* sound.

f   *b*

You will learn one more new letter sound today. This letter makes the *h* sound (as in *hush*). This is a very soft sound. Say the *h* sound as I point to the letter.

h

Let's see how well you remember the words you learned in the last lesson. (Retrieve the cards from the previous lesson.)

I will put all the little cards in one pile and the big cards in another pile. Pick a little card and a big card. Put them together to make a word.

(Help the child to place the cards in the proper order. You may wish to draw a small box and a large box on a piece of paper to enable him to place the cards in proper order. The words you will make are shown below.)

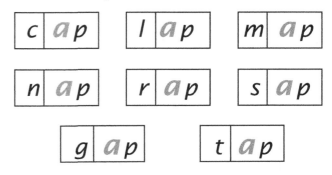

Example: What sound does the little card make? What sound does the big card make? Now put the two sounds together to make a word. Great! The word is *gap*.

g	*a p*

Now choose another small card and another big card.

(Continue in the same manner until all the cards are used.)

Look at the letters below. Point to each letter as I say the sound it makes. (Say the letter sounds in random order.)

m   *g*   *p*   *f*   *c*   *d*

39

Here are some more letters you have learned. Point to each letter as I say the sound it makes. (Say the letter sounds in random order.)

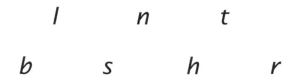

You are doing very well. Soon you will be reading lots of different words.

Look at the letters below. Tell me the sound each letter makes as I point to it.

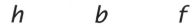

Let's take a break and read a book. Would you like to pick a book for me to read?

(Review the material before moving on to the next lesson. Use the index cards for review. Review the material from the previous lesson as well. A typical schedule is to complete three lessons per week with review between lessons.)

Lesson 11

Materials: reading manual, blank index cards, pen, gray crayon, and black crayon.

Instructions: In today's lesson, the child will review the sounds made by the following letters: *f, h,* and *b.* He will also review the following letter combinations: *ap, at, ag, am, an,* and *ad.* He will read the following words using index cards: *cat, bat, fat, rat, hat, pat, mat,* and *sat.* In preparation for the lesson, write the following words on index cards. Use gray for the letter *a* and black for the consonants. Cut the index cards where indicated below. Label the first card with the lesson number for future use. Place a rubber band around the cards when not in use.

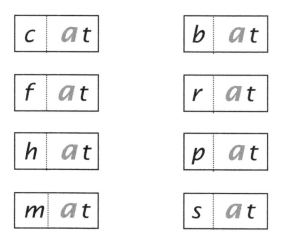

Next, the child will review the following words from the previous lesson: *cap, lap, map, nap, rap, sap, gap,* and *tap.* He will be introduced to the long vowel sound for the letter *a.* This letter makes the *a* sound as in *cake.* This letter will be represented by the bold black letter *a* as shown below. We will refer to this as the bold *a* sound.

a

Today the child will learn to read his first sentence and complete a variety of exercises based on the sentence: *a cat sat.*

Dialogue: Look at the letters at the top of the next page. Let's see if you can remember the sounds for these letters. Say the sound each letter makes as I point to it. (Repeat the letter sounds if the child has trouble.)

f   h   b

Look at the letters below and tell me what sound each group of letters makes.

ap   ag   at

am   ad   an

(Retrieve index cards you prepared for today's lesson.)

Today you are going to learn some new words. You will make words using cards like we did before. Pick a small card and a big card. Place them on the table to make a word.

Example: | f | at |

What sound does the small card make? What sound does the big card make? Put the two sounds together to make a word. Very good, the word is fat. Pick another small card and another big card.

(Continue until all the cards have been used.)

Look at the words below. These are the words you learned in the last two lessons. Read each word as I point to it.

cap   lap

map   nap

rap   sap

gap   tap

Did you know that now you can read 16 words! That's a lot of words.

Look at the letter below. What sound does this letter make? (*aaa* as in *cat*.)

a

That's correct, it says *aaa*.

Notice this letter is printed in the color gray.

Now I will show you the same letter printed in a bold black. If you see this letter printed this way, it says *a* (as in *cake*). We call this the bold *a* sound. Say *a* as I point to the letter.

a

Read the following words as I point to them. (Assist the child if he experiences difficulty with the *aaa* sounds and the bold *a.* sound.)

cat   sat   **a**

You are doing so well I think you can read an entire sentence. A sentence is usually made up of several words. You have learned many words so far.

Read the sentence at the top of the next page, and then I will show you a picture to go with the sentence.

Read each word as I point to it.

*a   c*a*t   s*a*t.*

Very good! Can you read the sentence a little faster this time?

Great. You read, "a cat sat." The dot at the end of the sentence is called a period. It means this is where the sentence ends. The sentence is finished. (Capitalization will be introduced in a future lesson.)

Now I will show you a picture of the cat.

What is the cat sitting on? Yes, he is sitting on the bone. Do you think the dog is happy? Do you think the cat is happy? Do you think the bone belongs to the dog? Yes, it is probably the dog's bone.

Copy Work: (The copy work is optional for children who have difficulty with writing.)

I will write the sentence you just read on a piece of paper.

(Neatly write the sentence with a pen, paying close attention to letter spacing, formation, and size. Make the letters large enough for the child to easily copy. Allow space for the child to write his letters directly under yours. An alternate method is to allow the child to trace over your letters.)

Now you can copy what I wrote.

*a   c*a*t   s*a*t.*

I will trace over the bold *a* sound (as in *cake*) with a black crayon. I will trace over the *aaa* sounds (as in *cat*) with a gray crayon.

(Trace over the letters you wrote. If the child wants, he can trace over his letters with the proper colors.)

I would like for you to read your sentence once more. Very good! Would you like to draw a picture to go with your sentence?

Now let's read a book together.

(Review the material before moving on to the next lesson. Use the index cards for review. Review the material from the previous lesson as well. A typical schedule is to complete three lessons per week with review between lessons.)

Lesson 12

Materials: reading manual, blank index cards, pen, gray crayon, and black crayon.

Instructions: In today's lesson, the child will review the sounds made by the following letters: *f, h,* and *b.* He will learn two new letter sounds: *w* and *z.* To isolate the sound for the letter *w,* say the word *now* and lift the *w* sound from the end of the word. Remember, we do not want *wuh.* To isolate the sound for the letter *z,* say the word *buzz* and lift the *zzz* sound from the end of the word.

Next, the child will review the following words from the previous two lessons: *tap, cap, map, gap, lap, nap, fat, sat, bat, rat, pat,* and *hat.* The sound for the bold letter *a* will be reviewed as well. The sight word *has* will be introduced.

The child will read the following words using index cards: *bag, rag, sag, wag, nag, tag, zag,* and *lag.* In preparation for the lesson, write the words on index cards. Use gray for the letter *a* and black for the consonants. Cut the index cards where indicated in the diagram. Label the first card with the lesson number for future use. Place a rubber band around the cards when not in use.

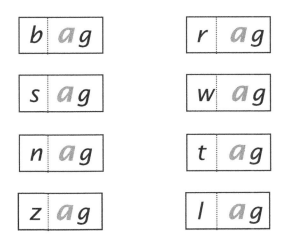

Finally, the child will read a second sentence: *a rat has a cap.* Comprehension exercises will follow as well as an optional exercise in which he copies the sentence.

Dialogue: Tell me the sound each letter makes as I point to it.

f   h   b

Look at the letters below and tell me what sound each group of letters makes.

a p   a g   a t

a m   a d   a n

Today you are going to learn two new letter sounds. The first sound is *w* (as in *now*). Say the *w* sound as I point to the letter below. (Say the letter sound, not the letter name.)

w

Repeat the *w* sound.

The next letter makes the *zzz* sound (as in *buzz*). Say the *zzz* sound as I point to the letter. (Say the letter sound, not the letter name.)

z

Look at the letters below. Which letter makes the *zzz* sound? Which letter makes the *w* sound?

w   z

Read the words below.

t a p   c a p   m a p

g a p   l a p   n a p

f a t   s a t   b a t

r*a*t   p*a*t   h*a*t

Now you are going to learn to read some new words. You will make words using cards like we did before.

(Retrieve the cards you prepared for this lesson. Place the small cards in one pile and the big cards in another pile.)

Pick a small card and a big card. Place them on the table to make a word.

Example: | b | *a* g |

What sound does the small card make? What sound does the big card make? Put the two sounds together to make a word. Very good, the word is *bag*. Pick another small card and another big card.

(Continue until all the cards have been used.)

What sound does this letter make? Remember, it is written in bold print. (*a* as in *cake*.)

a

Very good! The letter says *a* (as in *cake*).

Today you will learn a special word that we call a *sight word*. It is sort of funny because you cannot exactly sound it out. Look at the word at the top of the page as I read it. The word is *has*. (Point to the letter *s* in the word.) This letter does not make the *sss* sound (as in *glass*). It makes a *zzz* sound (as in *buzz*).

has

Repeat the word *has* as I point to it. Very good! We underlined this word because it is a sight word.

Today you will read another sentence. After you read the sentence, I will show you a picture to go with the sentence. First, let's go over a couple of words again. You read the words as I point to them.

a   has

Very good! Now read the sentence below. (Run your finger under each word as the child reads.)

a r*a*t has *a* c*a*p.

Can you read the sentence again, but this time read it a little faster. Great! The sentence is *a rat has a cap*. Notice the dot at the end of the sentence. Do you remember what that is called? Good! It is called a period, and it means the sentence is finished.

Now I will show you the picture of the rat.

What does the rat have on his head?
That's right, he has a cap on his head.
What does the rat have in his hand? Yes,
he has a bat in his hand. What do you
think he is going to do?

Copy Work: (The copy work is optional for children who have difficulty with writing.)

I will write the sentence you just
read on a piece of paper.

(Neatly write the sentence with a pen, paying close attention to letter spacing, formation, and size. Make the letters large enough for the child to easily copy. Allow space for the child to write his letters directly under yours. An alternate method is to allow the child to trace over your letters.)

Now you can copy what I wrote.

a r*a*t <u>*has*</u> *a* c*a*p.

I will trace over the bold *a* sounds
(as in *cake*) with a black crayon. I will
trace over the *aaa* sounds (as in *cat*) with a
gray crayon. I will underline the sight
word *has* with a black crayon.

(Trace over the letters you wrote. If the child wants, he can trace over his letters with the proper colors.)

I would like for you to read the
sentence once more. Very good! Would
you like to draw a picture to go with
your sentence?

Now let's read a book together.

(Review the material before moving on to the next lesson. Use the index cards for review. From time to time, review the material from some of the previous lessons as well. A typical schedule is to complete three lessons per week with review between lessons.)

Lesson 13

Materials: reading manual, blank index cards, pen, gray crayon, and black crayon.

Instructions: In today's lesson, the child will review the sounds for the letters *w* and *z*. He will review the following letter combinations: *ap, at, ag, an, am,* and *ad*. He will review the bold *a* sound as in *cake*, and he will review the sight word *has*.

He will be introduced to the sound for the letter *v*. To correctly isolate the sound for the letter *v*, say the word *have* and lift the *v* sound from the end of the word. Remember, we do not want to add a vowel sound such as *vuh*.

Next, the child will review the following selected words from the previous lessons: *rap, sap, lap, nap, cat, mat, hat, pat, bag, wag, zag,* and *tag*.

Today the child will use index cards to read the following words: *ran, fan, man, tan, pan, can, ban,* and *van*. In preparation for the lesson, write the following words on index cards. Use gray for the letter *a* and black for the consonants. Cut the index cards where indicated in the diagram. Label the first card with the lesson number for future use. Place a rubber band around the cards when not in use.

r	a n		f	a n		m	a n

t	a n		p	a n		c	a n

b	a n		v	a n

The child will be introduced to the sight word *the*. He will read the following sentence and complete a variety of exercises based on the sentence: *a man has a bag*.

Dialogue: Look at the letters at the top of the page. Which letter makes the *fff* sound? Which letter makes the *w* sound? Which letter makes the *h* sound? Which letter makes the *zzz* sound? Which letter makes the *b* sound?

---

f   z   b   w   h

As I point to each letter, say the sound the letter makes. Very good!

(If the child experiences difficulty with any of these sounds, repeat the exercise. Then have the child say the letter sounds as you point to each letter.)

Now you are going to learn a new letter sound. Look at the letter below. This letter makes the *v* sound (as in *have*). As I point to the letter, make the *v* sound. Very good! Say the *v* sound once more. (Say the letter sound, not the letter name.)

v

Look at the letters below, and tell me what sound each group of letters makes.

ad   at   am

an   ag   ap

Read the following words.

rap   sap   lap

nap   cat   mat

hat   pat   bag

wag   zag   tag

Look at the letters below. Which letter makes the v sound? Which letter makes the zzz sound? Which letter makes the w sound? Say the sound for each letter as I point to it.

w   v   z

Now you are going to learn to read some new words. You will make words using cards like we did in the last few lessons.

(Retrieve the cards you prepared for this lesson. Place the small cards in one pile and the big cards in another pile.)

Pick a small card and a big card. Place them on the table to make a word.

Example: | t | a n |

What sound does the small card make? What sound does the big card make? Put the two sounds together to make a word. Very good, the word is tan. Pick another small card and another big card.

(Continue until all the cards have been used.)

What sound does this bold letter make? (**a** as in *cake*.)

a

Read the sight word. Remember, a sight word is a word that's a little bit funny. You can't exactly sound it out.

has

Today you will learn a new sight word. This word is *the*. Say *the* as I point to the word. Great! Say *the* again.

the

Read the following words.

a   the   has

Today you will read another sentence. After you read the sentence, I will show you a picture to go with the sentence. Now read the sentence. (Run your finger under each word as the child reads.)

a man has a bag.

Can you read the sentence again, but this time read it a little faster. Great! The sentence is a *man has a bag*. What does the dot at the end of the sentence tell us? Do you remember what it is called? Good. It is called a period, and it means the sentence is finished.

Now I will show you the picture of a man with the bag.

What is in the bag? That's right, there is food in the bag. Where do you think he has been? Yes, he has probably been to the grocery store. Do you like to help shop for groceries?

Copy Work: (The copy work is optional for children who have difficulty with writing.)

I will write the sentence you just read on a piece of paper.

(Neatly write the sentence with a pen, paying close attention to letter spacing, formation, and size. Make the letters large enough for the child to easily copy. Allow space for the child to write his letters directly under yours. An alternate method is to allow the child to trace over your letters.)

Now you can copy what I wrote.

a m*a*n <u>has</u> *a*

b*a*g.

I will trace over the bold *a* sounds (as in *cake*) with a black crayon. I will trace over the *aaa* sounds (as in *cat*) with a gray crayon. I will underline the sight word *has* with a black crayon.

(Trace over the letters you wrote. If the child wants, he can trace over his letters with the proper colors.)

I would like for you to read the sentence once more. Very good! Would you like to draw a picture to go with your sentence?

Now let's read a book together.

(Review the material before moving on to the next lesson. Use the index cards for review. From time to time, review the material from some of the previous lessons as well. A typical schedule is to complete three lessons per week with review between lessons.)

Lesson 14

Materials: reading manual, blank index cards, pen, gray crayon, and black crayon.

Instructions: In today's lesson, the child will review the sounds for the letters *w, z,* and *v*. He will review the following letter combinations: *ap, ag, at, am, ad,* and *an*. He will review the bold *a* sound as in *cake*.

He will review the sight word *has* and the sight word *the*. Next, the child will review the following selected words from the previous lessons: *cap, map, gap, tap, rat, sat, hat, bat, wag, zag, nag, lag, can, fan, van,* and *pan*.

He will be introduced to the sounds for the following letters: *y* and *j*. To correctly isolate the sound for the letter *y* say the word *yes,* and lift the *y* sound from the beginning of the word. Remember not to add a vowel sound to the letter resulting in *yuh*. To correctly isolate the sound for the letter *j* say the word *jet,* and lift the *j* sound from the beginning of the word. Do not add a vowel sound to the letter resulting in *juh*.

Today the child will use index cards to read the following words: *ham, pam, sam, ram, yam, bam, jam,* and *dam*. In preparation for the lesson, write the following words on index cards. Use gray for the letter *a* and black for the consonants. Cut the index cards where indicated in the diagram. Label the first card with the lesson number for future use. Place a rubber band around the cards when not in use.

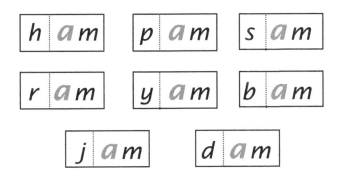

He will read the following sentence and complete a variety of exercises based on the sentence: *the ram has a can*.

Dialogue: Look at the letters at the top of the page. Which letter makes the

v sound? Which letter makes the *w* sound? Which letter makes the *zzz* sound?

v z w

Look at the letters below. As I point to each letter, say the sound the letter makes.

(If the child experiences difficulty with this exercise, tell him the sound for each letter in random order, and have him point to the correct letter as you say the sound the letter makes.)

b f w z h v

Look at the letters below and tell me what sound each group of letters makes.

a g	a t	a m
a p	a n	a d

Read the following words.

c a p	m a p	g a p
t a p	r a t	s a t
h a t	b a t	w a g
z a g	n a g	l a g
c a n	f a n	v a n
	p a n	

Now you are going to learn a new letter sound. Look at the letter below. This letter makes the y sound (as in *yes*). As I point to the letter, make the y sound. Very good! Say the y sound once more. (Say the letter sound, not the letter name.)

y

The next letter you are going to learn makes the j sound (as in *jet*). As I point to the letter below, make the j sound. Very good! Say the j sound once more. (Say the letter sound, not the letter name.)

j

Look at the letters below. Which letter makes the j sound? Which letter makes the y sound? Which letter makes the w sound? Which letter makes the v sound? Which letter makes the zzz sound?

j   w   z   y   v

Look at the two letters below. Say the sound the letter makes as I point it.

j   y

Now you are going to learn to read some new words. You will make words using cards like we did in the last few lessons.

(Retrieve the cards you prepared for this lesson. Place the small cards in one pile and the big cards in another pile.)

Pick a small card and a big card. Place them on the table to make a word.

Example: | y | a m |

What sound does the little card make? (Assist the child, especially if this is a new letter sound.) What sound does the big card make? Put the two sounds together to make a word. Very good! The word is yam. Pick another small card and another big card.

(Continue until all the cards have been used.)

What sound does this bold letter make? (a as in *cake*.)

a

Read the two sights words below. Remember, a sight word is a word that's a little bit funny. You can't exactly sound it out.

has   the

Today you will read another sentence. After you read the sentence, I will show you a picture to go with the sentence. Now read the sentence. (Run your finger under each word as the child reads.)

the ram has a can.

Can you read the sentence again, but this time read it a little faster? Great! The sentence is *the ram has a can.* What does the dot at the end of the sentence tell us? Do you remember what it is called? Good. It is called a period and it means the sentence is finished.

Now I will show you the picture of the ram with the can.

Where is the can? That's right, it is on the ram's horn. How do you think it got there? Yes, the ram probably got the can from the pile of cans under the tree.

Copy Work: (The copy work is optional for children who have difficulty with writing.)

I will write the sentence you just read on a piece of paper.

(Neatly write the sentence with a pen, paying close attention to letter spacing, formation, and size. Make the letters large enough for the child to easily copy. Allow space for the child to write his letters directly under yours. An alternate method is to allow the child to trace over your letters.)

Now you can copy what I wrote.

the ram has a can.

I will trace over the *aaa* sounds (as in *cat*) with a gray crayon. I will trace over the bold *a* sound (as in *cake*) with a black crayon. I will underline the sight words *the* and *has* with a black crayon.

(Trace over the letters you wrote. If the child wants, he can trace over his letters with the proper colors.)

I would like for you to read the sentence once more. Very good! Would you like to draw a picture to go with your sentence?

Now let's read a book together.

(Review the material before moving on to the next lesson. Use the index cards for review. From time to time, review the material from some of the previous lessons as well. A typical schedule is to complete three lessons per week with review between lessons.)

Lesson 15

Materials: reading manual, blank index cards, pen, gray crayon, and black crayon.

Instructions: In today's lesson, the child will review the sounds for the letters *w, z, v, y,* and *j*. He will review the bold *a* sound as in *cake*. He will review the sight word *has* and the sight word *the*. He will be introduced to the new sight word *was*. He will review the following letter combinations: *ap, at, am, ag, ad,* and *an*.

Next the child will review the following selected words from the previous lessons: *lap, sap, rap, cat, fat, pat, wag, zag, tag, man, van, ran, jam, yam,* and *ham*. So far the child has learned the typical sounds for all the consonants of the alphabet with the exception of the following three letters: *k, q,* and *x*. These letters will be introduced in future lessons.

Today you will introduce the meaning of uppercase and lowercase letters, explaining that uppercase letters are used at the beginning of a sentence. The child will read the following sentence: *the cat was sad*. He will then read the sentence again with conventional punctuation: *The cat was sad*. This sentence will be written on index cards, and the child will complete a variety of exercises based on the sentence. (Refer to page 10, point 4 in the Introduction.)

Today the child will use index cards to read the following words: *bad, sad, mad, dad, had, lad, pad,* and *tad*. In preparation for the lesson, write the following words on index cards. Use gray for the letter *a* and black for the consonants. Cut the index cards where indicated in the diagram. Label the first card with the lesson number for future use. Place a rubber band around the cards when not in use.

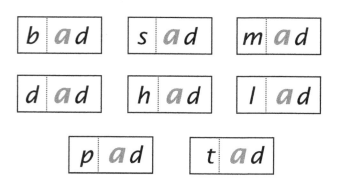

Dialogue: Look at the letters below. Say the letter sound as I point to each letter.

z   v   w   y   j

(If the child experiences difficulty with this exercise, tell him the sound for each letter in random order, and have him point to the correct letter as you say the sound the letter makes.)

Read the following words.

a   has   the

Today you will learn a new sight word. Remember, a sight word is a word you cannot exactly sound out. It is a little bit funny. The new sight word is was. Say the word was as I point to it.

was

Very good! Now you point to the word and read it again. Great!

Look at the letters below, and tell me what sound each group of letters makes.

at   ap   ad   ag
am   an

Read the following words.

lap   sap   rap
cat   fat   pat

wag   zag   tag

man   van   ran

jam   yam   ham

Now you are going to learn to read some new words. You will make words using index cards like we did in the last few lessons.

(Retrieve the cards you prepared for this lesson. Place the small cards in one pile and the big cards in another pile.)

Pick a small card and a big card. Place them on the table to make a word.

Example: | *h* | *a d* |

What sound does the small card make? What sound does the big card make? Put the two sounds together to make a word. Very good! The word is *had*. Pick another small card and another big card.

(Continue until all the cards have been used.)

Read the sight words below once more.

<u>was</u>   <u>has</u>   <u>the</u>

Today you will read another sentence. After you read the sentence, I will show you a picture to go with the sentence. Now read the sentence. (Run your finger under each word as the child reads.)

<u>the</u> c*a*t <u>was</u> s*a*d.

Read the sentence again, but this time read it a little faster. Great! The sentence is *the cat was sad*. What is the dot at the end of the sentence called? Very good! It is called a *period*.

Now I will show you a picture of the sad cat.

Why do you think the cat is sad? Yes, he is probably sad because he can see the rat, but he cannot get the rat. What do you think the rat is going to do?

Look at the letter below. What sound does the letter make? (*t* as in *bat*.)

t

Yes, that's right, it makes the *t* sound. It is called the letter *t*.

(Say the letter's name. The child may or may not know the names for the letters. Since the child knows the sounds for most of the letters of the alphabet, you can now introduce the names for the letters as they appear in future lessons.)

This letter is called a lowercase letter *t*. (Point to the letter *t* below.)

t

Sometimes we need to write an uppercase letter *T*. It looks like this. (Point to the uppercase letter *T* below.) This letter still makes the *t* sound. (Point to the uppercase letter *T* and say the *t* sound.)

T

Look at the two words below. They both say the same thing. (Point to each word as you read it.)

the   The

There are special times when we want to use uppercase letters. One special time is at the beginning of a sentence. The first word of each sentence should be written with an uppercase letter. Let's look at the sentence you just read again. This time it is written with an uppercase letter *T* for the word *The*.

The cat was sad.

I am going to write the words from this sentence on index cards.

(Have the child watch as you write each word with a pen. Label the first card with the lesson number for future use.)

I am going to write the first word of the sentence with an uppercase letter.

| The | cat | was |

| sad. |

Did you notice I put a dot after the word sad? What is this dot called? That's right it is called a *period*. Why do we need it? Good, it tells us this is the end of the sentence.

I am going to underline the sight words with a black crayon. The sight words are *the* and *was*. I am going to trace over the *aaa* sounds (as in *cat*) with a gray crayon.

Read the sentence. Very good! Today you learned the first word of a sentence begins with an uppercase letter. (Point to the card with the word *The* written on it.)

Now I am going to mix the cards. I want you to put the cards in the proper order to make the sentence again.

How do you know which card will come first? That's right, because it is written with an uppercase letter. How do you know which card will come last? Good, because it has the period after the word. Now try to figure out where to put the other two cards. Read the first card. What word would make sense next?

(Assist the child as needed to place the cards in proper order.)

Now that the cards are in the right order, read the sentence again.

Copy Work: (The copy work is optional for children who have difficulty with writing.)

54

(Neatly write the sentence with a pen, paying close attention to letter spacing, formation, and size. Make the letters large enough for the child to easily copy. Allow space for the child to write his letters directly under yours. An alternate method is to allow the child to trace over your letters.)

Now you can copy what I wrote.

The cat was sad.

I will trace over the *aaa* sounds with a gray crayon. I will underline the sight words *the* and *was* with a black crayon.

(Trace over the letters you wrote. If the child wants, he can trace over his letters with the proper colors.)

I would like for you to read the sentence once more. Very good! Would you like to draw a picture to go with your sentence?

Now let's read a book together. As we read, let's look for uppercase letters.

(As you read with your child, point out some uppercase letters. Find a lowercase letter for each uppercase letter found. Teach the names for the letters at this time if your child does not know them. Discuss whether or not the uppercase letters resemble the lowercase letters.

Go over only three or four uppercase letters and their corresponding lowercase letters each day. Have the child say the sound the letter makes as well as the name for each letter. Keep a list of the uppercase letters and their corresponding lower case letters that you review.

Review the material from the lesson using the index cards. Refer to Teaching Tips page 21.)

Lesson 16

Materials: reading manual, blank index cards, pen, gray crayon, and black crayon.

Instructions: In today's lesson, the child will review the sight words *the, has,* and *was.* He will review the following letter combinations: *ap, at, am, ag, ad,* and *an.* He will review the following words by playing a game called *I'm Thinking of a Word*: *sad, pan, bag, map, hat, jam, bat, cat, fan, ram, wag,* and *rat.*

Today the child will read the following sentence and complete a variety of exercises based on the sentence: *The man has a map.*

Dialogue: Read the following words:

the has was a

Look at the letters below, and tell me what sound each group of letters makes.

at   am   ap

an   ad   ag

We are going to play a game. It is called, *I'm Thinking of a Word.* Look at the words in the box below. Try to tell me of which word I am thinking. I will give you a hint for each word.

sad	pan
bag	map

I'm thinking of a word. You fry eggs in this. What is it? (pan)

I'm thinking of a word. If you are not happy, then you are this. What is it? (sad)

I'm thinking of a word. You use this to find places. What is it? (map)

I'm thinking of a word. You put groceries in this. What is it? (bag)

We are going to play the game again. Look at the words in the box below. Try to tell me of which word I am thinking.

hat	*jam*
bat	*cat*

I'm thinking of a word. You put this on toast. What is it? (jam)

I'm thinking of a word. You put this on your head. What is it? (hat)

I'm thinking of a word. It has a long tail. What is it? (cat)

I'm thinking of a word. You use this to hit a ball. What is it? (bat)

We are going to play the game one more time. Look at the words in the box below. Try to tell me of which word I am thinking.

fan	*ram*
wag	*rat*

I'm thinking of a word. It looks like a big mouse. What is it? (rat)

I'm thinking of a word. You use this to keep cool. What is it? (fan)

I'm thinking of a word. A dog does this with his tail. What is it? (wag)

I'm thinking of a word. This is an animal that has big, curly horns. What is it? (ram)

Today you will read another sentence. After you read the sentence I will show you a picture to go with the sentence. Now read the sentence. (Run your finger under each word as the child reads.)

<u>The</u> man <u>has</u> a

map.

Read the sentence again, but this time read it a little faster. Great! The sentence is The *man has a map.* What is the dot at the end of the sentence called? Good. It is called a *period.*

Now I will show you a picture of the man with the map.

What is the man doing? That's right, he is riding on a camel. He is looking at a map. What is funny about this picture? Yes, he is riding the camel backwards.

I am going to write the words from the sentence you read on index cards.

(Have the child watch as you write each word with a pen. Label the first card with the lesson number for future use.)

I am going to write the first word of the sentence with an uppercase letter.

The	man	has

a	map.

Did you notice I put a dot after the word *map*? What is this dot called? That's right, it is called a *period*. Why do we need it? Good, it tells us this is the end of the sentence.

I am going to underline the sight words with a black crayon. The sight words are *the* and *has*. I am going to trace over the *aaa* sounds (as in *cat*) with a gray crayon. I am going to trace over the bold *a* sound (as in *cake*) with a black crayon.

Read the sentence. Very good! In the last lesson you learned the first word of a sentence begins with an uppercase letter. I am going to mix these cards. I want you to put the cards in the proper order to make the sentence again.

How do you know which card will come first? That's right, because it is written with an uppercase letter. How do you know which card will come last? Good, because it has the period after the word. Now try to figure out where to put the other cards. Read the first card. What word would make sense next?

(Assist the child as needed to place the cards in proper order.)

Now the cards are in the right order, read the sentence again.

Copy Work: (The copy work is optional for children who have difficulty with writing.)

I will write the sentence you just read on a piece of paper.

(Neatly write the sentence with a pen, paying close attention to letter spacing, formation, and size. Make the letters large enough for the child to easily copy. Allow space for the child to write his letters directly under yours. An alternate method is to allow the child to trace over your letters.)

Now you can copy what I wrote.

The man has a map.

I will trace over the *aaa* sounds with a gray crayon. I will trace over the bold *a* sound with a black crayon. I will underline the sight words *the* and *has* with a black crayon.

(Trace over the letters you wrote. If the child wants, he can trace over his letters with the proper colors.)

I would like for you to read the sentence once more. Very good! Would you like to draw a picture to go with your sentence?

Now let's read a book together. As we read, let's look for uppercase letters.

(Review the material before moving on to the next lesson. Use the index cards for review. From time to time, review the material from some of the previous lessons as well. Refer to Teaching Tips on page 21.)

Lesson 17

Materials: reading manual, blank index cards, pen, gray crayon, and black crayon.

Instructions: In today's lesson, the child will review the bold *a* sound. He will also review the following sight words: *the, has,* and *was*. He will review the following selected words from the previous lessons: *map, gap, bat, hat, wag, zag, van, man, yam, jam, dad,* and *lad*.

He will be introduced to the sound made by the following letter combination: *ck* as in *back*. The letter *c* will be printed in regular black type while the letter *k* will be printed in a dotted fashion. If a letter is dotted, it makes no sound. We say it is silent.

c*k*

Today the child will use index cards to read the following words: *back, sack, rack, jack, hack, lack, pack,* and *tack*. In preparation for the lesson, write the following words on index cards. Use a gray crayon for the letter *a*. Write the letter *k* with a black crayon in a dotted fashion as shown below. Use black for the consonants. Cut the index cards where indicated in the diagram. Label the first card with the lesson number for future use. Place a rubber band around the cards when not in use.

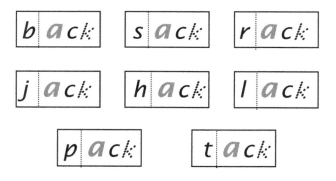

The child will read the following sentence and complete a variety of exercises based on the sentence: *The bat has a sack.*

Dialogue: Read the words below.

m a p   g a p   b a t

h a t   w a g   z a g

van   man   yam

jam   dad   lad

What sound does this letter make? (*c* as in *topic*.)

c

Very good! It says c. (Say the letter sound, not the letter name.) Some words have the letter c and the letter k written together. (Say the letter names for *c* and *k*. Point to the letter combination below.) When this happens, the letter k does not make a sound. We say it is silent.

Since it makes no sound, we will write it like this. The letter k is dotted. When you see a letter that is dotted in this book, remember it does not make a sound.

c*k*

Now practice saying the c sound as I point to the letters above. (Say the letter sound, not the letter name.)

What sound does this letter make? (*aaa* as in *cat*.)

a

What sound do these letters make? (*ck* as in *back*.)

c*k*

Very good! Now let's see what sound is made when we put the three letters together. The letters say *aaack* (as in *back*). (Point to the letters below as you make the sound.) Remember, the *k* is silent.

a c k

Now you are going to learn to read some new words. You will make words using cards like we did in the last few lessons.

(Retrieve the cards you prepared for this lesson. Place the small cards in one pile and the big cards in another pile.)

Pick a small card and a big card. Place them on the table to make a word.

Example: | s | a c k |

What sound does the little card make? (Assist the child, especially if this is a new letter sound.) What sound does the big card make? Put the two sounds together to make a word. Very good! The word is *sack*. Pick another small card and another big card. (Continue until all the cards have been used.)

Remember, the *k* is silent. It makes no sound.

What sound does this bold letter make? (*a* as in *cake*.)

a

Read the sight words at the top of the next page.

Read the sight words at the top of the next page.

has   the   was

Today you will read another sentence. After you read the sentence, I will show you a picture to go with the sentence. Now read the sentence. (Run your finger under each word as the child reads.)

The bat has a sack.

Can you read the sentence again, but this time read it a little faster? Great! The sentence is *The bat has a sack.*

Now I will show you a picture of the bat with a sack.

What do you think the bat has in the sack? That's right, he has apples in the sack. Do you think the sack is heavy? Why? Yes, the sack is heavy and apples are falling through a hole in the bottom of the sack.

I am going to write the words from the sentence you read on index cards.

(Have the child watch as you write each word with a pen. Label the first card with the lesson number for future use.)

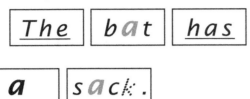

I am going to underline the sight words with a black crayon. The sight words are *the* and *has*. I am going to trace over the *aaa* sounds (as in *cat*) with a gray crayon. I am going to trace over the bold *a* sound (as in *cake*) with a black crayon.

I am going to make dotted lines over the letter *k* in the word *sack*. Can you tell me why I dotted this letter? That's right. I dotted the letter *k*, because it is silent. It makes no sound.

Read the sentence. Very good! Now I am going to mix these cards. I want you to put the cards in the proper order to make the sentence again.

How do you know which card comes first? That's right, because it is written with an uppercase letter. How do you know which card will come last? Good, because it has a period after the word. Now try to figure out where to put the other three cards. What word would make sense next?

(Assist the child as needed to place the cards in proper order.)

Now that the cards are in the right order, read the sentence again.

Copy Work: (The copy work is optional for children who have difficulty with writing.)

I will write the sentence you just read on a piece of paper.

(Neatly write the sentence with a pen, paying close attention to letter spacing, formation, and size. Make the letters large enough for the child to easily copy. Allow space for the child to write his letters directly under yours. An alternate method is to allow the child to trace over your letters.)

Now you can copy what I wrote.

The bat has a sack.

I will trace over the *aaa* sounds with a gray crayon. I will trace over the bold *a* sound with a black crayon. I will underline the sight words *the* and *has* with a black crayon. I will make dotted lines over the letter *k* in the word *sack*.

(Trace over the letters you wrote. If the child wants, he can trace over his letters with the proper colors.)

I would like for you to read the sentence once more. Very good! Would you like to draw a picture to go with your sentence?

Now let's read a book together.

(Remember to look for uppercase and lowercase letters as you read. Help your child to recognize the letters by name. Review the material before moving on to the next lesson. Use the index cards for review. Refer to Teaching Tips on page 21.)

Lesson 18

Materials: reading manual, blank index cards, pen, gray crayon, and black crayon.

Instructions: In today's lesson, the child will review the following words from previous lessons: *wag, hat, tap, fan, yam, lad, rack, pack, sack, jack,* and *back*. He will also review the sight words learned so far: *has, was,* and *the*.

The child will read a number of words containing the bold ***a*** sound as in *cake*. The following words will be introduced: *nail, sail, pail, hail, fail, tail, gain, pain,* and *rain*. The letter *i* will be dotted and taught as a silent letter as shown in the word below.

t a i l

The child will read the following sentence and complete a variety of exercises based on the sentence: *The cat has a tail.*

Dialogue: Read the words below. Remember, the dotted letters are silent. They make no sound.

w a g   h a t   t a p

f a n   y a m   l a d

r a c k   p a c k   s a c k

j a c k   b a c k

Look at the letter below. What sound does this bold letter make? (*a* as in *cake*.)

a

Very good! This letter says *a*.

Next, I will show you a word that has the same bold *a* sound (as in *cake*). This word also has a silent letter.

Look at the word below. See the bold letter. It makes the bold *a* sound. See the dotted letter. It makes no sound. It is silent. The word is *tail*. (Run your finger under the word as you sound out each letter.)

Say the word as I point to it.

t a i l

Very good! The word is *tail*.

Read the following words. Each word has a bold *a* sound. Each word also has a silent letter. Remember to say *a* (as in *cake*) when you see the bold letter *a*. Remember, the dotted letters are silent. They make no sound.

n a i l   s a i l   p a i l

h a i l   f a i l   t a i l

g a i n   p a i n   r a i n

Read the sight words below.

has   was   the

Today you will read another sentence. After you read the sentence, I will show you a picture to go with the sentence. Now read the sentence. (Run your finger under each word as the child reads.)

61

The cat has a tail.

The cat has a

Can you read the sentence a little faster this time? Great! The sentence is *The cat has a tail.*

Now I will show you a picture of the cat and his tail.

What is funny about this picture? That's right, the cat has a very long tail. Have you ever seen a cat with such a long tail? Do you think it would be good for a cat to have such a long tail? Do you know the purpose of a cat's tail? He uses it to help him balance.

I am going to write the words from the sentence you read on index cards.

(Have the child watch as you write each word with a pen. Label the first card with the lesson number for future use.)

The | cat | has |
a | tail.

Did you notice I put a special mark after the word *tail?* What is this special mark called? That's right it is a period. Why do we need it? Good, it tells us this is the end of the sentence.

I am going to underline the sight words with a black crayon. The sight words are *the* and *has.* I am going to trace over the *aaa* sound (as in *cat*) with a gray crayon and the bold *a* sounds (as in *cake*) with a black crayon.

I will make dotted lines over the letter *i* in the word *tail* with a black crayon. Do you know why I am dotting this letter? That's right, because the letter *i* in this word is silent. It makes no sound.

Read the sentence. Very good! I am going to mix these cards. I want you to put the cards in the proper order to make the sentence again.

How do you know which card will come first? That's right, because it is written with an uppercase letter. How do you know which card will come last? Good, because it has the period after the word. Now try to figure out where to put the other cards. Read the first card. What word would make sense next?

(Assist the child as needed to place the cards in proper order.)

Now that the cards are in the right order, read the sentence again.

Copy Work: (The copy work is optional for children who have difficulty with writing.)

I will write the sentence you just read on a piece of paper.

(Neatly write the sentence with a pen, paying close attention to letter spacing, formation, and size. Make the letters large enough for the child to easily copy. Allow space for the child to write his letters directly under yours. An alternate method is to allow the child to trace over your letters.)

Now you can copy what I wrote.

The cat has a tail.

I will trace over the *aaa* sounds with a gray crayon. I will trace over the bold *a* sounds with a black crayon. I will make dotted lines over the letter *i* in the word *tail* with a black crayon. Do you know why I am doing this? That's right, because the letter *i* in this word is silent. It makes no sound. I will underline the sight words *the* and *has* with a black crayon.

(Trace over the letters you wrote. If the child wants, he can trace over his letters with the proper colors.)

I would like for you to read the sentence once more. Very good! Would you like to draw a picture to go with your sentence?

Now let's read a book together.

(Review the material before moving on to the next lesson. Use the index cards for review. From time to time, review the material from some of the previous lessons as well. Refer to Teaching Tips on page 21.)

Lesson 19

Materials: reading manual, index cards, pen, gray crayon, and black crayon.

Instructions: In today's lesson, the child will review the following sight words: *has, the,* and *was*. He will be introduced to the new sight word *is*. He will also review the following words from previous lessons: *bag, fat, nap, man, ram, had, tack,* and *zack.*

He will practice reading additional words containing the bold *a* sound as in *cake*. The following words will be introduced: *wave, pave, save, gave, Dave, cave, same, came, game, lame, name,* and *tame.*

We will use this opportunity to explain that proper names begin with an uppercase letter. Each new word contains a silent *e* at the end that will be printed in a dotted type as shown below.

cave

The child will also read the following sentence and complete a variety of exercises based on the sentence: *The ram was at the game.*

Dialogue: Read the sight words below.

has   was   the

Today you will learn a new sight word. The sight word is *is*. (Point to the word below.)

is

Say *is* as I point to the word. Very good! The letter *s* (point to the letter *s*) makes a *zzz* sound just like in the sight words *has* and *was*. (Point to the word above and say *is* once more.)

Read the words below.

bag   fat   nap

man   ram   had

tack   zack

You are doing such a good job reading words with the *aaa* sound.

Let's work on reading some words with the bold *a* sound. The dotted letters are silent. They make no sound. I will read the first word for you. It is *wave*. Read the words below.

wave	pave
save	gave
dave	cave
same	came
game	lame
name	tame

Let's look at one of the words again. The word is *dave*. (Point to the word below.)

dave

Dave is a boy's name. When we write names, we begin the name with an uppercase letter. This is how we should write the name *Dave*. (Point to the word below.)

Dave

See the uppercase letter *D*? Say the word as I point to it. (Point to the word above.)

Can you tell me another time when we use an uppercase letter? (Pause for response.) That's right. We begin a sentence with an uppercase letter.

Read the sight words below.

has   the   was   is

Now read this word. It has the *aaa* sound in it. It is a very short word.

at

That's right. The word is *at*.

Today you will read another sentence. After you read the sentence, I will show you a picture to go with the sentence. Now read the sentence. (Run your finger under each word as the child reads.)

The ram was at the game.

Now I will show you a picture of the ram at the game.

What kind of game is the ram playing? That's right, he is playing football. Look at his funny helmet. Do you think rams really play football? No, they do not.

I am going to write the words from the sentence you read on index cards. (Have the child watch as you write each word with a pen. Label the first card with the lesson number for future use.)

The	ram	was	at

the	game.

Did you notice I put a special mark after the word *game*? What is this special mark called? That's right it is a period. Why do we need it? Good, it tells us this is the end of the sentence.

I am going to underline the sight words with a black crayon. The sight words are *the* and *was*. I am going to

trace over the *aaa* sounds (as in *cat*) with a gray crayon and the bold *a* sound (as in *cake*) with a black crayon.

I will make dotted lines over the letter *e* at the end of the word *game* with a black crayon. Do you know why I am dotting this letter? That's right, because the letter *e* in this word is silent. It makes no sound.

Read the sentence. Very good! I am going to mix these cards. I want you to put the cards in the proper order to make the sentence again.

How do you know which card will come first? That's right, because it is written with an uppercase letter. How do you know which card will come last? Good, because it has a period after the word. Now try to figure out where to put the other cards. Read the first card. What word would make sense next?

(Assist the child as needed to place the cards in proper order.)

Now that the cards are in the right order, read the sentence again.

Copy Work: (The copy work is optional for children who have difficulty with writing.)

I will write the sentence you just read on a piece of paper.

(Neatly write the sentence with a pen, paying close attention to letter spacing, formation, and size. Make the letters large enough for the child to easily copy. Allow space for the child to write his letters directly under yours. An alternate method is to allow the child to trace over your letters.)

Now you can copy what I wrote.

The ram was at the game.

I will trace over the *aaa* sounds with a gray crayon. I will trace over the bold *a* sound with a black crayon. I will make dotted lines over the letter *e* at the end of the word *game* with a black crayon. Do you know why I am doing this? That's right, because the letter *e* in this word is silent. It makes no sound. I will underline the sight words *the* and *was* with a black crayon.

(Trace over the letters you wrote. If the child wants, he can trace over his letters with the proper colors.)

I would like for you to read the sentence once more. Very good! Would you like to draw a picture to go with your sentence?

Now let's read a book together.

(Review the material before moving on to the next lesson. Use the index cards for review. From time to time, review the material from some of the previous lessons as well. Refer to Teaching Tips on page 21.)

Lesson 20

Materials: reading manual, index cards, pen, gray crayon, and black crayon.

Instructions: In today's lesson, the child will review the following words from previous lessons: *fat, rag, lap, pan, jam, mad, sack,* and *rack*. He will review the sight words *has, was, is,* and *the*.

Next, he will practice reading additional words containing the bold *a* sound as in *cake*. The following words will be introduced: *bake, cake, lake, rake, make, take, ate, date, fate, gate, late,* and *hate*. We will introduce the *k* sound as in the word *bake* as well. Prior to this lesson the letter *k* was presented only as a silent letter following the letter *c* as in *back*. Each new word contains a silent *e* at the end, which will be printed in a dotted type as shown below.

cake

The child will also read the following sentences and complete a variety of exercises based on the sentences: *The rat ate the cake. The rat is fat.*

Dialogue: Read the *aaa* words below.

fat   rag   lap

pan   jam   mad

sack   rack

Read the sight words below.

was   has   is   the

Look at the word below. (Point to the letter *k*.) You know this letter is silent, because it is printed in a dotted type. This letter makes no sound. Read the word.

sack

Look at the letter below. (Point to the letter.) This time it makes a sound, because it is not dotted. It says *k* (as in *bake*). (Say the letter sound not the letter name.)

Say *k* as I point to the letter.

k

Can you think of another letter that says *k* (as in *bake*)? (Say the letter sound not the letter name.)

Look at the letters below. Both of these letters say *k*. Say the letter sounds as I point to each letter.

c   k

Look at the words below. These words have the bold *a* sound (as in *cake*). Remember, the dotted letters are silent. They make no sound. I will read the first word for you. It is *bake*. (Repeat the first word.)

Now read the words below. (Run your finger under each word as the child reads.)

bake   cake   lake

rake   make   take

ate   date   fate

gate   late   hate

You are doing so well that today you are going to read two new sentences. After you read the sentences, I will show you a picture to go with the sentences. Now read the sentences. (Run your finger under each word as the child reads.)

The rat ate the cake.

The rat is fat.

Now I will show you a picture of the rat.

Do you think the rat is happy? No, he does not look happy. Why not? Yes, the rat is sick from eating too much cake. Do you like cake? Yes, cake is good, but it is not good to eat too much.

I am going to write the words from the first sentence you read on index cards.

(Have the child watch as you write each word with a pen. Label the first card with the lesson number for future use.)

| The | rat | a̤te̤ |
| the | ca̤ke̤. |

I'm going to underline the sight words with a black crayon. I am going to trace over the aaa sound (as in cat) with a gray crayon and the bold a sounds (as in cake) with a black crayon.

I will make dotted lines over the letter e at the end of the word ate with a black crayon. I will also make dotted lines over the letter e at the end of the word cake with a black crayon. Why am I dotting these letters? That's right, I am dotting them, because they make no sound. They are silent.

Read the sentence. Great! Now I am going to mix the cards. I want you to put the cards in proper order to make the sentence again.

(Assist the child with putting the cards in proper order. Remind him, if necessary, a sentence begins with an uppercase letter and ends with a period.)

Now read the sentence.

Copy Work: (The copy work is optional for children who have difficulty with writing.)

I will write the first sentence you just read on a piece of paper.

(Neatly write the sentence with a pen, paying close attention to letter spacing, formation, and size. Make the letters large enough for the child to easily copy. Allow space for the child to write his letters directly under yours. An alternate method is to allow the child to trace over your letters.)

Now you can copy what I wrote.

The rat a̤te̤ the ca̤ke̤.

I will trace over the aaa sound with a gray crayon. I will trace over the bold a sounds with a black crayon. I will make dotted lines over the letter e at the end of the words ate and cake with a black crayon. Do you know why I am doing this? That's right, because the letter e is silent in these words. It makes no sound. I will underline the sight words with a black crayon.

(Trace over the letters you wrote. If the child wants, he can trace over his letters with the proper colors.)

I would like for you to read the sentence once more. Very good! Would you like to draw a picture to go with your sentence?

Now let's read a book together.

(Review the material before moving on to the next lesson. Use the index cards for review. From time to time, review the material from some of the previous lessons as well. Refer to Teaching Tips on page 21.)

Lesson 21

Materials: reading manual, index cards, pen, gray crayon, and black crayon.

Instructions: In today's lesson, the child will review the following words from previous lessons: *map, pat, wag, yam, bad, man, zack, tail, rain, lake, name, wave,* and *fate*. He will also review the following sight words: *the, has, is,* and *was*. The child will be introduced to the new sight word *to*.

He will practice reading additional words containing the bold *a* sound as in *cake*. The following words will be introduced: *pay, say, way, may, Kay, Fay, day, ray, bay, hay,* and *lay*.

We will use this opportunity to repeat that names begin with an uppercase letter. Each new word contains a silent *y* at the end that will be printed in a dotted type as shown in the word below.

ha*y*

The child will read the following sentences and complete a variety of exercises based on the sentences: *The cat ate the hay. The cat had a pain. The cat was sad.*

Dialogue: Read the words below. Remember, the dotted letters are silent. They make no sound.

map	pat	wag
yam	bad	man
	zack	
tail	rain	lake
name	wave	fate

Read the sight words below.

the   has   is   was

Today you will learn a new sight word. It is the word *to*. (Point to the word below.)

to

Say *to* as I point to the word. Very good!

Let's work on reading some words that have the bold *a* sound. Remember, the dotted letters are silent. I will read the first word for you. It is *pay*. (Repeat the first word.) Now, read the words below. (Run your finger under each word as the child reads.)

pay	say	way
may	Kay	Fay
day	ray	bay
hay		lay

Did you notice some of the words you read begin with an uppercase letter? Why do you think these begin this way? (Pause for a response.) That's right, because these are names. Names begin with an uppercase letter. (Point to the names above and read them aloud.)

Read the sentences, and then I will show you a picture to go with the sentences. (Run your finger under each word as the child reads.)

The cat ate the hay.

The cat had a pain.

The cat was sad.

Now I will show you a picture of the cat.

Do you think hay is good for cats? Can you name an animal that eats hay? That's a good answer. A horse eats hay. Cows eat hay too. Cats should not eat hay.

I am going to write the words from the first sentence you read on index cards.

(Have the child watch as you write each word with a pen. Label the first card with the lesson number for future use.)

The | cat | ate
the | hay.

I'm going to underline the sight words with a black crayon. I am going to trace over the aaa sound (as in cat) with a gray crayon and the bold a sounds (as in cake) with a black crayon.

I will make dotted lines over the letter e at the end of the word ate with a black crayon. I will make dotted lines over the letter y at the end of the word hay with a black crayon. Why am I dotting these letters? That's right, because these letters make no sound. They are silent.

Now read the sentence. Very good! I am going to mix the cards. I want you to put the cards in proper order to make the sentence again.

(Assist the child with putting the cards in proper order. Remind him, if necessary, a sentence begins with an uppercase letter and ends with a period.)

Now read the sentence.

Copy Work: (The copy work is optional for children who have difficulty with writing.)

I will write the first sentence you just read on a piece of paper.

(Neatly write the sentence with a pen, paying close attention to letter spacing, formation, and size. Make the letters large enough for the child to easily copy. Allow space for the child to write his letters directly under yours. An alternate method is to allow the child to trace over your letters.)

Now you can copy what I wrote.

The cat ate the hay.

I will trace over the *aaa* sound with a gray crayon. I will trace over the bold *a* sounds with a black crayon. I will make dotted lines over the letter *e* at the end of the word *ate* and over the letter *y* at the end of the word *hay* with a black crayon. Do you know why I am doing this? That's right, because these letters are silent. They make no sound. I will underline the sight words with a black crayon.

(Trace over the letters you wrote. If the child wants, he can trace over his letters with the proper colors.)

I would like for you to read the sentence once more. Very good! Would you like to draw a picture to go with your sentence?

Now let's read a book together.

(Review the material before moving on to the next lesson. Use the index cards for review. From time to time, review the material from some of the previous lessons as well. Refer to Teaching Tips on page 21.)

Lesson 22

Materials: reading manual, index cards, pen, gray crayon, and black crayon.

Instructions: In today's lesson, the child will review the following words from previous lessons: *nap, hat, rag, ham, dad, pan, sack, back, sail, pain, game, gave, rake, late, hay, say, day, may, way,* and *pay.* He will also review the following sight words: *is, was, to, has,* and *the.*

The child will read the following sentences and complete a variety of exercises based on the sentences: *The rat is sad. The rat has a rake. The rat can rake the hay.*

Dialogue: Read the words below. Remember, the dotted letters are silent. They make no sound.

nap   hat   rag

ham   dad   pan

sack   back

sail   pain   game

gave   rake   late

hay   say   day

may   way   pay

Read the sight words below.

is   was   to

has   the

Read the sentences below, and then I will show you a picture to go with the sentences. (Run your finger under each word as the child reads.)

The rat is sad.

The rat has a rake.

The rat can rake the hay.

Now I will show you the picture of the rat.

What is the rat holding? That's right, he is holding a rake. What is the rat doing with the rake? Yes, he is raking the hay. Why do you think the rat is sad? Yes, he is probably sad, because he

has a lot of hay to rake. It will take him a long time.

I am going to write the words from the last sentence you read on index cards.

(Have the child watch as you write each word with a pen. Label the first card with the lesson number for future use.)

The **rat** **can** **rake** **the** **hay.**

I'm going to underline the sight words with a black crayon. I am going to trace over the *aaa* sounds (as in *cat*) with a gray crayon and the bold *a* sounds (as in *cake*) with a black crayon.

I will make dotted lines over the letter *e* at the end of the word *rake* with a black crayon. I will make dotted lines over the letter *y* at the end of the word *hay* with a black crayon. Why am I dotting these letters? That's right, because these letters are silent. They make no sound.

Read the sentence. Great! Now I am going to mix the cards. I want you to put the cards in proper order to make the sentence again.

(Assist the child with putting the cards in proper order. Remind him, if necessary, a sentence begins with an uppercase letter and ends with a period.)

Now read the sentence.

Copy Work: (The copy work is optional for children who have difficulty with writing.)

I will write the last sentence you just read on a piece of paper.

(Neatly write the sentence with a pen, paying close attention to letter spacing, formation, and size. Make the letters large enough for the child to easily copy. Allow space for the child to write his letters directly under yours. An alternate method is to allow the child to trace over your letters.)

Now you can copy what I wrote.

The rat can rake the hay.

I will trace over the *aaa* sounds with a gray crayon. I will trace over the bold *a* sounds with a black crayon. I will make dotted lines over the letter *e* at the end of the word *rake* and over the letter *y* at the end of the word *hay* with a black crayon. Do you know why I am doing this? That's right, because these letters are silent. They make no sound. I will underline the sight words with a black crayon.

(Trace over the letters you wrote. If the child wants, he can trace over his letters with the proper colors.)

I would like for you to read the sentence once more. Very good! Would you like to draw a picture to go with your sentence?

Now let's read a book together.

(Review the material before moving on to the next lesson. Use the index cards for review. From time to time, review the material from some of the previous lessons as well. Refer to Teaching Tips on page 21.)

Lesson 23

Materials: reading manual, index cards, pen, gray crayon, and black crayon.

Instructions: Today the child will review the following sight words: *the, has, is, was,* and *to*. He will review the bold *a* sound as in *cake* by reading the following words: *mail, pail, rain, pain, game, name, save, wave, bake,* and *lake*. He will be introduced to the short vowel sound for the letter *i*. This letter makes the *iii* sound as in *pig*. It will appear in a gray print as shown below.

i

The child will learn to read the following letter combinations: *ip, it, ig, in, im,* and *id*. He will learn to read various words using these letter combinations.

In preparation for today's lesson, write the following words on index cards, and cut the cards where indicated in the diagram. Write the letter *i* with a gray crayon and the other letters with a black crayon. Label the first card with the lesson number for future use. Place a rubber band around the cards when not in use.

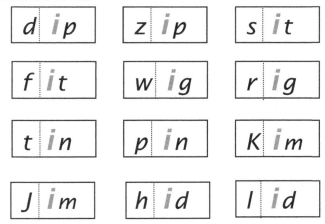

He will read the following sentences and complete a variety of exercises based on the sentences: *The cat hid. The cat hid in the bag. The bag was big.*

Dialogue: What sound does the letter below make? (*a* as in *cake*.)

a

Good, the letter makes the bold *a* sound.

Read the words below. These words all have the bold *a* sound. Remember, the dotted letters are silent. They make no sound.

m a i l	p a i l
r a i n	p a i n
g a m e	n a m e
s a v e	w a v e
b a k e	l a k e

Read the sight words below:

the   **has**   **is**

was   **to**

Look at the letter below. This letter makes the *iii* sound (as in *pig*). Say *iii* as I point to the letter. Notice this letter is gray.

i

Now say *iii* again. (Point to the letter above.)

(Retrieve the cards you prepared for today's lesson. Put the small cards aside and place the big cards face down in pile on the table.)

Now you are going to read some cards that have the *iii* sound. Pick up a card from the pile and read it.

Example: Look at the letters on the card. What sound do the letters make? Good, the letters say *iiig* (as in *pig*).

ig

(Continue until all the cards have been read. There will be two cards for each letter combination. If the child is having trouble with the *iii* sound, as in *pig,* assist him in reading the cards.)

Now you are going to make some new words using the big cards and the small cards.

(Place the small cards in a pile face down on the table next to the pile of big cards)

Pick a small card and a big card. Put them together to make a word. Sometimes you may make a funny word. Let's see if you make a real word or a funny word.

Example: What does the small card say? What does the big card say? Put the sounds together to make a word. What is the word?

z ip

Very good, the word is *zip*. Zip is a real word. Now try making another word. (Continue until all the cards have been used.)

Read the sentences, and then I will show you a picture to go with the sentences. (Encourage the child to run his finger under each word as he reads.)

The cat hid.

The cat hid in the bag.

The bag was big.

Now I will show you a picture of the cat.

Look at the picture. How do you know a cat is hiding in the bag? What part of his body is sticking out? Do you think the cat is playing? Cats like to play.

I am going to write the words from one of the sentences you just read on index cards.

(Have the child watch as you write each word with a pen. Label the first card with the lesson number for future use.)

The	cat	hid	in

the	bag.

I'm going to underline the sight words with a black crayon. I am going to trace over the *aaa* sounds (as in *cat*) and the *iii* sounds (as in *pig*) with a gray crayon.

Read the sentence. Great! Now I will mix the cards, and you can put them in proper order to make the sentence again.

(Assist the child with putting the cards in proper order. Remind him, if necessary, a sentence begins with an uppercase letter and ends with a period.)

Now read the sentence.

Copy Work: (The copy work is optional for children who have difficulty with writing.)

I will write the sentence you just read on a piece of paper.

(Neatly write the sentence with a pen, paying close attention to letter spacing, formation, and size. Make the letters large enough for the child to easily copy. Allow space for the child to write his letters directly under yours. An alternate method is to allow the child to trace over your letters.)

Now you can copy what I wrote.

The cat hid in the bag.

I will trace over the *aaa* sounds and the *iii* sounds with a gray crayon. I will underline the sight words with a black crayon.

(Trace over the letters you wrote. If the child wants, he can trace over his letters with the proper colors.)

I would like for you to read the sentence once more. Very good! Would you like to draw a picture to go with your sentence?

Now let's read a book together.

(Review the material before moving on to the next lesson. Use the index cards for review. From time to time, review the material from some of the previous lessons as well. Refer to Teaching Tips on page 21.)

Lesson 24

Materials: reading manual, index cards, pen, gray crayon, and black crayon.

Instructions: In today's lesson, the child will review the following sight words: *has, was, the, to,* and *is*. He will be introduced to the word *his*. Next, he will review the bold *a* sound as in *cake* by reading the following words: *make, rake, rain, gain, pale, sale, made, fade, gate, hate, bay,* and *way*. He will review the *iii* sound as in *pig* by reading the following words: *zip, hip, fit, sit, wig, pig, fin, pin, hid, lid, rim,* and *Tim*.

He will read the following sentences and complete a variety of exercises based on the sentences. *The man has a pig. The pig is in the hay. His name is Jake.*

Dialogue: Read the sight words below:

has   *was*   *the*

to   *is*

If we put the *h* sound (as in hush) with the sight word *is*, we get *his*. (Point to the word below as you say it.)

his

This word also has the *iii* sound in it (as in *pig*). Say the word as I point to it.

his

What sound does this bold letter make? (*a* as in *cake.*)

a

76

Read the words below with the bold *a* sound. Remember, the dotted letters are silent. They make no sound.

m**a**ke   r**a**ke

r**a**in   g**a**in

p**a**le   s**a**le

m**a**de   f**a**de

g**a**te   h**a**te

b**a**y   w**a**y

What sound does the letter below make? (*iii* as in *pig*).

i

That's right. This letter makes the *iii* sound. Read the words below that have the *iii* sound.

z**i**p   h**i**p   f**i**t

s**i**t   w**i**g   p**i**g

f**i**n   p**i**n   h**i**d

l**i**d   r**i**m   T**i**m

Did you notice the last word begins with an uppercase letter? (Point to the word *Tim* below.) Why? That's right, because we begin names with an uppercase letter. The name is *Tim*.

Read the sentences below, and then I will show you a picture to go with the sentences. (Encourage the child to run his finger under each word as he reads.)

<u>The</u> m**a**n <u>has</u> **a** p**i**g.

<u>The</u> p**i**g <u>is</u> **i**n <u>the</u> h**a**y.

H**i**s n**a**me <u>is</u> J**a**ke.

Now I will show you a picture of the pig.

Look at the picture. Where is the pig? That's right, he is in the hay. The pig has a funny tail. What is funny about his tail? Yes, it is very curly. What kind of work do you think the man does? Yes, he looks like a farmer.

I am going to write the words from one of the sentences you just read on index cards.

(Have the child watch as you write each word with a pen. Label the first card with the lesson number for future use.)

The	pig	is	in

the	hay.

I am going to underline the sight words with a black crayon. I am going to trace over the iii sounds (as in *pig*) with a gray crayon and the bold *a* sound (as in *cake*) with a black crayon.

I will make dotted lines over the letter y at the end of the word hay. Can you tell me why I dotted this letter? Good. I dotted it, because it is a silent letter. It makes no sound.

Read the sentence. Very good! Now I will mix the cards, and you can put them in proper order to make the sentence again.

(Assist the child with putting the cards in proper order. Remind him, if necessary, a sentence begins with an uppercase letter and ends with a period.)

Now read the sentence.

Copy Work: (The copy work is optional for children who have difficulty with writing.)

I will write the sentence you just read on a piece of paper.

(Neatly write the sentence with a pen, paying close attention to letter spacing, formation, and size. Make the letters large enough for the child to easily copy. Allow space for the child to write his letters directly under yours. An alternate method is to allow the child to trace over your letters.)

Now you can copy what I wrote.

The pig is in the hay.

I will trace over the iii sounds with a gray crayon. I will trace over the bold *a* sound with a black crayon. I will make dotted lines over the letter y at the end of the word hay. I will underline the sight words with a black crayon.

(Trace over the letters you wrote. If the child wants, he can trace over his letters with the proper colors.)

I would like for you to read the sentence once more. Very good! Would you like to draw a picture to go with your sentence?

Now let's read a book together.

(Review the material before moving on to the next lesson. Use the index cards for review. From time to time, review the material from some of the previous lessons as well. Refer to Teaching Tips on page 21.)

Lesson 25

Materials: reading manual, index cards, pen, gray crayon, and black crayon.

Instructions: In today's lesson, the child will review the following sight words: *has, was, the, to,* and *is.* He will also be introduced to the new sight word *I.*

He will review the bold *a* sound as in *cake* by reading the following words: *lake, make, pail, sail, gate, mate, rain,* and *pain.* He will review the *iii* sound as in *pig* by reading the following words: *pig, fig, sin, win, dim, rim, fit, pit, sip, lip, hid,* and *bid.*

He will be introduced to the long vowel sound for the letter *i as* in *bike.* This will be referred to as the bold *i* sound and will be represented with a bold letter as shown below.

i

He will read the following words containing the bold *i* sound: *bike, hike, ride, side, mine, fine, time, dime, mile, file, pie,* and *die.*

He will read the following sentences and complete a variety of exercises based on the sentences: *I can ride a bike. I like to ride. I can ride to the lake.*

Dialogue: Read the sight words below.

has   was   the

to   is

Today you will learn a new sight word. It is the word I. (Point to the word below as you say it.) You use this when you are talking about yourself. You might say, I am going to the park. Look at the word below and say I as I point to it.

I

Now read the sentence below.

I had a cat.

Very good!

What sound does this bold letter make? (*a* as in *cake.*)

a

Read the words below that have the bold *a* sound. Remember, the dotted letters are silent. They make no sound.

lake   make

pail   sail

gate   mate

rain   pain

Read the words below that have the *iii* sound (as in *pig*).

pig   fig   sin

win   dim   rim

fit   pit   sip

lip   hid   bid

You are doing very well!

Now you are going to learn a new sound. Look at the letter below. This bold letter makes the *i* sound (as in *bike*).

i

Say *i* as I point to the letter. Very good!

Now read the words below that have the bold *i* sound (as in *bike*). Remember, the dotted letters are silent. They make no sound. I will read the first word for you. It is *bike*. (Point to the word as you read it.)

bike   *hike*

ride   *side*

mine   *fine*

time   *dime*

mile   *file*

pie   *die*

Read the sentences below, and then I will show you a picture to go with the sentences. (Encourage the child to run his finger under each word as he reads.)

<u>I</u> can ride a bike.

<u>I</u> like <u>to</u> ride.

<u>I</u> can ride <u>to</u> <u>the</u> lake.

Now I will show you a picture of the lake.

Look at the picture. The boy and girl are riding their bikes by the lake. They are not the only ones at the lake. Who else do you see? Why do you think the ducks are interested in the children? Do you think they want the children to give them food? Have you ever fed ducks at a lake or pond?

I am going to write the words from one of the sentences you just read on index cards.

(Have the child watch as you write each word with a pen. Label the first card with the lesson number for future use.)

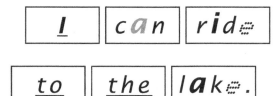

I am going to underline the sight words with a black crayon. Today our sentence has three sight words. What are they? I am going to trace over the *aaa* sound (as in *cat*) with a gray crayon. I am going to trace over the bold *i* sound (as in *bike*) with a black crayon. I am going to trace over the bold *a* sound (as in *cake*) with a black crayon too.

I will make dotted lines over the letter *e* at the end of the words *ride* and *lake*. Can you tell me why I dotted these letters? Good. I dotted them because they are silent letters. They make no sound.

Read the sentence. Great! Now I will mix the cards, and you can put them in proper order to make the sentence again.

(Assist the child with putting the cards in proper order. Remind him, if necessary, a sentence begins with an uppercase letter and ends with a period.)

Now read the sentence.

Copy Work: (The copy work is optional for children who have difficulty with writing.)

I will write the sentence you just read on a piece of paper.

(Neatly write the sentence with a pen, paying close attention to letter spacing, formation, and size. Make the letters large enough for the child to easily copy. Allow space for the child to write his letters directly under yours. An alternate method is to allow the child to trace over your letters.)

Now you can copy what I wrote.

I can ride to the lake.

I will trace over the *aaa* sound with a gray crayon. I will trace over the bold *i* sound with a black crayon. I will trace over the bold *a* sound with a black crayon. I will make dotted lines over the letter *e* at the end of the words *ride* and *lake*. I will underline the sight words with a black crayon.

(Trace over the letters you wrote. If the child wants, he can trace over his letters with the proper colors.)

I would like for you to read the sentence once more. Very good! Would you like to draw a picture to go with your sentence?

Now let's read a book together.

(Review the material before moving on to the next lesson. Use the index cards for review. From time to time, review the material from some of the previous lessons as well. Refer to Teaching Tips on page 21.)

Lesson 26

Materials: reading manual, index cards, pen, gray crayon, and black crayon.

Instructions: In today's lesson, the child will review the following sight words: *has, was, the, to, is,* and *I.* He will also be introduced to the new sight word *you.*

He will review the *aaa* sound as in *cat.* Today he will focus on words containing the *aaa* sound that have the *nd* sound at the end of the word as in *land.* He will read the following words: *and, land, hand, sand,* and *band.* The child may need assistance in blending the letters *nd* together.

He will also review the bold *a* sound as in *cake* by reading the following words: *bake, make, pail,* and *mail.* He will review the *iii* sound as in *pig* by reading the following words: *pig, dig, win,* and *fin.* Next, he will review the bold *i* sound as in *bike* by reading the following words: *pile, file, like,* and *hike.*

He will read the following sentences and complete a variety of exercises based on the sentences: *I can dig. I can dig in the sand. I can make a pile. I can make a pile in the pail.*

Dialogue: Read the sight words below.

has   was   the

to   is   I

Today you will learn a new sight word. It is the word *you.* (Point to the word below as you say it.) Now say *you* as I point to the word.

you

Now let's use this new sight word in a sentence. Read the sentence at the top of the next page.

You can pat the pig.

Very good!

Look at the letter below. What sound does this letter make? (*aaa* as in *cat.*)

a

That is right. This letter makes the *aaa* sound. Now you are going to read some new words that have the *aaa* sound. Look at the word below. I will read it. The word is *and.* (Sound out the word slowly at first and then repeat it a little faster.)

and

Say *and* as I point to the word. Great!

Now read the words below that have the *and* sound (as in *land*).

and   land   hand

sand   band

Read the words below with the bold *a* sound (as in *cake*).

bake   make

pail   mail

Read the words below that have the *iii* sound (as in *pig*).

pig   dig

win   fin

Read the words below that have the bold *i* sound (as in *bike*).

pile   file

like   hike

Read the sentences below, and then I will show you a picture to go with the sentences. (Encourage the child to run his finger under each word as he reads.)

I can dig.

I can dig in <u>the</u> sand.

I can make a pile.

I can make a pile in <u>the</u> pail.

Now I will show you a picture of the pail in the sand.

Look at the picture. The boy and girl are playing in the sandbox. What is unusual about the pail they are filling? Have you ever seen such a big pail?

I am going to write the words from one of the sentences you just read on index cards.

(Have the child watch as you write each word with a pen. Label the first card with the lesson number for future use.)

<u>I</u>	can	make	a

pile	in	<u>the</u>	pail.

I am going to underline the sight words with a black crayon. Today our sentence has two sight words. What are they? I am going to trace over the *aaa* sound (as in *cat*) and the *iii* sound (as in *pig*) with a gray crayon. I will trace over the bold *a* sounds (as in *cake*) with a black crayon. I am going to trace over the

83

bold *i* sound (as in *bike*) with a black crayon too.

I will make dotted lines over the letter *e* at the end of the word *make* with a black crayon. I will also make dotted lines over the letter *e* at the end of the word *pile* with a black crayon. I will make dotted lines over the letter *i* in the word *pail* with a black crayon. Can you tell me why I dotted these letters? Good. I dotted them, because they are silent letters. They make no sound.

Read the sentence. Very good! Now I will mix the cards, and you can put them in proper order to make the sentence again.

(Assist the child with putting the cards in proper order. Remind him, if necessary, a sentence begins with an uppercase letter and ends with a period.)

Now read the sentence.

Copy Work: (The copy work is optional for children who have difficulty with writing.)

I will write the sentence you just read on a piece of paper.

(Neatly write the sentence with a pen, paying close attention to letter spacing, formation, and size. Make the letters large enough for the child to easily copy. Allow space for the child to write his letters directly under yours. An alternate method is to allow the child to trace over your letters.)

Now you can copy what I wrote.

I can make a pile in the pail.

I will trace over the *aaa* sound and the *iii* sound with a gray crayon. I will trace over the bold *a* sounds and the bold *i* sound with a black crayon.

I will make dotted lines over the letter *e* at the end of the word *make* and at the end of the word *pile* with a black crayon. I will make dotted lines over the letter *i* in the word *pail* with a black crayon. I will underline the sight words with a black crayon.

(Trace over the letters you wrote. If the child wants, he can trace over his letters with the proper colors.)

I would like for you to read the sentence once more. Very good! Would you like to draw a picture to go with your sentence?

Now let's read a book together.

(Review the material before moving on to the next lesson. Use the index cards for review. From time to time, review the material from some of the previous lessons as well. Refer to Teaching Tips on page 21.)

Lesson 27

Materials: reading manual, index cards, pen, gray crayon, and black crayon.

Instructions: In today's lesson, the child will review the following sight words: *has, was, the, to, is, I,* and *you.* He will review the *iii* sound as in *pig* as he reads various words that end in the *ck* sound such as *pick.* He will read the following words: *pick, sick, lick, Dick, Rick, kick, Nick, tick, Vick,* and *wick.*

He will review the bold *a* sound as in *cake* as he reads the following words: *main, gain, late,* and *gate.* He will also review the bold *i* sound as in *bike* as he reads the following words: *white, bite, mine,* and *fine.*

He will be introduced to the short vowel sound for the letter *o.* This letter makes the *ooo* sound as in *hot.* It will appear in a gray print as shown below.

o

The child will learn to read the following letter combinations: *op, ot, og, om, od* and *ock.* He will learn to read various words using these letter combinations. In preparation for today's lesson, write the following words on index cards, and cut the cards where indicated in the diagram. Write the letter *o* with a gray crayon and the other letters with a black crayon. Label the first card with the lesson number for future use. Place a rubber around the cards when not in use.

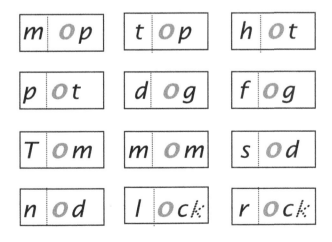

He will read the following sentences and complete a variety of exercises based on the sentences: *The dog sat. The dog sat on the rock. The dog sat in the rain. The dog was white.*

We are no longer using clues to assist the child with reading the copy work. It is important for the child to read the text located in this segment of the lesson even if he does not copy the sentences. This will give him an opportunity to practice reading text printed in a regular type.

Dialogue: Read the sight words below:

<u>h a s</u>   <u>w a s</u>   <u>t h e</u>

<u>t o</u>   <u>i s</u>   <u>I</u>   <u>y o u</u>

Read the words below that have the *iii* sound (as in *pig*). These words also have a silent letter. It is the letter *k*. It is dotted, because it makes no sound.

pick   sick   lick

Dick   Rick   kick

Nick   tick   Vick

wick

Why do some of the words begin with uppercase letters? That's right, because these are special words. They are names. (Point to the names above and read them.)

Read the following words that have the bold *a* sound. Remember, the dotted letters are silent. They make no sound.

85

m**a**̤n   g**a**̤n

l**a**t̤e   g**a**t̤e

Read the words below that have the bold *i* sound. The first word is unusual, because it has two silent letters.

Remember, the dotted letters are silent. They make no sound.

wh̤**i**t̤e   b**i**t̤e

m**i**n̤e   f**i**n̤e

Look at the letter below. This letter makes the *ooo* sound (as in *hot*). Say *ooo* as I point to the letter. Notice this letter is gray.

o

(Retrieve the cards you prepared for today's lesson. Put the small cards aside and place the big cards face down in pile on the table.)

Now you are going to read some cards that have the *ooo* sound (as in *hot*). Pick a card from the pile and read it.

Example: What sound do the letters make? Good, the letters say *ooog* (as in *dog*).

| o g |

(Continue until all the cards have been read. There will be two cards for each letter combination. If the child is having trouble with the *ooo* sound as in *hot,* assist him in reading the cards.)

Now you are going to make some new words using the big cards and the small cards.

(Place the small cards in a pile face down on the table next to the pile of big cards.)

Pick a small card and a big card. Put them together to make a word. Sometimes you may make a funny word. Let's see if you make a real word or a funny word.

Example: What does the small card say? What does the big card say? Put the sounds together to make a word. What is the word?

| t | op |

Very good, the word is *top*. *Top* is a real word. Now try making another word. (Continue until all the cards have been used.)

Read the word below. It has the *ooo* sound in it (as in *hot*). It is a very short word.

o n

Now read the sentence below. It has the new word *on* in it.

The pig is on the ma**t.**

Read the following sentences, and then I will show you a picture to go

86

with the sentences. (Encourage the child to run his finger under each word as he reads.)

The dog sat.

The dog sat on the rock.

The dog sat in the rain.

The dog was white.

Now I will show you a picture of the dog.

Look at the picture. The dog is sitting in the rain. He is on the rock.

What is the dog holding? That's right, he is holding an umbrella. It is a good thing he has an umbrella. Why do you think he is sitting on the rock? That's right. He is sitting on the rock, because he doesn't want to step in the puddle.

The story said the dog was white. Is he plain white? No, he isn't. What color spots does the dog have? That's right, he has black spots.

I am going to write the words from one of the sentences you just read on index cards.

(Have the child watch as you write each word with a pen. Label the first card with the lesson number for future use.)

| The | dog | sat | on |
| the | rock. | | |

I am going to underline the sight words with a black crayon. Today our sentence has two sight words. They are the same word. What is the word? I am going to trace over the *ooo* sounds (as in *hot*) with a gray crayon. I am going to trace over the *aaa* sound (as in *cat*) with a gray crayon too.

I will make dotted lines over the letter *k* at the end of the word *rock*. Can you tell me why I dotted this letter? Good. I dotted it, because it is a silent letter. It makes no sound.

Read the sentence. Very good! Now I will mix the cards, and you can put them in proper order to make the sentence again.

(Assist the child with putting the cards in proper order. Remind him, if necessary, a sentence begins with an uppercase letter and ends with a period.)

Now read the sentence.

(**Note**: We are no longer using clues to assist the child with reading the copy work. It is important for the child to read the text located in this segment of the lesson even if he does not copy the sentences. This will give him an opportunity to practice reading text printed in a regular type.)

Copy Work: (The copy work is optional for children who have difficulty with writing.)

I will write the sentence you just read on a piece of paper.

(Neatly write the sentence with a pen, paying close attention to letter spacing, formation, and size. Make the letters large enough for the child to easily copy. Allow space for the child to write his letters directly under yours. An alternate method is to allow the child to trace over your letters.)

Now you can copy what I wrote.

The dog sat on the rock.

I would like for you to read the sentence once more. Very good! Would you like to draw a picture to go with your sentence?

Now let's read a book together.

(Review the material before moving on to the next lesson. Use the index cards for review. From time to time, review the material from some of the previous lessons as well. Refer to Teaching Tips on page 21.)

Lesson 28

Materials: reading manual, index cards, pen, gray crayon, and black crayon.

Instructions: In today's lesson, the child will review the following sight words: *I, the, is, you, has, was,* and *to.* He will review the *ooo* sound as in *hot* as he reads various words that end in the letters *ck* as in *lock.* He will read the following words: *lock, dock, sock, mock, rock,* and *tock.* He will review the *iii* sound as in *pig* as he reads the following words: *hit, sit, give, live, pig,* and *wig.*

He will review the bold *a* sound as in *cake* as he reads the following words: *save, wave, bay, way, lake,* and *bake.* He will review the bold *i* sound as in *bike* as he reads the following words: *bike, hike, time, lime, die,* and *pie.*

He will review the *aaa* sound as in *cat* as he reads words that end in the letters *nd* as in *land.* He will read the following words: *sand, hand, land,* and *band.*

He will read the following sentences and complete a variety of exercises based on the sentences: *I can bake. I can bake a pie. The pie is hot. I like pie.*

We are no longer using clues to assist the child with reading the copy work. It is important for the child to read the text located in this segment of the lesson even if he does not copy the sentences. This will give him an opportunity to practice reading text printed in a regular type.

Dialogue: Read the sight words below:

I   the   is   you
has   was   to

Look at the letter below. What sound does this letter make? (*ooo* as in *hot.*)

o

That is right. This letter makes the *ooo* sound.

Read the following words that have the *ooo* sound. These words also have a silent letter. It is the letter *k*. It is dotted, because it makes no sound.

lock   dock   sock

mock   rock   tock

Read the words below that have the *iii* sound (as in *pig*).

hit   sit

give   live

pig   wig

Read the words below that have the *bold a* sound (as in *cake*). Remember, the dotted letters are silent. They make no sound.

save   wave

bay   way

lake   bake

Look at the letter below. What sound does this letter make? (*i* as in *bike*.)

i

Good, the letter makes the bold *i* sound.

Read the words below that have the bold *i* sound (as in *bike*). Remember, the dotted letters are silent. They make no sound.

bike   hike

time   lime

die   pie

Now you are going to read some words that have the *aaa* sound (as in *cat*). Look at the letters below. What sound do these letters make? (*aaa* as in *land*.)

and

Very good! These letters make the *and* sound.

Read the words below that have the *and* sound.

sand   hand

land   band

Read the sentences below, and then I will show you a picture to go with the sentences. (Encourage the child to run his finger under each word as he reads.)

I can bake.

I can bake a pie.

The pie is hot.

I like pie.

Now I will show you a picture of the pie.

Look at the picture. Does the pie look like it is hot? How can you tell the pie is hot? That's right, you can see steam rising from the pie. Do you like pie? What is your favorite kind of pie?

I am going to write the words from one of the sentences you just read on index cards.

(Have the child watch as you write each word with a pen. Label the first card with the lesson number for future use.)

| The | pi**e** | is |
| hot. |

I am going to underline the sight words with a black crayon. Today our sentence has two sight words. What are they? I will trace over the bold *i* sound (as in *bike*) with a black crayon. I am going to trace over the *ooo* sound (as in *hot*) with a gray crayon.

I will make dotted lines over the letter *e* at the end of the word *pie*. Can you tell me why I dotted this letter? Good. I dotted it, because it is a silent letter. It makes no sound.

Read the sentence. Very good! Now I will mix the cards, and you can put them in proper order to make the sentence again.

(Assist the child with putting the cards in proper order. Remind him, if necessary, a sentence begins with an uppercase letter and ends with a period.)

Now read the sentence.

(**Note**: We are no longer using clues to assist the child with reading the copy work. It is important for the child to read the text located in this segment of the lesson even if he does not copy the sentences. This will give him an opportunity to practice reading text printed in a regular type.)

Copy Work: (The copy work is optional for children who have difficulty with writing.)

I will write the sentence you just read on a piece of paper.

(Neatly write the sentence with a pen, paying close attention to letter spacing, formation, and size. Make the letters large enough for the child to easily copy. Allow space for the child to write his letters directly under yours. An alternate method is to allow the child to trace over your letters.)

Now you can copy what I wrote.

The pie is hot.

I would like for you to read the sentence once more. Very good! Would you like to draw a picture to go with your sentence?

Now let's read a book together.

(Review the material before moving on to the next lesson. Use the index cards for review. From time to time, review the material from some of the previous lessons as well. Refer to Teaching Tips on page 21.)

Lesson 29

Materials: reading manual, index cards, pen, gray crayon, and black crayon.

Instructions: Today the child will review the *ooo* sound as in *hot* by reading the following words: *mop, top, hot, pot, dog, fog, Tom, mom, sod, nod, lock, rock,* and *on*.

He will review the *aaa* sound as in *cat* as he reads various words that end in the *ang* sound as in *rang*. He will read the following words: *rang, sang, hang, fang, gang, pang, tang,* and *bang*. The child may need assistance in blending the letters *ng* together.

He will review the following sight words: *has, I, to, is, the, was* and *you*. He will be introduced to the new sight word *do*. He will review the bold *i* sound as in *bike* by reading the following words: *file, while, dime, time, white,* and *kite*.

We will introduce the use of question marks. This is only an introduction, and we do not expect the child to master this concept.

The sentences the child will read will take on a new aspect. We will now refer to them as stories. Each story will have a title.

The child will read the following story and complete a variety of exercises based on the story.

Title: *"The Band"*

Story: *I can bang. I can bang on the pot. I can bang on the pan. I can bang on the lid. I can bang in the band.*

We are no longer using clues to assist the child with reading the copy work. It is important for the child to read the text located in this segment of the lesson even if he does not copy the sentences. This will give him an opportunity to practice reading text printed in a regular type.

Dialogue: What sound does this letter make? (*ooo* as in *hot*.)

o

Read the following words that have the *ooo* sound.

mop   top   hot

pot   dog   fog

Tom   mom   sod

nod   lock   rock

on

Now you are going to learn some new words that have the *aaa* sound (as in *cat*). Look at the letters below. The letters say *ang* (as in *rang*). Say *ang* as I point the letters.

ang

Look at the words below that have the *ang* sound. I will read the first word for you. It is *rang*. Now read the words below that have the *ang* sound.

rang   sang

hang   fang

gang   pang

tang   bang

Read the sight words below.

has I to is

the was you

Today you will learn a new sight word. Look at the word below. It is the word *do*. (Point to the word.) Say *do* as I point to the word.

do

Now you can read a sentence that has the word *do* in it.

Do you have a cat?

Look at the mark at the end of the sentence you just read. It is not a period. It is called a question mark. We use it when we are asking a question. I will read the sentence again. I will make it sound like I am asking a question. (Read the sentence as you point to each word with your finger. Emphasize the question.)

Read the words below. These words have the bold *i* sound (as in *bike*).

file   while

dime   time

white   kite

Today you are going to read a story. A story has a title. A title is like the story's name.

Read the title below.

"The Band"

Read the story below. Then I will show you a picture to go with the story.

"The Band"

I can bang.

I can bang on the pot.

I can bang on the pan.

I can bang on the lid.

I can bang in the band.

Now I will show you a picture of the pot and pan band.

Look at the picture. The little boy is sitting on the floor. Can you guess what room he is in? That's right he is in the kitchen. Did you like to bang on pots when you were little?

I am going to write the words from one of the sentences you just read on index cards.

(Have the child watch as you write each word with a pen. Label the first card with the lesson number for future use.)

I	can	bang

on	the	pot.

93

I am going to underline the sight words with a black crayon. Today our sentence has two sight words. Can you tell me what they are?

I am going to trace over the *aaa* sounds (as in *cat*) and the *ooo* sounds (as in *hot*) with a gray crayon.

Read the sentence. Great! Now I will mix the cards, and you can put them in proper order to make the sentence again.

(Assist the child with putting the cards in proper order. Remind him, if necessary, a sentence begins with an uppercase letter and ends with a period.)

Now read the sentence.

(**Note**: We are no longer using clues to assist the child with reading the copy work. It is important for the child to read the text located in this segment of the lesson even if he does not copy the sentences. This will give him an opportunity to practice reading text printed in a regular type.)

Copy Work: (The copy work is optional for children who have difficulty with writing.)

I will write the sentence you just read on a piece of paper.

(Neatly write the sentence with a pen, paying close attention to letter spacing, formation, and size. Make the letters large enough for the child to easily copy. Allow space for the child to write his letters directly under yours. An alternate method is to allow the child to trace over your letters.)

Now you can copy what I wrote.

I can bang on the pot.

I would like for you to read the sentence once more. Very good! Would you like to draw a picture to go with your sentence?

Now let's read a book together.

(Review the material before moving on to the next lesson. Use the index cards for review. From time to time, review the material from some of the previous lessons as well. Refer to Teaching Tips on page 21.)

Lesson 30

Materials: reading manual, index cards, pen, gray crayon, and black crayon.

Instructions: Today the child will review the *ooo* sound as in *hot as* he reads the following words: *mop, fog,* and *rock*. He will also review the *ooo* sound as in *hot* as he reads various words that end in the letters *ng* as in *long*. He will read the following words: *long, song, gong, tong, pong,* and *dong*.

He will review the *aaa* sound as in *cat* as he reads various words that end in *ank* sound as in *bank*. He will read the following words: *bank, Hank, rank, sank, tank,* and *yank*.

The child will review the *iii* sound as in *pig* as he reads various words that end in the letters *ll* as in *hill*. He will read the following words: *hill, fill, kill, Bill, dill, mill, gill, Jill, will* and *pill*. He will review the following sight words: *has, was, the, to, is, I, you* and *do*.

The child will read the following story and perform a variety of exercises based on the story.

Title: *"At the Mill"*

Story: *Jill sang a song. Jill sang at the mill. The mill was on the hill.*

We are no longer using clues to assist the child with reading the copy work. It is important for the child to read the text located in this segment of the lesson even if he does not copy the sentences. This will give him an opportunity to practice reading text printed in a regular type.

Dialogue: Read the following words that have the *ooo* sound (as in *hot*).

mop   fog   rock

That was very good! Now you are going to learn some new words that have the *ooo* sound (as in *hot*). Look at the letters below. These letters say *ong* (as in *long*). (Point to the letters as you sound them out.)

ong

Say *ong* as I point to the letters. Good!

Read the words below. These words have the *ong* sound (as in *long*). I will read the first word for you. It is *long*. (Point to the word as you say it.)

long   song   gong
tong   pong   dong

Now you are going to learn some new words that have the *aaa* sound (as in *cat*). Look at the letters below. These letters say *ank* (as in *bank*). (Point to the letters as you sound them out.)

ank

Say *ank* as I point to the letters. Good!

Now look at the words below. These words have the *ank* sound (as in *bank*). I will read the first word for you. It is *bank*. (Point to the word as you say it.) Read the words below.

bank   Hank   rank
sank   tank   yank

Did you notice one of the words begins with an uppercase letter? Which word is it? Why does it start with an uppercase letter? That's right, because it is a name.

Read the sentence below. This sentence has a word with the *ank* sound (as in *bank*).

Dad <u>is</u> at <u>the</u> bank.

Now you are going to learn some new words that have the *iii* sound (as in *pig*). Look at the letters below. These letters say *iill* (as in *hill*). (Point to the letters as you sound them out.)

ill

Say *iill* as I point to the letters. Good!

Now look at the words below. These words have the *iill* sound (as in *hill*). I will read the first word for you. It is *hill*. (Point to the word as you say it.) Read the words below.

hill   fill   kill

Bill   dill   mill

gill   Jill   will

pill

Did you notice two of the words begin with an uppercase letter? Which words are they? That's right. They are the words Bill and Jill. Why do they start with an uppercase letter? That's right, because they are names.

Read the sight words below.

<u>has</u>   <u>was</u>   <u>the</u>   <u>to</u>

<u>is</u>   <u>I</u>   <u>you</u>   <u>do</u>

Read the story below. Then I will show you a picture to go with the story.

"At <u>the</u> Mill"

Jill sang **a** song.

Jill sang at <u>the</u> mill.

<u>The</u> mill <u>was</u> on <u>the</u> hill.

Now I will show you a picture of the mill.

Look at the picture. What does Jill have in her hand? That's right. She has a bag. Why do you think she needs a bag? Can you see where is she going? Yes, she is going to the mill. She can put the flour from the mill in her bag.

I am going to write the words from one of the sentences you just read on index cards.

(Have the child watch as you write each word with a pen. Label the first card with the lesson number for future use.)

| Jill | sang | at |

| the | mill. |

I am going to underline the sight word with a black crayon. Today our

sentence has only one sight word. Can you tell me what it is? I am going to trace over the *iii* sounds (as in *pig*) and the *aaa* sounds (as in *cat*) with a gray crayon.

Read the sentence. Great! Now I will mix the cards, and you can put them in proper order to make the sentence again.

(Assist the child with putting the cards in proper order. Remind him, if necessary, a sentence begins with an uppercase letter and ends with a period.)

Now read the sentence.

(**Note**: We are no longer using clues to assist the child with reading the copy work. It is important for the child to read the text located in this segment of the lesson even if he does not copy the sentences. This will give him an opportunity to practice reading text printed in a regular type.)

Copy Work: (The copy work is optional for children who have difficulty with writing.)

I will write the sentence you just read on a piece of paper.

(Neatly write the sentence with a pen, paying close attention to letter spacing, formation, and size. Make the letters large enough for the child to easily copy. Allow space for the child to write his letters directly under yours. An alternate method is to allow the child to trace over your letters.)

Now you can copy what I wrote.

Jill   sang   at   the   mill.

I would like for you to read the sentence once more. Very good! Would you like to draw a picture to go with your sentence?

Now let's read a book together.

(Review the material before moving on to the next lesson. Use the index cards for review. From time to time, review the material from some of the previous lessons as well. Refer to Teaching Tips on page 21.)

Lesson 31

Materials: reading manual, index cards, pen, gray crayon, and black crayon.

Instructions: Today the child will be introduced to the letter *x*. He will read the following words: *tax, wax, lax, fix, mix, six, fox,* and *box.*

He will learn about adding the letter *s* to the end of words. For example, *dog* becomes *dogs* when we add an *s* to it. He will read the following words that have the letter *s* added to them: *hats, bats, racks, packs, fans, vans, digs, wigs, ticks, licks, pins, wins, mops, hops, dots, cots, rocks, socks, dogs, hogs, likes, bikes, cakes,* and *bakes.* This will allow him to review the *aaa* sound, the *iii* sound, the *ooo* sound, the bold *i* sound and the bold *a* sound.

He will review the following sight words: *has, was, the, to, is, I, you,* and *do.* He will be introduced to the new sight word *what.*

The child will read the following story and complete a variety of exercises based on the story.

Title: *"Six Dogs"*

Story: *I have six dogs. You can pat the dogs. The dogs like you. The dogs do not like cats.*

We are no longer using clues to assist the child with reading the copy work. It is important for the child to read the text located in this segment of the lesson even if he does not copy the sentences. This will give him an opportunity to practice reading text printed in a regular type.

Dialogue: Look at the letter below. It is the letter *x*. It makes the sound *cks* (as in *fox*). (Point to the letter as you say its sound.)

x

Say *cks* as I point to the letter. Good!

Now read the words below that have the *cks* sound (as in fox). I will read the first word for you. It is *tax*. (Point to the word as you sound it out.)

t a x   w a x   l a x

fix   mix   six

fox   box

Read the word below.

cat

Sometimes we want to talk about more than one cat. If we want to do this, we say cats. Look at the word below. We put an s at the end of cat to make cats. (Point to the word as you read it.)

cats

Read the words below. These words all have an s at the end.

hats   bats

racks   packs

fans   vans

digs   wigs

ticks   licks

pins   wins

mops   hops

dots   cots

rocks   socks

dogs   hogs

likes   bikes

cakes   bakes

Read the sight words below.

__has__   __was__   __the__   __to__

__is__   __I__   __you__   __do__

Today you will learn a new sight word. Look at the word below. It is the word what. (Point to the word as you read it.)

__what__

Read the sentence below. It begins with the new sight word.

__What__   __is__   __the__ dog's name?

(We will not discuss the reason for the use of the apostrophe as in the word dog's. We will just include it when needed.)

Read the story. Then I will show you a picture to go with the story.

"Six Dogs"

I have six dogs.

You can pat the dogs.

The dogs like you.

The dogs do not like cats.

Now I will show you a picture of the dogs.

Look at the picture. What can you tell me about the dogs? Yes, there are big dogs, and medium sized dogs, and little dogs. How many dogs can you see? How many big dogs are there? How many medium sized dogs are there? How many little dogs are there?

I am going to write the words from one of the sentences you just read on index cards.

(Have the child watch as you write each word with a pen. Label the first card with the lesson number for future use.)

I	have	six

dogs.

I am going to underline the sight word with a black crayon. Today our sentence has one sight word. Can you tell me what it is? I am going to trace over the *aaa* sound (as in *cat*), the *iii* sound (as in *pig*), and the *ooo* sound (as in *hot*) with a gray crayon.

I will make dotted lines over the letter *e* at the end of the word have. Can you tell me why I dotted this letter? That's right. It is a silent letter. It makes no sound.

100

Read the sentence. Now I will mix the cards, and you can put them in proper order to make the sentence again.

(Assist the child with putting the cards in proper order. Remind him, if necessary, a sentence begins with an uppercase letter and ends with a period.)

Now read the sentence.

(**Note**: We are no longer using clues to assist the child with reading the copy work. It is important for the child to read the text located in this segment of the lesson even if he does not copy the sentences. This will give him an opportunity to practice reading text printed in a regular type.)

Copy Work: (The copy work is optional for children who have difficulty with writing.)

I will write the sentence you just read on a piece of paper.

(Neatly write the sentence with a pen, paying close attention to letter spacing, formation, and size. Make the letters large enough for the child to easily copy. Allow space for the child to write his letters directly under yours. An alternate method is to allow the child to trace over your letters.)

Now you can copy what I wrote.

I have six dogs.

I would like for you to read the sentence once more. Very good! Would you like to draw a picture to go with your sentence?

Now let's read a book together.

(Review material between lessons.)

Lesson 32

Materials: reading manual, index cards, pen, gray crayon, black crayon, and a photocopy of the *Sight Word Bingo Game Boards* found on pages 508 and 509 in the Appendix.

Instructions: Today the child will review the bold *i* sound as in *bike* as he reads the following words: *bike, Mike, pipe,* and *ripe*. He will also review the bold *i* sound as in *bike* as he reads various words that end in the letters *nd* as in *find*. He will read the following words: *find, wind, mind, kind, hind, rind* and *bind*.

He will review the following sight words: *has, was, the, to, is, you, I, do,* and *what*. To help him learn his sight words more easily, you will play a game called *Sight Word Bingo*. In preparation for today's lesson, photocopy pages 508 and 509 from the Appendix. These pages will be your game boards. (See the sample game boards on the next page.)

Next, cut five index cards in half. Write a sight word on each card. You will need place markers of some sort. Buttons, pennies, or other small objects will do. M & M's, chocolate chips, raisins, or some other treat can be substituted for place markers.

Place the cards with the sight words written on them in a pile face down on the table. You and the child will take turns reading the cards. Each time a card is read, each player places a marker on the corresponding space on his game board. The first person to have a marker on three words in a row is the winner. The row can run vertically, horizontally, or diagonally.

Play the game several times to ensure the child wins a sufficient number of times. This also ensures he reviews each word several times. Try to keep the winning aspect of the game to a minimum. Some children are easily upset if they do not win. Save the game for review.

is	the	has
was	I	you
what	do	to

I	to	was
do	is	what
has	you	the

The child will review adding the letter *s* to the end of words. For example: *mop* becomes *mops* when we add an *s* to it. He will also review the vowel sounds learned so far as he reads a number of words that have the letter *s* added to them. The child will review the sound for the letter *x* as in the word *fox*.

The child will read the following story and complete a variety of exercises based on the story.

Title: *"The Cake"*

Story: *I can mix a cake. I can bake a cake. I like white cake. What kind do you like?*

We are no longer using clues to assist the child with reading the copy work. It is important for the child to read the text located in this segment of the lesson even if he does not copy the sentences. This will give him an opportunity to practice reading text printed in a regular type.

Dialogue: Read the following words that have the bold *i* sound (as in *bike*).

bike   Mike

pipe   ripe

That was very good! Now you are going to learn some new words that have the bold *i* sound. Look at the letters below. These letters say *ind* (as in *find*). (Point to the letters as you sound them out.)

ind

Say *ind* as I point to the letters. Good!

Read the words below that have the *ind* sound (as in *find*). The first word is *find*. (Point to the word as you say it.)

find   wind

mind   kind

hind   rind

bind

Read the following sight words. You have learned many sight words.

<u>has</u>   <u>was</u>   <u>the</u>

<u>to</u>   <u>is</u>   <u>you</u>

<u>I</u>   <u>do</u>   <u>what</u>

102

Today we are going to play a game. It is called *Sight Word Bingo*.

(Retrieve the game boards and playing cards you made in preparation for today's lesson. Shuffle the playing cards, and place them face down on the table. You will need place markers also.)

Choose a game board. I will use the other game board. You pick the first card from the top of the pile and read it. Good. Now find that word on your game board. Place a marker on the word. I will place a marker on the same word on my game board.

Now, I will pick the next card and read it. The word is _____. Now we must both put a marker on that word on our game card. The first person to have markers on three words in a row is the winner. That was fun, let's play the game again. This time I will go first. (Play the game several times.)

Read the word below.

m o p

Now read the word after we put the letter s at the end.

m o p s

Very good! Read the following words that have the letter s at the end.

(This will offer a review of the sounds the child has recently learned. These sounds appear at the end of the words: *nd, nk, ll,* and *ng.* Assist the child if he has difficulty blending these consonant sounds.)

h a n d s	b a n d s
s o n g s	t o n g s
t a n k s	b a n k s
p i l l s	h i l l s
b a n g s	h a n g s
m i n d s	f i n d s

Look at the word below. This word is *fox*. The letter *x* says *cks* (as in *fox*). Say the word as I point to it.

f o x

Read the words below that have the *cks* sound at the end.

f o x	b o x
t a x	w a x
f i x	s i x

Read the story. Then I will show you a picture to go with the story.

"The Cake"

I can mix a cake.

I can bake a cake.

I like white cake.

What kind do you like?

Now I will show you a picture of the cake.

Look at the picture. The children have made a cake. Now they are making the frosting to decorate the cake. Have you ever seen such a large cake?

I am going to write the words from one of the sentences you just read on index cards.

(Have the child watch as you write each word with a pen. Label the first card with the lesson number for future use.)

What | kind | do | you | like?

I am going to underline the sight words with a black crayon. Today our sentence has three sight words. Can you tell me what they are? I am going to trace over the bold *i* sounds (as in *bike*) with a black crayon.

I will make dotted lines over the letter *e* at the end of the word *like*. Can you tell me why I dotted this letter? That's right. It is a silent letter. It makes no sound.

This sentence does not end in a period. What is the mark called at the end of this sentence? Very good! It is a question mark. This sentence asks a question. Can you answer the question?

Read the sentence. Great! Now I will mix the cards, and you can put them in proper order to make the sentence again.

(Assist the child with putting the cards in proper order. Remind him, if necessary, a sentence begins with an uppercase letter and ends with a period, or as in this case, a question mark.)

Now read the sentence.

(**Note**: We are no longer using clues to assist the child with reading the copy work. It is important for the child to read the text located in this segment of the lesson even if he does not copy the sentences. This will give him an opportunity to practice reading text printed in a regular type.)

Copy Work: (The copy work is optional for children who have difficulty with writing.)

I will write the sentence you just read on a piece of paper.

(Neatly write the sentence with a pen, paying close attention to letter spacing, formation, and size. Make the letters large enough for the child to easily copy. Allow space for the child to write his letters directly under yours. An alternate method is to allow the child to trace over your letters.)

Now you can copy what I wrote.

What kind do you like?

I would like for you to read the sentence once more. Very good! Would you like to draw a picture to go with your sentence?

Now let's read a book together.

(Review material between lessons.)

Lesson 33

Materials: reading manual, index cards, pen, gray crayon, black crayon, and *Sight Word Bingo Game Boards* from Lesson 32.

Instructions: Today the child will be introduced to the *sh* sound as in *ship*. He will read the following words that begin with the *sh* sound: *ship, shop, shame, shot, shine, shack, shade,* and *shape*. He will read the following words that end with the *sh* sound: *sash, mash, hash, wish, dish, fish, bash, cash,* and *rash*.

He will review the following sight words: *has, to, you, do, the, was, I, is,* and *what*. You will play the *Sight Word Bingo* game with the child again. He will be introduced to the new sight word *they*.

The child will read the following story and complete a variety of exercises based on the story.

Title: *"The Ship"*

Story: *The ship is in the sand. It can not sail. The man is on the ship. The man is sad.*

We are no longer using clues to assist the child with reading the copy work. It is important for the child to read the text located in this segment of the lesson even if he does not copy the sentences. This will give him an opportunity to practice reading text printed in a regular type.

Dialogue: Look at the letters below. These letters make the *sh* sound (as in *ship*). You will notice a gray ring around the letters that make the *sh* sound. This ring will help you to see the letters more easily.

Say *sh* (as in *ship*) as I point to the letters. Good!

Look at the word below. This word has the *sh* sound. The word is *ship*.

Read the following words that have the *sh* sound (as in *ship*) at the beginning.

Remember, the dotted letters are silent.

ship   shop

shame   shot

shine   shack

shade   shape

Look at the word below. This word has the *sh* sound (as in *ship*) at the end. The word is *dash*.

dash

Read the following words that have the *sh* sound (as in *ship*) at the end.

sash   mash   hash

wish   dish   fish

bash   cash   rash

Read the following sight words.

has   to   you

do   the   was

I   is   what

(Retrieve the game boards, cards, and place markers for *Sight Word Bingo*.)

Let's play the *Sight Word Bingo* game again. Pick the game board you want to use. I will use the other game board. You may go first. Select a card from the top of the pile. Read the card. (Play the game several times if desired.)

You have learned a lot of sight words so far. You have learned nine sight words. Today you will learn another sight word. Look at the word below. The word is *they*. (Point to the word as you read it.)

they

Read the sentences below. The sentences contain the new sight word.

They have a dog.

They have a cat.

They have a pig.

What do they have?

106

The last sentence has three sight words in it. What else is unusual about this sentence? What kind of mark does it have at the end? That's right. It has a question mark, because it asks a question. Can you answer the question?

What do they have? That's right, they have a dog, a cat, and a pig.

Read the story below. Then I will show you a picture to go with the story.

"The Ship"

The ship is in the sand.

It can not sail.

The man is on the ship.

The man is sad.

Now I will show you a picture of the man and the ship.

Look at the picture. The man in the ship is sad. The ship is stuck in the

sand. See the water behind the ship. What is wrong with the ship? Yes, it has a hole in it. Can a ship float with a hole in it? No, it would sink. Why do you think the ship has a hole in it? Maybe it ran into the rocks near the shoreline.

I am going to write the words from one of the sentences you just read on index cards.

(Have the child watch as you write each word with a pen. Label the first card with the lesson number for future use.)

The	ship	is
in	the	sand.

I am going to underline the sight words with a black crayon. Today our sentence has three sight words. Can you tell me what they are? I am going to trace over the *iii* sounds (as in *pig*) and the *aaa* sound (as in *cat*) with a gray crayon.

I am going to draw a gray ring around the *sh* sound in the word *ship*.

Read the sentence. Great! Now I will mix the cards, and you can put them in proper order to make the sentence again.

(Assist the child with putting the cards in proper order. Remind him, if necessary, a sentence begins with an uppercase letter and ends with a period or other form of punctuation.)

Now read the sentence.

(**Note**: We are no longer using clues to assist the child with reading the copy work. It is important for the child to read the text located in this segment of the lesson even if he does not copy the sentences. This will give him an opportunity to practice reading text printed in a regular type.)

Copy Work: (The copy work is optional for children who have difficulty with writing.)

I will write the sentence you just read on a piece of paper.

(Neatly write the sentence with a pen, paying close attention to letter spacing, formation, and size. Make the letters large enough for the child to easily copy. Allow space for the child to write his letters directly under yours. An alternate method is to allow the child to trace over your letters.)

Now you can copy what I wrote.

The ship is in the sand.

I would like for you to read the sentence once more. Very good! Would you like to draw a picture to go with your sentence?

Now let's read a book together.

(Review material between lessons.)

Lesson 34

Materials: reading manual, index cards, pen, gray crayon, and black crayon.

Instructions: Today the child will review the *sh* sound as in *ship*. He will read the following words that begin with the *sh* sound: *ship, shake,* and *shock.* He will read the following words that end with the *sh* sound: *wish, cash,* and *mash.* He will review the following sight words: *they, was, what, you, is, do,* and *to.*

The child will review the *ang* sound (as in *rang*) by reading the following words: *rang, sang, bang,* and *hang.* He will review the *ong* sound (as in *song*) by reading the following words: *song, long, gong,* and *dong.*

He will review the *cks* sound made by the letter *x* by reading the following words: *tax, fix, fox, wax, mix,* and *box.* He will also review the *ind* sound (as in *find*) by reading the following words: *find, mind, kind,* and *wind.*

The child will read the following story and complete a variety of exercises based on the story.

Title: *"The Big Box"*

Story: *I have a box. You have a box. They have a big box. What is in the big box?*

We are no longer using clues to assist the child with reading the copy work. It is important for the child to read the text located in this segment of the lesson even if he does not copy the sentences. This will give him an opportunity to practice reading text printed in a regular type.

Dialogue: Look at the letters below. What sound do these letters make? (*sh as in ship.*)

s h

Good. These letters say *sh.*

Read the following words that have the *sh* sound at the beginning.

s h i p   s h a k e

s h o c k

Read the following words that have the *sh* sound at the end.

w i s h   c a s h

m a s h

Read the sight words below.

they   was   what

you   is   do   to

Look at the letters below. What sound do these letters make? (*ang* as in *rang.*)

a n g

Very good! They make the *ang* sound. Read the words below that have the *ang* sound.

r a n g   s a n g

b a n g   h a n g

Look at the letters below. What sound do these letters make? (*ong* as in *song.*)

o n g

Very good! They make the *ong* sound. Read the words below that have the *ong* sound.

s o n g   l o n g

gong   dong

Look at the letter below. What sound does this letter make? (*cks* as in *fox.*)

x

Good! It makes the *cks* sound. Read the following words that have the *cks* sound.

tax   fix   fox

wax   mix   box

Look at the letters below. What sound do these letters make? (*ind* as in *find.*)

ind

Very good! They make the *ind* sound. Read the words below that have the *ind* sound.

find   mind

kind   wind

Read the story below. Then I will show you a picture to go with the story.

"The Big Box"

I have a box.

You have a box.

They have a big box.

What is in the big box?

Now I will show you a picture of the box.

Look at the picture. What is in the big box? That's right, kittens are in the big box. What do you think the children are doing with the kittens? Yes, they are selling the kittens.

Can you read the sign by the big box? What does it say? That's right. It says *SALE*.

I am going to write the words from one of the sentences you just read on index cards.

(Have the child watch as you write each card with a pen. Label the first card with the lesson number for future use.)

What	is	in
the	big	box?

I am going to underline the sight words with a black crayon. Today our sentence has three sight words. Can you tell me what they are? I am going to

trace over the *iii* sounds (as in *pig*) and the *ooo* sound (as in *hot*) with a gray crayon.

Can you tell me what we call the special mark at the end of the sentence? That's right. It is called a question mark. We use it when someone asks a question.

Read the sentence. Great! Now I will mix the cards, and you can put them in proper order to make the sentence again.

(Assist the child with putting the cards in proper order.)

Now read the sentence.

(**Note**: We are no longer using clues to assist the child with reading the copy work. It is important for the child to read the text located in this segment of the lesson even if he does not copy the sentences. This will give him an opportunity to practice reading text printed in a regular type.)

Copy Work: (The copy work is optional for children who have difficulty with writing.)

I will write the sentence you just read on a piece of paper.

(Neatly write the sentence with a pen, paying close attention to letter spacing and formation.)

Now you can copy what I wrote.

What is in the big box?

I would like for you to read the sentence once more. Very good! Would you like to draw a picture to go with your sentence?

Now let's read a book together.

(Review material between lessons.)

Lesson 35

Materials: reading manual, index cards, pen, gray crayon, black crayon, *Sight Word Worm* pattern found on page 510 of the Appendix, and 11 construction paper circles.

Instructions: Today the child will review the following sight words: *to, is, do, the, what, you, was they, has,* and *I*. He will complete an activity to help him learn his sight words. He will make *a Sight Word Worm*.

In preparation for today's lesson, trace or photocopy the *Sight Word Worm* pattern found in the Appendix on page 510. Cut 11 circles out of construction paper using the pattern as a guide. Write one sight word on each colored circle. Draw a face on the large circle. (See diagram below.)

Glue the circles on a large piece of paper to form a worm. A half of a sheet of poster board works well. Pipe cleaners may be used to make the antenna or they can be drawn with a black crayon or marker. Draw feet to complete the worm. More circles can be added as the child is introduced to new sight words.

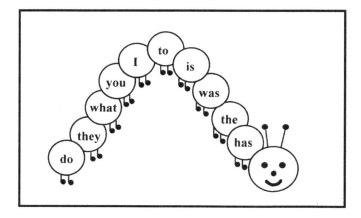

Next the child will review the *sh* sound as in *ship* by reading the following words: *ship, shop, dish, shack, shine, shame,* and *mash.*

The child will be introduced to the long vowel sound for the letter *o* as in *hope.* This will be referred to as the bold *o* sound and will be represented with a bold letter as shown below.

o

He will read the following words containing the bold *o* sound: *hope, rope, note, vote, cone, bone, home, dome, coke, joke, rose, hose, boat, goat, toad,* and *road.*

The child will read the following story and complete a variety of exercises based on the story.

Title: *"The Toad"*

Story: *The toad sat on the bank. His home is in the lake. The toad sang a song. The toad likes his home.*

We are no longer using clues to assist the child with reading the copy work. It is important for the child to read the text located in this segment of the lesson even if he does not copy the sentences. This will give him an opportunity to practice reading text printed in a regular type.

Dialogue: Read the sight words below.

to	is	do
the	what	you
was	they	has

I

(Retrieve the construction paper circles you made for today's lesson.)

Today you are going to make a *Sight Word Worm*. I have written the sight words listed above on the circles. We will use these circles to make the worm's body. The larger circle is for the worm's head. You can help me glue the circles on the poster board to make the worm. Then we can add feet and antenna.

(Assist the child in making the worm as shown in the diagram at the beginning of the lesson.)

Now look at the *Sight Word Worm*, and read the sight words to me. Very good! Now when you learn a new sight word, we will add it to the worm. One day he will be very long!

Look at the letters below. What sound do these letters make? (*sh* as in *ship*.)

(sh)

Very good! These letters make the *sh* sound.

Read the words below that have the *sh* sound.

(sh)ip   (sh)op   di(sh)

(sh)ack   (sh)ine

(sh)ame   ma(sh)

Now you are going to learn a new sound. Look at the letter below. This bold letter makes the *o* sound (as in *hope*).

o

Say *o* (as in *hope*) as I point to the letter. Very good!

Now read the following words that have the bold *o* sound. Remember, the dotted letters are silent. They make no sound. I will read the first word for you. It is *hope*.

h**o**pe	r**o**pe
n**o**te	v**o**te
c**o**ne	b**o**ne
h**o**me	d**o**me
c**o**ke	j**o**ke
r**o**se	h**o**se
b**o**at	g**o**at
t**o**ad	r**o**ad

Read the story below. Then I will show you a picture to go with the story.

"The T**o**ad"

The t**o**ad sat on the bank.

His h**o**me is in the lake.

113

The toad sang a song.

The toad likes his home.

Now I will show you a picture of the toad.

Look at the picture. What is the toad sitting on? Yes, he is sitting on a lawn chair. Does he look comfortable? Name four things the toad has to help him to feel comfortable. That's right, he has a lawn chair, an umbrella, sunglasses, and a cool drink. What do you think he might be drinking? What kinds of drinks do you like to have when it is hot?

I am going to write the words from one of the sentences you just read on index cards.

(Have the child watch as you write each word with a pen. Label the first card with the lesson number for future use.)

The toad likes his home.

I am going to underline the sight word with a black crayon. Today our sentence has one sight word. What is it? I am going to trace over the bold *o* sounds (as in *hope*) with a black crayon. I am also going to trace over the bold *i* sound (as in *bike*) with a black crayon. I will trace over the *iii* sound (as in *pig*) with a gray crayon.

I will make dotted lines over the letter *a* in the word *toad*. I will make dotted lines over the letter *e* in the word *likes*. I will also make dotted lines over the letter *e* at the end of the word *home*. Can you tell me why I dotted these letters? That's right. They are silent. They make no sound.

Read the sentence. Great! Now I will mix the cards, and you can put them in proper order to make the sentence again.

(Assist the child with putting the cards in proper order. Remind him, if necessary, a sentence begins with an uppercase letter and ends with a period or other form of punctuation.)

Now read the sentence.

(**Note**: We are no longer using clues to assist the child with reading the copy work. It is important for the child to read the text located in this segment of the lesson even if he does not copy the sentences. This will give him an opportunity to practice reading text printed in a regular type.)

Copy Work: (The copy work is optional for children who have difficulty with writing.)

I will write the sentence you just read on a piece of paper.

(Neatly write the sentence with a pen, paying close attention to letter spacing, formation, and size. Make the letters large enough for the child to easily copy. Allow space for the child to write his letters directly under yours. An alternate method is to allow the child to trace over your letters.)

Now you can copy what I wrote.

The toad likes his home.

I would like for you to read the sentence once more. Very good! Would you like to draw a picture to go with your sentence?

Now let's read a book together.

(Review material between lessons.)

Lesson 36

Materials: reading manual, index cards, pen, gray crayon, black crayon, and one construction paper circle.

Instructions: Today the child will review the following sight words: *the, has, was, to, I, you, do, is, what,* and *they*. He will play a game to help him review his sight words. The game is called *Sight Word Memory*. In preparation for today's lesson, write each sight word on an index card. Make two identical sets of sight word cards.

Place the cards face down on the table in random order as shown in the diagram below, being sure to keep each set separate. The object of the game is to match a sight word card from one set with the same sight word card from the other set.

Have the child turn over one card from the set on the right. Then have him turn over one card from the set on the left. Encourage him to read the words on the cards as he turns them over. If the cards match, he can place them together face up on the table. If the cards do not match, he must turn both cards face down and leave them in their places.

Have the child turn over another card from the set on the right. Then have him turn over another card from the set on the left. Continue playing until all the cards have been matched. (To simplify the game, use only half of the cards at one time.)

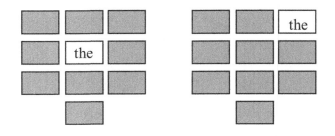

He will also be introduced to the new sight word *are*. Cut a circle out of construction paper. Write the new sight word *are* on the circle. Have the child glue the circle on the *Sight Word Worm* when you introduce the new word.

The child will review the bold *o* sound as in *hope*. He will read the following words with the bold *o* sound: *soap, moan, coat, roam, robe, mole, pole,* and *rode*. He will also be introduced to some additional words containing the bold *o* sound as in *old* by reading the following words: *old, cold, mold, hold, bold, sold, fold, gold,* and *told.*

The child will read the following story and complete a variety of exercises based on the story. This story is part one in a series of four stories about some farm animals and a rose.

Title: *"The Goat"*

Story: *The goat had a hat. The hat was old. The hat had a rose on it. The goat ate the hat. The goat gave the rose to the pig.*

We are no longer using clues to assist the child with reading the copy work. It is important for the child to read the text located in this segment of the lesson even if he does not copy the sentences. This will give him an opportunity to practice reading text printed in a regular type.

Dialogue: Today we are going to play a game. It is called *Sight Word Memory.* (Retrieve the cards you prepared for today's lesson.)

I have two sets of cards. Each card has a sight word written on it. Both sets of cards are the same. I am going to lay the cards on the table. I will put one set of cards face down on the right side of the table and one set of cards face down on the left side of the table. (See diagram on previous page.)

Turn over one card from the set on the right. (Point to the set.) Leave the card you have chosen face up in its place. Read the sight word on the card. Now turn over a card from the set on the left. (Point to the set.) Leave this card face up in its place also. Read the sight word on this card. Are the words the same, or are the words different?

(If the words are the same, have the child put the cards together face up on the table. If the words are different, have him turn the cards face down and

leave them in their places. Continue playing until all cards are matched.)

Now you are going to learn a new sight word. It is the word *are.* (Point to the word at the top of the page.)

are

Say *are* as I point to the word. Very good! Let's add the new word to your *Sight Word Worm.*

(Retrieve the circle you prepared earlier with the word *are* written on it. Have the child frequently review the sight words on the *Sight Word Worm.* Have him read the words in random order.)

Read the words below with the bold *o* sound (as in *hope*). Remember, the dotted letters are silent. They make no sound.

s**o**⬚p	m**o**⬚n
c**o**⬚t	r**o**⬚m
r**o**b⬚	m**o**l⬚
p**o**l⬚	r**o**d⬚

The next word also has the bold *o* sound. It is the word *old.*

(Point to the word as you say it. Slowly sound it out again emphasizing each letter sound. The letters *l* and *d* may be difficult for the child to blend together.)

old

The following words also have the same sound as the word *old*. Read the words.

c**o**ld	m**o**ld
h**o**ld	b**o**ld
s**o**ld	f**o**ld

g**o**ld   t**o**ld

Very good!

Read the story below, and then I will show you a picture to go with the story.

"<u>The</u> G**O**at"

<u>The</u> g**o**at h**a**d **a** h**a**t.

<u>The</u> h**a**t <u>was</u> **o**ld.

<u>The</u> h**a**t h**a**d **a** r**o**se on it.

<u>The</u> g**o**at **a**te <u>the</u> h**a**t.

<u>The</u> g**o**at g**a**ve <u>the</u> r**o**se <u>to</u> <u>the</u> p**i**g.

Now I will show you a picture of the goat.

117

Look at the picture. On what is the goat sitting? Yes, he is sitting on a tractor. Do you think he likes the hat? Would you like to eat a hat? No, you would not like to eat a hat. Goats eat many strange things.

This goat did not want to eat the rose. To whom did he give the rose? Do you think the pig wants to eat the rose? What do you think the pig wants to do with the rose? That's right. The pig put the rose behind its ear.

I am going to write the words from one of the sentences you just read on index cards.

(Have the child watch as you write each word with a pen. Label the first card with the lesson number for future use.)

The goat gave the rose to the pig.

I am going to underline the sight words with a black crayon. Today our sentence has four sight words. Three of the sight words are the same. What are they?

I am going to trace over the bold *o* sounds (as in *hope*) with a black crayon. I am also going to trace over the bold *a* sound (as in *cake*) with a black crayon. I will trace over the *iii* sound (as in *pig*) with a gray crayon.

I will make dotted lines over the letter *a* in the word *goat*. I will also make dotted lines over the letter *e* in the words *gave* and *rose*. Can you tell me why I dotted these letters? That's right. They are silent letters.

Read the sentence. Very good! Now I will mix the cards, and you can put them in proper order to make the sentence again.

(Assist the child with putting the cards in proper order. Remind him, if necessary, a sentence begins with an uppercase letter and ends with a period or other form of punctuation.)

Now read the sentence.

(**Note**: We are no longer using clues to assist the child with reading the copy work. It is important for the child to read the text located in this segment of the lesson even if he does not copy the sentences.

This will give him an opportunity to practice reading text printed in a regular type.)

Copy Work: (The copy work is optional for children who have difficulty with writing.) (You may now encourage the child to copy the sentence directly from the model below. If this is too difficult, continue as directed.)

I will write the sentence you just read on a piece of paper.

(Neatly write the sentence with a pen, paying close attention to letter spacing, formation, and size. Make the letters large enough for the child to easily copy. Allow space for the child to write his letters directly under yours. An alternate method is to allow the child to trace over your letters.)

Now you can copy what I wrote.

The goat gave the rose to the pig.

I would like for you to read the sentence once more. Very good! I would like for you to draw a picture to go with your sentence. Here is a picture of a goat you can draw.

(Assist the child with drawing the picture if necessary. The picture has been drawn with bold lines so the child may trace it if he likes.)

Make up a sentence about the goat you drew. Tell me the sentence, and I will write it on a piece of paper. Now you can copy the sentence at the bottom of your picture.

(Draw lines if necessary for the child to write his sentence at the bottom of his picture.)

Read the sentence you just wrote.

Now let's read a book together.

(Review material between lessons.)

Lesson 37

Materials: reading manual, index cards, pen, gray crayon, black crayon and two construction paper circles.

Instructions: Today the child will review the following sight words: *I, you, do, the, has, is, was, to, what, they,* and *are.* He will be introduced to the sight words *said* and *of.* Cut two circles out of construction paper. Write the new sight words *said* and *of* on the circles. Have the child glue the circles on the *Sight Word Worm* when you introduce the new words.

He will be introduced to the *st* sound as in *mist.* He will read the following words containing the *st* sound at the end: *fist, list, mist, last, past, fast, lost, cost, paste, waste, taste, host, most, post, roast, toast* and *coast.* He will read the following words containing the *st* sound at the beginning: *stock, still, stick, stiff, stack, stab, stand, state, stay, stove, stone,* and *stole.*

The child will read the following story and complete a variety of exercises based on the story. This story is part two in a series of four stories about some farm animals and a rose. Our desire is to stimulate an interest in an on going story to strengthen thinking skills.

We will introduce the use of quotation marks when a character is speaking. This is only an introduction, and we do not expect the child to master this concept. We will discuss the reason for using quotation marks in the next lesson.

Title: *"The Pig"*

Story: *The pig lost the rose.*

The pig said to the cat, "Do you have the rose?"

"I do not have the rose," said the cat.

"The rose is in his tail," said the goat.

Dialogue: See how quickly you can find the sight words as I read them. Point to the correct word as I read it. (Read the sight words in random order.)

I   you   do   the

has   is   was   to
what   they   are

You are doing very well.

Next you will learn a new sight word. Look at the word below. The word is said. Remember, sight words are funny words. You cannot sound them out, because they are spelled in a funny way. (Point to the word as you say it.)

said

Say *said* as I point to the word. Very good!

Now read the sentence below that has *said* in it.

Pat said, "The dog is sick."

Great!

Now you are going to learn another new sight word. Look at the word below. The word is *of.* (Point to the word as you say it.)

of

Say *of* as I point to the word. Very good! This is another funny sight word.

Now read the sentence that has the word *of* in it.

What is the name of the pig?

Let's add the new words to your *Sight Word Worm*. (Retrieve the circles you prepared earlier with the words *said* and *of* written on them.)

Now you are going to learn a new sound. Look at the letters below. (Point to the letters as you make the sound.) These letters make the *st* sound (as in *mist*). You will find these letters have a gray ring around them to help you see them better.

(st)

Say *st* as I point to the letters.
Very good!

Read the words below that have the *st* sound at the end. I will read the first word for you. It is *fist*. Remember, the dotted letters are silent. They make no sound.

f i(st)   l i(st)   m i(st)

l a(st)   p a(st)   f a(st)

l o(st)   c o(st)

p a(st)e   w a(st)e

t a(st)e

h o(st)   m o(st)

p o(st)   r o a(st)

t o a(st)   c o a(st)

Sometimes the *st* sound comes at the beginning of a word. Look at the word below. It begins with the *st* sound. The word is *stop*. (Point to the word as you read it.)

(st)o p

Read the words below that have the *st* sound at the beginning.

(st)o c k   (st)i l l

(st)i c k   (st)i f f

(st)a c k   (st)a b

(st)a n d   (st)a t e

(st)a y   (st)o v e

(st)o n e   (st)o l e

Before you read today's story, let's turn back to the last story you read.

(Turn to the previous lesson and have the child read the story. Then return to this part of today's lesson. If the child is overwhelmed by the amount of reading, help him by reading every other sentence from the previous story, or read the entire previous story to him.)

Today's story tells us some more about the goat and the pig. Read the story below, and then I will show you a picture to go with the story.

"The Pig"

The pig lo(st) the rose.

The pig said to the cat,

"Do you have the rose?"

"I do not have the rose,"

said the cat.

"The rose is in his tail,"

said the goat.

Now I will show you a picture of the pig with the rose.

Look at the picture. Where is the rose? Why do you think the pig cannot see the rose? That's right, the rose is in the pig's tail. The pig has a curly tail. Have you ever seen a real pig? Did it have a curly tail?

I am going to write the words from one of the sentences you just read on index cards.

(Have the child watch as you write each word with a pen. Label the first card with the lesson number for future use.)

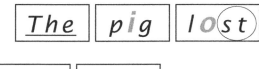

I am going to underline the sight words with a black crayon. Today our sentence has two sight words. The sight words are the same. What are they?

I will trace over the *iii* sound (as in *pig*) with a gray crayon. I will also trace over the *ooo* sound (as in *hot*) with a gray crayon. I am going to trace over the bold *o* sound (as in *hope*) with a black crayon.

I will make dotted lines over the letter *e* at the end of the word *rose*. Can you tell me why I dotted this letter? That's right. It is a silent letter. It makes no sound. I am going to draw a gray ring around the *st* sound (as in *mist*) in the word *lost*.

Read the sentence. Great! Now I will mix the cards, and you can put them in proper order to make the sentence again.

(Assist the child with putting the cards in proper order. Remind him, if necessary, a sentence begins with an uppercase letter and ends with a period or other form of punctuation.)

Now read the sentence.

(**Note**: We are no longer using clues to assist the child with reading the copy work. It is important for the child to read the text located in this segment of the lesson even if he does not copy the sentences. This will give him an opportunity to practice reading text printed in a regular type.)

Copy Work: (The copy work is optional for children who have difficulty with writing.) (You may now encourage the child to copy the sentence directly from the model below. If this is too difficult, continue as directed.)

I will write the sentence you just read on a piece of paper.

(Neatly write the sentence with a pen, paying close attention to letter spacing, formation, and size. Make the letters large enough for the child to easily copy. Allow space for the child to write his letters directly under yours. An alternate method is to allow the child to trace over your letters.)

Now you can copy what I wrote.

The   pig   lost   the   rose.

I would like for you to read the sentence once more. Very good! I would like for you to draw a picture to go with your sentence. Here is a picture of a pig you can draw.

(Assist the child with drawing the picture if necessary. The picture has been drawn with bold lines so the child may trace it if he likes.)

Make up a sentence about the pig you drew. Tell me the sentence, and I will write it on a piece of paper. Now you can copy the sentence at the bottom of your picture.

(Draw lines if necessary for the child to write his sentence at the bottom of his picture.)

Read the sentence you just wrote.

Now let's read a book together.

(Review material between lessons.)

Lesson 38

Materials: reading manual, index cards, pen, gray crayon, black crayon, and one construction paper circle.

Instructions: Today the child will be introduced to the sight word *put*. Prepare a construction paper circle with the new sight word written on it. He will review the following sight words as you write them on index cards: *the, has, was, to, you, do, is, what, they, are, said, of,* and *I*.

The child will review the *sh* sound as in *ship* by reading the following words: *dish, fish, bash, cash, rash, ship, shop, shame,* and *shot.* He will also review the *st* sound as in *mist* by reading the following words: *list, last, lost, taste, most, roast, stock, still, stab, state, stay, stove,* and *stone.* Next, he will review the bold *o* sound as in *old* by reading the following words: *cold, mold, hold, bold, sold, fold, gold,* and *told.*

The child will read the following story and complete a variety of exercises based on the story. This story is part three in a series of four stories pertaining to some farm animals and a rose.

Title: *"The Cat"*

Story: *The pig said to the cat, "Can you hold the rose?"*

The cat said, "I can hold the rose. The rose is not big."

"I will give it to you," said the pig. "I do not like it."

Dialogue: Today you are going to learn a new sight word. Look at the word below. The word is *put*. (Point to the word as you read it.)

put

Say *put* as I point to the word.

Very good! Now read the sentence at the top of the next page that has the word *put* in it.

Put the cat in the sack.

Let's add the new sight word to your *Sight Word Worm*.

Next, let's review all the sight words you have learned so far. I will write each word on an index card. As I write each word, try to read the word as quickly as you can.

(Label the first card with the lesson number for future use. Place a rubber band around the cards when not in use.)

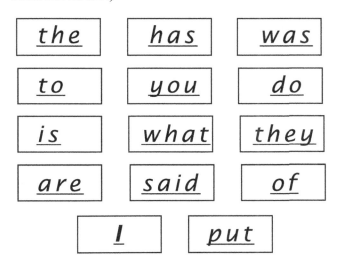

the	has	was
to	you	do
is	what	they
are	said	of

I	put

Very good! Look at the letters below. Remember, these letters make the *sh* sound (as in *ship*).

(sh)

Read the words below that have the sh sound at the end.

d i(sh)   fi(sh)   ba(sh)

ca(sh)   ra(sh)

Read the words below that have the sh sound at the beginning.

(sh)ip   (sh)op
(sh)ame   (sh)ot

Read the words below that have the st sound (as in *mist*) at the end.

li(st)   la(st)   lo(st)

ta(st)e   mo(st)

ro(st)

Read the words below that have the st sound at the beginning.

(st)ock   (st)ill   (st)ab

(st)ate   (st)ay

(st)ove   (st)one

Read the word below that has the bold *o* sound.

old

Very good! The following words also have the same bold *o* sound as the word *old*. Read the words.

c**o**ld   m**o**ld

125

hold   bold | gold   told

sold   fold | Read the story below, and then I will show you a picture to go with the story.

"The Cat"

The pig said to the cat,

"Can you hold the rose?"

The cat said, "I can hold the rose.

The rose is not big."

"I will give it to you,"

said the pig.

"I do not like it."

Now I will show you a picture of the cat with the rose.

Look at the picture. How is the cat holding the rose? That's right he's holding it in his mouth. Do you remember how the pig was holding the rose in the last lesson? Yes, he was holding it in his tail.

Pigs and cats do not have hands like we do. God has made our hands very special. We can do many wonderful things with our hands. Can you think of something you can do with your hands that an animal cannot do?

I am going to write the words from one of the sentences you just read on index cards.

(Have the child watch as you write each word with a pen. Label the first card with the lesson number for future use.)

The	cat	said,

"I	can	hold	the

rose."

I am going to underline the sight words with a black crayon. Today our sentence has four sights word. Two of the sight words are the same. What are they? I will trace over the *aaa* sounds (as in *cat*) with a gray crayon. I am going to trace over the bold *o* sounds (as in *hope*) with a black crayon.

I will make dotted lines over the letter *e* at the end of the word *rose*. Can you tell me why I dotted this letter? That's right. It is silent. It makes no sound.

Read the sentence. Great! *The cat said, "I can hold the rose."* The words the cat says are enclosed in something we call *quotation marks*. (Point to the quotation marks on the index cards.)

Whenever someone speaks, we put the words they say in these special marks.

Now I will mix the cards, and you can put them in proper order to make the sentence again.

(Assist the child with putting the cards in proper order. Remind him, if necessary, a sentence begins with an uppercase letter and ends with a period or other form of punctuation.)

Now read the sentence.

(**Note**: We are no longer using clues to assist the child with reading the copy work. It is important for the child to read the text located in this segment of the lesson even if he does not copy the sentences. This will give him an opportunity to practice reading text printed in a regular type.)

Copy Work: (The copy work is optional for children who have difficulty with writing.) (You may now encourage the child to copy the sentence directly from the model below. If this is too difficult, continue as directed.)

I will write the sentence you just read on a piece of paper.

(Neatly write the sentence with a pen, paying close attention to letter spacing, formation, and size. Make the letters large enough for the child to easily copy. Allow space for the child to write his letters directly under yours. An alternate method is to allow the child to trace over your letters.)

Now you can copy what I wrote.

The cat said, "I can hold the rose."

I would like for you to read the sentence once more. Very good! I would like for you to draw a picture to go with your sentence. Here is a picture of a simple cat you can draw.

(Assist the child with drawing the picture if necessary. The picture has been drawn with bold lines so the child may trace it if he likes.)

Make up a sentence about the cat you drew. Tell me the sentence, and I will write it on a piece of paper. Now you can copy the sentence at the bottom of your picture.

(Draw lines if necessary for the child to write his sentence at the bottom of his picture.)

Read the sentence you just wrote.

Now let's read a book together.

(Review material between lessons.)

Lesson 39

Materials: reading manual, index cards, pen, gray crayon, black crayon, and *Sight Word Bingo Game Boards* found on pages 511 and 512 in the Appendix.

Instructions: Today the child will review the following sight words by playing *Sight Word Bingo*: *the, has, was, to, I, you, do, is, what, they, are, said, of,* and *put*. In preparation for today's lesson, photocopy pages 511 and 512 from the Appendix. (See sample game boards below.)

Cut seven index cards in half. Write a sight word on each card. You will need place markers of some sort. Buttons, pennies, or other small objects will do. M & M's, chocolate chips, peanuts, or some other treat can be substituted for place markers. Place the cards with the sight words written on them face down in a pile on the table. You and the child will take turns reading the cards.

Each time a card is read, a player places a marker on the corresponding word on his game board. Each player may begin the game by placing a marker on the free spaces. The first person to have markers on four spaces in a row is the winner. The row can run vertically, horizontally, or diagonally.

Play the game several times to ensure the child wins a sufficient number of times. This also ensures he reviews each word several times. Try to keep the winning aspect of the game to a minimum. Save the game for review.

has	put	of	are
to	said	(free)	what
do	you	is	I
(free)	the	was	they

He will review various letter sounds by reading the following words: *band, sand, hang, sang, bank, sank, hill, will, mind, kind, long, song, lost, cost, stop, stick, fish, dish, shop,* and *shack.*

The child will read the following story and complete a variety of exercises based on the story. This is the final story in the series pertaining to some farm animals and a rose.

Title: *"The Rose"*

Story: *The pig gave the rose to the cat.*

The cat said, "I can take the rose. I can take it home. I will put it in a vase. I will take care of it."

Dialogue: Today we are going to review the sight words you have learned so far. We are going to play a game. It is called *Sight Word Bingo*.

(Retrieve the game boards and playing cards you made in preparation for today's lesson. Shuffle the playing cards, and place them face down on the table. You will also need place markers.)

Choose a game board. I will use the other game board. We can place a marker on each free space on our board. (Point to the free spaces.) You pick the first card from the top of the pile and read it. Good! Now find that word on your game board. Place a marker on the word. I will place a marker on the same word on my game board.

Now, I will pick the next card and read it. The word is _____. Now we must both put a marker on that word

(free)	to	was	I
you	are	do	said
what	they	(free)	put
the	has	is	of

on our game board. The first person to have markers on four words in a row is the winner. That was fun, let's play the game again. This time I will go first.

(Play the game several times.)

Read the following words. These are words you have read before.

band	sand
hang	sang
bank	sank
hill	will

mind	kind
long	song
lost	cost
stop	stick
fish	dish
shop	shack

Read the story below. Then I will show you a picture to go with the story.

"The Rose"

The pig gave the rose to the cat.

The cat said, "I can take the rose.

I can take it home.

I will put it in a vase.

I will take care of it."

Now I will show you a picture of the cat with the rose.

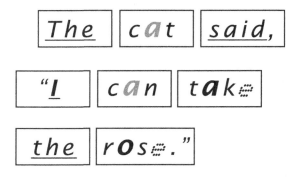

Look at the picture. What is the cat doing with the rose? That's right, he is putting it in a vase. You have read four short stories about this rose. This is the last story about the rose.

Can you remember who had the rose in the very beginning? That's right the goat had it. Then to whom did the goat give the rose? Did the pig want the rose? No, he didn't want it.

Where was the rose when the pig could not find it? Yes, it was in his tail. Isn't that funny? To whom did the pig give the rose? That's right. He gave it to the cat. Did the cat want the rose? Yes, he liked the rose.

I am going to write the words from one of the sentences you just read on index cards.

(Have the child watch as you write each word with a pen. Label the first card with the lesson number for future use.)

I am going to underline the sight words with a black crayon. Today our sentence has three different sight words. Can you tell me what they are?

I'm going to trace over the *aaa* sounds (as in *cat*) with a gray crayon. I am going to trace over the bold *a* sound (as in *cake*) with a black crayon. I will also trace over the bold *o* sound (as in *hope*) with a black crayon.

I am going to make dotted lines over the letter *e* at the end of the word *take* and at the end of the word *rose*. Can you tell me why I dotted these letters? Good! I dotted them because they are silent letters. They make no sound.

Read the sentence. Very good! *The cat said, "I can take the rose."* The words the cat says are enclosed in something we call *quotation marks*. (Point to the quotation marks on the index cards.)

Whenever someone speaks, we put the words they say in these special marks.

Now I will mix the cards, and you can put them in proper order to make the sentence again.

(Assist the child with putting the cards in proper order. Remind him, if necessary, a sentence begins with an uppercase letter and ends with a period or other form of punctuation.)

Now read the sentence.

Copy Work: (The copy work is optional for children who have difficulty with writing.) (You may now encourage the child to copy the sentence directly from the model below. If this is too difficult, continue as directed.)

I will write the sentence you just read on a piece of paper.

(Neatly write the sentence with a pen, paying close attention to letter spacing, formation, and size. Make the letters large enough for the child to easily copy. Allow space for the child to write his letters directly under yours. An alternate method is to allow the child to trace over your letters.)

Now you can copy what I wrote.

The cat said, "I can take the rose."

I would like for you to read the sentence once more. Very good! I would you like for you to draw a picture to go with your sentence. Here is a picture of a simple rose you can draw.

(Assist the child with drawing the picture if necessary. The picture has been drawn with bold lines so the child may trace it if he likes.)

Make up a sentence about the rose you drew. Tell me the sentence, and I will write it on a piece of paper. Now you can copy the sentence at the bottom of your picture.

(Draw lines if necessary for the child to write his sentence at the bottom of his picture.)

Read the sentence you just wrote.

Now let's read a book together.

(Review material between lessons.)

Lesson 40

Materials: reading manual, index cards, pen, gray crayon, and black crayon.

Instructions: Today the child will review the following sight words: *what, they, are, said, of, was* and *put*. He will review the bold *o* sound as in *hope* by reading the following words: *hope, rope, coat,* and *boat*.

He will also review the bold *o* sound as in *old* by reading the following words: *fold, cold, bold,* and *hold*. The child will review the *st* sound as in *mist* by reading the following words: *stop, still, stone, stay, last, lost,* and *list*.

The child will read the following story and complete a variety of exercises based on the story.

Title: *"The Coat"*

Story: *The old dog said, "It is cold."*

The big dog said, "Put on the coat. You will not shake."

The old dog put on the coat. The old dog did not shake.

Dialogue: Read the sight words below.

what   **they**   **are**

said   **of**   **was**

put

Read the words below that have the bold *o* sound (as in *hope*).

h o p e   **r o p e**

c o a t   **b o a t**

Look at the letters below. What sound do these letters make?

o l d

Good! They make the *old* sound. Read the words below that have the *old* sound.

f o l d   **c o l d**

b o l d   **h o l d**

Look at the letters below. What sound do these letters make? (*st* as in *mist*.)

s t

Good! They make the *st* sound. Read the words below that have the *st* sound.

s t o p   **s t i l l**

s t o n e   **s t a y**

l a s t   **l o s t**

l i s t

Read the story below, and then I will show you a picture to go with the story.

"The Coat"

The old dog said, "It is cold."

The big dog said, "Put on the coat.

You will not (shake)."

The old dog put on the coat.

The old dog did not (shake).

Now I will show you a picture of the dogs.

Look at the picture. Does it look like it is cold in this picture? What makes you think it is cold? That's right, there is snow and a snowman in the picture. What is the big dog doing? That's right. He is helping the old dog put on the coat. Have you ever seen a real dog in a coat?

I am going to write the words from one of the sentences you just read on index cards.

(Have the child watch as you write each word with a pen. Label the first card with the lesson number for future use.)

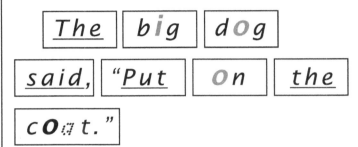

I am going to underline the sight words with a black crayon. Today our sentence has three different sight words. Can you tell me what they are?

I'm going to trace over the *iii* sound (as in *pig*) with a gray crayon. I'm going to trace over the *ooo* sounds (as in *hot*) with a gray crayon. I am going to trace over the bold *o* sound (as in *hope*) with a black crayon.

I am going to make dotted lines over the letter a in the word *coat*. Can you tell me why I dotted this letter? Good! I dotted it because it is a silent letter. It makes no sound.

Read the sentence. Great! *The big dog said, "Put on the coat."* The words the big dog says are enclosed in something we call *quotation marks*. (Point to the quotation marks on the index cards.)

Whenever someone speaks, we put the words they say in these special marks.

Now I will mix the cards, and you can put them in proper order to make the sentence again.

(Assist the child with putting the cards in proper order. Remind him, if necessary, a sentence begins with an uppercase letter and ends with a period or other form of punctuation.)

Now read the sentence.

(**Note**: We are no longer using clues to assist the child with reading the copy work. It is important for the child to read the text located in this segment of the lesson even if he does not copy the sentences. This will give him an opportunity to practice reading text printed in a regular type.)

Copy Work: (The copy work is optional for children who have difficulty with writing.) (You may now encourage the child to copy the sentence directly from the model below. If this is too difficult, continue as directed.)

I will write the sentence you just read on a piece of paper.

(Neatly write the sentence with a pen, paying close attention to letter spacing, formation, and size. Make the letters large enough for the child to easily copy. Allow space for the child to write his letters directly under yours. An alternate method is to allow the child to trace over your letters.)

Now you can copy what I wrote.

The big dog said, "Put on the coat."

I would like for you to read the sentence once more. Very good! I would like for you to draw a picture to go with your sentence. Here is a picture of a simple dog you can draw.

(Assist the child with drawing the picture if necessary. The picture has been drawn with bold lines so the child may trace it if he likes.)

Make up a sentence about the dog you drew. Tell me the sentence, and I will write it on a piece of paper. Now you can copy the sentence at the bottom of your picture.

(Draw lines if necessary for the child to write his sentence at the bottom of his picture.)

Read the sentence you just wrote.

Now let's read a book together.

(Review material between lessons.)

Lesson 41

Materials: reading manual, index cards, pen, gray crayon, black crayon and the *Sight Word Bingo Game Boards* from lesson 39.

Instructions: Today the child will review the following sight words by playing *Sight Word Bingo*: *the, has, was, to, I, you, do, is, what, they, are, said, of,* and *put*.

He will be introduced to the long vowel sound for the letter *e* as in *heat*. This letter will be referred to as the bold *e* sound and will be represented with a bold letter as shown below.

e

The child will learn to read the following words containing the bold *e* sound: *he, me, we, be, she,* and *see*.

He will read the following story and complete a variety of exercises based on the story.

Title: *"The Bone"*

Story: *The old dog had a bone. He put it in a hole. He put sand in the hole. The bad dog did not find the bone. The old dog hid it. It was not lost.*

Dialogue: Today you are going to review your sight words. We will play the Sight Word Bingo Game. (Retrieve the game boards you used in lesson 39 and continue with the game.)

Look at the letter below. This bold letter says *e* (as in *heat*). (Point to the letter as you say its sound.)

e

Say *e* as I point to the letter. Very good!

Now read the following words that have the bold *e* sound (as in *heat*). I will read the first word for you. It is *he*.

he   me   we

be   (she)   see

Read the sentence below.

He can see me.

Read the story below, and then I will show you a picture to go with the story.

"The Bone"

The old dog had a bone.

He put it in a hole.

He put sand in the hole.

The bad dog did not find the bone.

The old dog hid it.

136

Now I will show you a picture of the old dog and the bad dog.

Look at the picture. Why do you think the old dog hid the bone? Do you think the bad dog likes to take the old dog's bones? Does the old dog look happy or sad? Why do you think he is happy? Does the bad dog look happy or sad? Why do you think he is sad?

I am going to write the words from one of the sentences you just read on index cards.

(Have the child watch as you write each word with a pen. Label the first card with the lesson number for future use.)

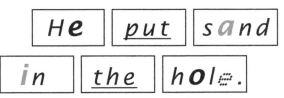

I am going to underline the sight words with a black crayon. Today our sentence has two sight words. Can you tell me what they are?

I am going to trace over the bold *e* sound (as in *heat*) with a black crayon. I will also trace over the bold *o* sound (as in *hope*) with a black crayon.

I'm going to trace over the *aaa* sound (as in *cat*) with a gray crayon. I will also trace over the *iii* sound (as in *pig*) with a gray crayon.

I am going to make dotted lines over the letter *e* at the end of the word *hole*. Can you tell me why I dotted this letter? Good! I dotted it, because it is a silent letter. It makes no sound.

Read the sentence. Very good! Now I will mix the cards, and you can put them in proper order to make the sentence again.

(Assist the child with putting the cards in proper order. Remind him, if necessary, a sentence begins with an uppercase letter and ends with a period or other form of punctuation.)

Now read the sentence.

(**Note**: We are no longer using clues to assist the child with reading the copy work. It is important for the child to read the text located in this segment of the lesson even if he does not copy the sentences. This will give him an opportunity to practice reading text printed in a regular type.)

Copy Work: (The copy work is optional for children who have difficulty with writing.) (You may now encourage the child to copy the sentence directly from the model below. If this is too difficult, continue as directed.)

I will write the sentence you just read on a piece of paper.

(Neatly write the sentence with a pen, paying close attention to letter spacing, formation, and size. Make the letters large enough for the child to easily copy. Allow space for the child to write his letters directly under yours. An alternate method is to allow the child to trace over your letters.)

Now you can copy what I wrote.

He put sand in the hole.

I would like for you to read the sentence once more. Very good! I would like for you to draw a picture to go with your sentence. Here is a picture of a simple dog you can draw.

(Assist the child with drawing the picture if necessary. The picture has been drawn with bold lines so the child may trace it if he likes.)

Make up a sentence about the dog you drew. Tell me the sentence, and I will write it on a piece of paper. Now

you can copy the sentence at the bottom of your picture.

(Draw lines if necessary for the child to write his sentence at the bottom of his picture.)

Read the sentence you just wrote.

Now let's read a book together.

(Review material between lessons.)

Lesson 42

Materials: reading manual, index cards, pen, gray crayon, and black crayon.

Instructions: Today the child will review the following words containing the bold *e* sound: *he, me, we, be, she*, and *see*. He will also read the following new words containing the bold *e* sound: *ear, tear, year, dear, near, fear, hear, rear, eat, seat, meat, neat, peat, heat, wheat*, and *beat*.

He will review the following sight words: *the, has, was, to, I, you, do, what, is, put, are, of, said* and *they*.

The child will also read the following story and complete a variety of exercises based on the story.

Title: *"Jane and Tim"*

Story: *Jane put the pie on the dish. She gave it to Tim.*

He said, "I am cold. I will sit near the stove. I will eat the pie. I will not be cold."

Dialogue: Look at the letter below. What sound does this bold letter make? (*e* as in *heat*.)

e

Good! This letter makes the *e* sound.

Read the words below that have the bold *e* sound.

he   **me**   **we**

be   (**she**)   **see**

Here are some new words that have the bold *e* sound. They also have letters that are dotted. Remember, the dotted letters are silent. They make no sound.

ear   **tear**

year   **dear**

near   **fear**

hear   **rear**

Read the sentence below. It has one of the words in it you just read. This word has the bold *e* sound in it. Can you find the word?

Did you hear the cat?

Read the words below. These words also have the bold *e* sound. Remember, the dotted letters are silent. They make no sound.

eat   **seat**

meat   **neat**

peat   **heat**

wheat   **beat**

Read the sentence on the next page. It has one of the words in it you just read. This word has the bold *e* sound in it. Can you find the word?

The cat sat on the seat.

You are doing great!

Let's see how fast you can read the sight words below. You have learned a lot of sight words. You have learned 14 sight words so far.

the   has   was

to   I   you

do   what   is

put   are   of

said   they

Read the story below, and then I will show you a picture to go with the story.

"Jane and Tim"

Jane put the pie on the dish.

She gave it to Tim.

He said, "I am cold.

I will sit near the stove.

I will eat the pie.

I will not be cold."

Now I will show you a picture of Tim by the stove.

Look at the picture. Do you have a stove that looks like the one in the picture? Have you ever seen a stove like this one? It is an old-fashioned stove. Your great, great grandmother may have cooked on a stove like this one. Often the stove was not only used for cooking, but it was used for heating the house as well. Why does Tim want to sit near the stove? That's right. He wants to sit near the stove to get warm.

I am going to write the words from two of the sentences you just read on index cards.

(Have the child watch as you write each word with a pen. Label the first card with the lesson number for future use.)

He	said,	"I

am	cold.

I	will	sit

near	the	stove."

I am going to underline the sight words with a black crayon. Today our sentences have three different sight words. Can you tell me what they are?

I'm going to trace over the *aaa* sound (as in *cat*) with a gray crayon. I will also trace over the *iii* sounds (as in *pig*) with a gray crayon. I am going to trace over the bold *e* sounds (as in *heat*) with a black crayon. I will also trace over the bold *o* sounds (as in *hope*) with a black crayon.

I am going to make dotted lines over the letter *a* in the word *near* and over the letter *e* at the end of the word *stove*. Can you tell me why I dotted these letters? Good! I dotted them, because they are silent letters. They make no sound. I will also draw a gray ring around the *st* sound (as in *mist*) in the word *stove*.

Read the sentences. Great! *He said, "I am cold. I will sit near the stove."* The words the boy says are enclosed in something we call *quotation marks.* (Point to the quotation marks on the index cards.)

Whenever someone speaks, we put the words they say in these special marks.

Now I will mix the cards, and you can put them in proper order to make the sentences again.

(Assist the child with putting the cards in proper order. Keep the cards from each sentence separate. Remind him, if necessary, a sentence begins with an uppercase letter and ends with a period or other form of punctuation.)

Now read the sentences.

(**Note**: We are no longer using clues to assist the child with reading the copy work. It is important for the child to read the text located in this segment of the lesson even if he does not copy the sentences. This will give him an opportunity to practice reading text printed in a regular type.)

Copy Work: (The copy work is optional for children who have difficulty with writing.) (You may now encourage the child to copy the sentences directly from the model below. If this is too difficult, continue as directed.)

I will write the sentences you just read on a piece of paper.

(Neatly write the sentences with a pen, paying close attention to letter spacing, formation, and size. Make the letters large enough for the child to easily copy. Allow space for the child to write his letters directly under yours. An alternate method is to allow the child to trace over your letters.)

Now you can copy what I wrote.

He said, "I am cold.

I will sit near the stove."

I would like for you to read the sentences once more.

Very good! I would you like for you to draw a picture to go with your sentences. Here is a picture of an old-fashioned stove you can draw.

(Assist the child with drawing the picture if necessary. The picture has been drawn with bold lines so the child may trace it if he likes.)

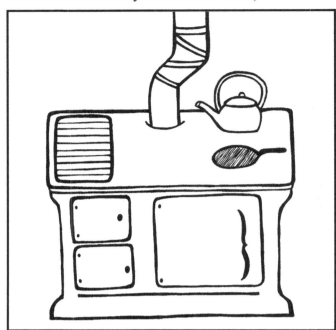

Make up a sentence about the stove you drew. Tell me the sentence, and I will write it on a piece of paper. Now you can copy the sentence at the bottom of your picture.

(Draw lines if necessary for the child to write his sentence at the bottom of his picture.)

Read the sentence you just wrote.

Now let's read a book together.

Lesson 43

Materials: reading manual, index cards, pen, gray crayon, black crayon, and one construction paper circle.

Instructions: Today the child will review the following words containing the bold *e* sound as in *heat*: *he, she, we, me, near, fear, heat, meat,* and *seat*.

He will be introduced to the *kw* sound made by the letters *qu* as in *queen*. He will read the following words beginning with the *kw* sound: *quack, quick, quit, quilt, quote,* and *quake*.

Today the child will read the following new words containing the bold *e* sound: *queen, feed, keep, jeep, see, beef, feet, weed, meet, beep,* and *bee*.

He will be introduced to the new sight word *does*. Prepare a construction paper circle with the new sight word written on it. If you find your *Sight Word Worm* growing too large, begin a new one. He will also review the following sight words: *said, put, what,* and *do*.

The child will also read the following story and complete a variety of exercises based on the story.

Title: *"The Queen Bee"*

Story: *The queen bee is big. She lives in a hive. The hive is made of wax. The hive has a lot of bees in it. The bees feed the queen. They take care of the queen.*

Dialogue: Look at the letter below. What sound does this bold letter make? (*e* as in *heat*.)

e

Good! This letter makes the bold *e* sound.

Read the words below that have the bold *e* sound.

he　　she　　we

me　　near　　fear

---

heat　　meat　　seat

Now you are going to learn a new sound. Look at the letters below. These letters make the *kw* sound (as in *queen*). (Point to the letters.)

When we put the letter q with the letter u (say the letter names) we get the *kw* sound (as in *queen*). You will notice the letters that make the *kw* sound have a gray ring around them. This is to help you see the letters more easily.

qu

This is a lowercase letter q.

q

This is an uppercase letter Q.

Q

The letters below make the *kw* sound (as in *queen*).

Qu　　qu

Say *kw* (as in *queen*) as I point to each group of letters.

Read the following words that have the *kw* sound.

quack　　quick

quit　　quilt

quote　　quake

Look at the word at the top of the next page. It begins with the *kw* sound (as in *queen*). It also has the bold *e* sound (as in *heat*). The word is *queen*. (Point to the word as you read it.)

q**ueen**

Read the following words that have the bold *e* sound.

f**ee**d	k**ee**p
j**ee**p	s**ee**
b**ee**f	f**ee**t
w**ee**d	m**ee**t
b**ee**p	b**ee**

You are doing really well. You have learned many, many new words. Here is another new word. It is a sight word. The word is *does*.

does

Say *does* as I point to the word.

Read the sentence at the top of the page that has the word *does* in it.

What does he have in his hand?

What do we call the mark at the end of this sentence? That's right. It is called a question mark, because it is asking us a question.

Let's add the new sight word to your *Sight Word Worm*.

Read the following sight words.

said   put   what

do   does

Read the following story, and then I will show you a picture to go with the story.

(Assist the child with any sounds he finds difficult. For example, he may need help with the *cks* sound as in the word *wax*. He may also need assistance with the *s* ending in various words such as *lives* and *bees*. These topics have been covered in past lessons, but may require review.)

"The Qu**een** B**ee**"

The qu**een** b**ee** is big.

Sh**e** liv**e**s in **a** hiv**e**.

The hiv**e** is mad**e** of w**a**x.

The hiv**e** has **a** lot of b**ee**s in it.

The b**ee**s f**ee**d the qu**een**.

They take care of the (qu)een.

Now I will show you a picture of a bee.

Look at the picture. This is a special kind of bee. Do you know what this special kind of bee makes? That's right. It makes honey. Do you like honey?

I am going to write the words from two of the sentences you just read on index cards.

(Have the child watch as you write each word with a pen. Label the first card with the lesson number for future use.)

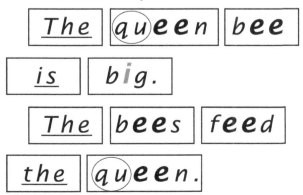

I am going to underline the sight words with a black crayon. Today our sentence has two different sight words. Can you tell me what they are?

I am going to trace over the bold *e* sounds (as in *heat*) with a black crayon. I will trace over the *iii* sound (as in *pig*) with a gray crayon. I will also draw a gray ring around the *kw* sound (as in *queen*) in the word *queen*.

Read the sentences. Great! Now I will mix the cards, and you can put them in proper order to make the sentences again.

(Assist the child with putting the cards in proper order. Keep the cards from each sentence separate. Remind him, if necessary, a sentence begins with an uppercase letter and ends with a period or other form of punctuation.)

Now read the sentences.

(**Note**: We are no longer using clues to assist the child with reading the copy work. It is important for the child to read the text located in this segment of the lesson even if he does not copy the sentences. This will give him an opportunity to practice reading text printed in a regular type.)

Copy Work: (The copy work is optional for children who have difficulty with writing.) (You may now encourage the child to copy the sentences directly from the model below. If this is too difficult, continue as directed.)

I will write the sentences you just read on a piece of paper.

(Neatly write the sentences with a pen, paying close attention to letter spacing, formation, and size. Make the letters large enough for the child to easily copy. Allow space for the child to write his letters directly under yours. An alternate method is to allow the child to trace over your letters.)

Now you can copy what I wrote.

The queen bee is big.

The bees feed the queen.

I would like for you to read the sentences once more. Very good! I would like for you to draw a picture to go with your sentences. Here is a picture of a bee and a beehive you can draw.

(Assist the child with drawing the picture if necessary. The picture has been drawn with bold lines so the child may trace it if he likes.)

Make up a sentence about the bee and the beehive you drew. Tell me the sentence, and I will write it on a piece of paper. Now you can copy the sentence at the bottom of your picture.

(Draw lines if necessary for the child to write his sentence at the bottom of his picture.)

Read the sentence you just wrote.

Now let's read a book together.

(Review material between lessons.)

Lesson 44

Materials: reading manual, index cards, pen, gray crayon, and black crayon.

Instructions: Today the child will review the following words containing the bold *e* sound as in *heat*: *me, she, rear, hear, seat, weed, queen,* and *feet*.

He will also read the following new words containing the bold *e* sound: *read, bean, tea, mean, team, peak, lean, leap, seed, seen, sheet, sheep, steep, steel, steam,* and *Steve*.

The child will be introduced to the *pl* sound as in *play*. He will read the following words containing the *pl* sound: *plot, plod, plan, plant, plaid, plane, play, plate, plead, please,* and *pleat*.

The child will review the following sight words: *does, you, I, the, was, to, they, are, of, has,* and *is*.

He will read the following story and complete a variety of exercises based on the story.

Title: *"The Sheep"*

Story: *See the sheep. They are on the steep hill. The sheep are fat. They have on coats. They are not cold. The sheep like to play. They like to leap.*

Dialogue: Look at the bold letter below. What sound does this bold letter make? (*e* as in *heat*).

e

Very good! It makes the bold *e* sound.

Read the words below that have the bold *e* sound. You have read these words before.

me   (sh)e

rear   hear

seat   weed

(qu)een   feet

Now read some new words that have the bold *e* sound.

read   bean

tea   mean

team   peak

lean   leap

seed   seen

(sh)eet   (sh)eep

(st)eep   (st)eel

(st)eam   (St)eve

Now look at the letters below. These letters make the *pl* sound (as in *play*). (Point to the letters as you say the sound.)

You will notice the letters that make the *pl* sound have a gray ring around them. This is to help you see the letters more easily.

(pl)

Say *pl* as I point to the letters.
Very good! Now read the words below that have the *pl* sound.

(pl)ot   (pl)od

(pl)an

(pl)ant   (pl)aid

plane play

plate plead

please pleat

Read the following sight words.

does   you   I

---

the   was   to

they   are   of

has   is

Read the story below, and I will show you a picture to go with the story.

"The Sheep"

See the sheep.

They are on the steep hill.

The sheep are fat.

They have on coats.

They are not cold.

The sheep like to play.

They like to leap.

Now I will show you a picture of the sheep.

Look at the picture. The story said the sheep have on coats. What are their coats made of? That's right, their coats are made of wool.

Can they take off their coats? No, not by themselves, but the people who tend the sheep can. They can shear the sheep. That means they give them a hair cut. Then the wool is used to make clothes and blankets and other things. After a while, the sheep grow new coats.

Can you find anything in your home made out of wool? What can you find?

I am going to write the words from two of the sentences you just read on index cards.

(Have the child watch as you write each word with a pen. Label the first card with the lesson number for future use.)

| The | sheep | like |

| to | play. |

| They | like | to |

| leap. |

I am going to underline the sight words with a black crayon. Today our sentences have three different sight words. Can you tell me what they are?

I am going to trace over the bold *e* sounds (as in *heat*) with a black crayon. I will also trace over the bold *i* sounds (as in *bike*) and the bold *a* sound (as in *cake*) with a black crayon.

I will make dotted lines over the letter *e* in the word *like* and over the letter *y* in the word *play*. I will also make dotted lines over the letter *a* in the word *leap*. Can you tell me why I dotted these letters? That's right. I dotted them, because they are silent. They make no sound.

I will draw a gray ring around the *sh* sound (as in *ship*) in the word *sheep* and the *pl* sound (as in *play*) in the word *play*.

Read the sentences. Very good! Now I will mix the cards, and you can put them in proper order to make the sentences again.

(Assist the child with putting the cards in proper order. Keep the cards from each sentence separate. Remind him, if necessary, a sentence begins with an uppercase letter and ends with a period or other form of punctuation.)

Now read the sentences.

(**Note**: We are no longer using clues to assist the child with reading the copy work. It is important for the child to read the text located in this segment of the lesson even if he does not copy the sentences. This will give him an opportunity to practice reading text printed in a regular type.)

Copy Work: (The copy work is optional for children who have difficulty with writing.) (You may now encourage the child to copy the sentences directly from the model below. If this is too difficult, continue as directed.)

I will write the sentences you just read on a piece of paper.

(Neatly write the sentences with a pen, paying close attention to letter spacing, formation, and size. Make the letters large enough for the child to easily copy. Allow space for the child to write his letters directly under yours. An alternate method is to allow the child to trace over your letters.)

Now you can copy what I wrote.

The sheep like to play.
They like to leap.

I would like for you to read the sentences once more. Very good! I would like for you to draw a picture to go with your sentences. Here is a picture of a sheep you can draw.

(Assist the child with drawing the picture if necessary. The picture has been drawn with bold lines so the child may trace it if he likes.)

Make up a sentence about the sheep you drew. Tell me the sentence, and I will write it on a piece of paper. Now you can copy the sentence at the bottom of your picture.

(Draw lines if necessary for the child to write his sentence at the bottom of his picture.)

Read the sentence you just wrote.

Now let's read a book together.

(Review material between lessons.)

Lesson 45

Materials: reading manual, index cards, pen, gray crayon, black crayon, and two construction paper circles.

Instructions: In today's lesson, the child will read the following words containing the bold *e* sound as in *heat*: *real, meal, seal, east, feast,* and *yeast.*

The child will be introduced to the *bl* sound as in *black.* He will read the following words containing the *bl* sound: *black, blast, block, blond, bliss, blaze, blame, bloat, bleed,* and *bleat.*

The child will review the following sight words: *does, they, what, said, are, put,* and *was.* He will also be introduced to the new sight words *some* and *come.* Prepare two construction paper circles with the new sight words written on them.

He will read the following story and complete a variety of exercises based on the story.

Title: *"Jack and the Blocks"*

Story: *Jack had some blocks. He put the blocks on the mat.*

He said, "I can make a box. I can put the dog in the box. The dog is black. It will not bite me. It is not real."

Jack put the black dog in the box.

He said, "The dog can play in the box."

Dialogue: Read the words below that have the bold *e* sound.

re𝒶l   me𝒶l   se𝒶l

e𝒶st   fe𝒶st

ye𝒶st

Now look at the letters at the top of the page. These letters make the *bl* sound (as in *black*). (Point to the letters as you say the sound.) You will notice the letters that make the *bl* sound have a gray ring around them. This is to help you see the letters more easily.

bl

Say *bl* (as in *block*) as I point to the letters.

Very good! Now read the words below that have the *bl* sound.

black   blast

block   blond

bliss   blaze

blame   bloat

bleed   bleat

Read the sight words below:

does   they   what

said   are   put

was

Today you are going to learn two new sight words. Look at the word below. The word is *some.*

some

Say *some* as I point to the word. Very good!

Now look at the next sight word. It is the word *come*.

come

Say *come* as I point to the word. Very good!

The new sight words are almost the same. Look at the new sight words as I read them. (Point to each word as you read it.)

some   come

Now you read the new sight words as I point to them.

Very good! You have learned lots of sight words. Let's add these new sight words to your *Sight Word Worm*. Now read all of the words on your *Sight Word Worm*.

Read the story below, and then I will show you a picture to go with the story.

"Jack and the Blocks"

Jack had some blocks.

He put the blocks on the mat.

He said, "I can make a box.

I can put the dog in the box.

The dog is black.

It will not bite me. It is not real."

Jack put the black dog in the box.

He said, "The dog can

play in the box."

Now I will show you a picture of Jack and the blocks.

152

Look at the picture. The story said Jack was going to put the black dog in the box. He said the dog was not real. Do you have any toy dogs or other toy animals?

Then Jack said the dog could play in the box. Can the dog really play in the box? No, he cannot really play in the box. We say Jack is pretending the dog can play. Do you like to pretend? Do you like to play with blocks? What kind of things do you make with your blocks?

I am going to write the words from two of the sentences you just read on index cards.

(Have the child watch as you write each word with a pen. Label the first card with the lesson number for future use.)

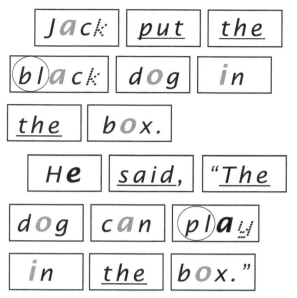

I am going to underline the sight words with a black crayon. Today our sentences have three different sight words. Can you tell me what they are?

I am going to trace over the *aaa* sounds (as in *cat*) with a gray crayon. I will also trace over the *ooo* sounds (as in *hot*) and the *iii* sounds (as in *pig*) with a gray crayon.

I will trace over the bold *e* sound (as in *heat*) with a black crayon. I will trace over the bold *a* sound (as in *cake*) with a black crayon.

I will make dotted lines over the letter *k* in the word *black* and over the letter *y* in the word *play*. Can you tell me why I dotted these letters? That's right. I dotted them, because they are silent. They make no sound.

I will draw a gray ring around the *bl* sound (as in *black*) in the word *black*. I will also draw a gray ring around the *pl* sound (as in *play*) in the word *play*.

Read the sentences. Great! He said, "The dog can play in the box." The words spoken by the boy are put inside special marks. (Point to the quotation marks on the index cards.) Can you remember what these special marks are called? They are called quotation marks. We use them when a person speaks.

Now I will mix the cards, and you can put them in proper order to make the sentences again.

(Assist the child with putting the cards in proper order. Keep the cards from each sentence separate. Remind him, if necessary, a sentence begins with an uppercase letter and ends with a period.)

Now read the sentences.

(**Note**: We are no longer using clues to assist the child with reading the copy work. It is important for the child to read the text located in this segment of the lesson even if he does not copy the sentences. This will give him an opportunity to practice reading text printed in a regular type.)

Copy Work: (The copy work is optional for children who have difficulty with writing.) (You may now encourage the child to copy the sentences directly from the model below. If this is too difficult, continue as directed.)

I will write the sentences you just read on a piece of paper.

(Neatly write the sentences with a pen, paying close attention to letter spacing, formation, and size. Make the letters large enough for the child to easily copy. Allow space for the child to write his letters directly under yours. An alternate method is to allow the child to trace over your letters.)

Now you can copy what I wrote.

Jack   put   the   black   dog   in   the   box.

He   said,   "The   dog   can   play   in   the   box."

I would like for you to read the sentences once more. Very good! I would like for you to draw a picture to go with your sentences. Here is a picture of a dog you can draw.

(Assist the child with drawing the picture if necessary. The picture has been drawn with bold lines so the child may trace it if he likes.)

Make up a sentence about the dog you drew. Tell me the sentence, and I will write it on a piece of paper. Now you can copy the sentence at the bottom of your picture.

(Draw lines if necessary for the child to write his sentence at the bottom of his picture.)

Read the sentence you just wrote.

154

Now let's read a book together.

(An interesting poem to read to the child is entitled "Block City" by Robert Louis Stevenson. You can find this at your public library.)

(Review material between lessons.)

Lesson 46

Materials: reading manual, index cards, pen, gray crayon, and black crayon.

Instructions: In today's lesson, the child will read the following words containing the bold *e* sound as in *heat*: *me, she, year, fear, eat, seat, east, feast, deal, seal, meet,* and *feet.*

The child will review the *bl* sound as in *black* by reading the following words: *block, bloat, blaze,* and *bleed.* He will review the *pl* sound as in *play* by reading the following words: *play, plate, pleat,* and *plot.*

He will review the *kw* sound as in *queen* by reading the following words: *queen, quick, quack,* and *quake.* He will review the *st* sound as in *stop* by reading the following words: *steam, stack, stove,* and *stay.* He will review the following sight words: *does, they, what, some, come, put,* and *was.*

The child will read the following story and complete a variety of exercises based on the story.

Title: *"The Quick Seal"*

Story: *The seal can play. The seal can play on the block. The seal can eat. The seal can eat the fish. The fish is on the plate. Can you see the seal? The seal is quick.*

Dialogue: Read the words below. These words have the bold *e* sound (as in *heat*).

me	*she*
year	*fear*
eat	*seat*
east	*feast*
deal	*seal*
meet	*feet*

Look at the letters below. What sound do these letters make? (*bl* as in *black*.)

(bl)

Very good! They make the *bl* sound. Read the words below that have the *bl* sound.

(bl)ock   (bl)oat

(bl)aze   (bl)eed

Look at the letters below. What sound do these letters make? (*pl* as in *play*.)

(pl)

Very good! They make the *pl* sound. Read the words below that have the *pl* sound.

(pl)ay   (pl)ate

(pl)eat   (pl)ot

Look at the letters below. What sound do these letters make? (*kw* as in *queen*.)

(qu)

Very good! They make the *kw* sound.

Read the words below that have the *kw* sound.

(qu)een   (qu)ick

(qu)ack   (qu)ake

Look at the letters below. What sound do these letters make? (*st* as in *stop*.)

(st)

Very good! They make the *st* sound. Read the words below that have the *st* sound.

(st)eam   (st)ack

(st)ove   (st)ay

Read the sight words below.

<u>does</u>   <u>they</u>   <u>what</u>

<u>some</u>   <u>come</u>   <u>put</u>

<u>was</u>

Read the story below, and then I will show you a picture to go with the story.

"<u>The</u> (Qu)ick Seal"

<u>The</u> seal can (pl)ay.

<u>The</u> seal can (pl)ay on <u>the</u> (bl)ock.

<u>The</u> seal can eat.

156

The seal can eat the fish.

The fish is on the plate.

Can you see the seal?

The seal is quick.

Now I will show you a picture of the seal.

Look at the picture. What is the seal doing? Yes, he is eating the fish and floating on a block of ice. Have you ever seen a seal at the zoo? Seals are very good at doing tricks. They are smart like dogs too.

Baby seals are born on land, but they can swim and dive almost immediately after they are born. Seals are excellent swimmers. They live in cold waters. Seals have a thick layer of fat that helps to keep them warm.

I am going to write the words from two of the sentences you just read on index cards.

(Have the child watch as you write each word with a pen. Label the first card with the lesson number for future use.)

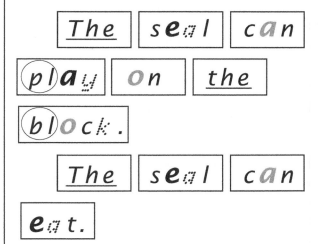

The seal can play on the block. The seal can eat.

I am going to underline the sight words with a black crayon. I will trace over the bold e sounds (as in *heat*) with a black crayon. I will trace over the bold a sound (as in *cake*) with a black crayon.

I am going to trace over the *aaa* sounds (as in *cat*) with a gray crayon. I will also trace over the *ooo* sounds (as in *hot*) with a gray crayon.

I will make dotted lines over the letter a in the words *seal* and *eat*. I will make dotted lines over the letter y in the word *play* and over the letter *k* in the word *block*. Can you tell me why I dotted these letters? That's right. I dotted them, because they are silent. They make no sound.

I will draw a gray ring around the *pl* sound (as in *play*) in the word *play*, and I will draw a gray ring around the *bl* sound (as in *black*) in the word *block*.

Read the sentences. Great! Now I will mix the cards, and you can put them in proper order to make the sentences again.

(Assist the child with putting the cards in proper order. Keep the cards from each sentence separate. Remind him, if necessary, a sentence begins with an uppercase letter and ends with a period or other form of punctuation.)

Now read the sentences.

(**Note**: We are no longer using clues to assist the child with reading the copy work. It is important for the child to read the text located in this segment of the lesson even if he does not copy the sentences. This will give him an opportunity to practice reading text printed in a regular type.)

Copy Work: (The copy work is optional for children who have difficulty with writing.) (You may now encourage the child to copy the sentences directly from the model below. If this is too difficult, continue as directed.)

I will write the sentences you just read on a piece of paper.

(Neatly write the sentences with a pen, paying close attention to letter spacing, formation, and size. Make the letters large enough for the child to easily copy. Allow space for the child to write his letters directly under yours. An alternate method is to allow the child to trace over your letters.)

Now you can copy what I wrote.

The seal can play on the block.
The seal can eat.

I would like for you to read the sentences once more. Very good! I would you like for you to draw a picture to go with your sentences. Here is a picture of a seal you can draw.

(Assist the child with drawing the picture if necessary. The picture has been drawn with bold lines so the child may trace it if he likes.)

Make up a sentence about the seal you drew. Tell me the sentence and I will write it on a piece of paper. Now you can copy the sentence at the bottom of your picture.

(Draw lines if necessary for the child to write his sentence at the bottom of his picture.)

Read the sentence you just wrote.

Now let's read a book together.

(Review material between lessons.)

Lesson 47

Materials: reading manual, index cards, pen, gray crayon, black crayon, and one construction paper circle.

Instructions: In today's lesson, the child will review the following sight words: *the, has, to, I, you, do, is, of, come,* and *some*. He will be introduced to the new sight word *from*. Prepare a construction paper circle with the new sight word written on it.

He will be introduced to the short vowel sound for the letter *e*. This letter makes the *eee* sound as in *wet*. It will appear in a gray print as shown below.

e

The child will learn to read the following words containing the *eee* sound as in *wet*: *net, met, pet, bet, wet, get, vet, fell, well, bell, yell, tell, yes, mess, bless, less, vest, nest, test, west, zest, went, sent, bent, shed, led, fed,* and *red*.

He will read the following story and complete a variety of exercises based on the story.

Title: *"The Red Vest"*

Story: *It was cold. It was wet and cold. The man and the dog went to the shed. They went to get a mop. The man had on a vest. His vest was black. The dog had on a vest. His vest was red. They did not get cold. They did not get wet.*

Dialogue: Read the following sight words:

the   has   to   I

you   do   is   of

come   some

Look at the word below. It is a new sight word. It is the word *from*. (Point to the word as you read it.)

from

Say *from* as I point to the word.

159

Very good!

Did you notice the new sight word rhymes with two of the sight words you already learned? Listen as I read the sight words below. (Point to each word as you read it.)

come   some   from

We say these words rhyme, because they have the same sound. Now, read the sight words as I point to each word. (Point to the sight words in random order.)

Very good!

Let's add the new sight word *from* to your *Sight Word Worm*. (Have the child frequently review the sight words on the *Sight Word Worm*. Have him read the words in random order.)

Look at the letter below. What sound does this letter make? (*e* as in *heat*.)

e

Great! This letter makes the bold *e* sound.

What color is this letter? That's right, it is black.

Next, you will learn a new sound. Look at the letter below. Notice this letter is gray. It says *eee* (as in *wet*). (Point to the letter as you say its sound. <u>Be sure to emphasize the *eee* sound as in *wet*, as it is difficult to hear.</u>)

e

The word below has the *eee* sound (as in *wet*). The word is *set*. (Point to the word as you read it.)

set

Read the word as I point to it. (Point to the word *set*.)

Very good! Now read the following words that have the *eee* sound (as in *wet*). I will read the first word for you. It is *net*.

n e t	m e t	p e t
b e t	w e t	g e t
v e t	f e l l	w e l l
b e l l	y e l l	t e l l

That was great! Now read some more words with *eee* sound (as in *wet*). I will read the first word for you. It is *yes*.

y e s	m e s s
b l e s s	l e s s
v e s t	n e s t
t e s t	w e s t
z e s t	w e n t
s e n t	b e n t
s h e d	l e d
f e d	r e d

That was a lot of work. You did a great job reading all of those words.

Read the story, and then I will show you a picture to go with the story.

160

"The Red Vest"

It was cold.

It was wet and cold.

The man and the dog

went to the shed.

They went to get a mop.

The man had on a vest.

His vest was black.

The dog had on a vest.

His vest was red.

They did not get cold.

They did not get wet.

Now I will show you a picture of the man and the dog.

161

Look at the picture. Why did the man and the dog go to the shed? Why do you think the man wanted a mop? Why do you think the man and the dog had on vests? That's right, they had on vests, because it was cold. Have you ever seen a real dog wearing a vest? What is funny about the way the dog is walking? Do real dogs walk this way? No, they do not. This is a pretend story.

The story said they did not get cold, and they did not get wet. What kept them from getting wet? That's right, the man had an umbrella. Do you think that maybe the man had a leak in his roof, and he needed to get the mop to clean up the water?

I am going to write the words from two of the sentences you just read on index cards.

(Have the child watch as you write each word with a pen. Label the first card with the lesson number for future use.)

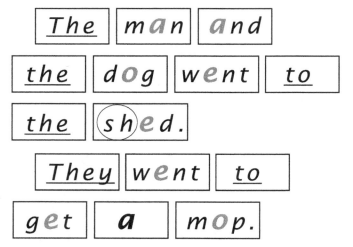

I am going to underline the sight words with a black crayon. Today our sentences have three different sight words. Can you tell me what they are?

I am going to trace over the *aaa* sounds (as in *cat*) with a gray crayon. I will also trace over the *ooo* sounds (as in *hot*) and the *eee* sounds (as in *wet*) with a gray crayon.

I will trace over the bold *a* sound (as in *cake*) with a black crayon. I will draw a gray ring around the *sh* sound (as in *ship*) in the word *shed*.

Read the sentences. Very good! Now I will mix the cards, and you can put them in proper order to make the sentences again.

(Assist the child with putting the cards in proper order. Keep the cards from each sentence separate. Remind him, if necessary, a sentence begins with an uppercase letter and ends with a period or other form of punctuation.)

Now read the sentences.

(**Note**: We are no longer using clues to assist the child with reading the copy work. It is important for the child to read the text located in this segment of the lesson even if he does not copy the sentences. This will give him an opportunity to practice reading text printed in a regular type.)

Copy Work: (The copy work is optional for children who have difficulty with writing.) (You may now encourage the child to copy the sentences directly from the model below. If this is too difficult, continue as directed.)

I will write the sentences you just read on a piece of paper.

(Neatly write the sentences with a pen, paying close attention to letter spacing, formation, and size. Make the letters large enough for the child to easily copy. Allow space for the child to write his letters directly under yours. An alternate method is to allow the child to trace over your letters.)

Now you can copy what I wrote.

The man and the dog went to the shed.

They went to get a mop.

I would like for you to read the sentences once more. Very good! I would like for you to draw a picture to go with your sentences. Here is a picture of a mop you can draw.

(Assist the child with drawing the picture if necessary. The picture has been drawn with bold lines so the child may trace it if he likes.)

Make up a sentence about the mop you drew. Tell me the sentence, and I will write it on a piece of paper. Now you can copy the sentence at the bottom of your picture.

(Draw lines if necessary for the child to write his sentence at the bottom of his picture.)

Read the sentence you just wrote.

Now let's read a book together.

(Review material between lessons.)

Lesson 48

Materials: reading manual, index cards, pen, gray crayon, and black crayon.

Instructions: In today's lesson, the child will review the following sight words: *the, has, to, I, you, do, is, of, come, some,* and *from*.

He will review the *eee* sound as in *wet* by reading the following words: *read, head, dead, stead, deaf, lead, bear, wear, tear,* and *pear*.

The child will also be introduced to the *cl* sound as in *clap*. He will read the following words containing the *cl* sound: *clear, clean, climb, close, clank, clang, clay, clash, cliff,* and *clock*.

He will also be introduced to the *sl* sound as in *slap*. He will read the following words containing the *sl* sound: *slap, slack, sled, slip, slosh, slay, sleeve, slate, slide,* and *slope*.

The child will read the following story and complete a variety of exercises based on the story:

Title: *"The Big Black Bear"*

Story: *The bear is at the lake. He is big and black. He will climb on the rock. He will slide in the lake. He will get wet. The bear will get a fish. He will eat it. He will go home. The bear lives in a den.*

Dialogue: Read the sight words below:

<u>the</u>	<u>has</u>	<u>to</u>
<u>I</u>	<u>you</u>	<u>do</u>
<u>is</u>	<u>of</u>	<u>come</u>
<u>some</u>		<u>from</u>

Look at the letter below. What sound does this letter make? (*eee* as in *wet*.)

e

Very good! This letter says *eee*.

Now read the words at the top of the page that have the *eee* sound.

Remember, the dotted letters are silent. They make no sound.

read	head
dead	(stead)
deaf	lead
bear	wear
tear	pear

That's great! You are learning to read really well.

Look at the letters below. These letters make the *cl* sound (as in *clap*). (Point to the letters as you make the sound.)

You will notice the letters that make the *cl* sound have a gray ring around them. This is to help you see the letters more easily.

(cl)

Say *cl* as I point to the letters above.

Now read the words below that have the *cl* sound. The first word is *clear*.

clear	clean
climb	close
clank	clang
clay	clash
cliff	clock

Look at the letters below. These letters make the sl sound (as in *slap*). (Point to the letters as you make the sound.) You will notice the letters that make the sl sound have a gray ring around them. This is to help you see the letters more easily.

sl

Say sl as I point to the letters above.

Now read the words below that have the sl sound. The first word is *slap*.

slap   slack

sled   slip

slosh   slay

sleeve   slate

slide   slope

Read the story below, and then I will show you a picture to go with the story.

"The Big Black Bear"

The bear is at the lake.

He is big and black.

He will climb on the rock.

He will slide in the lake.

He will get wet.

The bear will get a fish.

He will eat it.

He will go home.

The bear lives in a den.

Now I will show you a picture of the bear.

Look at the picture. Did you know bears are good fishermen? They catch fish with their paws and their teeth. Have you ever seen a bear at the zoo? They can grow to be very large. Do you think bears can swim? Yes, they are good swimmers too.

I am going to write the words from two of the sentences you just read on index cards.

(Have the child watch as you write each word with a pen. Label the first card with the lesson number for future use.)

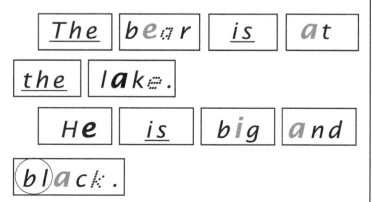

I am going to underline the sight words with a black crayon. Today our sentences have only two different sight words. Can you tell me what they are?

I am going to trace over the *eee* sound (as in *wet*) and the *aaa* sounds (as in *cat*) with a gray crayon. I will also trace over the *iii* sound (as in *pig*) with a gray crayon.

I will trace over the bold *a* sound (as in *cake*) and the bold *e* sound (as in *heat*) with a black crayon.

I will make dotted lines over the letter a in the word *bear* and over the letter e in the word *lake*. I will also make dotted lines over the letter *k* in the word *black*. Can you tell me why I dotted these letters? That's right. I dotted them, because they are silent. They make no sound.

I will draw a gray ring around the *bl* sound (as in *black*) in the word *black*.

Read the sentences. Great! Now I will mix the cards, and you can put them in proper order to make the sentences again.

(Assist the child with putting the cards in proper order. Keep the cards from each sentence separate. Remind him, if necessary, a sentence begins with an uppercase letter and ends with a period or other form of punctuation.)

Now read the sentences.

(**Note**: We are no longer using clues to assist the child with reading the copy work. It is important for the child to read the text located in this segment of the lesson even if he does not copy the sentences. This will give him an opportunity to practice reading text printed in a regular type.)

Copy Work: (The copy work is optional for children who have difficulty with writing.) (You may now encourage the child to copy the sentences directly from the model below. If this is too difficult, continue as directed.)

I will write the sentences you just read on a piece of paper.

(Neatly write the sentences with a pen, paying close attention to letter spacing, formation, and size. Make the letters large enough for the child to easily copy. Allow space for the child to write his letters directly under yours. An alternate method is to allow the child to trace over your letters.)

Now you can copy what I wrote.

The bear is at the lake.

He is big and black.

I would like for you to read the sentences once more. Very good! I would you like for you to draw a picture to go with your sentences. Here is a picture of a bear you can draw.

(Assist the child with drawing the picture if necessary. The picture has been drawn with bold lines so the child may trace it if he likes.)

Make up a sentence about the bear you drew. Tell me the sentence and I will write it on a piece of paper. Now you can copy the sentence at the bottom of your picture.

(Draw lines if necessary for the child to write his sentence at the bottom of his picture.)

Read the sentence you just wrote.

Now let's read a book together.

(Review material between lessons.)

Lesson 49

Materials: reading manual, index cards, pen, gray crayon, black crayon, and one construction paper circle.

Instructions: In today's lesson, the child will review the following sight words: *was, what, they, are, said, does, put, some, come,* and *from*. He will be introduced to the new sight word *want*. Prepare a construction paper circle with the new sight word written on it.

The child will review the *eee* sound as in *wet* by reading the following words: *wet, vet, rest, test, mess, less, head, read, bear, pear, well,* and *bell*.

The child will also be introduced to the *fl* sound as in *flag*. He will read the following words containing the *fl* sound: *flag, flap, flash, fled, flesh, flop, flake, flame, float,* and *fleet*.

The child will be introduced to the *gl* sound as in *glad*. He will read the following words containing the *gl* sound: *glad, glass, gloss, globe, gloat, glaze, gleam,* and *glide*.

The child will read the following story and complete a variety of exercises based on the story.

Title: "*The Boat*"

Story: *It was a clear day.*

Jim said, "I want to sail the boat. I can sail it on the lake. It will float. It will glide on the lake."

Jan said, "Can I come to the lake?"

Jim said, "Yes, you can sail the boat. It has a flag on the deck. We can tie a rope to the boat."

Dialogue: Read the sight words below.

<u>was</u>   <u>what</u>   <u>they</u>

<u>are</u>   <u>said</u>   <u>does</u>

<u>put</u>   <u>some</u>   <u>come</u>

<u>from</u>

Great! You have learned many sight words so far. Look at the next word. It is the sight word *want*. (Point to the word as you read it.)

want

Say *want* as I point to the word. Very good! Now read the sentences below containing the new sight word.

<u>I</u> <u>want</u> **a** p**e**t.

<u>I</u> <u>want</u> **a** p**i**g.

<u>I</u> <u>want</u> **a** p**e**t p**i**g.

Let's add the new sight word *want* to your *Sight Word Worm*.

Look at the letter below. What sound does this letter make? (*eee* as in *wet*.)

e

Very good! This letter says *eee*.

Now read the words below that have the *eee* sound.

w**e**t	v**e**t
r**e**(st)	t**e**(st)
m**e**ss	l**e**ss
h**e**ad	r**e**ad
b**e**ar	p**e**ar
w**e**ll	b**e**ll

Today you will learn a new sound. Look at the letters at the top of the next page. These letters make the *fl* sound (as in *flag*). (Point to the letters as you say the word.)

168

You will notice the letters that make the *fl* sound have a gray ring around them. This is to help you see the letters more easily.

(fl)

Say *fl* as I point to the letters above. Very good!

Now read the words containing the *fl* sound. I will read the first word for you. It is *flag*.

(fl)ag   (fl)ap
(fl)ash   (fl)ed
(fl)esh   (fl)op
(fl)ake   (fl)ame
(fl)oat   (fl)eet

Today you will learn another new sound. Look at the letters. These letters make the *gl* sound (as in *glad*). (Point to the letters as you say the word.)

You will notice the letters that make the *gl* sound have a gray ring around them. This is to help you see the letters more easily.

(gl)

Say *gl* as I point to the letters above. Very good!

Now read the words containing the *gl* sound. I will read the first word for you. It is *glad*.

(gl)ad   (gl)ass
(gl)oss   (gl)obe
(gl)oat   (gl)aze
(gl)eam   (gl)ide

Read the story below, and then I will show you a picture to go with the story.

"The Boat"

It was a (cl)ear day.

Jim said, "I want to sail the boat.

I can sail it on the lake.

It will (fl)oat.

It will (gl)ide on the lake."

169

Jan said, "Can I come to the lake?"

Jim said, "Yes, you can sail the boat.

It has a (flag) on the deck.

We can tie a rope to the boat."

Now I will show you a picture of the children with the boat.

Look at the picture. Can Jim and Jan sail in the boat? No, it is just a toy boat. Have you ever sailed a toy boat? Have you sailed a toy boat on a lake? Have you sailed a toy boat in the bathtub?

I am going to write the words from two of the sentences you just read on index cards.

(Have the child watch as you write each word with a pen. Label the first card with the lesson number for future use.)

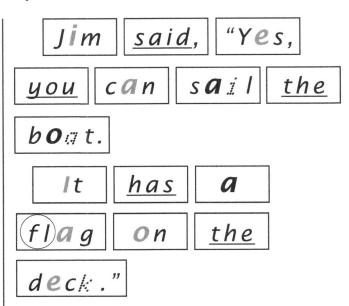

I am going to underline the sight words with a black crayon. Today our sentences have four different sight words. Can you tell me what they are?

I am going to trace over the *iii* sounds (as in *pig*) and the *eee* sounds (as in *wet*) with a gray crayon. I will also trace over the *aaa* sounds (as in *cat*) and the *ooo* sound (as in *hot*) with a gray crayon.

I will trace over the bold *a* sounds (as in *cake*) and the bold *o* sound (as in *hope*) with a black crayon.

I will make dotted lines over the letter *i* in the word *sail* and over the letter *a* in the word *boat*. I will make dotted lines over the letter *k* in the word *deck.* Can you tell me why I dotted these letters? That's right. I dotted them, because they are silent. They make no sound.

I will draw a gray ring around the *fl* sound (as in *flag*) in the word *flag.*

(Point to the quotation marks on the index cards.) Whenever someone speaks, we put the words they say in these special marks. Can you remember what these special marks are called? That's right, they are called quotation marks.

Read the sentence. Very good! Now I will mix the cards, and you can put them in proper order to make the sentences again.

(Assist the child with putting the cards in proper order. Keep the cards from each sentence separate. Remind him, if necessary, a sentence begins with an uppercase letter and ends with a period or other form of punctuation.)

Now read the sentences.

(**Note**: <u>We are no longer using clues to assist the child with reading the copy work. It is important for the child to read the text located in this segment of the lesson even if he does not copy the sentences. This will give him an opportunity to practice reading text printed in a regular type.</u>)

Copy Work: (The copy work is optional for children who have difficulty with writing.) (You may now encourage the child to copy the sentences directly from the model below. If this is too difficult, continue as directed.)

I will write the sentences you just read on a piece of paper.

(Neatly write the sentences with a pen, paying close attention to letter spacing, formation, and size. Make the letters large enough for the child to easily copy. Allow space for the child to write his letters

directly under yours. An alternate method is to allow the child to trace over your letters.)

Now you can copy what I wrote.

Jim said, "Yes, you can sail the boat. It has a flag on the deck."

I would like for you to read the sentences once more. Very good! I would like for you to draw a picture to go with your sentences. Here is a picture of a boat you can draw.

(Assist the child with drawing the picture if necessary. The picture has been drawn with bold lines so the child may trace it if he likes.)

Make up a sentence about the boat you drew. Tell me the sentence and I will write it on a piece of paper. Now

171

you can copy the sentence at the bottom of your picture.

(Draw lines if necessary for the child to write his sentence at the bottom of his picture.)

Read the sentence you just wrote.

Now let's read a book together.

(Review material between lessons.)

Lesson 50

Materials: reading manual, index cards, pen, gray crayon, and black crayon.

Instructions: In today's lesson, the child will review the following sight words: *from, come, some, want, the, has, to, I, you, is, of,* and *do.* He will review the *eee* sound as in *wet.* He will read the following words containing the *eee* sound: *sled, bed, lead, stead, wear, tear, fell, tell, vest,* and *best.*

The child will be introduced to the *dr* sound as in *dress.* He will read the following words containing the *dr* sound: *dress, dread, drag, drab, drip, drop, drape, drake, dream, drove,* and *drive.*

He will also be introduced to the *cr* sound as in *crab.* He will read the following words containing the *cr* sound: *crab, crack, crash, crop, cross, crest, crib, crave, crane, creek, creep,* and *croak.*

The child will read the following story and complete a variety of exercises based on the story.

Title: *"The Red Sled"*

Story: *Dad said, "I will drive the red sled to the creek. I can cross the creek. It is cold. The sled will not crash."*

Mom said, "Take care, Dad. Do not go fast."

Dad said, "I will not drive fast. I will cross the creek. I will not get wet. I will get a deer. We can eat the meat."

Dialogue: Read the sight words below.

from	come	some
want	the	has
to	I	you
is	of	do

Read the words below that have the *eee* sound (as in *wet*).

s(l)ed   bed

le(a)d   (s)te(a)d

we a r   te a r

fe ll   te ll

v e (st)   b e (st)

Look at the letters below. These letters make the *dr* sound (as in *dress*). (Point to the letters as you make the sound.)

You will notice the letters that make the *dr* sound have a gray ring around them. This is to help you see the letters more easily.

(dr)

Say *dr* as I point to the letters above.

Now read the words below that have the *dr* sound. The first word is *dress*.

(dr)ess   (dr)ead

(dr)ag   (dr)ab

(dr)ip   (dr)op

(dr)ape   (dr)ake

(dr)eam   (dr)ove

(dr)ive

Look at the letters below. These letters make the *cr* sound (as in *crab*). (Point to the letters as you make the sound.)

You will notice the letters that make the *cr* sound have a gray ring around them. This is to help you see the letters more easily.

(cr)

Say *cr* as I point to the letters above.

Now read the words below that have the *cr* sound.

(cr)ab   (cr)ack

(cr)ash   (cr)op

(cr)oss   (cr)est

(cr)ib   (cr)ave

(cr)ane   (cr)eek

(cr)eep   (cr)ook

Read the story below, and then I will show you a picture to go with the story.

"The Red (Sl)ed"

Dad said, "I will (dr)ive the red (sl)ed to the (cr)eek.

I can cross the creek.

It is cold.

The sled will not crash."

Mom said, "Take care, Dad.

Do not go fast."

Dad said, "I will not drive fast.

I will cross the creek.

I will not get wet.

I will get a deer.

We can eat the meat."

Now I will show you a picture of the man with the sled.

Look at the picture. Can you tell what time of year it is? That's right. It is wintertime. See all the snow on the ground.

Why do you think Dad can drive the sled across the creek without getting wet? That's right, because the creek is frozen. Long ago, before there were many bridges, people would cross rivers, creeks, and lakes in the wintertime when the water was frozen.

Why do you think Dad is going to get a deer? That's right. He's getting it to feed his family.

I am going to write the words from two of the sentences you just read on index cards.

(Have the child watch as you write each word with a pen. Label the first card with the lesson number for future use.)

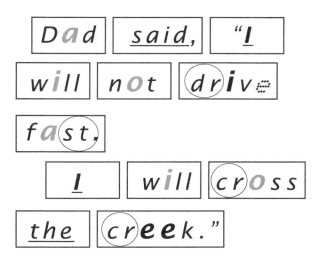

I am going to underline the sight words with a black crayon. Today our sentences have three different sight words. Can you tell me what they are?

I am going to trace over the *aaa* sounds (as in *cat*) with a gray crayon. I will also trace over the *iii* sounds (as in *pig*) and the *ooo* sounds (as in *hot*) with a gray crayon.

I will trace over the bold *i* sound (as in *bike*) and the bold *e* sounds (as in *heat*) with a black crayon.

I will make dotted lines over the letter *e* in the word *drive*. Can you tell me why I dotted this letter? That's right. I dotted it because it is silent. It makes no sound.

I will draw a gray ring around the *dr* sound (as in *dress*) in the word *drive* and around the *st* sound (as in *mist*) in the word *fast*. I will also draw a gray ring

around the *cr* sound (as in *crab*) in the word *cross* and in the word *creek*.

(Point to the quotation marks.) Whenever someone speaks, we put the words they say in these special marks. Do you remember what these marks are called? That's right. They are called quotation marks.

Read the sentences. Great! Now I will mix the cards, and you can put them in proper order to make the sentences again.

(Assist the child with putting the cards in proper order. Keep the cards from each sentence separate. Remind him, if necessary, a sentence begins with an uppercase letter and ends with a period or other form of punctuation.)

Now read the sentences.

(**Note**: We are no longer using clues to assist the child with reading the copy work. It is important for the child to read the text located in this segment of the lesson even if he does not copy the sentences. This will give him an opportunity to practice reading text printed in a regular type.)

Copy Work: (The copy work is optional for children who have difficulty with writing.) (You may now encourage the child to copy the sentences directly from the model below. If this is too difficult, continue as directed.)

I will write the sentences you just read on a piece of paper.

(Neatly write the sentences with a pen, paying close attention to letter spacing, formation, and size. Make the letters large enough for the child to easily copy. Allow space for the child to write his letters directly under yours. An alternate method is to allow the child to trace over your letters.)

Now you can copy what I wrote.

175

Dad said, "I will not drive fast. I will cross the creek."

I would like for you to read the sentences once more. Very good! I would like for you to draw a picture to go with your sentences. Here is a picture of a sled you can draw.

(Assist the child with drawing the picture if necessary. The picture has been drawn with bold lines so the child may trace it if he likes.)

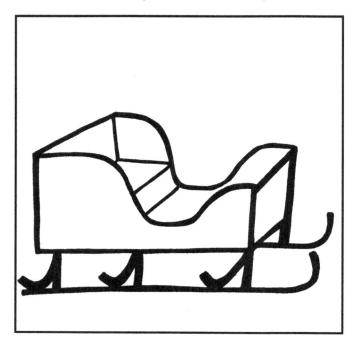

Make up a sentence about the sled you drew. Tell me the sentence, and I will write it on a piece of paper. Now you can copy the sentence at the bottom of your picture.

(Draw lines if necessary for the child to write his sentence at the bottom of his picture.)

Read the sentence you just wrote.

Now let's read a book together.

(Review material between lessons.)

Lesson 51

Materials: reading manual, index cards, pen, gray crayon, black crayon, and three construction paper circles.

Instructions: In today's lesson, the child will review the following sight words: *want, was, what, they, are, said, does, put, some, come,* and *from*. He will be introduced to the following new sight words: *could, should,* and *would*. Prepare three construction paper circles with the new sight words written on them.

He will be introduced to the *fr* sound as in *frog*. He will read the following words containing the *fr* sound: *frog, frock, frost, fresh, frill, frame, frail,* and *free*.

He will also be introduced to the *gr* sound as in *grass*. He will read the following words containing the *gr* sound: *grass, grab, grand, grip, grin, Greg, grape, gray, green,* and *groan*.

The child will read the following story and complete a variety of exercises based on the story.

Title: *"The Green Frog"*

Story: *The green frog sat on the bank.*

He said to the gray toad, "We should go home. See the frost on the trees. See the frost on the grass. It is cold. We do not like the cold."

The gray toad said, "Come, green frog. I will take you home. We will not be cold. We will be glad."

Dialogue: Read the sight words below.

want was what

they are said

does put some

come from

Look at the new sight word below. It is the word *could*. (Point to the word as you read it.)

could

Say *could* as I point to the word. Very good!

Now you will learn two more new sight words. These words rhyme with *could*. (Point to the word *could*.)

The new sight words are *should* and *would*. (Point to the words below.)

should would

Now read the three new sight words as I point to them.

should could

would

Let's add the new sight words to your *Sight Word Worm*.

Look at the letters below. These letters make the *fr* sound (as in *frog*). (Point to the letters as you make the sound.)

You will notice the letters that make the *fr* sound have a gray ring around them. This is to help you see the letters more easily.

fr

Say *fr* as I point to the letters above.

Now read the words below that have the *fr* sound. The first word is *frog*.

frog frock

frost fresh

frill frame

frail free

177

Look at the letters below. These letters make the *gr* sound (as in *grass*). (Point to the letters as you make the sound.)

You will notice the letters that make the *gr* sound have a gray ring around them. This is to help you see the letters more easily.

(gr)

Say *gr* as I point to the letters above.

Now read the words below that have the *gr* sound. The first word is *grass*.

(gr)ass   (gr)ab

(gr)and   (gr)ip

(gr)in   (Gr)eg

(gr)ape   (gr)ay

(gr)een   (gr)oan

Read the story below, and then I will show you a picture to go with the story.

"The (Gr)een (Fr)og "

The (gr)een (fr)og sat on the bank.

He said to the (gr)ay toad,

"We should go home.

See the (fr)ost on the (tr)ees.

See the (fr)ost on the (gr)ass.

It is cold.

We do not like the cold."

The (gr)ay toad said, "Come, (gr)een (fr)og.

I will take you home.

178

We will not be cold.

We will be (gl)ad."

Now I will show you a picture of the frog and the toad.

Look at the picture. See the frog and the toad sitting on the bank. The frog is smaller than the toad. What does he have in his hand? That's right, he has a fishing rod. What do you think he has been doing? Did he catch a fish? Yes, he caught a fish. What do you think they will do with the fish? That's right, they will eat it.

I am going to write the words from two of the sentences you just read on index cards.

(Have the child watch as you write each word with a pen. Label the first card with the lesson number for future use.)

The | (gr)ee(n) | (fr)o(g)

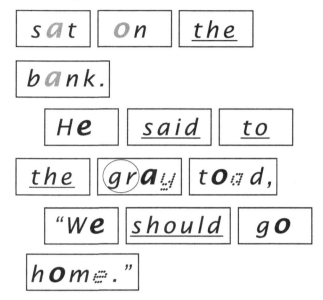

s(a)t | on | the
b(a)nk.
He | said | to
the | (gr)a(y) | to(a)d,
"We | should | go
h(o)m(e)."

I am going to underline the sight words with a black crayon. Today our sentences have four different sight words. Can you tell me what they are? I am going to trace over the *ooo* sounds (as in *hot*) *and the* *aaa* sounds (as in *cat*) with a gray crayon.

I will trace over the bold *e* sounds (as in *heat*) and the bold *a* sound (as in *cake*) with a black crayon. I will also trace over the bold *o* sounds (as in *hope*) with a black crayon.

I will make dotted lines over the letter *y* in the word *gray*. I will also make dotted lines over the letter *a* in the word *toad*, and I will make dotted lines over the letter *e* in the word *home*. Can you tell me why I dotted these letters? That's right. I dotted them because they are silent. They make no sound.

179

I will draw a gray ring around the *gr* sound (as in *grass*) in the word *green* and in the word *gray*. I will also draw a gray ring around the *fr* sound (as in *frog*) in the word *frog*.

(Point to the quotation marks on the index cards.) Whenever someone speaks, we put the words they say in these special marks. Do you remember what they are called? That's right. They are called quotation marks.

Read the sentences. Very good! Now I will mix the cards, and you can put them in proper order to make the sentences again.

(Assist the child with putting the cards in proper order. Keep the cards from each sentence separate. Remind him, if necessary, a sentence begins with an uppercase letter and ends with a period or other form of punctuation.)

Now read the sentences.

(**Note**: We are no longer using clues to assist the child with reading the copy work. It is important for the child to read the text located in this segment of the lesson even if he does not copy the sentences. This will give him an opportunity to practice reading text printed in a regular type.)

Copy Work: (The copy work is optional for children who have difficulty with writing.) (You may now encourage the child to copy the sentences directly from the model below. If this is too difficult, continue as directed.)

I will write the sentences you just read on a piece of paper.

(Neatly write the sentences with a pen, paying close attention to letter spacing, formation, and size. Make the letters large enough for the child to easily copy. Allow space for the child to write his letters directly under yours. An alternate method is to allow the child to trace over your letters.)

Now you can copy what I wrote.

The green frog sat on the bank. He said to the gray toad, "We should go home."

I would like for you to read the sentences once more. Very good! I would like for you to draw a picture to go with your sentences. Here is a picture of a frog you can draw.

(Assist the child with drawing the picture if necessary. The picture has been drawn with bold lines so the child may trace it if he likes.)

Make up a sentence about the frog you drew. Tell me the sentence and I will write it on a piece of paper. Now you can copy the sentence at the bottom of your picture.

(Draw lines if necessary for the child to write his sentence at the bottom of his picture.)

Read the sentence you just wrote.

Now let's read a book together.

(Review material between lessons.)

Lesson 52

Materials: reading manual, index cards, pen, gray crayon, and black crayon.

Instructions: In today's lesson, the child will review the following sight words: *could, should, would, put, some, come.* He will review a number of sounds learned so far by reading the following words: *dress, drape, close, clash, sled, slide, crib, crop, flame, fleet, glad, glass, frog, frost, green,* and *grass.*

The child will read the following story and complete a variety of exercises based on the story.

Title: *"Jill and Jane Can Slide"*

Story: *Jill said, "I want to slide. I want to slide on the hill."*

Jane said, "Do you have a sled?"

Jill said, "Yes, I have a sled. I have a green sled."

Jane said, "I do not have a sled."

Jill said, "Come to the hill. We can slide on the sled. The frost is on the hill. We can slide fast."

Dialogue: Read the sight words below.

<u>could</u>   <u>should</u>

<u>would</u>

<u>put</u>   <u>some</u>   <u>come</u>

Read the words below.

dress   drape

close   clash

sled   slide

crib   crop

flame   fleet

glad   glass

fr(o)g   fr(o)st
(gr)(ee)n   (gr)(a)ss

"Jill and Jane can (sl)(i)de"

Jill said, "I want to (sl)(i)de.

I want to (sl)(i)de on the hill."

Jane said, "Do you have a (sl)ed?"

Jill said, "Yes, I have a (sl)ed.

I have a (gr)(ee)n (sl)ed."

Jane said, "I do not have a (sl)ed."

Jill said, "Come to the hill.

We can (sl)(i)de on the (sl)ed.

The (fr)(o)st is on the hill.

We can (sl)(i)de f(a)st."

Now I will show you a picture of Jane and Jill and the sled.

Look at the picture. Do you think it is cold outside? Yes, it is cold. What can you see in the picture that lets you know it is cold outside? What is on the ground? That's right. Snow is on the ground. Since snow is on the ground, what season of the year do you think it is? Yes, it is probably wintertime, although in some parts of the world it also snows during other seasons of the year. Often snow covers the tops of very, very high mountains all year long.

What are the children wearing? That's right, they are wearing jackets, mittens, scarves, hats, and boots. They should be nice and warm with all those clothes.

Have you ridden on a sled before? What did the sled look like? What shape was the sled? What color was the sled?

I am going to write the words from three of the sentences you just read on index cards.

(Have the child watch as you write each word with a pen. Label the first card with the lesson number for future use.)

Jill said, "Come to the hill. We can slide on the sled. The frost is on the hill."

I am going to underline the sight words with a black crayon. Today our sentences have five different sight words. Can you tell me what they are?

I am going to trace over the *iii* sounds (as in *pig*) and *aaa* sound (as in *cat*) with a gray crayon. I will also trace over the *ooo* sounds (as in *hot*) and the *eee* sound (as in *wet*) with a gray crayon.

I will trace over the bold *e* sound (as in *heat*) and the bold *i* sound (as in *bike*) with a black crayon. I will make dotted lines over the letter *e* in the word *slide*. Can you tell me why I dotted this letter? That's right. I dotted it, because it is silent. It makes no sound.

I will draw a gray ring around the *sl* sound (as in *sled*) in the word *slide* and in the word *sled*. I will draw a gray ring around the *fr* sound (as in *frog*) in the word *frost*. I will also draw a gray ring

183

around the *st* sound (as in *mist*) in the word *frost.*

(Point to the quotation marks on the index cards.) Whenever someone speaks, we put the words they say in these special marks. Do you remember what they are called? That's right. They are called quotation marks.

Read the sentences. Great! Now I will mix the cards, and you can put them in proper order to make the sentences again.

(Assist the child with putting the cards in proper order. Keep the cards from each sentence separate. Remind him, if necessary, a sentence begins with an uppercase letter and ends with a period or other form of punctuation.)

Now read the sentences.

(**Note**: We are no longer using clues to assist the child with reading the copy work. It is important for the child to read the text located in this segment of the lesson even if he does not copy the sentences. This will give him an opportunity to practice reading text printed in a regular type.)

Copy Work: (The copy work is optional for children who have difficulty with writing.) (You may now encourage the child to copy the sentences directly from the model below. If this is too difficult, continue as directed.)

I will write the sentences you just read on a piece of paper.

(Neatly write the sentences with a pen, paying close attention to letter spacing, formation, and size. Make the letters large enough for the child to easily copy. Allow space for the child to write his letters directly under yours. An alternate method is to allow the child to trace over your letters.)

Now you can copy what I wrote.

Jill said, "Come to the hill. We can slide on the sled. The frost is on the hill."

I would like for you to read the sentences once more. Very good! I would like for you to draw a picture to go with your sentences. Here is a picture of a sled you can draw.

(Assist the child with drawing the picture if necessary. The picture has been drawn with bold lines so the child may trace it if he likes.)

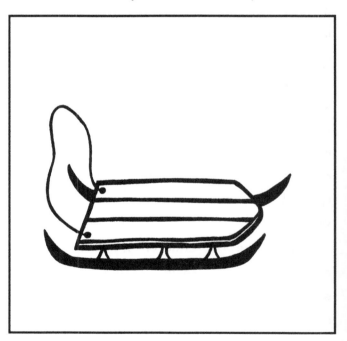

Make up a sentence about the sled you drew. Tell me the sentence and I will write it on a piece of paper. Now you can copy the sentence at the bottom of your picture.

(Draw lines if necessary for the child to write his sentence at the bottom of his picture.)

Read the sentence you just wrote.

Now let's read a book together.

(Review material between lessons.)

Lesson 53

Materials: reading manual, index cards, pen, gray crayon, and black crayon.

Instructions: In today's lesson, the child will review the following sight words: *want, what, from, come, some, could, should,* and *would.*

He will be introduced to the *pr* sound as in *prick.* He will read the following words containing the *pr* sound: *prick, print, prop, press, pray, praise, prize,* and *prose.* He will also be introduced to the *br* sound as in *brass.* He will read the following words containing the *br* sound: *brass, brake, brag, bread, brick, breeze, bride,* and *broke.*

The child will be introduced to the *tr* sound as in *trick.* He will read the following words containing the *tr* sound: *trick, trip, track, trap, tread, trot, tree, tray, trade,* and *train.*

The child will read the following story and complete a variety of exercises based on the story.

Title: *"The Big Train"*

Story: *Jane said, "The big train will come on the track. It will come on time. It will not be late. The man will put on the brake. The train will stop."*

Pat said, "I want to ride on the train. I want to go fast. Do you want to go?"

Jane said, "Yes, I would like to go. We could share a seat."

Pat said, "We should pack the bags. I will press the pants. You can fold the tops."

Dialogue: Read the sight words below.

<u>want</u>   <u>what</u>

<u>from</u>   <u>come</u>

<u>some</u>   <u>could</u>

<u>should</u>   <u>would</u>

Look at the letters at the top of the next page. These letters make the *pr* sound (as in *prick*). (Point to the letters as you make the sound.)

You will notice the letters that make the *pr* sound have a gray ring around them. This is to help you see the letters more easily.

(pr)

Say *pr* (as in *prick*) as I point to the letters above.

Now read the words below that have the *pr* sound. The first word is *prick*.

(pr)ick   (pr)int

(pr)op   (pr)ess

(pr)ay   (pr)aise

(pr)ize   (pr)ose

Look at the letters below. These letters make the *br* sound (as in *brass*). (Point to the letters as you make the sound.)

You will notice the letters that make the *br* sound have a gray ring around them. This is to help you see the letters more easily.

(br)

Say *br* (as in *brass*) as I point to the letters above.

Now read the words below that have the *br* sound. The first word is *brass*.

(br)ass   (br)ake

(br)ag   (br)ead

(br)ick   (br)eeze

(br)ide   (br)oke

Look at the letters below. These letters make the *tr* sound (as in *trick*). (Point to the letters as you make the sound.)

You will notice the letters that make the *tr* sound have a gray ring around them. This is to help you see the letters more easily.

(tr)

Say *tr* (as in *trick*) as I point to the letters above.

Now read the words below that have the *tr* sound.

(tr)ick   (tr)ip

(tr)ack   (tr)ap

(tr)ead   (tr)ot

(tr)ee   (tr)ay

(tr)ade   (tr)ain

Read the story, and then I will show you a picture to go with the story.

"The Big Train"

Jane said, "The big train

will come on the track.

It will come on time.

It will not be late.

The man will put on the brake.

The train will stop."

Pat said, "I want to

ride on the train.

I want to go fast. Do you want to go?"

Jane said, "Yes, I would like to go.

We could share a seat."

Pat said, "We should pack the bags.

I will press the pants.

You can fold the tops."

Now I will show you a picture of
the girls packing their bags for the train
ride.

Look at the picture. The girls are getting ready to go on a train ride. They are packing their bags. Do you think they will be gone for a long time or a short time? What makes you think so?

They will probably be gone for a long time because they are packing many bags. Have you ever been on a train? Where did you go, or where would you like to go?

I am going to write the words from two of the sentences you just read on index cards.

(Have the child watch as you write each word with a pen. Label the first card with the lesson number for future use.)

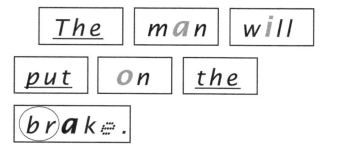

The ⟨tr⟩a⟨i⟩n wi⟨ll⟩

⟨st⟩op.

I am going to underline the sight words with a black crayon. Today our sentences have two different sight words. Can you tell me what they are?

I am going to trace over the aaa sound (as in cat) with a gray crayon. I am going to trace over the iii sounds (as in pig) and the ooo sounds (as in hot) with a gray crayon.

I will trace over the bold a sounds (as in cake) with a black crayon. I will make dotted lines over the letter e in the word brake. I will make dotted lines over the letter i in the word train. Can you tell me why I dotted these letters? That's right. I dotted them because they are silent. They make no sound.

I will draw a gray ring around the br sound (as in brass) in the word brake. I will also draw a gray ring around the tr sound (as in trick) in the word train. I will draw a gray ring around the st sound (as in stop) in the word stop.

Read the sentences. Great! Now I will mix the cards, and you can put them in proper order to make the sentences again.

(Assist the child with putting the cards in proper order. Keep the cards from each sentence separate. Remind him, if necessary, a sentence begins with an uppercase letter and ends with a period or some other form of punctuation.)

Now read the sentences.

(**Note**: We are no longer using clues to assist the child with reading the copy work. It is important for the child to read the text located in this segment of the lesson even if he does not copy the sentences. This will give him an opportunity to practice reading text printed in a regular type.)

Copy Work: (The copy work is optional for children who have difficulty with writing.) (You may now encourage the child to copy the sentences directly from the model below. If this is too difficult, continue as directed.)

I will write the sentences you just read on a piece of paper.

(Neatly write the sentences with a pen, paying close attention to letter spacing, formation, and size. Make the letters large enough for the child to easily copy. Allow space for the child to write his letters directly under yours. An alternate method is to allow the child to trace over your letters.)

Now you can copy what I wrote.

The man will put on the brake. The train will stop.

I would like for you to read the sentences once more. Very good! I would like for you to draw a picture to go with your sentences. Here is a picture of a train you can draw.

(Assist the child with drawing the picture if necessary. The picture has been drawn with bold lines so the child may trace it if he likes.)

Make up a sentence about the train you drew. Tell me the sentence, and I will write it on a piece of paper. Now you can copy the sentence at the bottom of your picture.

(Draw lines if necessary for the child to write his sentence at the bottom of his picture.)

Read the sentence you just wrote. Now let's read a book together.

(Review material between lessons.)

Lesson 54

Materials: reading manual, index cards, pen, gray crayon, black crayon, and two construction paper circles.

Instructions: In today's lesson, the child will review the following sight words: *does, do, are, they, want, put, from, come, some, could, would,* and *should.* He will be introduced to the new sight words *there* and *where.* Prepare two construction paper circles with the new sight words written on them.

He will be introduced to the *sc* sound as in *scat.* He will read the following words containing the *sc* sound: *scat, scan, scab, scoff, scale,* and *scope.*

He will also be introduced to *sk* sound as in *skate.* He will read the following words containing the *sk* sound: *skin, skill, skip, skit, skim, skate, bask, mask, disk,* and *risk.*

The child will read the following story and complete a variety of exercises based on the story.

Title: *"Joe and Jill"*

Story: *Joe and Jill like to play. Joe can skate. Jill can skate. They can skate on the tile. They can go fast. They wear pads. They play safe. They like to skip rope. They can skip fast. Top can not skate. Top can not skip. He can not play. He is sad.*

Joe said to Top, "Come here. Come to me. You and I can play tag. We can play in the grass. I will take off the skates."

Jill said, "Can I play tag in the grass?"

Joe said, "Yes, you can play. You can tag me and Top."

Dialogue: Read the sight words below.

<u>does</u>   <u>do</u>   <u>are</u>

<u>they</u>   <u>want</u>   <u>put</u>

<u>from</u>   <u>come</u>   <u>some</u>

<u>could</u>   <u>would</u>

<u>should</u>

Look at the new sight word. It is the word *there.* (Point to the word below.)

<u>there</u>

Say *there* as I point to the word. Very good!

Now look at the next new sight word. It rhymes with *there.* Can you read this new sight word? (Point to the word below.)

<u>where</u>

Read the two new sight words again.

<u>there</u>   <u>where</u>

Read the sentences below that contain the new sight words.

"<u>Where</u> <u>is</u> <u>the</u> fr(o)g?" <u>said</u> Tom.

"He <u>is</u> <u>there</u>," <u>said</u> Jack. "He <u>is</u> <u>in</u> <u>the</u> pond. He <u>is</u> <u>wet</u>."

Let's add the new sight words to your *Sight Word Worm.*

Look at the letters at the top of the next page. These letters make the *sc* sound (as in *scat*). (Point to the letters as you make the sound.)

You will notice the letters that make the *sc* sound (as in *scat*) have a gray ring around them. This is to help you see the letters more easily.

(s c)

Say *sc* as I point to the letters.

Now read the following words that have the sc sound. The first word is scat.

sc at   sc an

sc ab   sc off

sc a le   sc o pe

Look at the letters below. These letters also make the *sk* sound (as in *skate*). (Point to the letters as you make the sound.)

You will notice the letters that make the *sk* sound (as in *skate*) have a gray ring around them. This is to help you see the letters more easily.

sk

Say *sk* as I point to the letters.

Now read the words below that have the *sk* sound. The first word is *skin*

s k in   s k ill

s k ip   s k it

s k im   s k a te

Sometimes the *sk* sound comes at the end of words. Read the words below. The first word is *bask*.

b a sk   m a sk

d i sk   r i sk

Read the story below, and then I will show you a picture to go with the story.

"Jo e   and   Jill"

Jo e   and   Jill   like   to   pl a y.

Jo e   can   sk a te.   Jill   can   sk a te.

They   can   sk a te on   the   ti le.

They   can   g o   fa st.   They   we a r   p a ds.

They   pl a y   s a fe.

They   like   to   sk ip   ro pe.

They   can   sk ip   fa st.

Top   can   not   sk a te.

Top can not skip.

He can not play. He is sad.

Joe said to Top, "Come here.

Come to me. You and I can play tag.

We can play in the grass.

I will take off the skates."

Jill said, "Can I play

tag in the grass?"

Joe said, "Yes, you can play.

You can tag me and Top."

Now I will show you a picture of Joe, Jill and Top.

Look at the picture. What are Joe and Jill wearing on their knees? That's

192

right. They are wearing kneepads. Why are they wearing kneepads? That's right. They wear them to protect their knees if they fall.

Who is Top? Yes, he is the dog in the story. Do you think he wants the children to play with him?

I am going to write the words from two of the sentences you just read on index cards.

(Have the child watch as you write each word with a pen. Label the first card with the lesson number for future use.)

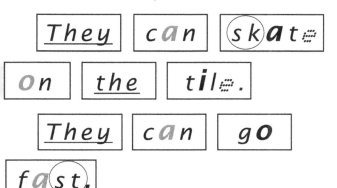

(**Note**: You may eliminate some of the print clues from the index cards with which your child is familiar. Be sure to include the print clues for sounds that have been recently introduced.)

I am going to underline the sight words with a black crayon. Today our sentences have two different sight words. Can you tell me what they are?

I am going to trace over the *aaa* sounds (as in *cat*) and the *ooo* sound (as in *hot*) with a gray crayon.

I will trace over the bold *a* sound (as in *cake*) with a black crayon. I will also trace over the bold *i* sound (as in *bike*) and the bold *o* sound (as in *hope*) with a black crayon.

I will make dotted lines over the letter *e* in the word *skate* and over the letter *e* in the word *tile*. Can you tell me why I dotted these letters? That's right. I dotted them because they are silent. They make no sound.

I will draw a gray ring around the *sk* sound (as in *skate*) in the word *skate*. I will also draw a gray ring around the *st* sound (as in *mist*) in the word *fast*.

Read the sentences. Very good! Now I will mix the cards, and you can put them in proper order to make the sentences again.

(Assist the child with putting the cards in proper order. Keep the cards from each sentence separate. Remind him, if necessary, a sentence begins with an uppercase letter and ends with a period or some other form of punctuation.)

Now read the sentences.

(**Note**: We are no longer using clues to assist the child with reading the copy work. It is important for the child to read the text located in this segment of the lesson even if he does not copy the sentences. This will give him an opportunity to practice reading text printed in a regular type.)

Copy Work: (The copy work is optional for children who have difficulty with writing.) (You may now encourage the child to copy the sentences directly from the model below. If this is too difficult, continue as directed.)

I will write the sentences you just read on a piece of paper.

(Neatly write the sentences with a pen, paying close attention to letter spacing and formation.)

Now you can copy what I wrote.

They can skate on the tile. They can go fast.

I would like for you to read the sentences once more. Very good! I would like for you to draw a picture to go with your sentences. Here is a picture of a dog you can draw.

(Assist the child with drawing the picture if necessary. The picture has been drawn with bold lines so the child may trace it if he likes.)

(**Note**: You may choose to encourage the child to dictate a short story to you about the picture he drew instead of only one sentence.)

Make up a story about the dog you drew. Tell me the story, and I will write it on a piece of paper. Now you can copy one sentence from your story at the bottom of your picture.

(Draw lines if necessary for the child to write his sentence at the bottom of his picture.)

Read the story you dictated to me. (Assist the child by reading any difficult words for him. If the story is long, have him read part of it and you read part of it.)

Now let's read a book together.

(Review material between lessons.)

Lesson 55

Materials: reading manual, index cards, pen, gray crayon, and black crayon.

Instructions: In today's lesson, the child will review the following sight words: *from, come, some, should, would, want, could, there,* and *where.*

He will be introduced to the *sm* sound as in *smoke.* He will read the following words containing the *sm* sound: *smoke, smell, smack, smock, smash, smear,* and *smile.*

He will also be introduced to the *sp* sound as in *spill.* He will read the following words containing the *sp* sound: *spill, spin, speck, spend, spot, speak, speed, spank, spoke,* and *spike.*

The child will read the following story and complete a variety of exercises based on the story.

Title: *"The Big Fire"*

Story: *Fred said, "Can you smell the smoke?"*

Pam said, "Yes, I can smell the smoke. Is it a fire?"

Fred said, "Let's go see."

They ran to the smoke. It was not a fire. It was Dad. Dad had meat on the grill.

Dad said, "Could you smell the meat?"

Fred and Pam spoke, "We could smell the smoke. We are glad it is not a fire."

Dad said, "Fred, get the milk. Pam, get the bread. It is time to eat."

Dialogue: Read the sight words below.

from   come   some

should   would

want   could

there   where

Look at the letters at the top of the next page. These letters make the *sm* sound (as in *smoke*). (Point to the letters as you make the sound.)

You will notice the letters that make the *sm* sound have a gray ring around them. This is to help you see the letters more easily.

(sm)

Say *sm* as I point to the letters above. Now read the words below that have the *sm* sound (as in *smoke*). The first word is *smoke*.

(sm)oke   (sm)ell

(sm)ack   (sm)ock

(sm)a(sh)   (sme)ar

(sm)ile

Look at the letters below. These letters make the *sp* sound (as in *spill*). (Point to the letters as you make the sound.)

You will notice the letters that make the *sp* sound have a gray ring around them. This is to help you see the letters more easily.

(sp)

Say *sp* as I point to the letters above. Now read the words below that

have the *sp* sound (as in *spill*). The first word is *spill*.

(sp)ill   (sp)in

(sp)eck   (sp)end

(sp)ot   (sp)eak

(sp)eed   (sp)ank

(sp)oke   (sp)ike

Read the words below. (Assist the child with reading any unfamiliar words. These words will appear in today's story.)

milk   fire

(Fr)ed   let's

(gr)ill   (gl)ad

(br)ead   meat

Read the story below, and then I will show you a picture to go with the story.

"The Big Fire"

(Fr)ed <u>said</u>, "Can <u>you</u> (sm)ell <u>the</u> (sm)oke?"

Pam <u>said</u>, "Yes, <u>I</u> can (sm)ell <u>the</u> (sm)oke. <u>Is</u> it a fire?"

Fred said, "Let's go see."

They ran to the smoke.

It was not a fire. It was Dad.

Dad had meat on the grill.

Dad said, "Could you smell the meat?"

Fred and Pam spoke,

"We could smell the smoke.

We are glad it is not a fire."

Dad said, "Fred, get the milk.

Pam, get the bread. It is time to eat."

Now I will show you a picture of Fred and Pam looking at the smoke.

Look at the picture. Can you see why Fred and Pam are worried? What do they see? That's right, they see smoke coming from behind the house. What is making the smoke? That's right, it is the grill. What is Dad cooking on the grill?

I am going to write the words from two of the sentences you just read on index cards.

(Have the child watch as you write each word with a pen. Label the first card with the lesson number for future use.)

Dad	had	meat
on	the	grill.

196

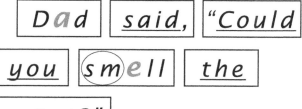

(**Note**: You may eliminate some of the print clues from the index cards with which your child is familiar. Be sure to include the print clues for sounds that have been recently introduced.)

I am going to underline the sight words with a black crayon. Today our sentences have four different sight words. Can you tell me what they are?

I am going to trace over the *aaa* sounds (as in *cat*) and the *ooo* sound (as in *hot*) with a gray crayon. I will also trace over the *iii* sound (as in *pig*) and the *eee* sound (as in *wet*) with a gray crayon.

I will trace over the bold *e* sounds with a black crayon. I will make dotted lines over the letter a in the word *meat*. Can you tell me why I dotted this letter? That's right. I dotted it, because it is silent. It makes no sound.

I will draw a gray ring around the *gr* sound (as in *grass*) in the word *grill*. I will also draw a gray ring around the *sm* sound (as in *smoke*) in the word *smell*.

Dad said, "Could you smell the meat?" (Point to the index cards containing this sentence.) Remember, when a person speaks we put the words he says in quotation marks. (Point to the quotation marks.)

What do we call the mark at the end of the second sentence? (Point to the question mark.) That's right, we call that a question mark. We use this mark when someone asks a question.

Read the sentences. Great! Now I will mix the cards, and you can put them in proper order to make the sentences again.

(Assist the child with putting the cards in proper order. Keep the cards from each sentence separate. Remind him, if necessary, a sentence begins with an uppercase letter and ends with a period or some other form of punctuation.)

Now read the sentences.

(**Note**: We are no longer using clues to assist the child with reading the copy work. It is important for the child to read the text located in this segment of the lesson even if he does not copy the sentences. This will give him an opportunity to practice reading text printed in a regular type.)

Copy Work: (The copy work is optional for children who have difficulty with writing.) (You may now encourage the child to copy the sentences directly from the model below. If this is too difficult, continue as directed.)

I will write the sentences you just read on a piece of paper.

(Neatly write the sentences with a pen, paying close attention to letter spacing and formation.)

Now you can copy what I wrote.

Dad had meat on the grill. Dad said, "Could you smell the meat?"

I would like for you to read the sentences once more. Very good! I would like for you to draw a picture to go

197

with your sentences. Here is a picture of a grill you can draw.

(Assist the child with drawing the picture if necessary. The picture has been drawn with bold lines so the child may trace it if he likes.)

(**Note**: You may choose to encourage the child to dictate a short story to you about the picture he drew instead of only one sentence.)

Make up a story about the grill you drew. Tell me the story, and I will write it on a piece of paper. Now you can copy one sentence from your story at the bottom of your picture.

(Draw lines if necessary for the child to write his sentence at the bottom of his picture.)

Read the story you dictated to me.

(Assist the child by reading any difficult words for him. If the story is long, have him read part of it and you read part of it.)

Now let's read a book together.

(Review material between lessons.)

Lesson 56

Materials: reading manual, index cards, pen, gray crayon, black crayon, and one construction paper circle.

Instructions: In today's lesson, the child will review the following sight words: *could, should, would, from, come, some, there, where, said, what,* and *they.* He will be introduced to the new sight word *your.* Prepare one construction paper circle with the new sight word written on it.

He will also be introduced to the *sn* sound as in *snake.* He will read the following words containing the *sn* sound: *snake, snail, sneeze, sneak, snap, snag, snack,* and *snip.*

The child will be introduced to the *sw* sound as in *sweet.* He will read the following words containing the *sw* sound: *sweet, sweep, swine, swell, swam,* and *swish.*

The child will read the following story and complete a variety of exercises based on the story.

Title: *"The Swine and the Snake."*

Story: *The swine said to the snake, "What is your name?"*

The snake said, "It is Sam. What is your name?"

The swine said, "It is Pig Pen."

Sam said, "Do you want to play a game?"

Pig Pen said, "Yes, I would like to play a game."

Sam said, "We can play hide and seek. I will hide. I can swish in the grass."

The snake hid in the grass. The swine could not find him.

Pig Pen said, "Where are you? I can not find you"

Sam said, "Here I am. I am green. The grass is green. Can you see me?"

Pig Pen said, "Yes, I can see you."

Dialogue: Read the sight words below.

could   should

would   from

198

come   some
there   where
said   what
                  they

Today you will learn a new sight word. The word is *your*. (Point to the word as you say it.)

your

Say *your* as I point to the word. Very good!

Now read the sentence below with the new sight word *your*.

What is your name?

Let's add the new sight word to your *Sight Word Worm*. (Have the child frequently review the sight words on the *Sight Word Worm*. Have him read the words in random order.)

Look at the letters below. These letters make the *sn* sound (as in *snake*). (Point to the letters as you make the sound.)

You will notice the letters that make the *sn* sound have a gray ring around them. This is to help you see the letters more easily.

sn

Say *sn* as I point to the letters above. Now read the words below that have the *sn* sound (as in *snake*). The first word is *snake*.

snake   snail

sneeze   sneak
snap   snag
snack   snip

Look at the letters below. These letters make the *sw* sound (as in *sweet*). (Point to the letters as you make the sound.)

You will notice the letters that make the *sw* sound have a gray ring around them. This is to help you see the letters more easily.

sw

Say *sw* as I point to the letters above. Now read the words below that have the *sw* sound (as in *sweet*). The first word is *sweet*.

sweet   sweep
swine   swell
swam   swish

Read the words below.

(Assist the child with reading any unfamiliar words. These words will appear in today's story.)

pen   seek
find   swish
here   green
grass   Sam

199

Read the story, and then I will show
you a picture to go with the story.

"The Swine and the Snake"

The swine said to the snake,

"What is your name?"

The snake said, "It is Sam.

What is your name?"

The swine said, "It is Pig Pen."

Sam said, "Do you want

to play a game?"

Pig Pen said, "Yes, I would

like to play a game."

Sam said, "We can play

hide and seek. I will hide.

I can swish in the grass."

The snake hid in the grass.

The swine could not find him.

Pig Pen said, "Where are you?

200

I *can* *not* **find** *you*."

Sam *said*, "Here **I** *am*. **I** *am* gr**ee**n.

The gr**a**ss **is** gr**ee**n. **Can** *you* s**ee** *me*?"

Pig Pen *said*, "Yes, **I** *can* s**ee** *you*."

Now I will show you a picture of the swine and the snake.

Look at the picture. What are the swine and the snake playing? That's right. They are playing hide and seek. Why do you think the swine is having a hard time finding the snake? That's right. The snake is hiding in the grass.

Do you think the snake would be hard to find if he was green like the grass? Maybe you could color the snake and the grass green. Then the snake would really be hard to find. What color would you make the swine?

Do you like to play hide and seek? Where is your favorite place to hide?

I am going to write the words from two of the sentences you just read on index cards.

(Have the child watch as you write each word with a pen. Label the first card with the lesson number for future use.)

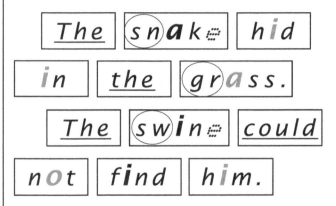

(**Note**: You may eliminate some of the print clues from the index cards with which your child is familiar. Be sure to include the print clues for sounds that have been recently introduced.)

I am going to underline the sight words with a black crayon. Today our sentences have two different sight words. Can you tell me what they are?

I am going to trace over the *iii* sounds (as in *pig*) and the *aaa* sound (as in *cat*) with a gray crayon. I will also trace over the *ooo* sound (as in *hot*) with a gray crayon.

I will trace over the bold *a* sound (as in *cake*) with a black crayon. I will also trace over the bold *i* sounds (as in *bike*) with a black crayon.

I will make dotted lines over the letter *e* in the word *snake* and over the letter *e* in the word *swine*. Can you tell me why I dotted these letters? That's right. I dotted them, because they are silent. They make no sound. I will draw a gray ring around the *sn* sound (as in *snake*) in the word *snake*. I will also draw a gray ring around the *gr* sound (as in *grass*) in the word *grass* and around the *sw* sound (as in *sweet*) in the word *swine*

Read the sentences. Great! Now I will mix the cards, and you can put them in proper order to make the sentences again.

(Assist the child with putting the cards in proper order. Keep the cards from each sentence separate. Remind him, if necessary, a sentence begins with an uppercase letter and ends with a period or some other form of punctuation.)

Now read the sentences.

(**Note**: <u>We are no longer using clues to assist the child with reading the copy work. It is important for the child to read the text located in this segment of the lesson even if he does not copy the sentences. This will give him an opportunity to practice reading text printed in a regular type.</u>)

Copy Work: (The copy work is optional for children who have difficulty with writing.) (You may now encourage the child to copy the sentences directly from the model below. If this is too difficult, continue as directed.)

I will write the sentences you just read on a piece of paper.

(Neatly write the sentences with a pen, paying close attention to letter spacing and formation.)

Now you can copy what I wrote.

The snake hid in the grass. The swine could not find him.

I would like for you to read the sentences once more.

Very good! I would like for you to draw a picture to go with your sentences. Here is a picture of a snake you can draw.

(Assist the child with drawing the picture if necessary. The picture has been drawn with bold lines so the child may trace it if he likes.)

(**Note**: You may choose to encourage the child to dictate a short story to you about the picture he drew instead of only one sentence.)

Make up a story about the snake you drew. Tell me the story, and I will write it on a piece of paper. Now you can copy one sentence from your story at the bottom of your picture.

(Draw lines if necessary for the child to write his sentence at the bottom of his picture.)

Read the story you dictated to me.

(Assist the child by reading any difficult words for him. If the story is long, have him read part of it and you read part of it.)

Now let's read a book together.

(Review material between lessons.)

Lesson 57

Materials: reading manual, index cards, pen, gray crayon, and black crayon.

Instructions: In today's lesson, the child will review the following sight words: *of, there, where, from, come, some, your, should, would, could, want,* and *does*.

The child will be introduced to the bold *o* sound as in *snow*. He will read the following words containing the bold *o* sound as in *snow*: *snow, blow, grow, row, tow, mow, bow, low, crow, flow, slow,* and *glow*.

He will also be introduced to the *ow* sound as in *cow*. He will read the following words with the *ow* sound as in *cow*: *cow, now, wow, plow, town, gown, down, brown, clown, crown,* and *frown*.

To help the child recognize when to use the bold *o* sound as in *snow* or the *ow* sound as in *cow*, we will use the following clues. First, the bold *o* sound as in *snow* will be represented with a bold *o* and the silent letter *w* as shown below. Secondly, the *ow* sound as in *cow* will be represented with a gray ring around the letters *ow* as shown below.

The child will read the following story and complete a variety of exercises based on the story. This is part one of a three-part story.

Title: *"The Cow in the Snow"*

Story: *The cow was in the snow.*

She said, "It is cold in the snow. I do not like the snow. I will go home. I will go to the shed."

She did not see the shed.

"How can I get home?" she said.

A man came in the snow.

He said to the cow, "I will take you home. I will show you the way to go."

They went home.

The cow said, "I will stay here now. I will not leave."

The man said, "It is cold. We can not go to town. We can not plow the field. We will stay near the stove."

Dialogue: Read the sight words below.

<u>of</u>   <u>there</u>

203

where   _from_

come   _some_

your   _should_

would   _could_

want   _does_

Look at the word below. This word has the bold _o_ sound (as in _snow_). It is the word _snow_. (Point to the word as you read it.)

The letter _w_ is dotted. Can you tell me why this letter is dotted? That's right, it is dotted, because it is silent. It makes no sound. Say the word as I point to it.

s n(O)ⁱⁱⁱ

Read the words below that have the bold _o_ sound (as in _snow_).

(s n)**O**ⁿ   (b l)**O**ⁿ

(g r)**O**ⁿ   r**O**ⁿ

t**O**ⁿ   m**O**ⁿ

b**O**ⁿ   l**O**ⁿ

(c r)**O**ⁿ   (f l)**O**ⁿ

(s l)**O**ⁿ   (g l)**O**ⁿ

Look at the letters at the top of the page. These letters make the _ow_ sound (as in _cow_). (Point to the letters as you make the sound.)

You will notice the letters that make the _ow_ sound (as in _cow_) have a gray ring around them. This is to help you see the letters more easily.

(o w)

Say _ow_ (as in _cow_) as I point to the letters above.

Now read the words below that have the _ow_ sound. The first word is _cow_.

(If a word, such as _plow_, has two or more phonetic combinations side-by-side, we will put a gray ring around the newest combination the child is learning. For example, we will not put a gray ring around the _pl_ sound in the word _plow_, but we will put a gray ring around the _ow_ sound in the word _plow_. Two consecutive gray rings would be more confusing than helpful.)

c(o w)   n(o w)

w(o w)   p l(o w)

t(o w)n   g(o w)n

d(o w)n   b r(o w)n

c l(o w)n   c r(o w)n

f r(o w)n

Read the words below. (Assist the child with reading any unfamiliar words. These words will appear in today's story.)

(s h)e d   w e n t   s t(**a**)y

h e r̲e̲   l e a v e   t(o w)n

plow   field   near

Read the story below, and then I will show you a picture to go with the story.

"The Cow in the Snow"

The cow was in the snow.

She said, "It is cold in the snow.

I do not like snow. I will go home.

I will go to the shed."

She did not see the shed.

"How can I get home?" she said.

A man came in the snow.

He said to the cow,

"I will take you home.

I will show you the way to go."

They went home.

The cow said, "I will stay here now.

I will not leave."

The man said, "It is cold.

We can not go to town.

We can not plow the field.

We will stay near the stove."

Now I will show you a picture of the man and the cow.

Look at the picture. Why do you think the man and the cow are standing near the stove? That's right. They want to get warm.

Why do you think the cow was out in the snow? Maybe she wandered out of the shed while the man was away. The cow did not like the snow. Have you seen snow? Do you like snow?

I am going to write the words from two of the sentences you just read on index cards.

(Have the child watch as you write each word with a pen. Label the first card with the lesson number for future use.)

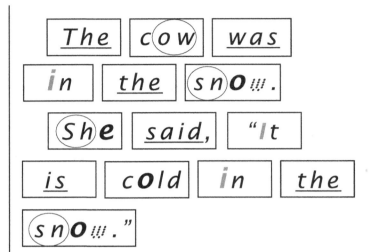

(**Note**: You may eliminate some of the print clues from the index cards with which your child is familiar. Be sure to include the print clues for sounds that have been recently introduced.)

I am going to underline the sight words with a black crayon. Today our sentences have four different sight words. Can you tell me what they are?

I am going to trace over the *iii* sounds (as in *pig*) with a gray crayon. I will trace over the bold *o* sounds (as in *hope* and *snow*) with a black crayon. I will also trace over the bold *e* sound (as in *heat*) with a black crayon.

I will make dotted lines over the letter *w* in the word *snow*. Can you tell me why I dotted this letter? That's right. I dotted it, because it is silent. It makes no sound.

I will draw a gray ring around the *ow* sound (as in *cow*) in the word *cow*. I will draw a gray ring around the *sn* sound (as in *snake*) in the word *snow*. I will also draw a gray ring around the *sh* sound (as in *ship*) in the word *she*.

Read the sentences. Very good! (Point to the quotation marks on the cards.) *She said, "It is cold in the snow."* What do we call these special marks? That's right, they are called quotation marks. We use them when someone is speaking.

Now I will mix the cards, and you can put them in proper order to make the sentences again.

(Assist the child with putting the cards in proper order. Keep the cards from each sentence separate. Remind him, if necessary, a sentence begins with an uppercase letter and ends with a period or some other form of punctuation.)

Now read the sentences.

(**Note**: We are no longer using clues to assist the child with reading the copy work. It is important for the child to read the text located in this segment of the lesson even if he does not copy the sentences. This will give him an opportunity to practice reading text printed in a regular type.)

Copy Work: (The copy work is optional for children who have difficulty with writing.) (You may now encourage the child to copy the sentences directly from the model below. If this is too difficult, continue as directed.)

I will write the sentences you just read on a piece of paper.

(Neatly write the sentences with a pen, paying close attention to letter spacing and formation.)

Now you can copy what I wrote.

The cow was in the snow.

She said, "It is cold in the snow."

I would like for you to read the sentences once more. Very good! I would like for you to draw a picture to go with your sentences. Here is a picture of a cow you can draw.

(Assist the child with drawing the picture if necessary. The picture has been drawn with bold lines so the child may trace it if he likes.)

Make up a story about the cow you drew. Tell me the story, and I will write it on a piece of paper. Now you can copy one sentence from your story at the bottom of your picture.

(Draw lines if necessary for the child to write his sentence at the bottom of his picture.)

Read the story you dictated to me. (Assist the child by reading any difficult words for him. If the story is long, have him read part of it and you read part of it.)

Now let's read a book together.

Lesson 58

Materials: reading manual, index cards, pen, gray crayon, and black crayon.

Instructions: In today's lesson, the child will review the following sight words: *from, come, some, want, what, was, said, does, of, put,* and *your.*

The child will be introduced to the short vowel sound for the letter *u* as in *cub*. This letter makes the *uuu* sound as in *cub*. It will appear in a gray print as shown below.

u

The child will read the following words containing the *uuu* sound as in *cub*: *sub, rub, cub, tub, bus, fuss, bug, dug, hug, mug, rug, tug, bun, run, fun, gun, sun, hut, nut,* and *cut.*

He will review the bold *o* sound as in *snow* by reading the following words: *bow, row, crow, flow, glow,* and *snow*. The child will review the *ow* sound as in *cow* by reading the following words: *cow, now, wow, plow, town,* and *brown.*

The child will read the following story and complete a variety of exercises based on the story. This is part two of a three-part story.

Title: *"The Bug and the Cow"*

Story: *The cow was glad to be in the shed.*

She said to the man, "I like it here. I like it near the stove. I am not cold."

The man said, "It is not fun to be cold."

A bug sat on a rug.

He said to the cow, "I want to see the snow."

The cow said, "But the snow is cold. You do not want to be cold."

The bug said, "Let me sit on your back. I can see the snow. I will stay in the shed. It will be lots of fun."

Dialogue: Read the sight words below.

from   come   some

want   what   was

said   does   of

put   your

Look at the letter below. This letter makes the *uuu* sound (as in *cub*). (Point to the letter as you make the sound.)

u

Say *uuu* as I point to the letter. Very good! Now look at the word below. This word has the *uuu* sound (as in *cub*). The word is *cub*. (Point to the word as you read it.)

cub

Read the words below that have the *uuu* sound (as in *cub*).

sub   rub   cub

tub   bus   fuss

bug   dug   hug

mug   rug   tug

bun   run   fun

gun   sun   hut

nut   cut

Read the words below that have the bold *o* sound (as in *snow*).

bow   row

crow   flow

glow   snow

Look at the letters below. These letters say ow (as in *cow*).

(ow)

Read the words below that have the ow sound (as in *cow*).

c(ow)   n(ow)

w(ow)   pl(ow)

t(ow)n   br(ow)n

Read the following words.
(Assist the child with reading any unfamiliar words. These words will appear in today's story.)

bug   rug

ne*a*r   her*e*

c*o*ld   (sh)ed

lots   (gl)ad

This is part two of our story.
(If you like you can turn to part one of our story in the last lesson and read part one again.)

Now, read the story below, and then I will show you a picture to go with the story.

"The Bug and the C(ow)"

The c(ow) was (gl)ad to be in the (sh)ed.

(Sh)e said to the man, "I like it her*e*.

I like it near the (st)ove.

I am not c*o*ld."

The man said,

"It is not fun to be cold."

A bug sat on *a* rug.

He said to the c(ow),

209

"I want to see the snow."

The cow said, "But the snow is cold.

You do not want to be cold."

The bug said,

"Let me sit on your back.

I can see the snow.

I will stay in the shed.

It will be lots of fun."

Now I will show you a picture of the cow and the bug.

Look at the picture. Why did the bug want to get on the cow's back? That's right, he wanted to see the snow. Could the bug see out of the window when he was on the rug? No, he could not, because the window was up too high.

Why do you think the bug wanted to look out of the window? Maybe he had never seen snow.

I am going to write the words from two of the sentences you just read on index cards.

(Have the child watch as you write each word with a pen. Label the first card with the lesson number for future use.)

A	bug	sat	on

a	rug.

He	said	to	the

cow,	"I	want	to

see	the	snow."

(**Note**: You may eliminate some of the print clues from the index cards with which your child is familiar. Be sure to include the print clues for sounds that have been recently introduced.)

I am going to underline the sight words with a black crayon. Today our sentences have five different sight words. Can you tell me what they are?

I am going to trace over the *uuu* sounds (as in *cub*) with a gray crayon. I am also going to trace over the *aaa* sound (as in *cat*) and the *ooo* sound (as in *hot*) with a gray crayon.

I will trace over the bold *a* sounds (as in *cake*) with a black crayon. I will also trace over the bold *e* sounds (as in *heat*) and the bold *o* sound (as in *snow*) with a black crayon.

I will make dotted lines over the letter *w* in the word *snow*. Can you tell me why I dotted this letter? That's right. I dotted it, because it is silent. It makes no sound. I will draw a gray ring around the *ow* sound (as in *cow*) in the word *cow*. I will draw a gray ring around the *sn* sound (as in *snake*) in the word *snow*.

Read the sentences. Great! (Point to the quotation marks on the index cards.) *He said to the cow, "I want to see the snow."* When a character speaks, we put special marks around the words he says. Can you remember what these special marks are called? That's right. They are called quotation marks.

Now I will mix the cards, and you can put them in proper order to make the sentences again.

(Assist the child with putting the cards in proper order. Keep the cards from each sentence separate. Remind him, if necessary, a sentence begins with an uppercase letter and ends with a period or some other form of punctuation.)

Now read the sentences.

(**Note**: We are no longer using clues to assist the child with reading the copy work. It is important for the child to read the text located in this segment of the lesson even if he does not copy the sentences. This will give him an opportunity to practice reading text printed in a regular type.)

Copy Work: (The copy work is optional for children who have difficulty with writing.) (You may now encourage the child to copy the sentences directly from the model below. If this is too difficult, continue as directed.)

I will write the sentences you just read on a piece of paper.

(Neatly write the sentences with a pen, paying close attention to letter spacing and formation.)

Now you can copy what I wrote.

A bug sat on a rug.

He said to the cow, "I want to see the snow."

I would like for you to read the sentences once more. Very good! I would like for you to draw a picture to go with your sentences. Here is a picture of a bug you can draw.

(Assist the child with drawing the picture if necessary. The picture has been drawn with bold lines so the child may trace it if he likes.)

211

(**Note**: You may choose to encourage the child to dictate a short story to you about the picture he drew instead of only one sentence.)

Make up a story about the bug you drew. Tell me the story, and I will write it on a piece of paper. Now you can copy one sentence from your story at the bottom of your picture.

(Draw lines if necessary for the child to write his sentence at the bottom of his picture.)

Read the story you dictated to me.

(Assist the child by reading any difficult words for him. If the story is long, have him read part of it and you read part of it.)

Now let's read a book together.

(Review material between lessons.)

Lesson 59

Materials: reading manual, index cards, pen, gray crayon, and black crayon.

Instructions: In today's lesson, the child will review the following sight words: *where, there, they, would, should, could, you, has,* and *are.*

The child will review the *uuu* sound as in *cub* by reading the following words: *plug, slug, stun, stuck, shut, drug, drum, truck, rush, brush, blush,* and *plum.*

He will also be introduced to the *oo* sound as in *cook.* He will read the following words containing the *oo* sound as in *cook: cook, book, look, took, nook, shook, brook, crook, wood, good, hood,* and *foot.*

Next, the child will be introduced to the *oo* sound as in *boot.* He will read the following words containing the *oo* sound as in *boot: boot, shoot, root, food, room, boom, zoom, bloom, gloom, cool, pool, tool, spool, moon, noon, soon, spoon,* and *roof.*

To assist the child in recognizing when to use the *oo* sound as in *cook* and when to use the *oo* sound as in *boot,* we will use the following clues. First, the *oo* sound as in *cook* will be represented with a gray ring around the letters. Secondly, the *oo* sound as in *boot* will be represented with a shaded gray ring around the letters.

The child will read the following story and complete a variety of exercises based on the story. This is part three of a three-part story.

Title: *"The Cub in the Snow"*

Story: *The cow said, "I see a cub in the snow."*

"Look, the cub is stuck," said the bug.

The man said, "I will get the cub."

The man dug in the snow. He got the cub.

He said to the cub, "I will take you in the shed. You will not be cold."

The cub said, "I feel sick."

The man said, "You need to eat. I will cook you some food."

The man gave the cub some food. He gave some food to the cow and the bug.

They said, "The food is good. You are a good cook."

Dialogue: Read the sight words below.

<u>where</u>   <u>there</u>

<u>they</u>   <u>would</u>

<u>should</u>   <u>could</u>

<u>you</u> <u>has</u>   <u>are</u>

Very good! Now look at the letter below. What sound does this letter make? (*uuu* as in *cub.*)

u

That's right, this letter makes the *uuu* sound.

Read the words below that have the *uuu* sound (as in *cub*).

p(l)ug   s(l)ug

s(t)un   s(t)uck

(sh)ut   (dr)ug

(dr)um   (tr)uck

r(us h)   b(r us h)

b(l)(us h)   p(l)um

Look at the letters at the top of the page. They make the oo sound (as in *cook*). (Point to the letters as you make the sound.)

You will notice the letters that make the oo sound have a gray ring around them. This is to help you see the letters more easily.

Say oo (as in *cook*) as I point to the letters.

Now read the words below that have the oo sound (as in *cook*). I will read the first word for you. It is *cook*.

(If a word, such as *shook,* has two or more phonetic combinations side-by-side, we will put a gray ring around the newest combination the child is learning. For example, we will not put a gray ring around the *sh* sound in the word *shook*, but we will put a gray ring around the *oo* sound in the word *shook*. Two consecutive rings would be more confusing than helpful.)

c(oo)k   b(oo)k

l(oo)k   t(oo)k

n(oo)k   sh(oo)k

br(oo)k   cr(oo)k

w(oo)d   g(oo)d

h(oo)d   f(oo)t

Look at the letters below. These letters make the oo sound (as in *boot*). (Point to the letters as you make the sound.)

You will notice this time the letters have a shaded gray ring around them. This is to help you to know these letters make the oo sound (as in *boot*.)

Say oo (as in *boot*) as I point to the letters above. Now read the words that have the oo sound. I will read the first word for you. It is *boot*.

bt

r**oo**t

r**oo**m

z**oo**m

gl**oo**m

p**oo**l

sp**oo**l

sh**oo**t

f**oo**d

b**oo**m

bl**oo**m

c**oo**l

t**oo**l

m**oo**n

n**oo**n

sp**oo**n

s**oo**n

r**oo**f

Read the words below.

(Assist the child with reading any unfamiliar words. These words will appear in today's story.)

s**h**ed   e**a**t   c**oo**k

f**oo**d   g**oo**d   f**ee**l

n**ee**d   s**i**ck   c**ow**

Read the story below, and then I will show you a picture to go with the story. This is the last part of our story.

"The Cub in the Sn**o**w"

The c**ow** said,

"**I** s**ee** **a** cub in the sn**o**w."

"L**oo**k, the cub is st**u**ck," said the bug.

The m**a**n said, "**I** will get the cub."

The m**a**n dug in the sn**o**w.

He got the cub.

He said to the cub,

"**I** will t**a**ke you in the sh**e**d.

214

You will not be cold."

The cub said, "I feel sick."

The man said, "You need to eat.

I will cook you some food."

The man gave the cub some food.

He gave some food to the

cow and the bug.

They said, "The food is good.

You are a good cook."

Now I will show you a picture of the man, the cub, the bug, and the cow.

Look at the picture. What did the cow and the bug see when they looked

out the window? That's right, they saw a bear cub. Who saved the cub? Yes, the man saved the cub. What did he give the cub after he took him in the shed? That's right he gave him some food.

I am going to write the words from two of the sentences you just read on index cards.

(Have the child watch as you write each word with a pen. Label the first card with the lesson number for future use.)

(**Note**: You may eliminate some of the print clues from the index cards with which your child is familiar. Be sure to include the print clues for sounds that have been recently introduced.)

I am going to underline the sight words with a black crayon. Today our sentences have six different sight words. Can you tell me what they are?

I will trace over the bold *a* sound (as in *cake*) with a black crayon. I will draw a shaded gray ring around the oo sound (as in *boot*) in the word *food*. I will draw a gray ring around the oo sound (as in *cook*) in the word *good* and in the word *cook*.

Read the sentences. Great! (Point to the quotation marks on the index cards.) They said, "The food is good. You are a good cook." When a character speaks, we put special marks around the words he says. Can you remember what these special marks are called? That's right. They are called quotation marks.

Now I will mix the cards, and you can put them in proper order to make the sentence again.

(Assist the child with putting the cards in proper order. Keep the cards from each sentence separate. Remind him, if necessary, a sentence begins with an uppercase letter and ends with a period or some other form of punctuation.)

Now read the sentences.

(**Note**: We are no longer using clues to assist the child with reading the copy work. It is important for the child to read the text located in this segment of the lesson even if he does not copy the sentences. This will give him an opportunity to practice reading text printed in a regular type.)

Copy Work: (The copy work is optional for children who have difficulty with writing.) (You may now encourage the child to copy the sentences directly from the model below. If this is too difficult, continue as directed.)

I will write the sentences you just read on a piece of paper.

(Neatly write the sentences with a pen, paying close attention to letter spacing and formation.)

Now you can copy what I wrote.

They said, "The food is good. You are a good cook."

I would like for you to read the sentences once more. Very good! I would like for you to draw a picture to go with your sentences. Here is a picture of a cub you can draw.

(Assist the child with drawing the picture if necessary. The picture has been drawn with bold lines so the child may trace it if he likes.)

(**Note**: You may choose to encourage the child to dictate a short story to you about the picture he drew instead of only one sentence.)

Make up a story about the cub you drew. Tell me the story, and I will write it on a piece of paper. Now you can copy one sentence from your story at the bottom of your picture.

(Draw lines if necessary for the child to write his sentence at the bottom of his picture.)

Read the story you dictated to me. (Assist the child by reading any difficult words for him. If the story is long, have him read part of it and you read part of it.)

Now let's read a book together.

(Review material between lessons.)

Lesson 60

Materials: reading manual, index cards, pen, gray crayon, and black crayon.

Instructions: In today's lesson, the child will review the following sight words: *where, there, from, put, would, should, could, your,* and *want.*

The child will review the *uuu* sound as in *cub* by reading the following words: *bug, dug, hug, run, fun, sun, stuck, duck, truck, plum, drum,* and *hum.*

He will review the *oo* sound as in *cook* by reading the following words: *stood, wood, good, hood, crook, brook, look,* and *took.*

Next, the child will review the *oo* sound as in *boot* by reading the following words: *broom, zoom, bloom, groom, gloom, boot, shoot, root, toot, hoot, drool, cool, pool, stool,* and *spool.*

The child will read the following poem and complete a variety of exercises based on the poem.

Title: *"I Can Hear and I Can See"*

Poem: *I can hear the train, I see it on the track.*
I can hear the crow, I see him he is black.
I can hear the snake, I see him in the grass.
I can hear the frog, I see him hop so fast.
I can hear the wind, I see it blow the tree.
I can hear the buzz, I see it is a bee.
I can hear the rain, I see it soak the land.
I can hear the bug, I see him in the sand.
I can hear the plane, I see it in the air.
I can hear the dog, I see him on the stair.
I can hear the fish, I see him swim and flip.
I can hear the bell, I see it on the ship.
I can hear the swine, I see it in the pen.
I can hear the cluck, I see it is a hen.

Dialogue: Read the sight words below.

where   there   from

put   would   should

could   your   want

Look at the letter below. What sound does this letter make? (*uuu* as in *cub*.)

u

That's right. This letter makes the *uuu* sound.

Read the words below that have the *uuu* sound (as in *cub*).

b u g   d u g

h u g   r u n

f u n   s u n

s t u c k   d u c k

t r u c k   p l u m

d r u m   h u m

Look at the letters below. What sound do these letters make? (*oo* as in *cook*.)

o o

That's right, this letter makes the *oo* sound (as in *cook*).

Read the words below that have the *oo* sound (as in *cook*).

(If a word, such as *stood,* has two or more phonetic combinations side-by-side, we will put a gray ring around the newest combination the child is learning. For example we will not put a gray ring around the *st* sound in the word *stood,* but we will put a gray ring around the *oo* sound in the word *stood.* Two consecutive rings would be more confusing than helpful.)

s t o o d   w o o d

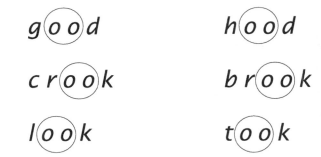

g o o d   h o o d

c r o o k   b r o o k

l o o k   t o o k

Look at the letters below. What sound do these letters make? (*oo* as in *boot*.)

That's right, this letter makes the *oo* sound (as in *boot*).

Read the words below that have the *oo* sound (as in *boot*).

b r o o m   z o o m

b l o o m   g r o o m

g l o o m   b o o t

s h o o t   r o o t

t o o t   h o o t

d r o o l   c o o l

p o o l   s t o o l

s p o o l

Read the poem, and then I will show you a picture to go with the poem.

(Assist the child with reading the poem if necessary. For example, you read two lines, and then he reads two lines and so on. On the following day as a review, alternate this process and have him read two lines, and then you read two lines and so on. On another review day, have him read the entire poem by himself.)

"I Can Hear and I Can See"

I can hear the train,

I see it on the track.

I can hear the crow,

I see him he is black.

I can hear the snake,

I see him in the grass.

I can hear the frog,

I see him hop so fast.

I can hear the wind,

I see it blow the tree.

I can hear the buzz,

I see it is a bee.

I can hear the rain,

I see it soak the land.

I can hear the bug,

I see him in the sand.

I can hear the plane,

_I_ s**ee** it in _the_ **a**ir.

_I_ can he**a**r _the_ dog,

_I_ s**ee** him on _the_ (st)**a**ir.

_I_ can he**a**r _the_ fi(sh),

_I_ s**ee** him (sw)im and (fl)ip.

_I_ can he**a**r _the_ bell,

_I_ s**ee** it on _the_ (sh)ip.

_I_ can he**a**r _the_ (sw)**i**ne,

_I_ s**ee** it in _the_ pen.

_I_ can he**a**r _the_ (cl)uck,

_I_ s**ee** it _is_ **a** hen.

Now I will show you a picture of some of the animals found in the poem.

220

Look at the picture. Where do you think the child is standing? Yes, it looks like he is standing in a farmyard.

What kinds of animals can you see in the picture? That's right, there is a pig. Pigs are sometimes called *swine*. We can also see some hens. Hens are female chickens. Do you know what male chickens are called? That's right, they are called roosters.

Can you find the rooster in the picture? Where is he standing? That's right, he is standing on top of the tractor. Have you ever visited a farm? What is your favorite farm animal?

I am going to write the words from the last four lines of the poem you just read on index cards.

(Have the child watch as you write each word with a pen. Label the first card with the lesson number for future use.)

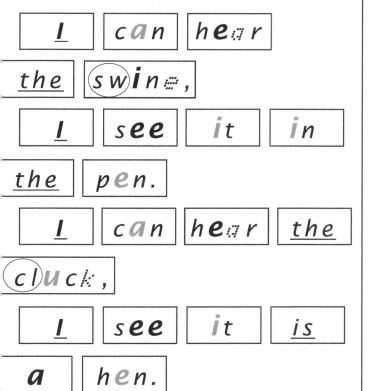

(**Note**: You may eliminate some of the print clues from the index cards with which your child is familiar. Be sure to include the print clues for sounds that have been recently introduced.)

I am going to underline the sight words with a black crayon. Today our sentences have three different sight words. Can you tell me what they are?

I will trace over the *aaa* sounds (as in *cat*) and the *iii* sounds (as in *pig*) with a gray crayon. I will also trace over the *eee* sounds (as in *wet*) and the *uuu* sound (as in *cub*) with a gray crayon.

I will trace over the bold *e* sounds (as in *heat*) and the bold *i* sound (as in *bike*) with a black crayon. I will also trace over the bold *a* sound (as in *cake*) with a black crayon.

I will make dotted lines over the letter a in the word *hear* and over the letter e in the word *swine*. I will also make dotted lines over the letter k in the word *cluck*. Can you tell me why I dotted these letters? That's right. I dotted them, because they are silent. They make no sound.

I will draw a gray ring around the sw sound (as in *sweet*) in the word *swine*. I will also draw a gray ring around the cl sound (as in *clap*) in the word *cluck*.

Read the sentences. Great! Now I will mix the cards, and you can put them in proper order to make the sentences again.

(Assist the child with putting the cards in proper order. Keep the cards from each sentence separate. Remind him, if necessary, a sentence begins with an uppercase letter and ends with a period or some other form of punctuation.)

Now read the sentences.

Copy Work: (The copy work is optional for children who have difficulty with writing.) (You may now encourage the child to copy the sentences directly from the model below. If this is too difficult, continue as directed.)

I will write the sentences you just read on a piece of paper.

(Neatly write the sentences with a pen, paying close attention to letter spacing and formation.)

Now you can copy what I wrote.

I can hear the swine,

I see it in the pen.

I can hear the cluck,

I see it is a hen.

I would like for you to read the sentences once more. Very good! I would like for you to draw a picture to go with your sentences. Here is a picture of a hen you can draw.

(Assist the child with drawing the picture if necessary. The picture has been drawn with bold lines so the child may trace it if he likes.)

(**Note**: You may choose to encourage the child to dictate a short story to you about the picture he drew instead of only one sentence.)

Make up a story about the hen you drew. Tell me the story, and I will write it on a piece of paper. Now you can copy one sentence from your story at the bottom of your picture.

(Draw lines if necessary for the child to write his sentence at the bottom of his picture.)

Read the story you dictated to me. (Assist the child by reading any difficult words for him. If the story is long, have him read part of it and you read part of it.)

Now let's read a book together.

Lesson 61

Materials: reading manual, index cards, pen, gray crayon, black crayon, and one construction paper circle.

Instructions: In today's lesson, the child will review the following sight words: *was, do, to, put, said, of, what, some, come, from, want,* and *your.* He will be introduced to the new sight word *one.* Prepare a construction paper circle with the new sight word written on it.

The child will review the *uuu* sound as in *cub* by reading the following words: *duck, yuck, buck, crumb, crust, must, bust, trunk, bunk, dunk, hunk, drunk, clunk,* and *flunk.*

The child will be introduced to the *ing* sound as in *sing.* He will read the following words containing the *ing* sound: *sing, wing, ring, ding, king, zing, bring, cling, fling, sling, swing,* and *sting.*

The child will read the following story and complete a variety of exercises based on the story.

Title: *"The White Duck"*

Story: *The white duck said to the green frog, "Can you sing?"*

The green frog said, "I can not sing. I can croak. I can croak in the pond."

The white duck said to the brown bee, "Can you sing?"

The brown bee said, "I can not sing. I can buzz. I can buzz in the hive."

The white duck said to the black crow, "Can you sing?"

The black crow said. "I can sing. I can sing in the tree."

The white duck said to the black crow, "Can you flap your wings and sing?"

The black crow said, "Yes, I can flap and sing."

Dialogue: Read the sight words below.

was	do
to	put
said	of

what   some

come   from

want   your

Look at the new sight word below. It is the word *one.* (Point to the word as you read it.)

one

Say *one* as I point to the word. Now read the sentence below that has the new sight word in it.

I have one dog and one cat.

Very good! Now, let's add the new sight word to your *Sight Word Worm.* (Have the child frequently review the sight words on the *Sight Word Worm.* Have him read the words in random order.)

Look at the letter below. What sound does this letter make? (*uuu* as in *cub*.)

u

That's right, this letter makes the *uuu* sound (as in *cub*).

Read the words below that have the *uuu* sound.

duck   yuck

buck   crumb

crust   must

223

b u(st)   tr(u)n k

b u n k   d u n k

h u n k   (dr)u n k

(cl)u n k   (fl)u n k

s(ing)	w(ing)
r(ing)	d(ing)
k(ing)	z(ing)
br(ing)	cl(ing)
fl(ing)	sl(ing)
sw(ing)	st(ing)

Look at the letters below. These letters make the *ing* sound (as in *sing*). (Point to the letters as you make the sound.)

You will notice the letters that make the *ing* sound have a gray ring around them. This is to help you see the letters more easily.

(i n g)

Say *ing* (as in *sing*) as I point to the letters above.

Now read the words at the top of the page that have the *ing* sound. I will read the first word for you. It is *sing*.

(If a word, such as *bring,* has two or more phonetic combinations side-by-side, we will only put a gray ring around the newest combination the child is learning. Two consecutive gray rings would be more confusing than helpful.)

Read the words below.

(Assist the child with reading any unfamiliar words. These words will appear in today's story.)

b r(ow)n	b u z z
w(ing)	s(ing)
(cr)o w	wh i te
(gr)e e n	(cr)o a k

Read the story below, and then I will show you a picture to go with the story.

"<u>The</u> Wh i te D u ck"

<u>The</u> wh i te d u ck <u>said</u> <u>to</u>

<u>the</u> (gr)e e n (fr)o g,

"C a n <u>you</u> s(ing)?"

224

The green frog said,

"I can not sing.

I can croak.

I can croak in the pond."

The white duck said

to the brown bee,

"Can you sing?"

The brown bee said,

"I can not sing.

I can buzz.

I can buzz in the hive."

The white duck said

to the black crow,

"Can you sing?"

The black crow said,

"I can sing.

I can sing in the tree."

The white duck said
to the black crow,
"Can you flap your
wings and sing?"
The black crow said,
"Yes, I can flap and sing."

Now I will show you a picture of some of the creatures found in the story.

Look at the picture. How many creatures can you see in the picture? That's right. There are three creatures in the picture. How many creatures did the duck talk to? Yes, he talked to three creatures.

Which creature is not shown in the picture that the duck talked to? That's right. The bee is not in the picture. Why do you think you cannot see the bee? That's right, he's probably in the hive.

I am going to write the words from one of the sentences you just read on index cards.

(Have the child watch as you write each word with a pen. Label the first card with the lesson number for future use.)

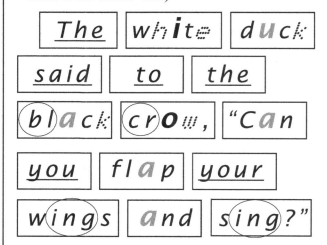

(**Note**: You may eliminate some of the print clues from the index cards with which your child is familiar. Be sure to include the print clues for sounds that have been recently introduced.)

226

I am going to underline the sight words with a black crayon. Today our sentence has five different sight words. Can you tell me what they are?

I will trace over the *uuu* sound (as in *cup*) and the *aaa* sounds (as in *cat*) with a gray crayon. I will trace over the bold *i* sound (as in *bike*) and the bold *o* sound (as in *snow*) with a black crayon.

I will make dotted lines over the letter *h* and the letter *e* in the word *white*. I will make dotted lines over the letter *k* in the word *duck* and in the word *black*. I will also make dotted lines over the letter *w* in the word *crow*. Can you tell me why I dotted all of these letters? That's right, I dotted them, because they are silent. They make no sound.

I will draw a gray ring around the *bl* sound (as in *black*) in the word *black*, around the *cr* sound (as in *crab*) in the word *crow*, and around the *fl* sound (as in flag) in the word *flap*. I will also draw a gray ring around the *ing* sound (as in *sing*) in the word *wings* and in the word *sing*.

Read the sentence. Very good! (Point to the quotation marks on the index cards.) *The white duck said to the black crow, "Can you flap your wings and sing?"* When a character speaks, we put special marks around the words he says. Can you remember what these special marks are called? That's right. They are called quotation marks.

Now I will mix the cards, and you can put them in proper order to make the sentence again.

(Since this is a long sentence, break it into two parts for this activity, dividing it at the comma. Assist the child with putting the cards in proper order. Remind him, if necessary, a sentence begins with an uppercase letter and ends with a period or some other form of punctuation.)

Now read the sentence.

(**Note**: We are no longer using clues to assist the child with reading the copy work. It is important for the child to read the text located in this segment of the lesson even if he does not copy the sentences. This will give him an opportunity to practice reading text printed in a regular type.)

Copy Work: (The copy work is optional for children who have difficulty with writing.) (You may now encourage the child to copy the sentences directly from the model below. If this is too difficult, continue as directed.)

I will write the sentence you just read on a piece of paper.

(Neatly write the sentence with a pen, paying close attention to letter spacing and formation.)

Now you can copy what I wrote.

The white duck said to the black crow, "Can you flap your wings and sing?"

I would like for you to read the sentence once more. Very good! I would like for you to draw a picture to go with your sentence. Here is a picture of a duck you can draw.

(Assist the child with drawing the picture if necessary. The picture has been drawn with bold lines so the child may trace it if he likes.)

(**Note**: You may choose to encourage the child to dictate a short story to you about the picture he drew instead of only one sentence.)

Make up a story about the duck you drew. Tell me the story, and I will write it on a piece of paper. Now you can copy one sentence from your story at the bottom of your picture.

(Draw lines if necessary for the child to write his sentence at the bottom of his picture.)

Read the story you dictated to me.

(Assist the child by reading any difficult words for him. If the story is long, have him read part of it and you read part of it.)

Now let's read a book together.

(Review material between lessons.)

Lesson 62

Materials: reading manual, index cards, pen, gray crayon, and black crayon.

Instructions: In today's lesson, the child will review the following sight words: *one, there, where, should, would, could, does, of, they,* and *put.*

The child will review the *uuu* sound as in *cub* by reading the following words: *plug, shut, drum, truck, mug, tub, must, fun,* and *pluck.* He will review the *ing* sound as in *sing* by reading the following words: *sing, ring, wing,* and *sting.*

He will be introduced to the bold *i* sound made by the letter *y* as in *fly.* He will read the following words containing bold *i* sound as in *fly*: *fly, my, try, by, sky, why, cry, fry, sly, spy, dry,* and *pry.* The bold *i* sound as in *fly* will be represented as shown below with a gray dot over the letter *y.*

●
y

The child will read the following story and complete a variety of exercises based on the story.

Title: *"What am I?"*

Story: *I can fly in the sky. I can flap my wings. I can sing in the trees. What am I? I can swim in the lake. I can swish my fins. I can eat bugs. What am I? I can float on a pad. I can swim in the pond. I can croak and croak. What am I? I can buzz in my hive. I can fly in the sky. I can sting. What am I? I can graze in the grass. I can put milk in the pail. I can say, " Moo, moo." What am I?*

Dialogue: Read the sight words below.

<u>one</u>	<u>there</u>
<u>where</u>	<u>should</u>
<u>would</u>	<u>could</u>
<u>does</u>	<u>of</u>
<u>they</u>	<u>put</u>

Read the words below that have the *uuu* sound (as in *cub*).

p l u g   s h u t

d r u m   t r u c k

m u g   t u b

m u s t   f u n

p l u c k

Look at the letters below. What sound do these letters make? (*ing* as in *sing*.)

i n g

Very good! These letters make the *ing* sound.

Read the words below that have the *ing* sound (as in *sing*).

s i n g   r i n g

w i n g   s t i n g

Look at the word at the top of the page. This is the word *fly*. The letter *y* (say the letter name) makes the bold *i* sound in this word. Notice the small gray dot

over the letter *y* (say the letter name, not the letter sound).

This is to help you remember to say *i* (say the letter name) when you see it written this way.

f l y

Read the words below that have the letter *y* that makes the bold *i* sound (as in *fly*).

f l y   m y

t r y   b y

s k y   w h y

c r y   f r y

s l y   s p y

d r y   p r y

Read the story below, and then I will show you a picture to go with the story.

"What am I?"

I can fly in the sky.

I can flap my wings.

I can sing in the trees.

What am I?

I can swim in the lake.

I can swish my fins. I can eat bugs.

What am I?

I can float on a pad.

I can swim in the pond.

I can croak and croak.

What am I?

I can buzz in my hive.

I can fly in the sky. I can sting.

What am I?

I can graze in the grass.

I can put milk in the pail.

I can say, "Moo, moo."

What am I?

Now I will show you a picture of
the creatures from the story.

Look at the picture. How many creatures can you see? That's right. There are five creatures. Which creature can sing in the trees? Yes, it's a bird. Which creature swishes its fins? Yes, it's a fish. Which creature croaks and croaks? Yes, it's a frog. Which creature can sting? Yes, it's a bee. Which creature can graze in the grass? Yes, it's a cow.

I am going to write the words from three of the sentences you just read on index cards.

(Have the child watch as you write each word with a pen. Label the first card with the lesson number for future use.)

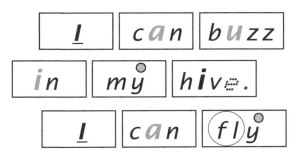

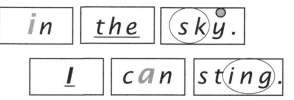

| I | can | sting. |

(**Note**: You may eliminate some of the print clues from the index cards with which your child is familiar. Be sure to include the print clues for sounds that have been recently introduced.)

I am going to underline the sight words with a black crayon. Today our sentences have two different sight words. Can you tell me what they are?

I will trace over the *aaa* sounds (as in *cat*) and the *uuu* sound (as in *cup*) with a gray crayon. I will also trace over the *iii* sounds (as in *pig*) with a gray crayon.

I will trace over the bold *i* sound (as in *bike*) with a black crayon. I will make dotted lines over the letter *e* in the word *hive*. Can you tell me why I dotted this letter? That's right. I dotted it, because it is silent. It makes no sound.

I will draw a gray ring around the *fl* sound (as in *flag*) in the word *fly* and around the *sk* sound (as in *skate*) in the word *sky*. I will also draw a gray ring around the *ing* sound (as in *sing*) in the word *sting*.

I will make a gray dot over the letter *y* in the word *my*, in the word *fly*, and in the word *sky*. The gray dot means the letter *y* makes the bold *i* sound in these words.

Read the sentences. Great! Now I will mix the cards, and you can put them in proper order to make the sentences again.

231

(Assist the child with putting the cards in proper order. Keep the cards from each sentence separate. Remind him, if necessary, a sentence begins with an uppercase letter and ends with a period or some other form of punctuation.)

Now read the sentences.

(**Note**: We are no longer using clues to assist the child with reading the copy work. It is important for the child to read the text located in this segment of the lesson even if he does not copy the sentences. This will give him an opportunity to practice reading text printed in a regular type.)

Copy Work: (The copy work is optional for children who have difficulty with writing.) (You may now encourage the child to copy the sentences directly from the model below. If this is too difficult, continue as directed.)

I will write the sentences you just read on a piece of paper.

(Neatly write the sentences with a pen, paying close attention to letter spacing and formation.)

Now you can copy what I wrote.

I can buzz in my hive.
I can fly in the sky.
I can sting.

I would like for you to read the sentences once more. Very good! I would like for you to draw a picture to go with your sentences. Here is a picture of a bee you can draw.

(Assist the child with drawing the picture if necessary. The picture has been drawn with bold lines so the child may trace it if he likes.)

(**Note**: You may choose to encourage the child to dictate a short story to you about the picture he drew instead of only one sentence.)

Make up a story about the bee you drew. Tell me the story, and I will write it on a piece of paper. Now you can copy one sentence from your story at the bottom of your picture.

(Draw lines if necessary for the child to write his sentence at the bottom of his picture.)

Read the story you dictated to me.

(Assist the child by reading any difficult words for him. If the story is long, have him read part of it and you read part of it.)

Now let's read a book together.

(Review material between lessons.)

Lesson 63

Materials: reading manual, index cards, pen, gray crayon, and black crayon.

Instructions: In today's lesson, the child will review the following sight words: *one, where, there, should, would, could, does, has, you,* and *your.*

He will review the *ing* sound as in *sing* by reading the following words: *sing, fling, ring, wing, cling,* and *king.*

He will review the *oo* sound as in *cook* by reading the following words: *cook, book, look, shook, took,* and *hook.* He will also review the *oo* sound as in *boot* by reading the following words: *boot, root, shoot, food, room,* and *gloom.*

Next the child will review the bold *i* sound made by the letter *y* as in *fly* by reading the following words: *try, my, by, fly, cry,* and *fry.*

The child will be introduced to the *or* sound as in *corn.* He will read the following words containing the *or* sound: *corn, born, horn, morn, torn, worn, pork, cork, fort, short, port, sort, scorn,* and *storm.*

The child will read the following story and complete a variety of exercises based on the story.

Title: *"The Bug in the Corn"*

Story: *The brown bug sat in the corn.*

He said, "I like to eat corn. Corn is sweet. I will take some corn to my home. I will try to pick up the corn."

He could not pick up the corn. A crow sat in a tree.

The crow said, "I can bring the corn to your home. I can pick it up in my beak. I can fly in the sky."

The bug said, "How can you pick up the corn?"

The crow said, "I will show you."

The crow bit the corn. He put some corn in his beak. The bug said, "Now I see how you did it."

Dialogue: Read the sight words below.

one   where

there   should

would   could

does   has

you   your

Look at the letters below. What sound do these letters make? (*ing* as in *sing.*)

ing

That's right, they make the *ing* sound.

Read the words below that have the *ing* sound (as in *sing*).

sing   fling   ring

wing   cling   king

Look at the letters below. What sound do these letters make? (*oo* as in *cook.*)

oo

That's right, they make the *oo* sound (as in *cook*).

Read the words below that contain the *oo* sound (as in *cook*).

cook   book   look

shook   took

hook

Look at the letters below. What sound do these letters make? (*oo* as in *boot.*)

oo

That's right, they make the *oo* sound (as in *boot*).

Read the words below that contain the oo sound (as in *boot*).

s h t   f o o d

   g l oo m

Look at the letter below. What sound does this letter make? (*i* as in *fly*.)

y

That's right, it makes the bold *i* sound (as in *fly*).

Read the words below that have the bold *i* sound (as in *fly*).

try   my   by
fly   cry   fry

Look at the letters below. These letters make the *or* sound (as in *corn*). You will notice these letters have a gray ring around them to help you see them more easily. (Point to the letters as you make the sound.)

(o r)

Say *or* as I point to the letters above.

Very good! Now read the words below that have the *or* sound (as in *corn*).

I will read the first word for you. It is *corn*.

c o r n   b o r n

h o r n   m o r n

t o r n   w o r n

p o r k   c o r k

f o r t   s h o r t

p o r t   s o r t

s c o r n   s t o r m

Read the words below.

(Assist the child with reading any difficult words. These words will appear in the story.)

b r o w n   s w e e t

b r i n g   b e a k

s h o w   c o r n

s k y

Read the story, and then I will show you a picture to go with the story.

"The Bug in the Corn"

The brown bug sat in the corn.

He said, "I like to eat corn.

Corn is sweet.

I will take some corn to my home.

I will try to pick up the corn."

He could not pick up the corn.

A crow sat in a tree.

The crow said, "I can bring

the corn to your home.

I can pick it up in my beak.

I can fly in the sky."

The bug said, "How can you

pick up the corn?"

The crow said, "I will show you."

The crow bit the corn.

He put some corn in his beak.

The bug said, "Now I see

how you did it."

Now I will show you a picture of the bug and the corn.

Look at the picture. What is the bug trying to do? That's right. He is trying to pick up the whole piece of corn. Can he pick it up? No, it is too big. How did the crow manage to pick up the corn? That's right. He bit some small pieces off the ear of corn and put them in his beak. He did not try to pick up the whole ear of corn.

I am going to write the words from two of the sentences you just read on index cards.

(Have the child watch as you write each word with a pen. Label the first card with the lesson number for future use.)

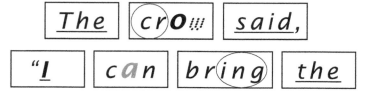

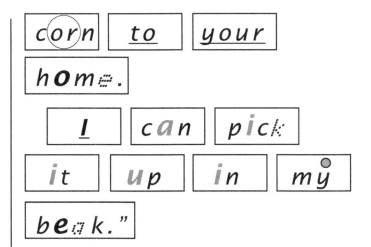

(**Note**: You may eliminate some of the print clues from the index cards with which your child is familiar. Be sure to include the print clues for sounds that have been recently introduced.)

I am going to underline the sight words with a black crayon. Today our sentences have five different sight words. Can you tell me what they are?

I will trace over the *aaa* sounds (as in *cat*) and the *iii* sounds (as in *pig*) with a gray crayon. I will also trace over the *uuu* sound (as in *cup*) with a gray crayon.

I will trace over the bold *o* sounds (as in *hope* and *snow*) with a black crayon. I will also trace over the bold *e* sound (as in *heat*) with a black crayon.

I will make dotted lines over the letter *w* in the word *crow*. I will make dotted lines over the letter *e* in the word *home*. I will make dotted lines over the letter *k* in the word *pick*. I will also make dotted lines over the letter *a* in the word *beak*. Can you tell me why I dotted these letters? That's right. I dotted them, because they are silent. They make no sound.

I will draw a gray ring around the *cr* sound (as in *crab*) in the word *crow* and around the *ing* sound (as in *sing*) in the word *bring*. I will also draw a gray ring around the *or* sound (as in *corn*) in the word *corn*. I will make a gray dot over the letter *y* in the word *my*. The gray dot means the letter *y* makes the bold *i* sound (as in *fly*) in this word.

Read the sentences. Great! Find the index cards with the quotation marks on them. When do we use quotation marks? That's right, we use them when a character speaks. Who is speaking in these sentences? That's right, the crow is speaking.

Now I will mix the cards, and you can put them in proper order to make the sentences again.

(Assist the child with putting the cards in proper order. Keep the cards from each sentence separate. Remind him, if necessary, a sentence begins with an uppercase letter and ends with a period or some other form of punctuation.)

Now read the sentences.

(**Note**: We are no longer using clues to assist the child with reading the copy work. It is important for the child to read the text located in this segment of the lesson even if he does not copy the sentences. This will give him an opportunity to practice reading text printed in a regular type.)

Copy Work: (The copy work is optional for children who have difficulty with writing.) (You may now encourage the child to copy the sentences directly from the model below. If this is too difficult, continue as directed.)

I will write the sentences you just read on a piece of paper.

(Neatly write the sentences with a pen, paying close attention to letter spacing and formation.)

Now you can copy what I wrote.

The crow said, "I can bring the corn to your home.

I can pick it up in my beak."

I would like for you to read the sentences once more. Very good! I would like for you to draw a picture to go with your sentences. Here is a picture of a bug you can draw.

(Assist the child with drawing the picture if necessary. The picture has been drawn with bold lines so the child may trace it if he likes.)

(**Note**: You may choose to encourage the child to dictate a short story to you about the picture he drew instead of only one sentence.)

Make up a story about the bug you drew. Tell me the story, and I will write it on a piece of paper. Now you can copy one sentence from your story at the bottom of your picture.

(Draw lines if necessary for the child to write his sentence at the bottom of his picture.)

Read the story you dictated to me.

(Assist the child by reading any difficult words for him. If the story is long, have him read part of it and you read part of it.)

Now let's read a book together.

(Review material between lessons.)

Lesson 64

Materials: reading manual, index cards, pen, gray crayon, and black crayon.

Instructions: In today's lesson, the child will review the following sight words: *would, could, should, what, said, your, put, some, come, from, there,* and *where.*

He will review the *ing* sound as in *sing* by reading the following words: *bring, sting, zing,* and *cling.*

He will review the *oo* sound as in *cook* by reading the following words: *crook, brook, snook,* and *book.* He will also review the *oo* sound as in *boot* by reading the following words: *zoom, broom, groom,* and *food.*

Next the child will review the bold *i* sound made by the letter *y* as in *fly* by reading the following words: *sky, my, fly,* and *cry.* The child will review the *or* sound as in *corn* by reading the following words: *born, storm, corn, morn, short,* and *scorn.*

We will introduce the use of exclamation points. This is only an introduction, and we do not expect the child to master this concept.

The child will read the following story and complete a variety of exercises based on the story.

Title: *"The Lost Boot"*

Story: *Steve said, "Look at the sky. Soon it will storm. I must find my boots."*

Steve could find just one boot.

"I can not wear just one boot. Where is my boot?"

Mom said, "Did you look in your bed room?"

"Yes," said Steve. "I could not find my boot."

"Look," said Mom. "Look at the dog. The dog has your boot!"

Steve said to the dog, "You can not wear my boot! It will not fit you."

Dialogue: Read the sight words below.

would	*could*
should	*what*
said	*your*

put   some

come   from

there   where

Read the words below that have the *ing* sound (as in *sing*).

b r ing   s t ing

z ing   c l ing

Read the words below that have the *oo* sound (as in *cook*).

c r oo k   b r oo k

s n oo k   b oo k

Read the words below that have the *oo* sound (as in *boot*).

z oo m   b r oo m

g r oo m   f oo d

Look at the letter below. What sound does this letter make? (*i* as in *fly*.)

y

That's right, it makes the bold *i* sound (as in *fly*).

Read the words at the top of the page that have the bold *i* sound.

sky   my

fly   cry

Look at the letters below. What sound do these letters make? (*or* as in *corn*.)

or

That's right, they make the *or* sound. Read the words below that have the *or* sound (as in *corn*). I will read the first word for you. It is *born*.

b or n   s t or m

c or n   m or n

s h or t   s c or n

Read the words below.

(Assist the child with reading any difficult words. These words will appear in the story.)

St e ve   m u st

j u st   one

find   we a r

Read the story, and then I will show you a picture to go with the story.

"The Lost Boot"

Steve said, "Look at the sky.

Soon it will storm.

I must find my boots."

Steve could find just one boot.

"I can not wear just one boot.

Where is my boot?"

Mom said, "Did you look

in your bed room?"

"Yes," said Steve.

"I could not find my boot."

"Look," said Mom. "Look at the dog.

The dog has your boot!"

Steve said to the dog,

"You can not wear my boot!

It will not fit you."

Now I will show you a picture of
Steve and his dog.

240

Look at the picture. What does Steve have on one of his feet? That's right. He has a boot. Who has on the other boot? Yes, the dog has on the other boot.

Have you ever seen a real dog with boots? Often dogs will chew on boots or shoes. Does it look like this dog has chewed on the boot? Yes, the boot on the dog's foot does not look as nice as the boot on the boy's foot.

I am going to write the words from two of the sentences you just read on index cards.

(Have the child watch as you write each word with a pen. Label the first card with the lesson number for future use.)

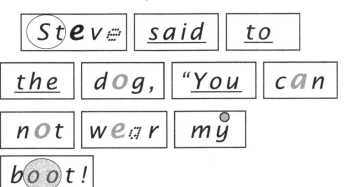

| It | will | not | fit |

| you." |

(**Note**: You may eliminate some of the print clues from the index cards with which your child is familiar. Be sure to include the print clues for sounds that have been recently introduced.)

I will underline the sight words with a black crayon. Today our sentences have four different sight words. Can you tell me what they are? I will trace over the bold *e* sound (as in *heat*) with a black crayon.

I will trace over the *ooo* sounds (as in *hot*) and the *aaa* sound (as in *cat*) with a gray crayon. I will also trace over the *eee* sound (as in *wet*) and the *iii* sounds (as in *pig*) with a gray crayon.

I will make dotted lines over the letter *e* at the end of the word *Steve* with a black crayon. I will also make dotted lines over the letter *a* in the word *wear* with a black crayon. Can you tell me why I dotted these letters? That's right, I dotted them, because they are silent. They make no sound.

I will make a gray dot over the letter *y* in the word *my*. Can you tell me why I did this? That's right, I did this, because the letter *y* makes a bold *i* sound (as in *fly*) in the word *my*.

I will draw a gray ring around the *st* sound (as in *mist*) in the word *Steve*. Next I will draw a shaded gray ring around the *oo* sound (as in *boot*) in the word *boot*.

Read the sentences. Very good! Find the index cards with the quotation marks on them. When do we use quotation marks? That's right, we use them when a character speaks.

Look at the card with the word *boot* written on it. There is a special mark after the word *boot*. This special mark is called an exclamation point. We use it when we want to show excitement or surprise. Do you think the boy was surprised to find his boot on the dog's foot? Yes, I am sure he was surprised.

Now I will mix the cards, and you can put them in proper order to make the sentences again.

(Assist the child with putting the cards in proper order. Keep the cards from each sentence separate. Remind him, if necessary, a sentence begins with an uppercase letter and ends with a period or some other form of punctuation.)

Now read the sentences.

(**Note**: We are no longer using clues to assist the child with reading the copy work. It is important for the child to read the text located in this segment of the lesson even if he does not copy the sentences. This will give him an opportunity to practice reading text printed in a regular type.)

Copy Work: (The copy work is optional for children who have difficulty with writing.) (You may now encourage the child to copy the sentences directly from the model below. If this is too difficult, continue as directed.)

I will write the sentences you just read on a piece of paper.

(Neatly write the sentences with a pen, paying close attention to letter spacing and formation.)

Now you can copy what I wrote.

Steve said to the dog, "You can not wear my boot! It will not fit you."

I would like for you to read the sentences once more. Very good! I would like for you to draw a picture to go with your sentences. Here is a picture of a dog you can draw.

(Assist the child with drawing the picture if necessary. The picture has been drawn with bold lines so the child may trace it if he likes.)

(**Note:** You may choose to encourage the child to dictate a short story to you about the picture he drew instead of only one sentence.)

Make up a story about the dog you drew. Tell me the story, and I will write it on a piece of paper. Now you can copy one sentence from your story at the bottom of your picture.

(Draw lines if necessary for the child to write his sentence at the bottom of his picture.)

Read the story you dictated to me.

(Assist the child by reading any difficult words for him. If the story is long, have him read part of it and you read part of it.)

Now let's read a book together.

(Review material between lessons.)

Lesson 65

Materials: reading manual, index cards, pen, gray crayon, black crayon, and one construction paper circle.

Instructions: In today's lesson, the child will review the following sight words: *are, said, what, put, some, come, from, one, was, do, to,* and *they.* He will also be introduced to the new sight word *many.* Prepare a construction paper circle with the new sight word written on it.

He will review the *or* sound as in *corn* by reading the following words: *born, scorn, pork, fork, horse, snort,* and *sport.*

The child will be introduced to the *all* sound as in *ball.* He will read the following words containing the *all* sound: *ball, call, fall, hall, wall, mall,* and *tall.*

The child will read the following story and complete a variety of exercises based on the story.

Title: *"The Frog and the Toad"*

Story: *The frog went to town to get a horn. The toad went to town to get a ball.*

The frog said, "I will share my horn. You can blow my horn."

The toad said, "I will share my ball. You can kick my ball."

The frog said, "You can play my horn. I will sing a song."

The toad said, "I will play the horn and you will sing. We can have fun."

The toad said, "Now, let us play ball. I will roll the ball and you can kick it."

The ball got stuck. It got stuck on the wall.

The toad said, "The wind will blow it down."

Dialogue: Read the sight words below.

are	said	what
put	some	come
from	one	was
do	to	they

Look at the new sight word below. It is the word *many*. (Point to the word as you read it.)

many

Say *many* as I point to the word. Very good! Now read the sentence with the new sight word.

The man has many cats in his room.

Let's add the new sight word to your *Sight Word Worm*.

Read the words below that have the *or* sound (as in corn).

b o r n   s c o r n

p o r k   f o r k

h o r s e   s n o r t

s p o r t

Look at the letters below. These letters make the *all* sound (as in *ball*). You will notice the letters have a gray ring around them. This is to help you see the letters more easily.

a l l

Say *all* as I point to the letters. Now read the words below that have the *all* sound (as in *ball*). I will read the first word for you. It is *ball*.

b a l l   c a l l

f a l l   h a l l

w a l l   m a l l

t a l l

Read the words below.

(Assist the child with any difficult words. These words will appear in the story.)

w e n t   t o w n

h o r n   b a l l

s h a r e   b l o w

s i n g   s o n g

s t u c k   w a l l

d o w n   r o l l

Read the story, and then I will show you a picture to go with the story.

"The Frog and the Toad"

The frog went to town to get a horn.

The toad went to town to get a ball.

The frog said, "I will share my horn.

You can blow my horn."

The toad said, "I will share my ball.

You can kick my ball."

The frog said, "You can play my horn.

I will sing a song.

The toad said, "I will play

the horn and you will sing.

We can have fun."

The toad said, "Now, let us play ball.

I will roll the ball and

you can kick it."

The ball got stuck.

It got stuck on the wall.

The toad said, "The wind

will blow it down."

Now I will show you a picture of the frog and the toad.

Look at the picture. What is the toad doing in the picture? That's right. He is rolling the ball to the frog. What do you think the frog will do? That's right. He will kick the ball.

According to the story, where does the ball go? That's right. It lands on the top of the wall. How did the toad say the ball would come down? Yes, he said the wind would blow it.

I am going to write the words from two of the sentences you just read on index cards.

(Have the child watch as you write each word with a pen. Label the first card with the lesson number for future use.)

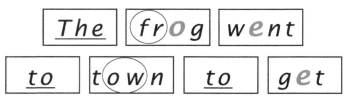

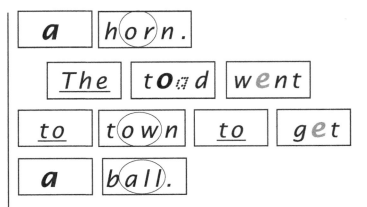

(**Note**: You may eliminate some of the print clues from the index cards with which your child is familiar. Be sure to include the print clues for sounds that have been recently introduced.)

I am going to underline the sight words with a black crayon. Today our sentences have two different sight words. Can you tell me what they are?

I will trace over the *ooo* sound (as in *hot*) and the *eee* sounds (as in *wet*) with a gray crayon. I will also trace over the bold *a* sounds (as in *cake*) and the bold *o* sound (as in *hope*) with a black crayon.

I will make dotted lines over the letter a in the word *toad*. Can you tell me why I dotted this letter? That's right. I dotted it, because it is silent. It makes no sound.

I will draw a gray ring around the *fr* sound (as in *frog*) in the word *frog* and around the *ow* sound (as in *cow*) in the word *town*. I will also draw a gray ring around the *or* sound (as in *corn*) in the word *horn* and around the *all* sound (as in *ball*) in the word *ball*.

Read the sentences. Great! Now I will mix the cards, and you can put them in proper order to make the sentences again.

(Assist the child with putting the cards in proper order. Keep the cards from each sentence separate. Remind him, if necessary, a sentence begins with an uppercase letter and ends with a period or some other form of punctuation.)

Now read the sentences.

(**Note**: We are no longer using clues to assist the child with reading the copy work. It is important for the child to read the text located in this segment of the lesson even if he does not copy the sentences. This will give him an opportunity to practice reading text printed in a regular type.)

Copy Work: (The copy work is optional for children who have difficulty with writing.) (You may now encourage the child to copy the sentences directly from the model below. If this is too difficult, continue as directed.)

I will write the sentences you just read on a piece of paper.

(Neatly write the sentences with a pen, paying close attention to letter spacing and formation.)

Now you can copy what I wrote.

The frog went to town to get a horn.

The toad went to town to get a ball.

I would like for you to read the sentences once more. Very good! I would like for you to draw a picture to go with your sentences. Here is a picture of a frog you can draw.

(Assist the child with drawing the picture if necessary. The picture has been drawn with bold lines so the child may trace it if he likes.)

(**Note:** You may choose to encourage the child to dictate a short story to you about the picture he drew instead of only one sentence.)

Make up a story about the frog you drew. Tell me the story, and I will write it on a piece of paper. Now you can copy one sentence from your story at the bottom of your picture.

(Draw lines if necessary for the child to write his sentence at the bottom of his picture.)

Read the story you dictated to me.

(Assist the child by reading any difficult words for him. If the story is long, have him read part of it and you read part of it.)

Now let's read a book together.

(Review material between lessons.)

247

Lesson 66

Materials: reading manual, index cards, pen, gray crayon, and black crayon.

Instructions: In today's lesson, the child will review the following sight words: *one, many, would, could, should, does, your, want, where, there*, and *you*.

He will review the *all* sound as in *ball* by reading the following words: *call, fall, wall, mall, hall*, and *tall*. He will review the *or* sound as in *corn* by reading the following words: *for, cord, stork, Lord, more*, and *born*.

The child will be introduced to the *ink* sound as in *drink*. He will read the following words containing the *ink* sound: *mink, ink, drink, blink, link, pink, rink, sink, stink*, and *wink*.

The child will read the following story and complete a variety of exercises based on the story.

Title: *"The Pink Pig"*

Story: *The pink pig sat in the mud.*

The pink pig said, "I do not like the mud. The mud is brown. I am pink. I want pink mud."

The cow sat in the grass.

The cow said, "Why do you want pink mud?"

The pink pig said, "I am pink, so I want pink mud."

The cow said, "I am brown, but I do not want brown grass. Brown grass is not good to eat. I like to eat green grass. Green grass is my food."

The pig said, "But I do not eat mud. I play in the mud."

The cow said, "What do you eat?"

The pig said, "I eat corn."

The cow said, "Is the corn pink?"

Dialogue: Read the sight words below.

one   many

would   could

should   does

your   want

where   there

---

you

Read the words below that have the *all* sound (as in *ball*). I will read the first word for you. It is *call*.

c(all)   f(all)   w(all)

m(all)   h(all)   t(all)

Read the words below that have the *or* sound (as in *corn*). I will read the first word for you. It is *for*.

f(or)   c(or)d

st(or)k   L(or)d

m(or)e   b(or)n

Look at the letters below. These letters make the *ink* sound (as in *drink*). (Point to the letters as you make the sound.)

You will notice the letters have a gray ring around them This is to help you see the letters more easily.

(ink)

Say *ink* (as in *drink*) as I point to the letters.

Very good! Now read the words below that have the *ink* sound (as in *drink*). I will read the first word for you. It is *mink*.

m(ink)   (ink)

dr(ink)   bl(ink)

link   pink | stink   wink

rink   sink | Read the story below, and then I will show you a picture to go with the story.

"The Pink Pig"

The pink pig sat in the mud.

The pink pig said, "I do not like the mud. The mud is brown.

I am pink. I want pink mud."

The cow sat in the grass.

The cow said,

"Why do you want pink mud?"

The pink pig said, "I am pink,

so I want pink mud."

The cow said, "I am brown,

but I do not want brown grass.

Brown grass is not good to eat.

I like to eat green grass.

Green grass is my food."

The pig said, "But I do not eat mud.

I play in the mud."

The cow said, "What do you eat?"

The pig said, "I eat corn."

The cow said, "Is the corn pink?"

Now I will show you a picture of the pig and the cow.

Look at the picture. Where is the pig. That's right. He is in the mud. Where is the cow? That's right, he is in the grass. Why do you think that the pig wants pink mud? Is the pig pink or brown? That's right, he is pink.

The cow says he is brown, but he does not want brown grass. Is brown grass good to eat? No, it is not good to eat. Green grass is good to eat. The

cow asks the pig what he eats. What does the pig say to this? That's right, he says he eats corn. What color is corn? That's right, it is yellow. It is not pink.

I am going to write the words from two of the sentences you just read on index cards.

(Have the child watch as you write each word with a pen. Label the first card with the lesson number for future use.)

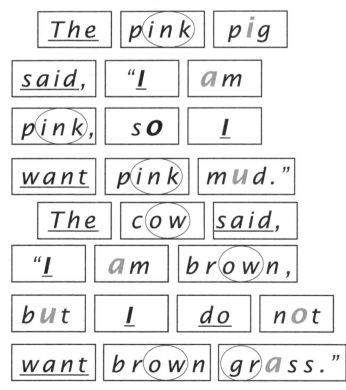

The pink pig said, "I am pink, so I want pink mud." The cow said, "I am brown, but I do not want brown grass."

250

(**Note**: You may eliminate some of the print clues from the index cards with which your child is familiar. Be sure to include the print clues for sounds that have been recently introduced.)

I am going to underline the sight words with a black crayon. Today our sentences have five different sight words. Can you tell me what they are?

I will trace over the *iii* sound (as in *pig*) and the *aaa* sounds (as in *cat*) with a gray crayon. I will also trace over the *uuu* sounds (as in *cub*) and the *ooo* sound (as in *hot*) with a gray crayon.

I will trace over the bold *o* sound (as in *hope*) with a black crayon. I will draw a gray ring around the *ink* sound (as in *drink*) in the word *pink*. I will draw a gray ring around the *ow* sound (as in *cow*) in the word *cow* and in the word *brown*. I will also draw a gray ring around the *gr* sound (as in *grass*) in the word *grass*.

Read the sentences. Great! Find the cards with the quotation marks? When do we use quotation marks? That's right, we use them when a character is speaking.

Now I will mix the cards, and you can put them in proper order to make the sentences again.

(Assist the child with putting the cards in proper order. Keep the cards from each sentence separate. Remind him, if necessary, a sentence begins with an uppercase letter and ends with a period or some other form of punctuation.)

Now read the sentences.

(**Note**: We are no longer using clues to assist the child with reading the copy work. It is important for the child to read the text located in this segment of the lesson even if he does not copy the sentences. This will give him an opportunity to practice reading text printed in a regular type.)

Copy Work: (The copy work is optional for children who have difficulty with writing.) (You may now encourage the child to copy the sentences directly from the model below. If this is too difficult, continue as directed.)

I will write the sentences you just read on a piece of paper.

(Neatly write the sentences with a pen, paying close attention to letter spacing and formation.)

Now you can copy what I wrote.

The pink pig said, "I am pink, so I want pink mud."

The cow said, "I am brown, but I do not want brown grass."

I would like for you to read the sentences once more. Very good! I would like for you to draw a picture to go with your sentences. Here is a picture of a pig you can draw.

(Assist the child with drawing the picture if necessary. The picture has been drawn with bold lines so the child may trace it if he likes.)

(**Note:** You may choose to encourage the child to dictate a short story to you about the picture he drew instead of only one sentence.)

Make up a story about the pig you drew. Tell me the story, and I will write it on a piece of paper. Now you can copy one sentence from your story at the bottom of your picture.

(Draw lines if necessary for the child to write his sentence at the bottom of his picture.)

Read the story you dictated to me.

(Assist the child by reading any difficult words for him. If the story is long, have him read part of it and you read part of it.)

Now let's read a book together.

(Review material between lessons.)

Lesson 67

Materials: reading manual, index cards, pen, gray crayon, and black crayon.

Instructions: In today's lesson, the child will review the following sight words: *many, one, come, from, some, what, they, put, are,* and *of*.

The child will review the *ing* sound as in *sing* by reading the following words: *sing, fling, zing,* and *bring*. The child will review the *ink* sound as in *drink* by reading the following words: *drink, wink, stink,* and *blink*.

He will be introduced to the *oy* sound as in *boy*. He will read the following words containing the *oy* sound: *boy, toy, Roy, coy, joy, soy,* and *ploy*. He will also be introduced to the *oi* sound as in *boil*. He will read the following words containing the *oi* sound: *boil, coil, oil, soil, coin, loin, join,* and *noise*.

The child will read the following story and complete a variety of exercises based on the story.

Title: *"Roy and Joy"*

Story: *Roy and Joy can play in the room.*

Roy said, "I will cook the food. I will boil the beans."

Joy said, "I will plant the seeds. I will put the seeds in the soil."

Roy said, "I will put the food on the plate. We can eat the food. It is good."

Joy said, "I will rake the seeds. Soon they will grow."

Roy said, "What kind of seeds did you plant?"

Joy said, "They are bean seeds."

"Good," said Roy. "I will cook the beans one day."

"Yes, one day they will grow," said Joy. "They will grow on a vine."

Dialogue: Read the sight words below.

many	*one*
come	*from*
some	*what*
they	*put*
are	*of*

252

Read the words below that have the *ing* sound (as in *sing*).

s(i n g)   fl(i n g)

z(i n g)   br(i n g)

Read the words below that have the *ink* sound (as in *drink*).

dr(i n k)   w(i n k)

st(i n k)   bl(i n k)

Look at the letters below. These letters make the *oy* sound (as in *boy*). (Point to the letters as you make the sound.)

You will notice the letters have a gray ring around them. This is to help you see the letters more easily.

(o y)

Say *oy* (as in *boy*) as I point to the letters above.

Very good! Now read the words below that have the *oy* sound (as in *boy*). I will read the first word for you. It is *boy*.

b(o y)   t(o y)

R(o y)   c(o y)

j(o y)   s(o y)

pl(o y)

Look at the letters below. These letters also make the *oi* sound (as in *boil*). (Point to the letters as you make the sound.)

You will notice the letters have a gray ring around them. This is to help you see the letters more easily.

(o i)

Say *oi* (as in *boil*) as I point to the letters above.

Very good! Now read the words below that have the *oi* sound. I will read the first word for you. It is *boil*.

b(o i)l   c(o i)l

(o i)l   s(o i)l

c(o i)n   l(o i)n

j(o i)n   n(o i)s⠑

Read the story, and then I will show you a picture to go with the story.

"R(o y) and J(o y)"

R(o y) and J(o y) can (pl a⠽) in <u>the</u> r(o)m.

253

Roy said, "I will cook the food.

I will boil the beans."

Joy said, "I will plant the seeds.

I will put the seeds in the soil."

Roy said, "I will put the

food on the plate.

We can eat the food. It is good."

Joy said, "I will rake the seeds.

Soon they will grow."

Roy said, "What kind of seeds

did you plant?"

Joy said, "They are bean seeds."

"Good," said Roy.

"I will cook the beans one day."

"Yes, one day they will grow," said Joy.

"They will grow on a vine."

Now I will show you a picture of
Roy and Joy.

254

Look at the picture. Roy and Joy are playing house. Roy is pretending to cook the food, and Joy is pretending to plant the seeds.

It is fun to pretend. Do you like to pretend? What do you like to pretend? Joy drew a picture of a vegetable garden on a big piece of paper and laid it on the floor. She is pretending it is a real garden. You can do this too.

What kinds of vegetables would you draw in your pretend garden? What kind of vegetables did Joy draw?

I am going to write the words from two of the sentences you just read on index cards.

(Have the child watch as you write each word with a pen. Label the first card with the lesson number for future use.)

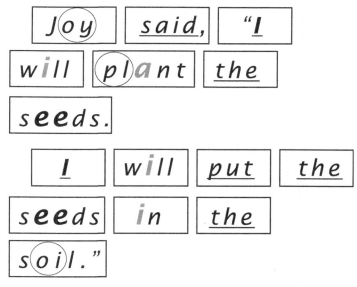

(**Note**: You may eliminate some of the print clues from the index cards with which your child is familiar. Be sure to include the print clues for sounds that have been recently introduced.)

I am going to underline the sight words with a black crayon. Today our sentences have four different sight words. Can you tell me what they are?

I will trace over the *iii* sounds (as in *pig*) and the *aaa* sound (as in *cat*) with a gray crayon. I will trace over the bold *e* sounds (as in *heat*) with a black crayon.

I will draw a gray ring around the *oy* sound (as in *boy*) in the word Joy. I will draw a gray ring around the *pl* sound (as in *play*) in the word *plant*. I will also draw a gray ring around the *oi* sound (as in *boil*) in the word *soil*.

Read the sentences. Very good! Find the index cards with the quotation marks written on them. Tell me why we use quotation marks. That's right, we use them when a character is speaking.

Now I will mix the cards, and you can put them in proper order to make the sentence again.

255

(Assist the child with putting the cards in proper order. Keep the cards from each sentence separate. Remind him, if necessary, a sentence begins with an uppercase letter and ends with a period or some other form of punctuation.)

Now read the sentences.

(**Note**: We are no longer using clues to assist the child with reading the copy work. It is important for the child to read the text located in this segment of the lesson even if he does not copy the sentences. This will give him an opportunity to practice reading text printed in a regular type.)

Copy Work: (The copy work is optional for children who have difficulty with writing.) (You may now encourage the child to copy the sentences directly from the model below. If this is too difficult, continue as directed.)

I will write the sentences you just read on a piece of paper.

(Neatly write the sentences with a pen, paying close attention to letter spacing and formation.)

Now you can copy what I wrote.

Joy said, "I will plant the seeds. I will put the seeds in the soil."

I would like for you to read the sentences once more. Very good! I would like for you to draw a picture to go with your sentences. Here is a picture of a rake you can draw.

(Assist the child with drawing the picture if necessary. The picture has been drawn with bold lines so the child may trace it if he likes.)

(**Note:** You may choose to encourage the child to dictate a short story to you about the picture he drew instead of only one sentence.)

Make up a story about the rake you drew. Tell me the story, and I will write it on a piece of paper. Now you can copy one sentence from your story at the bottom of your picture.

(Draw lines if necessary for the child to write his sentence at the bottom of his picture.)

Read the story you dictated to me. (Assist the child by reading any difficult words for him. If the story is long, have him read part of it and you read part of it.)

Now let's read a book together.

(Review material between lessons.)

Lesson 68

Materials: reading manual, index cards, pen, gray crayon, black crayon, and one construction paper circle.

Instructions: In today's lesson, the child will review the following sight words: *should, would, could, where, there, does, you,* and *your*. The child will be introduced to the new sight word *who*. Prepare one construction paper circle with the new sight word written on it.

He will review the *oi* sound as in *boil* by reading the following words: *oil, soil, foil,* and *noise*. He will also review the *oy* sound as in *boy* by reading the following words: *toy, soy, ploy,* and *boy*.

The child will be introduced to the *ou* sound as in *house*. He will read the following words containing the *ou* sound: *house, mouse, out, shout, pound, sound, cloud, loud, flour,* and *our*.

The child will read the following story and complete a variety of exercises based on the story.

Title: *"The Mouse House"*

Story: *"Look at the house," said the boy. "It is a toy house. It is pink."*

The man said, "It is not big. It is small. It is the size for a mouse."

"Does a mouse live in the house?" said the boy.

The man said, "Look in the house. Do you see a mouse?"

The boy said, "I do not see a mouse. But, I can hear a loud noise. Do you hear the sound?"

The man said, "Yes, I can hear the sound. Look in the bed room. What do you see?"

"I see one gray mouse on the rug," said the boy. "He has a drum."

Dialogue: Read the sight words below.

should   would

could   where

there   does

you   your

Look at the new sight word below. It is the word *who*. (Point to the word as you read it.)

who

Say *who* as I point to the word.

Very good! Now read the sentence below that has the new sight word in it.

Who has my hat?

Let's add the new sight word to your Sight Word Worm.

Read the words below that have the *oi* sound (as in *boil*).

o i l   s o i l

f o i l   n o i s e

Read the words below that have the *oy* sound (as in *boy*).

t o y   s o y

p l o y   b o y

Look at the letters below. These letters make the *ou* sound (as in *house*). (Point to the letters as you make the sound.)

You will notice the letters have a gray ring around them. This is to help you see the letters more easily.

o u

Say *ou* (as in *house*) as I point to the letters above.

Very good! Now read the words at the top of the next page that have the ou sound (as in *house*). I will read the first word for you. It is *house*.

h(ou)se   m(ou)se

(o)ut   sh(o)ut

p(ou)nd   s(ou)nd

cl(ou)d   l(ou)d

fl(ou)r   (o)ur

Read the words below.

(Assist the child with any difficult words. These words will appear in the story.)

l(oo)k   p(in)k   l(i)ve

l(ou)d   gr(a)y   r(u)g

r(oo)m   dr(u)m   he(a)r

Read the story below, and then I will show you a picture to go with the story.

"The M(ou)se H(ou)se"

"L(oo)k at the h(ou)se," said the b(oy).

It is a t(oy) h(ou)se. It is p(in)k."

The man said, "It is not big.

It is small.

It is the s(i)ze for a m(ou)se."

"Does a m(ou)se l(i)ve in the h(ou)se?"
said the b(oy).

The man said, "L(oo)k in the h(ou)se.

Do you s(ee) a m(ou)se?"

The b(oy) said, "I do not s(ee) a m(ou)se.

But, I can he(a)r a l(ou)d n(oi)se.

Do you hear the sound?"

The man said, "Yes, I

can hear the sound.

Look in the bed room.

What do you see?"

"I see one gray mouse on the rug,"

said the boy.

"He has a drum."

Now I will show you a picture of the mouse in the house.

Look at the picture. Do you see the toy house? What do you see on the rug in the bedroom? That's right, there is a mouse on the rug. What is he doing?

That's right he's playing a drum. Is he being loud? How do you know? That's right. It tells us in the story the boy hears a loud noise.

I am going to write the words from two of the sentences you just read on index cards.

(Have the child watch as you write each word with a pen. Label the first card with the lesson number for future use.)

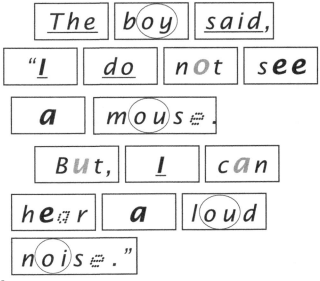

The boy said,
"I do not see
a mouse.
But, I can
hear a loud
noise."

259

(**Note**: You may eliminate some of the print clues from the index cards with which your child is familiar. Be sure to include the print clues for sounds that have been recently introduced.)

I am going to underline the sight words with a black crayon. Today our sentences have four different sight words. Can you tell me what they are?

I will trace over the *ooo* sound (as in *hot*), the *uuu* sound (as in *cub*), and the *aaa* sound (as in *cat*) with a gray crayon.

I will trace over the bold *e* sounds (as in *heat*) and the bold *a* sounds (as in *cake*) with a black crayon.

I will draw a gray ring around the *oy* sound (as in *boy*) in the word *boy*. I will draw a gray ring around the *ou* sound (as in *house*) in the word *mouse* and in the word *loud*. I will also draw a gray ring around the *oi* sound (as in *boil*) in the word *noise*.

Read the sentences. Great! Now I will mix the cards, and you can put them in proper order to make the sentences again.

(Assist the child with putting the cards in proper order. Keep the cards from each sentence separate. Remind him, if necessary, a sentence begins with an uppercase letter and ends with a period or some other form of punctuation.)

Now read the sentences.

(**Note**: <u>We are no longer using clues to assist the child with reading the copy work. It is important for the child to read the text located in this segment of the lesson even if he does not copy the sentences. This will give him an opportunity to practice reading text printed in a regular type.</u>)

Copy Work: (The copy work is optional for children who have difficulty with writing.) (You may now encourage the child to copy the sentences directly from the model below. If this is too difficult, continue as directed.)

I will write the sentences you just read on a piece of paper.

(Neatly write the sentences with a pen, paying close attention to letter spacing and formation.)

Now you can copy what I wrote.

The boy said, "I do not see a mouse. But, I can hear a loud noise."

I would like for you to read the sentences once more. Very good! I would like for you to draw a picture to go with your sentences. Here is a picture of a mouse you can draw.

(Assist the child with drawing the picture if necessary. The picture has been drawn with bold lines so the child may trace it if he likes.)

(**Note**: You may choose to encourage the child to dictate a short story to you about the picture he drew instead of only one sentence.)

Make up a story about the mouse you drew. Tell me the story, and I will write it on a piece of paper. Now you can copy one sentence from your story at the bottom of your picture.

(Draw lines if necessary for the child to write his sentence at the bottom of his picture.)

Read the story you dictated to me. (Assist the child by reading any difficult words for him. If the story is long, have him read part of it and you read part of it.)

Now let's read a book together.

(Review material between lessons.)

Lesson 69

Materials: reading manual, index cards, pen, gray crayon, black crayon, and two construction paper circles.

Instructions: In today's lesson, the child will review the following sight words: *who, come, from, some, what, they, are, was, has, do, is, said, of, put, want, many,* and *one*. He will be introduced to the following new sight words: *Mama* and *Papa*. Prepare two construction paper circles with the new sight words written on them. If you find your *Sight Word Worm* is growing too large, begin a new one.

The child will review the *ou* sound as in *house* by reading the following words: *out, ground, sour, spout, hound, cloud,* and *house*.

He will review the *all* sound as in *ball* by reading the following words: *ball, fall, mall, call, tall,* and *small*.

He will review the bold *i* sound made by the letter *y* as in *fly* by reading the following words: *fly, my, by,* and *why*.

He will be introduced to the *ar* sound as in *car*. He will read the following words containing the *ar* sound: *car, far, bar, star, park, dark, shark, bark, farm, harm, barn, yarn, hard,* and *yard*.

The child will read the following story and complete a variety of exercises based on the story.

Title: *"Who is in the Car?"*

Story: *Papa said, "Mama, did you park the car in the barn?"*

Mama said, "No, I did not park the car in the barn."

Papa said, "Where did you park the car?" Mama said, "I put it by the corn."

Papa said, "Come look and see. The car is in the barn."

Mama and Papa went to the barn. The car was in the barn. It was by the hay stack.

Mama said, "How did the car get in the barn? I did not park it in the barn. You did not park it in the barn."

Papa said, "Who could have put it there?" "Let's look in the car," said Mama.

Papa said, "The cow is in the car!"

Dialogue: Read the sight words below.

who   come   from

some   what   they

are   was   has

do   is   said

of   put   want

many   one

Look at the new sight word below. It is the word *Mama*. (Point to the word as you read it.)

Mama

Say *Mama* as I point to the word above. Very good!

Now let's look at another new sight word. It is the word *Papa*. (Point to the word as you read it.)

Papa

Say *Papa* as I point to the word above. Very good!

Now read the sentence below with the two new sight words.

Mama and Papa

have a black cat.

Let's add the new sight words to your *Sight Word Worm*.

Look at the letters below. Do you remember what sound these letters make? (*ou* as in *house*.)

ou

Very good! They make the ou sound. Read the words below that have the ou sound (as in *house*).

out   ground

sour   spout

hound   cloud

house

Look at the letters below. Do you remember what sound these letters make? (*all* as in *ball*.)

all

Very good! They make the *all* sound. Read the words below that have the *all* sound.

ball   fall

mall   call

tall   small

Read the words below. Remember, the letter y makes the bold *i* sound (as in *fly*).

fly   my

by   why

Look at the letters at the top of the next page. These letters make the ar sound (as in *car*). (Point to the letters as you make the sound.)

You will notice the letters have a gray ring around them. This is to help you see the letters more easily.

a r

Say ar (as in car) as I point to the letters.

Very good! Now read the words below that have the ar sound (as in car). I will read the first word for you. It is car.

c a r   f a r

b a r   s t a r

p a r k   d a r k

s h a r k   b a r k

f a r m   h a r m

b a r n   y a r n

h a r d   y a r d

Read the story, and then I will show you a picture to go with the story.

"Who is in the Car?"

Papa said, "Mama, did you park the car in the barn?"

Mama said, "No, I did not park the car in the barn."

Papa said, "Where did you park the car?"

Mama said, "I put it by the corn."

Papa said, "Come look and see. The car is in the barn."

Mama and Papa went to the barn.

263

The car was in the barn.

It was by the hay stack.

Mama said, "How did the

car get in the barn?"

I did not park it in the barn.

You did not park it in the barn."

Papa said, "Who could

have put it there?"

"Let's look in the car," said Mama.

Papa said, "The cow is in the car!"

Now I will show you a picture of the cow in the car.

Look at the picture. Who is sitting in the front seat of the car? That's right. The cow is sitting in the front seat. Do you think the farmer and his wife are surprised to see the cow in the front seat of the car?

Who do you think put the car in the barn? Yes, it was probably the cow. Can cows really drive? No, they cannot drive. This is a pretend story.

I am going to write two of the sentences you just read on index cards.

(Have the child watch as you write each word with a pen. Label the first card with the lesson number for future use.)

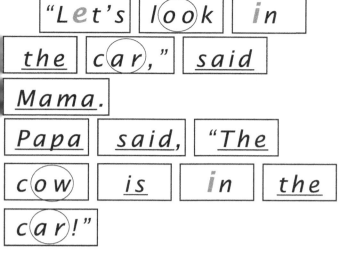

"Let's look in the car," said Mama.
Papa said, "The cow is in the car!"

(**Note**: You may eliminate some of the print clues from the index cards with which your child is familiar. Be sure to include the print clues for sounds that have been recently introduced.)

I am going to underline the sight words with a black crayon. Today our sentences have five different sight words. Can you tell me what they are?

I will trace over the *eee* sound (as in *wet*) and the *iii* sounds (as in *pig*) with a gray crayon.

I will draw a gray ring around the oo sound (as in *cook*) in the word *look*. I will draw a gray ring around the *ar* sound (as in *car*) in the word *car*. I will also draw a gray ring around the *ow* sound (as in *cow*) in the word *cow*.

The second sentence ends in the word *car*. (Point to the index card.) Look at the punctuation mark at the end of the sentence. This mark is called an exclamation point. We use it when we want to show surprise or excitement.

Read the sentences. Very good! Now I will mix the cards, and you can put them in proper order to make the sentences again.

(Assist the child with putting the cards in proper order. Keep the cards from each sentence separate. Remind him, if necessary, a sentence begins with an uppercase letter and ends with a period or some other form of punctuation.)

Now read the sentences. Be sure to read the second sentence with a surprised voice.

(**Note**: We are no longer using clues to assist the child with reading the copy work. It is important for the child to read the text located in this segment of the lesson even if he does not copy the sentences. This will give him an opportunity to practice reading text printed in a regular type.)

Copy Work: (The copy work is optional for children who have difficulty with writing.) (You may now encourage the child to copy the sentences directly from the model below. If this is too difficult, continue as directed.)

I will write the sentences you just read on a piece of paper.

(Neatly write the sentences with a pen, paying close attention to letter spacing and formation.)

Now you can copy what I wrote.

"Let's look in the car," said Mama.
Papa said, "The cow is in the car!"

I would like for you to read the sentences once more. Be sure to read the second sentence with a surprised voice. Very good! I would like for you to draw a picture to go with your sentences. Here is a picture of a car you can draw.

(Assist the child with drawing the picture if necessary. The picture has been drawn with bold lines so the child may trace it if he likes.)

(**Note:** You may choose to encourage the child to dictate a short story to you about the picture he drew instead of only one sentence.)

Make up a story about the car you drew. Tell me the story, and I will write it on a piece of paper. Now you can copy one sentence from your story at the bottom of your picture.

(Draw lines if necessary for the child to write his sentence at the bottom of his picture.)

Read the story you dictated to me. (Assist the child by reading any difficult words for him. If the story is long, have him read part of it and you read part of it.)

Now let's read a book together.

(Review material between lessons.)

Lesson 70

Materials: reading manual, index cards, pen, gray crayon, and black crayon.

Instructions: In today's lesson, the child will review the following sight words: *Mama, Papa, would, one, put, does, many, should, could, there, who,* and *what.*

He will review the *ar* sound as in *car* by reading the following words: *car, park, card, farm, yarn, star, barn,* and *far.*

The child will review the *ou* sound as in *house* by reading the following words: *house, mouse, out, shout, pound, sound, cloud, loud, flour,* and *our.*

The child will read the following story and complete a variety of exercises based on the story.

Title: *"A Trip to the Park"*

Story: *Mama and Papa took the boys to the park.*

The boys said, "We can go down the slide."

The boys ran to the slide.

Mama said to Papa, "Look. The boys can run fast."

Papa said, "Yes, they can run fast. I can not run fast like the boys."

The boys said, "We want to swing up to the sky."

The boys ran to the swing. They ran fast. Soon they could all hear a boom. They could all see a black cloud in the sky.

Papa and Mama said, "Quick. Run to the car. Soon it will storm."

The boys ran fast. Mama and Papa ran fast too.

Mama said to Papa, "You can run fast. You can run fast in a storm!"

Dialogue: Read the sight words below.

<u>Mama</u>   <u>Papa</u>

<u>would</u>   <u>one</u>

<u>put</u>   <u>does</u>

<u>many</u>   <u>should</u>

<u>could</u>   <u>there</u>

who   what

Look at the letters below. Do you remember what sound these letters make? (*ar* as in *car.*)

a r

Very good! They make the ar sound. Read the words below that have the ar sound (as in *car*).

c a r   p a r k

c a r d   f a r m

y a r n   s t a r

b a r n   f a r

Look at the letters below. Do you remember what sound these letters make? (*ou* as in *house.*)

o u

Very good! They make the ou sound.

Read the words below that have the ou sound (as in *house*).

h o u s e   m o u s e

o u t   s h o u t

p o u n d   s o u n d

c l o u d   l o u d

f l o u r   o u r

Read the words below.

(Assist the child with any difficult words. These words will appear in the story.)

d o w n   s l i d e

b o y s   s w i n g

s k y   s t o r m

Read the story, and then I will show you a picture to go with the story.

"A Trip to the Park"

Mama and Papa took the
boys to the park.
The boys said,
"We can go down the slide."
The boys ran to the slide.

Mama said to Papa,

"Look. The boys can run fast."

Papa said, "Yes, they can run fast.

I can not run fast like the boys."

The boys said,

"We want to swing up to the sky."

The boys ran to the swing.

They ran fast.

Soon they could all hear a boom.

They could all see a black

cloud in the sky.

Papa and Mama said, "Quick.

Run to the car. Soon it will storm."

The boys ran fast.

Mama and Papa ran fast too.

Mama said to Papa, "You can run fast.

You can run fast in a storm!"

Now I will show you a picture of
Mama and Papa and the boys.

Look at the picture. What do you see in the sky? That's right, you can see a dark cloud and lightning.

Papa said he could not run fast like the boys. Mama said he could run fast in a storm. Why do you think Papa was able to run fast in a storm? Yes, he could run fast, because he wanted to get out of the storm.

I am going to write two of the sentences you just read on index cards.

(Have the child watch as you write each word with a pen. Label the first card with the lesson number for future use.)

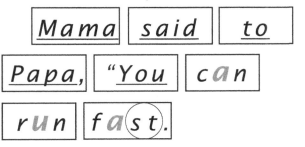

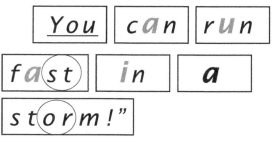

(**Note**: You may eliminate some of the print clues from the index cards with which your child is familiar. Be sure to include the print clues for sounds that have been recently introduced.)

I am going to underline the sight words with a black crayon. Today our sentences have five different sight words. Can you tell me what they are?

I will trace over the *aaa* sounds (as in *cat*), the *uuu* sounds (as in *cup*), and the *iii* sound (as in *pig*) with a gray crayon. I will trace over the bold *a* sound with a black crayon.

I will draw a gray ring around the *st* sound (as in *mist*) in the word *fast*. I will also draw a gray ring around the *or* sound (as in *corn*) in the word *storm*.

Read the sentences. Great!

The second sentence ends in the word *storm*. (Point to the index card.) Look at the punctuation mark at the end of the sentence. What is this mark called? That's right. This mark is called an exclamation point. We use it when we want to show surprise.

Can you find the index cards with the quotation marks? When do we use quotation marks? That's right, we use them when a character is speaking. Who is speaking in these sentences?

Now I will mix the cards, and you can put them in proper order to make the sentences again.

(Assist the child with putting the cards in proper order. Keep the cards from each sentence separate. Remind him, if necessary, a sentence begins with an uppercase letter and ends with a period or some other form of punctuation.)

Now read the sentences. Be sure to read the second sentence with a surprised voice.

(**Note**: We are no longer using clues to assist the child with reading the copy work. It is important for the child to read the text located in this segment of the lesson even if he does not copy the sentences. This will give him an opportunity to practice reading text printed in a regular type.)

Copy Work: (The copy work is optional for children who have difficulty with writing.) (You may now encourage the child to copy the sentences directly from the model below. If this is too difficult, continue as directed.)

I will write the sentences you just read on a piece of paper.

(Neatly write the sentences with a pen, paying close attention to letter spacing and formation.)

Now you can copy what I wrote.

Mama said to Papa, "You can run fast. You can run fast in a storm!"

I would like for you to read the sentences once more. Be sure to read the second sentence with a surprised voice. Very good!

I would like for you to draw a picture to go with your sentences. Here is a picture of a stormy sky you can draw.

(Assist the child with drawing the picture if necessary. The picture has been drawn with bold lines so the child may trace it if he likes.)

(**Note:** You may choose to encourage the child to dictate a short story to you about the picture he drew instead of only one sentence.)

Make up a story about the stormy sky you drew. Tell me the story, and I will write it on a piece of paper. Now you can copy one sentence from your story at the bottom of your picture.

(Draw lines if necessary for the child to write his sentence at the bottom of his picture.)

Read the story you dictated to me.

(Assist the child by reading any difficult words for him. If the story is long, have him read part of it and you read part of it.)

Now let's read a book together.

(Review material between lessons.)

Lesson 71

Materials: reading manual, index cards, pen, gray crayon, black crayon, and two construction paper circles.

Instructions: In today's lesson, the child will review the following sight words: *Mama, Papa, who, one, there, where, could, would, should, does, many,* and *of.* He will be introduced to the following new sight words: *people* and *that.* Prepare two construction paper circles with the new sight words written on them.

We will introduce the child to the use of the comma. This is only an introduction, and we do not expect him to master this concept. Although the child has already been reading material with commas, we have chosen not to discuss their use until now.

The child will review the *ar* sound as in *car* by reading the following words: *car, tar, star, ark, mark, bark, card, hard,* and *lard.*

He will review the *ing* sound as in *sing* by reading the following words: *sing, wing, ring, ding, fling,* and *sling.* He will be introduced to the *ing* sound when it is added to another word as in *taking* and *hopping.* He will read the following words: *calling, falling, crying, flying, baking, making, hopping, mopping, sitting, hitting,* and *having.*

The child will be introduced to the *fff* sound made by the letters *ph* as in *phone.* He will read the following words containing the *fff* sound as in *phone*: *phone, photo, graph,* and *phase.*

The child will read the following poem and complete a variety of exercises based on the poem.

Title: *"I Can"*

Poem: *I can hear the phone, I can hear it ring.*
I can hear the bell, I can hear it ding.
I can hear the sink, I can hear it drip.
I can hear the coin, I can hear it flip.
I can hear the rain, I can hear it fall.
I can hear the boys, as they hit the ball.
I can hear the horn, I can hear it blow.
I can hear the sound, of the big black crow.
I can see the sky, I can see the stars.
I can see the people, sitting in the cars.
I can see the moon, I can see the sun.
I can see the pups, having lots of fun.

I can see the pigs, I can see the sty.
I can see the bugs, that are running by.
I can see the grass, I can see the snake.
I can see the photo, that the man will take.

Dialogue: Read the sight words below.

Mama	*Papa*
who	*one*
there	*where*
could	*would*
should	*does*
many	*of*

Look at the new sight word below. It is the word *people.* (Point to the word as you read it.)

people

Say *people* as I point to the word. Very good! Now read the sentence below that has the new sight word in it.

Many people came to see the king.

Look at the next new sight word below. It is the word *that.* (Point to the word as you read it.)

that

Say *that* as I point to the word. Very good! Now read the sentence at the top of the next page that has the new sight word in it.

That man can hit the ball.

Let's add the new sight words to your _Sight Word Worm._

Look at the letters below. What sound do these letters make? (_ar_ as in _car._)

ar

Very good! They say _ar._

Read the words below that have the _ar_ sound (as in _car_).

car   tar

star   ark

mark   bark

card   hard

lard

Look at the letters below. What sound do these letters make? (_ing_ as in _sing._)

ing

Very good! They say _ing._

Read the words below that have the _ing_ sound (as in _sing_).

sing   wing   ring

ding   fling   sling

Read the words below.

call   fall

Now we will add the _ing_ sound (as in _sing_) to the end of the words _call_ and _fall._

Read the words below that have the _ing_ sound (as in _sing_) at the end.

calling   falling

Here are some more words that have the _ing_ sound (as in _sing_) at the end. Read the words below.

crying   flying

baking   making

hopping   mopping

sitting   hitting

having

Look at the letters below. These letters make the _fff_ sound (as in _phone_). You will notice these letters have a gray ring around them to help you see them more easily. (Point to the letters as you make the sound.)

ph

Say _fff_ (as in _phone_) as I point to the letters above. Very good!

Read the words below that have the _fff_ sound (as in _phone_).

phone   photo

graph   phase

Read the poem below, and then I will show you a picture to go with the poem.

(Assist the child with reading the poem if necessary. For example, you read four lines, and then he reads four lines and so on. On the following day as a review, alternate this process and have him read four lines, and then you read four lines and so on. On another review day, have him read the entire poem by himself.)

(**Note**: We are no longer underlining the sight words *I* and *the*.)

"I Can"

I can hear the phone,

I can hear it ring.

I can hear the bell,

I can hear it ding.

I can hear the sink,

I can hear it drip.

I can hear the coin,

I can hear it flip.

I can hear the rain,

I can hear it fall.

I can hear the boys,

As they hit the ball.

I can hear the horn,

I can hear it blow.

I can hear the sound,
Of the big black crow.
I can see the sky,
I can see the stars.
I can see the people,
Sitting in the cars.
I can see the moon,
I can see the sun.
I can see the pups,
Having lots of fun.
I can see the pigs,
I can see the sty.
I can see the bugs,
That are running by.
I can see the grass,
I can see the snake.
I can see the photo,
That the man will take.

Now I will show you a picture of the man taking the photo.

Look at the picture. What is the child doing? That's right, she is having her picture taken. The man taking the picture looks rather funny, doesn't he? That's because he is using an old-fashioned camera. He must put the black cloth over his head to take the picture. He does this, because he must keep the light from getting into the camera. What else do you see in the picture?

I am going to write four of the lines from the poem you just read on index cards.

(Have the child watch as you write each word with a pen. Label the first card with the lesson number for future use.)

I can see the
grass,

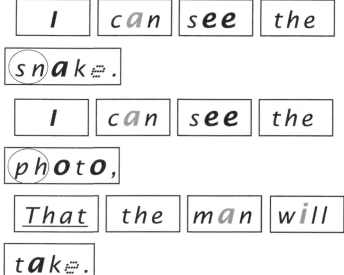

(**Note**: You may eliminate some of the print clues from the index cards with which your child is familiar. Be sure to include the print clues for sounds that have been recently introduced.)

I am only going to underline one sight word today with a black crayon. It is the new sight word *that.*

I will trace over the *aaa* sounds (as in *cat*) and the *iii* sound (as in *pig*) with a gray crayon.

I will trace over the bold *e* sounds (as in *heat*), the bold *a* sounds (as in *cake*), and the bold *o* sounds (as in *hope*) with a black crayon.

I will make dotted lines over the letter *e* in the word *snake* and in the word *take.* Can you tell me why I dotted these letters? That's right. I dotted them, because they are silent. They make no sound.

I will draw a gray ring around the *gr* sound (as in *grass*) in the word *grass* and around the *sn* sound (as in *snake*) in the word *snake.* I will also draw a gray ring around the *fff* sound (as in *phone*) in the word *photo*.

Find the card with the word *grass*. Now find the card with the word *photo*. Notice the mark at the end of each word. We call this mark a *comma*. Say *comma* as I point to the mark. We use a comma when we want to pause, or stop briefly. A period makes us come to a full stop, but a comma does not. Commas are often used in poems. (We will not discuss the many uses of the comma at this time.)

Read the four lines from the poem. Great! There are two words that rhyme in these lines from the poem. Can you tell me what they are? Very good! The word *snake* rhymes with the word *take*.

Now I will mix the cards, and you can put them in proper order to make the sentences again.

(Assist the child with putting the cards in proper order. Keep the cards from each sentence separate. Remind him, if necessary, a sentence begins with an uppercase letter and ends with a period or some other form of punctuation.)

Now read the lines from the poem.

(**Note**: We are no longer using clues to assist the child with reading the copy work. It is important for the child to read the text located in this segment of the lesson even if he does not copy the sentences. This will give him an opportunity to practice reading text printed in a regular type.)

Copy Work: (The copy work is optional for children who have difficulty with writing.) (You may now encourage the child to copy the sentences directly from the model below. If this is too difficult, continue as directed.)

I will write the lines from the poem you just read on a piece of paper.

(Neatly write the sentences with a pen, paying close attention to letter spacing and formation.)

Now you can copy what I wrote.

I   can   see   the   grass,
I   can   see   the   snake.
I   can   see   the   photo,
That   the   man   will   take.

I would like for you to read the lines from the poem once more. Very good! I would like for you to draw a picture to go with your sentences. Here is a picture of a snake you can draw.

(Assist the child with drawing the picture if necessary. The picture has been drawn with bold lines so the child may trace it if he likes.)

276

Make up a short poem about the snake you drew. Try to think of some words that rhyme with snake. This will help you to make up a poem. Tell me the poem, and I will write it on a piece of paper.

(Assist the child with finding words to rhyme with *snake*. His poem may be a brief as *The snake ate the cake*.)

Now you can copy one or two lines from your poem at the bottom of your picture.

(Draw lines if necessary for the child to write some lines from his poem at the bottom of his picture.)

Read the poem you just wrote.

(Assist the child by reading any difficult words for him. If the poem is long, have him read part of it and you read part of it.)

Now let's read a book together.

(Review material between lessons.)

Lesson 72

Materials: reading manual, index cards, pen, gray crayon, and black crayon.

Instructions: In today's lesson, the child will review the following sight words: *Mama, Papa, that, many, one, who,* and *people*.

He will review the *kw* sound made by the letters *qu* as in *queen* by reading the following words: *quick, quiz, quill, quilt, quack, quest, quote,* and *quail*.

He will be introduced to the *ch* sound as in *chip* and *patch*. He will read the following words containing the *ch* sound at the beginning: *chip, chick, check, chest, chime, child, cheese, cheap, chain,* and *choke*.

He will read the following words containing the *ch* sound at the end: *patch, match, lunch, punch, much, such, pitch,* and *ditch*.

The child will read the following story and complete a variety of exercises based on the story.

Title: *"The Quick Chick"*

Story: *The quick chick ran. He ran to the well to get a drink. A child was at the well.*

The child said, "Would you like a drink?"

The chick said, "Yes, I would like a drink. I would like a cold drink."

The child gave the chick a drink from the pail.

The chick said, "It is cold. It is cold and good."

The child said, "Would you like some food?"

The chick said, "Yes, I would like some corn. I like to eat corn."

The child said, "Come to the barn. I will give you some corn."

The child and the chick ran to the barn. The cow was in the barn.

The cow said, "May I have some hay?"

The child said, "Yes, I will give you some hay. I will give the chick some corn."

Dialogue: Read the sight words below.

Mama   Papa

that   many

one   who

people

Look at the letters below. Do you know what sound these letters make? (*kw* as in *queen*.)

(qu)

Very good! They make the *kw* sound (as in *queen*).

Read the words below that have the *kw* sound. I will read the first word for you. It is *quick*.

(**Note**: We are no longer dotting the letter *k* in the *ck* combination.)

(qu)ick   (qu)iz

(qu)ill   (qu)ilt

(qu)ack   (qu)est

(qu)ote   (qu)ail

Look at the letters below. These letters make the *ch* sound (as in *chip* and *patch*). You will notice these letters have a gray ring around them to help you see them more easily. (Point to the letters as you make the sound.)

(ch)

Say *ch* as I point to the letters.

Very good! Now read the words below that have the *ch* sound (as in *chip*) at the beginning. I will read the first word for you. It is *chip*.

(ch)ip   (ch)ick

(ch)eck   (ch)est

(ch)ime   (ch)ild

(ch)eese   (ch)eap

(ch)ain   (ch)oke

Very good! Now read the words below that have the *ch* sound (as in *patch*) at the end of the word. I will read the first word for you. It is *patch*. Remember, the letters that are dotted are silent. They make no sound.

pat(ch)   mat(ch)

lun(ch)   pun(ch)

mu(ch)   su(ch)

pit(ch)   dit(ch)

Read the words below.

(Assist the child with reading any difficult words. These words will appear in the story.)

(ch)ild   (qu)ick

(ch)ick   g(oo)d

dr(in)k   b(ar)n

f(oo)d   c(or)n

Read the story, and then I will show you a picture to go with the story.

(**Note**: We are no longer underlining the following sight words: *I, the,* and *is*. We are no longer dotting the letter *k* in the *ck* combination.)

"The Quick Chick"

The quick chick ran.

He ran to the well to get a drink.

A child was at the well.

The child said,

"Would you like a drink?"

The chick said,

"Yes, I would like a drink.

I would like a cold drink."

The child gave the chick a

drink from the pail.

The chick said, "It is cold.

It is cold and good."

The child said,

"Would you like some food?"

The chick said,

"Yes, I would like some corn.

I like to eat corn."

The child said, "Come to the barn.

I will give you some corn."

The child and the chick

ran to the barn.

The cow was in the barn.

The cow said, "May I have some hay?"

The child said,

"Yes, I will give you some hay.

I will give the chick some corn."

Now I will show you a picture of the child and the chick.

Look at the picture. The child is at the well. He can get water from the well. The chick is at the well too. Can he get the water from the well by himself? No, he needs help. Who helps the chick to get water? That's right. The child helps the chick.

What else does the child give the chick? That's right. He gives him corn. Where is the cow? Yes, she is in the barn. What does the child give the cow? Yes, he gives hay to the cow.

Next, I will write three of the sentences you just read on index cards.

(Have the child watch as you write each word with a pen. Label the first card with the lesson number for future use.)

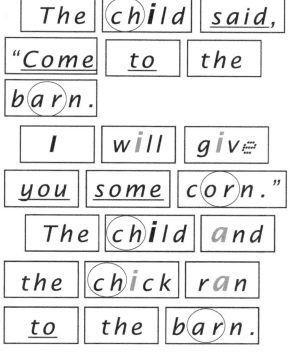

(**Note**: You may eliminate some of the print clues from the index cards with which your child is familiar. Be sure to include the print clues for sounds that have been recently introduced.)

I am going to underline five different sight words today with a black crayon. Can you read these sight words? I will trace over the *iii* sounds (as in *pig*) and the *aaa* sounds (as in *cat*) with a gray crayon.

I will trace over the bold *i* sounds (as in *bike*) with a black crayon. I will make dotted lines over the letter *e* in the word *give*. Can you tell me why I dotted this letter? That's right, I dotted it, because it is silent. It makes no sound.

I will draw a gray ring around the *ch* sound (as in *chip* and *patch*) in the word *child* and in the word *chick*. I will draw a gray ring around the *ar* sound (as in *car*) in the word *barn*, and I will also draw a

gray ring around the *or* sound (as in *corn*) in the word *corn*.

Read the sentences. Very good! Look at the first two sentences, *The child said, "Come to the barn. I will give you some corn."* (Point to the quotation marks on the index cards.) Do you notice the special marks used in these sentences? What are these special marks called? That's right. They are called quotation marks. We use them when a character is speaking.

Find the card with the word *said*. See the mark after the word. (Point to the comma.) Do you remember what this mark is called? That's right. It is called a *comma*. It tells us to pause before reading the next part of the sentence. A comma is used before quotation marks. (Point to the beginning quotation mark on the card with the word *Come*.)

Now I will mix the cards, and you can put them in proper order to make the sentences again.

(Assist the child with putting the cards in proper order. Keep the cards from each sentence separate. Remind him, if necessary, a sentence begins with an uppercase letter and ends with a period or some other form of punctuation.)

Now read the sentences.

(**Note**: We are no longer using clues to assist the child with reading the copy work. It is important for the child to read the text located in this segment of the lesson even if he does not copy the sentences. This will give him an opportunity to practice reading text printed in a regular type.)

Copy Work: (The copy work is optional for children who have difficulty with writing.) (You may now encourage the child to copy the sentences directly from the model below. If this is too difficult, continue as directed.)

I will write the sentences you just read on a piece of paper.

(Neatly write the sentences with a pen, paying close attention to letter spacing and formation.)

Now you can copy what I wrote.

The child said, "Come to the barn. I will give you some corn." The child and the chick ran to the barn.

I would like for you to read the sentences once more. Very good! I would like for you to draw a picture to go with your sentences. Here is a picture of a chick you can draw.

(Assist the child with drawing the picture if necessary. The picture has been drawn with bold lines so the child may trace it if he likes.)

(**Note:** You may choose to encourage the child to dictate a short story to you about the picture he drew instead of only one sentence.)

Make up a story about the chick you drew. Tell me the story, and I will write it on a piece of paper. Now you can copy one sentence from your story at the bottom of your picture.

(Draw lines if necessary for the child to write his sentence at the bottom of his picture.)

Read the story you dictated to me.

(Assist the child by reading any difficult words for him. If the story is long, have him read part of it and you read part of it.)

Now let's read a book together.

(Review material between lessons.)

Lesson 73

Materials: reading manual, index cards, pen, gray crayon, and black crayon.

Instructions: In today's lesson, the child will review the following sight words: *Mama, Papa, that, people, many, one, some,* and *who.*

He will review the *ch* sound as in *chip* and *patch* by reading the following words: *chick, chase, cheese, child, chop, patch, rich, reach,* and *munch.*

He will review the *fff* sound made by the letters *ph* as in *phone* by reading the following words: *phone, photo, phase,* and *graph.*

The child will be introduced to the *nnn* sound made by the letters *kn* as in *knee.* He will read the following words containing the *nnn* sound as in *knee*: *knee, knead, knock, know, knob, knot, knife,* and *knit.* The *nnn* sound as in *knee* will be represented as shown below, with the letter *k* dotted as a silent letter.

$$k \; n$$

The child will read the following story and complete a variety of exercises based on the story.

Title: *"Mama and Papa Mouse"*

Story: *Mama Mouse and Papa Mouse sat on a chair.*

Mama Mouse said, "Do you want some cheese?"

Papa Mouse said, "Yes, I would like some cheese."

Mama Mouse said, "I will climb up on the shelf. I can reach the cheese."

She got up on the shelf. She got the cheese.

She said, "I can jump down. I can jump on the chair."

Papa Mouse said, "I hear a noise. I hear a knock. It is a knock on the door. Quick! Jump to the floor. Run and hide in the hole. The hole is by the sink."

A man came in the room. A cat came in the room too.

Mama Mouse said, "I am glad we are safe in our hole."

Dialogue: Read the sight words below.

<u>Mama</u>   <u>Papa</u>

<u>that</u>   <u>people</u>

<u>many</u>   <u>one</u>

<u>some</u>   <u>who</u>

Look at the letters below. Can you tell me what sound these letters make? (*ch* as in *chip* and *patch*.)

ch

That's right. They make the *ch* sound. Read the words below that have the *ch* sound (as in *chip* and *patch*).

chick   chase

cheese   child

chop

patch   rich

reach   munch

Look at the letters below. Can you tell me what sound these letters make? (*fff* as in *phone*.)

ph

That's right. They make the *fff* sound.

Read the words below that have the *fff* sound (as in *phone*).

phone   photo

283

(ph)a s e   (gr)a(ph)

You are doing very well. You have learned to read many different words. You have found that sometimes words are strange. Sometimes they have silent letters. Usually the silent letters are at the end of a word or in the middle of the word. Now you will learn some words have a silent letter at the beginning of the word.

Look at the letters below. These letters make the *nnn* sound (as in *knee*). Notice the letter *k* is dotted. It is silent. It makes no sound.

k n

Read the words below that make the *nnn* sound (as in *knee*). Remember, the dotted letters are silent. They make no sound. I will read the first word for you. It is *knee*.

k n e e	k n e a d
k n o c k	k n o w
k n o b	k n o t
k n i f e	k n i t

Read the sentences that have some of the words you just read.

I like to knit.

I do not like to get a knot in my yarn.

Read the words below.

(Assist the child with reading any difficult words. These words will appear in story.)

(ch)e e s e	n(o)i s e
(sh)e l f	r e(a)(ch)
(ch)a i r	j u m p
h e a r	d(o)o r
f l o(o)r	s(i n k)
d(o w)n	(o u)r

Read the story, and then I will show you a picture to go with the story.

(**Note**: We are no longer underlining the sight words *I, the,* and *is*. We are no longer dotting the letter *k* in the blend *ck*. Also we are no longer drawing a ring around several beginning blends.)

"Mama and Papa M(ou)s e"

Mama and Papa M(ou)s e sat on a (ch)a i r.

Mama M(ou)s e said,

"Do you want some cheese?"
Papa Mouse said,
"Yes, I would like some cheese."
Mama Mouse said,
"I will climb up on the shelf.
I can reach the cheese."
She got up on the shelf.
She got the cheese.
She said, "I can jump down.
I can jump on the chair."
Papa Mouse said, "I hear a noise.
I hear a knock.
It is a knock on the door.
Quick. Jump to the floor.
Run and hide in the hole.
The hole is by the sink."
A man came in the room.
A cat came in the room too.

Mama M(ou)se said,

"I am glad we are safe in (ou)r hole."

Now I will show you a picture of the cat.

Look at the picture. Where is the mouse hole? That's right. It is under the sink. Do you think the cat knows the mice are in the hole?

What is the cat doing? Yes, that's right. He is sniffing the chair. Why do you think he is sniffing the chair? Do you think the chair smells like mice?

Does the man know mice have been in the room? What makes you think so? That's right, he sees the cheese on the floor. Maybe he thinks the mice put the cheese there.

Next, I will write three of the sentences you just read on index cards.

(Have the child watch as you write each word with a pen. Label the first card with the lesson number for future use.)

Papa M(ou)se said,

"I hear a noi(s)e.

I hear a knock.

It is a knock on the d(oo)r."

(**Note**: You may eliminate some of the print clues from the index cards with which your child is familiar. Be sure to include the print clues for sounds that have been recently introduced.)

I am going to underline two different sight words today with a black crayon. Can you read these sight words?

I will trace over the *ooo* sounds (as in *hot*) and the *iii* sound (as in *pig*) with a gray crayon. I will trace over the bold *e* sounds (as in *heat*) and the bold *a* sounds (as in *cake*) with a black crayon.

I will make dotted lines over the letter *e* in the word *mouse*, over the letter *a* in the word *hear*, and over the letter *e* in the word *noise*. I will also make dotted lines over letter *k* at the beginning of the word *knock* and over the first letter o in the word *door*. Can you tell me why I dotted these letters? That's right, I dotted them, because they are silent. They make no sound.

I will draw a gray ring around the *ou* sound (as in *house*) in the word *mouse*. I will draw a gray ring around the *oi* sound (as in *boil*) in the word *noise*. I will also draw a gray ring around the *or* sound (as in *corn*) in the word *door*.

Read the sentences. Great! Point to the quotation marks on the index cards. Can you tell me why we use these marks? That's right. We use quotation marks when a character is speaking. Who is speaking in these sentences? That's right. It is Papa Mouse who is speaking.

Find the index card with the word *said*. See the mark after the word. (Point to the comma.) Do you remember what this mark is called? That's right. It is called a *comma*. It tells us to pause before reading the next part of the sentence. A comma is used before quotation marks. (Point to the beginning quotation mark on the index card with the word *I*.)

Now I will mix the cards, and you can put them in the proper order to make the sentences again.

(Assist the child with putting the cards in proper order. Keep the cards from each sentence separate. Remind him, if necessary, a sentence begins with an uppercase letter and ends with a period or some other form of punctuation.)

Now read the sentences.

(**Note**: <u>We are no longer using clues to assist the child with reading the copy work. It is important for the child to read the text located in this segment of the lesson even if he does not copy the sentences. This will give him an opportunity to practice reading text printed in a regular type.</u>)

Copy Work: (The copy work is optional for children who have difficulty with writing.) (You may now encourage the child to copy the sentences directly from the model below. If this is too difficult, continue as directed.)

I will write the sentences you just read on a piece of paper.

(Neatly write the sentences with a pen, paying close attention to letter spacing and formation.)

Now you can copy what I wrote.

Papa Mouse said, "I hear a noise. I hear a knock. It is a knock on the door."

I would like for you to read the sentences once more. Very good! I would like for you to draw a picture to go with your sentences. Here is a picture of a mouse you can draw.

(Assist the child with drawing the picture if necessary. The picture has been drawn with bold lines so the child may trace it if he likes.)

(**Note:** You may choose to encourage the child to dictate a short story to you about the picture he drew instead of only one sentence.)

Make up a story about the mouse you drew. Tell me the story, and I will write it on a piece of paper. Now you can copy one sentence from your story at the bottom of your picture.

(Draw lines if necessary for the child to write his sentence at the bottom of his picture.)

Read the story you dictated to me.

(Assist the child by reading any difficult words for him. If the story is long, have him read part of it and you read part of it.)

Now let's read a book together.

(Review material between lessons.)

Lesson 74

Materials: reading manual, index cards, gray crayon, black crayon, and two construction paper circles.

Instructions: In today's lesson, the child will review the following sight words: *who, many, people, one, that, Mama,* and *Papa.* He will be introduced to the sight words *with* and *water.* Prepare two construction paper circles with the new sight words written on them.

He will review the *nnn* sound made by the letters *kn* as in *knee* by reading the following words: *knee, knob, know, knock, knit,* and *knot.*

He will review the *ch* sound as in *chip* and *patch* by reading the following words: *chest, chill, chose, lunch, punch,* and *much.*

He will review the *ing* sound as in *taking* and *hopping* by reading the following words: *calling, falling, hopping, mopping, raking, baking, sitting,* and *knitting.*

The child will be introduced to the bold *i* sound as in *night.* He will read the following words containing the bold *i* sound as in *night*: *night, right, sight, fight, light, might, tight, bright, flight, high,* and *sigh.* The bold *i* sound as in *night* will be represented as shown below. The letters *gh* are dotted as silent letters.

$$igh$$

The child will read the following story and complete a variety of exercises based on the story.

Title: *"The Deer"*

Story: *At night the deer go to the lake. They drink the water. They eat leaves from the trees. They can see by the light of the moon. The horns of the deer are tall. They can fight with the horns. The deer run if they hear a loud noise. The deer run if they see people. Deer can run fast. They can run far in to the woods. Deer have long legs. Have you seen a deer? I have seen a deer. I have seen a deer in the woods. I have seen a deer at the zoo. There are many kinds of deer at the zoo. There are many kinds of deer in the woods too.*

Dialogue: Read the sight words below.

who   many

<u>people</u>　　　　　<u>one</u>

<u>that</u>　　　　　<u>Mama</u>

<u>Papa</u>

Look at the new sight word below. It is *with*. (Point to the word as you read it.)

<u>with</u>

Say *with* as I point to the word. Very good! Now read the sentence that has the new sight word in it.

<u>You</u> can go <u>with</u>

me <u>to</u> the park.

Look at the new sight word below. It is *water*. (Point to the word as you read it.)

<u>water</u>

Say *water* as I point to the word. Very good! Now read the sentence that has the new sight word in it.

Can <u>you</u> <u>water</u>

the rose?

Now let's add the new sight words to your *Sight Word Worm*.

Read the words below that begin with the *nnn* sound (as in *knee*). Remember, the dotted letters are silent. They make no sound.

knee　　　　knob

know　　　　knock

---

knit　　　　knot

Read the words below that have the *ch* sound (as in *chip* and *patch*).

chest　　　chill

chose　　lunch

punch　　much

Look at the letters below. What sound do these letters make? (*ing* as in *sing*.)

ing

Very good! These letters make the *ing* sound.

Read the words below that have the *ing* sound (as in *sing*).

calling　　falling

hopping　　mopping

raking　　baking

sitting　　knitting

Look at the letters below. These letters make the bold *i* sound (as in *night*). (Point to the letters as you make the sound.)

The letters *g* and *h* are dotted because they are silent. They make no sound.

igh

Read the following words that have the bold *i* sound (as in *night*).

night　　right

sight   fight

light   might

tight   bright

flight   high

sigh

Read the words below.

(Assist the child with reading any difficult words. These words will appear in the story.)

night   water

leaves   woods

tall   hear

with   noise

kinds   loud

far   moon

drink   deer

Read the story below, and then I will show you a picture to go with the story.

(**Note**: We are no longer underlining the following sight words: *I, the,* and *is.* We are no longer dotting the letter *k* in the blend *ck* Also we are no longer drawing a ring around several beginning blends.)

"The Deer"

At night the deer go to the lake.

They drink the water.

They eat leaves from the trees.

They can see by the light of the moon.

The horns of the deer are tall.

They can fight with the horns.

The deer run if they

hear a loud noise.

The deer run if they see people.

Deer can run fast.

They can run far in to the woods.

Deer have long legs.

Have you seen a deer?

I have seen a deer.

I have seen a deer in the woods.

I have seen a deer at the zoo.

There are many kinds of

deer at the zoo.

There are many kinds of

deer in the woods too.

Now I will show you a picture of
the deer at the lake.

Look at the picture. What is the deer in the picture doing? That's right. He is eating leaves from the tree. He is standing near the lake.

A male deer is called a buck. A female deer is called a doe. A baby deer is called a fawn. Have you seen a deer in the woods or at the zoo?

Next I will write three of the sentences you just read on index cards.

(**Note**: Have the child watch as you write each word with a pen. Label the first card with the lesson number for future use.)

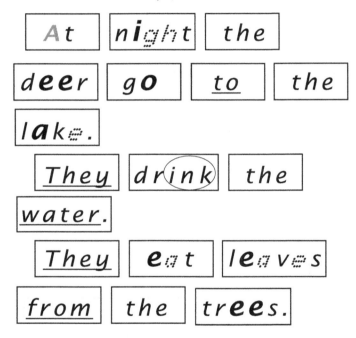

(**Note**: You may eliminate some of the print clues from the index cards with which your child is familiar. Be sure to include the print clues for sounds that have been recently introduced.)

I am going to underline four different sight words today with a black crayon. Can you read these sight words?

I will trace over the aaa sound (as in *cat*) with a gray crayon. I will trace over the bold *i* sound (as in *night*) and the bold *e* sounds (as in *heat*) with a black crayon.

I will also trace over the bold *o* sound (as in *hope*) and the bold *a* sound (as in *cake*) with a black crayon.

I will make dotted lines over the letters g and h in the word *night*. I will make dotted lines over the letter *e* in the word *lake* and in the word *leaves*. I will also make dotted lines over the letter a in the word *eat* and in the word *leaves*. Can you tell me why I dotted these letters? That's right, I dotted them, because they are silent. They make no sound.

I will draw a gray ring around the *ink* sound (as in *drink*) in the word *drink*.

Read the sentences. Very good! Now I will mix the cards, and you can put them in the proper order to make the sentences again.

(Assist the child with putting the cards in proper order. Keep the cards from each sentence separate. Remind him, if necessary, a sentence begins with an uppercase letter and ends with a period or some other form of punctuation.)

Now read the sentences.

(**Note**: We are no longer using clues to assist the child with reading the copy work. It is important for the child to read the text located in this segment of the lesson even if he does not copy the sentences. This will give him an opportunity to practice reading text printed in a regular type.)

Copy Work: (The copy work is optional for children who have difficulty with writing.) (You may now encourage the child to copy the sentences directly from the model below. If this is too difficult, continue as directed.)

I will write the sentences you just read on a piece of paper.

(Neatly write the sentences with a pen, paying close attention to letter spacing and formation.)

Now you can copy what I wrote.

At night the deer go to the lake.

They drink the water. They eat leaves from the trees.

I would like for you to read the sentences once more. Very good! I would like for you to draw a picture to go with your sentences. Here is a picture of a deer you can draw.

(Assist the child with drawing the picture if necessary. The picture has been drawn with bold lines so the child may trace it if he likes.)

(**Note:** You may choose to encourage the child to dictate a short story to you about the picture he drew instead of only one sentence.)

Make up a story about the deer you drew. Tell me the story, and I will write it on a piece of paper. Now you can copy one sentence from your story at the bottom of your picture.

(Draw lines if necessary for the child to write his sentence at the bottom of his picture.)

Read the story you dictated to me.

(Assist the child by reading any difficult words for him. If the story is long, have him read part of it and you read part of it.)

Now let's read a book together.

(Review material between lessons.)

Lesson 75

Materials: reading manual, index cards, pen, gray crayon, and black crayon.

Instructions: In today's lesson, the child will review the following sight words: *one, many, with, water, people, who, that, would, could,* and *should.*

He will review the bold *i* sound as in *night* by reading the following words: *right, sight, fight, tight, fright,* and *flight.*

He will review the *ch* sound as in *chip* and *patch* by reading the following words: *chin, chop, chill, batch, match,* and *hatch.*

The child will be introduced to the *th* sound as in *thick* or *this.* He will read the following words containing the *th* sound at the beginning: *thick, thin, thud, thump, this, then, than,* and *thy.* He will read the following words containing the *th* sound at the end: *bath, math, path,* and *moth.*

The child will read the following story and complete a variety of exercises based on the story.

Title: *"The Pig Takes a Bath"*

Story: *The pig took a bath. He took a bath in the mud.*

The pig said, "I like to take a bath in the mud. It is fun."

The duck said, "It is not good to take a bath in the mud. You will not be clean. You should take a bath in the water. Then you will be clean."

The pig said, "That is not the way I take a bath. That is not for me. I like mud. Mud will keep me cool. The sun is too hot. I do not like to be hot. Look at me. I can jump in the mud."

The duck said, "Stop! You got mud on my wing. I do not like mud."

The duck ran down the path. He ran to the water. The pig sat in the mud.

The pig said, "This is fun!"

Dialogue: Read the sight words below.

one   many

with   water

people   who

that   would

could   should

Read the words below that have the bold *i* sound (as in *night*). Remember, the dotted letters are silent. They make no sound.

right   sight

fight   tight

fright   flight

Read the words below that have the *ch* sound (as in *chip* and *patch*).

chin   chop

chill   batch

match   hatch

Look at the letters below. These letters make the *th* sound (as in *thick* or *this*). (Point to the letters as you make the sound.) You will notice these letters have a gray ring around them to help you see them more easily.

th

Read the words below that have the *th* sound (as in *thick* or *this*) at the beginning. I will read the first word for you. It is *thick.*

thick   thin

thud   thump

294

(th)is   (th)en

(th)an   (th)y

Sometimes the *th* sound (as in *thick* or *this*) comes at the end of the word. Look at the word below. The word is *bath*. (Point to the word as you read it.) The *th* sound comes at the end of the word *bath*.

b a (th)

Now read the words below that have the *th* sound (as in *thick* or *this*) at the end.

b a (th)   m a (th)

p a (th)   m o (th)

Now read the sentence below. You will find two words that have the *th* sound (as in *thick* or *this*).

The m o (th) can fly

in the (th)ick fog.

Read the words below.

(Assist the child with reading any difficult words. These words will appear in the story.)

t(oo)k   b a (th)

cle a n   water

k(ee)p   c(oo)l

that   jump

p a (th)   w(in)g

Read the story below, and then I will show you a picture to go with the story.

(**Note**: We are no longer underlining the following sight words: *I, the, is, to,* and *said*. We are no longer dotting the letter *k* in the blend *ck*. We are no longer dotting the letter *y* as in *way*. We are no longer drawing a ring around several beginning blends.)

"The Pig Tak e s a Ba(th)"

The pig t(oo)k a b a (th).

He t(oo)k a b a (th) in the mud.

The pig said,

"I like to take a b a (th) in the mud.

It is fun."

The duck said, "It is not g(oo)d to

295

take a bath in the mud.

You will not be clean.

You should take a bath in the water.

Then you will be clean."

The pig said,

"That is not the way I take a bath.

That is not for me. I like mud.

Mud will keep me cool.

The sun is too hot.

I do not like to be hot. Look at me.

I can jump in the mud."

The duck said, "Stop!

You got mud on my wing.

I do not like mud."

The duck ran down the path.

He ran to the water.

The pig sat in the mud.

The pig said, "This is fun!"

Now I will show you a picture of the pig in the mud.

Look at the picture. What is the pig doing? Yes, he is rolling in the mud. Does he look like he is having fun?

Look at the duck. Does the duck look like he is having fun? What happened to the duck?

Next, I will write three of the sentences you just read on index cards.

(Have the child watch as you write each word with a pen. Label the first card with the lesson number for future use.)

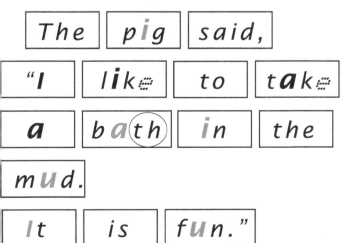

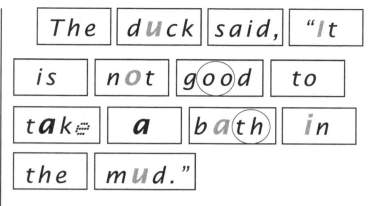

(**Note**: You may eliminate some of the print clues from the index cards with which your child is familiar. Be sure to include the print clues for sounds that have been recently introduced.)

(We are not underlining any of the sight words in this excerpt of the text, because the child should be well acquainted with the sight words used in this passage.)

I will trace over the *iii* sounds (as in *pig*), the *aaa* sounds (as in *cat*), the *uuu* sounds (as in *cup*), and the *ooo* sound (as in *hot*) with a gray crayon.

I will trace over the bold *i* sound (as in *bike*) and the bold *a* sounds (as in *cake*) with a black crayon.

I will make dotted lines over the letter *e* in the word *like* and in the word *take*. Can you tell me why I dotted these letters? That's right. I dotted them, because they are silent. They make no sound.

I will draw a gray ring around the *th* sound (as in *thick* or *this*) in the word *bath*. I will also draw a gray ring around the *oo* sound (as in *cook*) in the word *good*.

Read the sentences. Great! Find the index cards with the quotation marks. Why do we use these special marks? Who is speaking in these passages? That's right. The pig and the duck are speaking.

Look at the index cards from the first sentence. Find the index card with the comma. Very good! What does the comma tell us? That's right. It tells us to pause before reading the next part of the sentence. A comma is used before quotation marks. (Point to the beginning quotation mark on the card with the word *I*.) (Go over the use of the comma in the third sentence.)

Now I will mix the cards, and you can put them in the proper order to make the sentences again.

(Assist the child with putting the cards in proper order. Keep the cards from each sentence separate. Remind him, if necessary, a sentence begins with an uppercase letter and ends with a period or some other form of punctuation.)

Now read the sentences.

(**Note**: We are no longer using clues to assist the child with reading the copy work. It is important for the child to read the text located in this segment of the lesson even if he does not copy the sentences. This will give him an opportunity to practice reading text printed in a regular type.)

Copy Work: (The copy work is optional for children who have difficulty with writing.) (You may now encourage the child to copy the sentences directly from the model below. If this is too difficult, continue as directed.)

I will write the sentences you just read on a piece of paper.

(Neatly write the sentences with a pen, paying close attention to letter spacing and formation.)

Now you can copy what I wrote.

The pig said, "I like to take a bath in the mud. It is fun."

The duck said, "It is not good to take a bath in the mud."

I would like for you to read the sentences once more. Very good! I would like for you to draw a picture to go with your sentences. Here is a picture of a duck you can draw.

(Assist the child with drawing the picture if necessary. The picture has been drawn with bold lines so the child may trace it if he likes.)

Make up a story about the duck you drew. Tell me the story, and I will write it on a piece of paper. Now you can copy one sentence from your story at the bottom of your picture.

(Draw lines if necessary for the child to write his sentence at the bottom of his picture.)

Read the story you dictated to me.
Now let's read a book together.

Lesson 76

Materials: reading manual, index cards, pen, gray crayon, and black crayon.

Instructions: In today's lesson, the child will review the following sight words: *people, that, who, many, of, one, some, with,* and *water.*

He will review the bold *i* sound as in *night* by reading the following words: *bright, sight, fight, knight, tight,* and *night.*

He will review the *ch* sound as in *chip* and *patch* by reading the following words: *each, beach, such, much, chip, chop, cheap,* and *chime.*

He will review the *th* sound as in *thick* or *this* by reading the following words containing the *th* sound at the beginning: *this, then, them,* and *those.* He will read the following words containing the *th* sound at the end: *path, math, moth,* and *cloth.*

He will review the *ing* sound when it is added to the end of a word such as *taking* and *hopping* by reading the following words: *calling, falling, running, sunning, making, baking, fixing, mixing, cooking,* and *looking.*

The child will read the following story and complete a variety of exercises based on the story.

Title: *"God Save the King"*

Story: *The king came to the park. Many people came to see the king. The king rode on the path. He rode on a white horse. Many men rode with the king. Each man had a fine horse. Soon all the people could hear a noise. They could hear a horn. The horn was loud. Then a boy came running in to the park. The boy ran up to the king. He gave the king a note. The king read the note.*

Then the king said to his men, "Quick! We must go. There are bad men in the woods. We must fight them. We must save all the people."

The people said, "We have a good king. We know he will win the fight. May God save the king!"

Dialogue: Read the sight words below.

<u>people</u>   <u>that</u>

<u>who</u>   <u>many</u>

<u>of</u>   <u>one</u>

<u>some</u>   <u>with</u>

<u>water</u>

Read the words below that have the bold *i* sound (as in *night*). Remember, the dotted letters are silent. They make no sound.

bright   sight

fight   knight

tight   night

Read the words below that have the *ch* sound (as in *chip* and *patch*).

e a (ch)   be a (ch)

s u (ch)   m u (ch)

(ch) i p   (ch) o p

(ch) e a p   (ch) i m e

Look at the letters below. What sound do these letters make? (*th* as in *thick* or *this*).

(t h)

Yes. These letters make the *th* sound. (Point to the letters as you make the sound.)

Read the words below that have the *th* sound. I will read the first word for you. It is *this.*

(th) i s   (th) e n

(th) e m   (th) o s e

p a (th)   m a (th)

299

m o th   cl o th

Read the words below that have the
ing sound (as in *sing*).

calling   falling

running   sunning

making   baking

fixing   mixing

cooking   looking

Read the story below, and then I will
show you a picture to go with the
story.

(**Note**: We are no longer underlining the
following sight words: *I, the, is, to,* and *said.* We are
no longer dotting the letter *k* in the blend *ck.* We are
no longer dotting the letter *y* as in *way.* We are no
longer drawing a ring around several beginning
blends.)

"God Save the King"

The king came to the park.

Many people came to see the king.

The king rode on the path.

He rode on a white horse.

Many men rode with the king.

Each man had a fine horse.

Soon all the people

could hear a noise.

They could hear a horn.

The horn was loud.

Then a boy came running

300

in to the park.

The boy ran up to the king.

He gave the king **a** note.

The king read the note.

Then the king said to his men,

"Quick! We must go.

There are bad men in the woods.

We must fight them.

We must save all the people."

The people said, "We have **a** good king.

We know he will win the fight.

May God save the king!"

Now I will show you a picture of the king.

301

Look at the picture. What is the king wearing? Yes, he is wearing a suit of armor. Do you think he was expecting a fight? A good king is always ready to defend his people.

Next, I will write three of the sentences you just read on index cards.

(Have the child watch as you write each word with a pen. Label the first card with the lesson number for future use.)

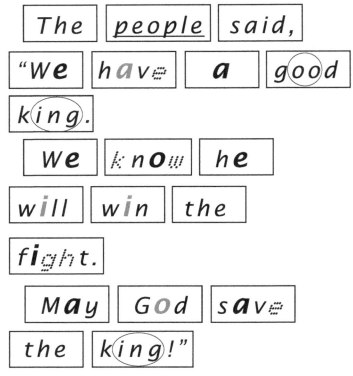

(**Note**: You may eliminate some of the print clues from the index cards with which your child is familiar. Be sure to include the print clues for sounds that have been recently introduced.)

(We are only underlining one of the sight words in this excerpt of the text, because the child should be well acquainted with most of the sight words used in this passage.)

I will underline one of the sight words with a black crayon. Read the sight word as I underline it.

I will trace over the aaa sound (as in cat), the iii sounds (as in pig), and the ooo sound (as in hot) with a gray crayon.

I will trace over the bold e sounds (as in heat) and the bold a sounds (as in cake) with a black crayon. I will also trace over the bold o sound (as in snow) and the bold i sound (as in fight) with a black crayon.

I will make dotted lines over the letter e in the word have and in the word save. I will make dotted lines over the letters k and w in the word know. I will also make dotted lines over the letters g and h in the word fight. Can you tell me why I dotted these letters? That's right. I dotted them, because they are silent. They make no sound.

I will draw a gray ring around the oo sound (as in cook) in the word good. I will draw a gray ring around the ing sound (as in sing) in the word king.

Read the sentences. Great! Find the index cards with the quotation marks. Why do we use these special marks? Who is speaking in these passages?

Find the index card with the exclamation point. Why do we use this special mark? That's right, we use an exclamation point when we want to show surprise. How are you supposed to read this sentence?

Now I will mix the cards, and you can put them in the proper order to make the sentences again.

(Assist the child with putting the cards in proper order. Keep the cards from each sentence separate. Remind him, if necessary, a sentence begins with an uppercase letter and ends with a period or some other form of punctuation.)

Now read the sentences.

Copy Work: (The copy work is optional for children who have difficulty with writing.) (You may now encourage the child to copy the sentences directly from the model below. If this is too difficult, continue as directed.)

I will write the sentences you just read on a piece of paper.

(Neatly write the sentences with a pen, paying close attention to letter spacing and formation.)

Now you can copy what I wrote.

The people said, "We have a good king. We know he will win the fight. May God save the king!"

I would like for you to read the sentences once more. Very good! I would like for you to draw a picture to go with your sentences. Here is a picture of a king you can draw.

(Assist the child with drawing the picture if necessary. The picture has been drawn with bold lines so the child may trace it if he likes.)

(**Note:** You may choose to encourage the child to dictate a short story to you about the picture he drew instead of only one sentence.)

Make up a story about the king you drew. Tell me the story, and I will write it on a piece of paper. Now you can copy one sentence from your story at the bottom of your picture.

(Draw lines if necessary for the child to write his sentence at the bottom of his picture.)

Read the story you dictated to me.

(Assist the child by reading any difficult words for him. If the story is long, have him read part of it and you read part of it.)

Now let's read a book together.

(Review material between lessons.)

Lesson 77

Materials: reading manual, index cards, pen, gray crayon, black crayon, and one construction paper circle.

Instructions: In today's lesson, the child will review the following sight words: *Mama, Papa, one, many, with, water, people, who, want,* and *that.* He will be introduced to the sight word *two.* Prepare one construction paper circle with the new sight word written on it.

He will review the *th* sound as in *thick* or *this* by reading the following words containing the *th* sound at the beginning: *thick, thump, this,* and *then.* He will read the following words containing the *th* sound at the end: *bath, path, moth,* and *fifth.*

The child will be introduced to the *aw* sound as in *saw.* He will read the following words containing the *aw* sound: *saw, paw, jaw, claw, draw, thaw, lawn, fawn,* and *dawn.*

He will review the *ch* sound as in *chip* and *patch* by reading the following words: *chime, chase, choose,* and *cheap.*

The child will read the following story and complete a variety of exercises based on the story.

Title: *"The Toy Ship"*

Story: *The boy said, "I can make a ship. I can make a toy ship. I can cut the wood with my saw. I can cut the wood on the lawn."*

Papa said, "I will help you. I will help you make a toy ship. Do you want a small ship or a tall ship?"

The boy said, "I would like a tall ship."

Papa said, "I will get the wood. You can get the nails and the saw."

The boy said, "Where are the tools?"

Papa said, "The tools are in the barn. The wood is in the shed."

The boy said, "I will look for the nails and the saw. I will look for them in the barn."

Papa said, "I will get the wood from the shed. I will choose a long plank."

Dialogue: Read the sight words below.

Mama   Papa

one   many

with   water

people   who

want   that

Look at the new sight word below. It is the word *two.* (Point to the word as you read it.)

two

Say *two* as I point to the word. Very good! Now read the sentence that has the new sight word in it.

I have two cats.

Now let's add the new sight word to your *Sight Word Worm.*

Look at the letters below. What sound do these letters make? (*th* as in *this* or *thick.*)

th

Very good! They make the *th* sound. Read the words below that have the *th* sound (as in *this* or *thick*) at the beginning.

thick   thump

this   then

Read the words below that have the *th* sound at the end of the word.

bath   path

moth   fifth

Look at the letters at the top of the next page. These letters make the *aw* sound (as in *saw*). You will notice these letters have a gray ring around them to help you see them more easily. (Point to the letters as you make the sound.)

(a w)

Say *aw* (as in *saw*) as I point to the letters.

Very good! Now read the words below that have the *aw* sound. I will read the first word for you. It is *saw*.

s(a w)   p(a w)

j(a w)   c l(a w)

d r(a w)   t h(a w)

l(a w)n   f(a w)n

d(a w)n

Read the words below that have the *ch* sound (as in *chip* and *patch*).

(c h)i m e   (c h)a s e

(c h)(o o)s e   (c h)e a p

Read the words below.

(Assist the child with reading any difficult words. These words will appear in the story.)

t(o y)   t(o o)ls

c u t   l o n g

s h i p   (c h)(o o)s e

p l a n k   b(a r)n

n a i l s

Read the story below, and then I will show you a picture to go with the story.

(**Note**: We are no longer underlining the following sight words: *I, the, is, to,* and *said.* We are no longer dotting the letter *k* in the blend *ck.* We are no longer dotting the letter *y* as in *way.* We are no longer drawing a ring around several beginning blends.)

"The T(o y) Ship"

The b(o y) said, "I can make a ship.

I can make a t(o y) ship.

I can cut the w(o o)d <u>with</u> my s(a w).

I can cut the w(o o)d on the l(a w)n."

<u>Papa</u> said, "I will help <u>you</u>.

305

I will help you make a toy ship.

Do you want a small

ship or a tall ship?"

The boy said, "I would

like a tall ship."

Papa said, "I will get the wood.

You can get the nails and the saw."

The boy said, "Where are the tools?"

Papa said, "The tools are in the barn.

The wood is in the shed."

The boy said, "I will look for

the nails and the saw.

I will look for them in the barn."

Papa said, "I will get the

wood from the shed.

I will choose a long plank."

Now I will show you a picture of the boy and his father.

Look at the picture. What is the boy doing? Yes, he is sawing the piece of wood. What is the boy making? That's right, he is making a ship. Is he making a small ship or a tall ship? Yes, he is making a tall ship. Who is helping him? That's right, his father is helping him.

Next, I will write three of the sentences you just read on index cards.

(Have the child watch as you write each word with a pen. Label the first card with the lesson number for future use.)

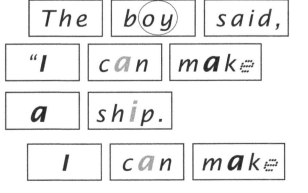

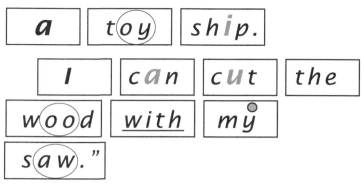

(**Note**: You may eliminate some of the print clues from the index cards with which your child is familiar. Be sure to include the print clues for sounds that have been recently introduced.)

Today we will underline the sight word *with*. Can you find the index card that has the word *with* on it?

I will trace over the *aaa* sounds (as in *cat*), the *iii* sounds (as in *pig*), and the *uuu* sound (as in *cup*) with a gray crayon.

I will trace over the bold *a* sounds (as in *cake*) with a black crayon. I will make dotted lines over the letter *e* in the word *make*. Can you tell me why I dotted this letter? That's right, it is silent. It makes no sound.

I will draw a gray ring around the *oy* sound (as in *boy*) in the word *boy* and in the word *toy*. I will draw a gray ring around the *oo* sound (as in *cook*) in the word *wood*. I will also draw a gray ring around the *aw* sound (as in *saw*) in the word *saw*.

I will put a gray dot over the letter *y* in the word *my*. Can you tell me why I put a gray dot over this letter? What sound does this letter make? That's right, it makes the bold *i* sound (as in *fly*).

Read the sentences. Very good! Can you find the index cards that have the quotation marks on them? Good, the cards with the word I and the word saw have the quotation marks on them. The boy said, "I can make a ship. I can make a toy ship. I can cut the wood with my saw." Remember, the words spoken by a character go inside the quotation marks.

Now I will mix the cards, and you can put them in the proper order to make the sentences again.

(Assist the child with putting the cards in proper order. Keep the cards from each sentence separate. Remind him, if necessary, a sentence begins with an uppercase letter and ends with a period or some other form of punctuation.)

Now read the sentences.

(**Note**: We are no longer using clues to assist the child with reading the copy work. It is important for the child to read the text located in this segment of the lesson even if he does not copy the sentences. This will give him an opportunity to practice reading text printed in a regular type.)

Copy Work: (The copy work is optional for children who have difficulty with writing.) (You may now encourage the child to copy the sentences directly from the model below. If this is too difficult, continue as directed.)

I will write the sentences you just read on a piece of paper.

(Neatly write the sentences with a pen, paying close attention to letter spacing and formation.)

Now you can copy what I wrote.

The boy said, "I can make a ship. I can make a toy ship. I can

cut the wood with my saw."

I would like for you to read the sentences once more. Very good! I would like for you to draw a picture to go with your sentences. Here is a picture of a toy ship you can draw.

(Assist the child with drawing the picture if necessary. The picture has been drawn with bold lines so the child may trace it if he likes.)

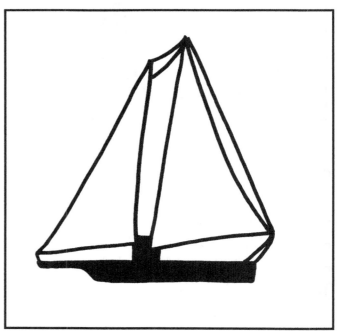

Make up a story about the toy ship you drew. Tell me the story, and I will write it on a piece of paper. Now you can copy one sentence from your story at the bottom of your picture.

(Draw lines if necessary for the child to write his sentence at the bottom of his picture.)

Read the story you dictated to me.

(Assist the child by reading any difficult words for him. If the story is long, have him read part of it and you read part of it.)

Now let's read a book together.

(Review material between lessons.)

Lesson 78

Materials: reading manual, index cards, pen, gray crayon, and black crayon.

Instructions: In today's lesson, the child will review the following sight words: *what, put, they, does, one, many, with, water, people, who, want, that,* and *two.*

He will review the *aw* sound as in *saw* by reading the following words: *saw, law, paw, jaw, flaw, thaw,* and *hawk.* The child will review the *all* sound as in *ball* as he reads the following words: *ball, fall, small, call,* and *wall.*

He will review the *ch* sound as in *patch.* He will read the following words with the *ch* sound at the end: *match, latch, catch, much, such, dutch,* and *clutch.*

He will be introduced to the *alk* sound as in *talk.* He will read the following words containing the *alk* sound: *talk, walk, chalk, stalk,* and *balk.*

The child will read the following story and complete a variety of exercises based on the story.

Title: *"The Small Ant and the Black Bug"*

Story: *The small ant was on the side walk. The black bug was on the side walk too. The small ant saw a big ball on the side walk.*

He said, "What is this?"

The black bug said, "It is a ball. It is a toy."

The small ant said, "Can I play with the ball?"

"No," said the black bug. "The ball is too big for you. It is too big for me. It is for people. People play with the ball. They are big."

"Look," said the small ant, "who is that in the grass?"

"That is a boy," said the black bug. "He will kick the ball. He will kick it in the grass. He will kick it to the man. The man can catch the ball."

Dialogue: Read the sight words below.

what   put

they   does

one   many

with   water

people   who

want   that

two

Look at the letters below. What sound do these letters make? (*aw* as in *saw.*)

aw

Very good! These letters make the *aw* sound.

Read the words below that have the *aw* sound (as in *saw*).

saw   law
paw   jaw
flaw   thaw
          hawk

Look at the letters below. What sound do these letters make? (*all* as in *ball.*)

all

Very good! These letters make the *all* sound.

Read the words below that have the *all* sound (as in *ball*).

ball   fall
small   call
          wall

Look at the letters below. What sound do these letters make? (*ch* as in *chip* and *patch.*)

ch

Very good! These letters make the *ch* sound.

Read the words below that have the *ch* sound at the end. I will read the first word for you. It is *match*. (Point to the word as you read it.) Remember, the dotted letters are silent. They make no sound.

m a t (ch)   l a t (ch)

c a t (ch)   m u (ch)

s u (ch)   d u t (ch)

c l u t (ch)

Look at the letters at the top of the page. These letters make the *alk* sound (as in *talk*). You will notice these letters have a gray ring around them to help you see them more easily. (Point to the letters as you make the sound.)

(alk)

Read the words below that have the *alk* sound (as in *talk*). I will read the first word for you. It is *talk*.

t (alk)   w (alk)

ch (alk)   st (alk)

b (alk)

Read the story below, and then I will show you a picture to go with the story.

(**Note**: We are no longer underlining the following sight words: *I, the, is, to, said,* and *you.* We are no longer dotting the letter *k* in the blend *ck.* We are no longer dotting the letter *y* as in *way.* We are no longer drawing a ring around several beginning blends.)

"The Sm(all) Ant and the Black Bug"

The sm(all) ant <u>was</u> on the side w(alk).

The black bug <u>was</u> on the side w(alk) t(oo).

The sm(all) ant s(aw) a big

b(all) on the side w(alk).

He said, "<u>What</u> is (th)is?"

The black bug said, "It is a b(all).

It is a t(oy)."

310

The small ant said,

"Can I play with the ball?"

"No," said the black bug.

"The ball is too big for you.

It is too big for me. It is for people.

People play with the ball. They are big."

"Look," said the small ant,

"Who is that in the grass?"

"That is a boy," said the black bug.

"He will kick the ball.

He will kick it in the grass.

He will kick it to the man.

The man can catch the ball."

Now I will show you a picture of
the ant and the bug.

311

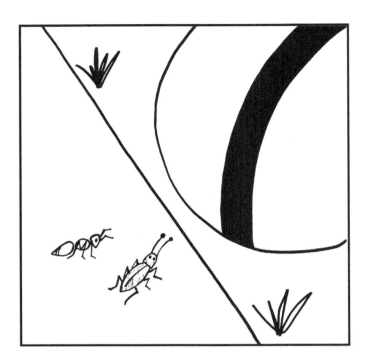

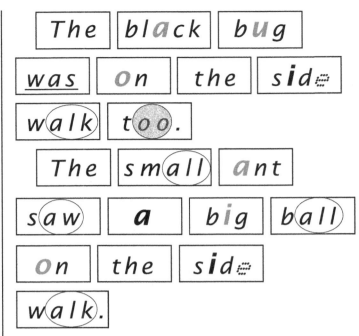

Look at the picture. What are the small ant and the black bug looking at? That's right, they are looking at a ball. Do they look little or big next to the ball? Yes, they look very small.

What does the small ant want to do with the ball? That's right. He wants to play with the ball. Do you think he is big enough to play with the ball? No, he is too small.

Next I will write three of the sentences you just read on index cards.

(Have the child watch as you write each word with a pen. Label the first card with the lesson number for future use.)

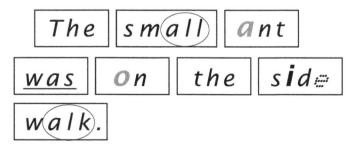

(**Note**: You may eliminate some of the print clues from the index cards with which your child is familiar. Be sure to include the print clues for sounds that have been recently introduced.)

I will underline the sight word *was* with a black crayon. This word appears two times in these sentences. I will trace over the *aaa* sounds (as in *cat*), the *ooo* sounds (as in *hot*), the *uuu* sound (as in *cup*), and the *iii* sound (as in *pig*) with a gray crayon.

I will trace over the bold *i* sounds (as in *bike*) and the bold *a* sound (as in *cake*) with a black crayon.

I will draw a gray ring around the *all* sound (as in *ball*) in the word *small* and in the word *ball*. I will draw a gray ring around the *alk* sound (as in *talk*) in the word *walk*. I will draw a shaded gray ring around the *oo* sound (as in *boot*) in the word *too*. I will also draw a gray ring around the *aw* sound (as in *saw*) in the word *saw*.

312

Read the sentences. Great! Now I will mix the cards, and you can put them in the proper order to make the sentences again.

(Assist the child with putting the cards in proper order. Keep the cards from each sentence separate. Remind him, if necessary, a sentence begins with an uppercase letter and ends with a period or some other form of punctuation.)

Now read the sentences.

(**Note**: We are no longer using clues to assist the child with reading the copy work. It is important for the child to read the text located in this segment of the lesson even if he does not copy the sentences. This will give him an opportunity to practice reading text printed in a regular type.)

Copy Work: (The copy work is optional for children who have difficulty with writing.) (You may now encourage the child to copy the sentences directly from the model below. If this is too difficult, continue as directed.)

I will write the sentences you just read on a piece of paper.

(Neatly write the sentences with a pen, paying close attention to letter spacing and formation.)

Now you can copy what I wrote.

The small ant was on the side walk. The black bug was on the side walk too. The small ant saw a big ball on the side walk.

I would like for you to read the sentences once more. Very good! I would like for you to draw a picture to go with your sentences. Here is a picture of an ant you can draw.

(Assist the child with drawing the picture if necessary. The picture has been drawn with bold lines so the child may trace it if he likes.)

(**Note:** You may choose to encourage the child to dictate a short story to you about the picture he drew instead of only one sentence.)

Make up a story about the ant you drew. Tell me the story, and I will write it on a piece of paper. Now you can copy one sentence from your story at the bottom of your picture.

(Draw lines if necessary for the child to write his sentence at the bottom of his picture.)

Read the story you dictated to me.

(Assist the child by reading any difficult words for him. If the story is long, have him read part of it and you read part of it.)

Now let's read a book together.

(Review material between lessons.)

Lesson 79

Materials: reading manual, index cards, pen, gray crayon, and black crayon.

Instructions: In today's lesson, the child will review the following sight words: *come, from, some, many, with, water, people, who, that,* and *two.*

He will review the *alk* sound as in *talk* by reading the following words: *talk, walk, chalk,* and *stalk.*

He will review the *ing* sound as in *sing* when added to the end of a word as in *hopping.* He will read the following words: *talking, walking, getting, hopping, batting, carting, making, trying, blowing, kneeling, plowing, counting, joining, winking,* and *snorting.*

The child will read the following poem and complete a variety of exercises based on the poem.

Title: *"One Day"*

Poem: *One day I saw a boy who was mopping,*
And a frog who was hopping.
An old man was raking,
And a good maid was baking.
A pink pig was walking,
And a big horse was talking.
A brown cow was plowing,
And a white goat was bowing.
A proud duck was winking,
And a wise owl was thinking.
A fat hen was laying,
And a small child was playing.
A red rose was blooming,
And a tan dog was grooming.
A black crow was singing,
And a brass bell was ringing.
The cold wind was blowing,
And then it was snowing.
Soon night time was falling,
And Mama was calling.
I had to start going,
For now it was growing, dark.

Dialogue: Read the sight words below.

come   from

some   many

with   water

people   who

that   two

Look at the letters below. What sound do these letters make? (*alk* as in *talk*.)

alk

Very good! These letters make the *alk* sound.

Read the words below that have the *alk* sound (as in *talk*).

talk   walk
chalk   stalk

Look at the letters below. What sound do these letters make? (*ing* as in *sing*)

ing

Very good! These letters make the *ing* sound.

Look at the word below.

talk

It is the word *talk*. We can add the *ing* sound to the end of the word to make a new word. Look at the new word below. It is the word *talking*.

talking

Read the words below that have the *ing* sound (as in *hopping*).

(Note: We are no longer dotting the letter *w* as in *blowing*.)

talking   walking

getting   hopping

batting   carting

making   trying

blowing   kneeling

plowing   counting

joining   winking

snorting

Read the poem below, and then I will show you a picture to go with the poem.

(**Note**: We are no longer underlining the following sight words: *I, the, is, to, said, was,* and *you.* We are no longer dotting the letter *k* in the blend *ck.* We are no longer dotting the letter *y* as in *way* or the letter *w* as in *crow.* We are no longer drawing a ring around several beginning blends.)

(Assist the child with reading the poem if necessary. For example, you read two lines, and then he reads two lines and so on. On the following day as a review, alternate this process and have him read two lines, and then you read two lines and so on. On another review day, have him read the entire poem by himself.)

"One Day"

One day I saw a boy who was mopping,

And a frog who was hopping.

An old man was raking,

And a good maid was baking.

A pink pig was walking,

And a big horse was talking.

A brown cow was plowing,

And a white goat was bowing.

A proud duck was winking,

315

And *a* wis*e* owl was thinking.

A fat h*e*n was l*a*ying,

And *a* small child was pl*a*ying.

A red r*o*s*e* was blooming,

And *a* tan d*o*g was gr*o*oming.

A black cr*o*w was singing,

And *a* brass b*e*ll was ringing.

The c*o*ld wind was bl*o*wing,

And then it was sn*o*wing.

S*oo*n night tim*e* was falling,

And _Mama_ was calling.

I had to st*a*rt g*o*ing,

For now it was gr*o*wing, d*a*rk.

Now I will show you a picture of
the boy from the poem.

Look at the picture. What is the boy doing? Yes, that's right. He is mopping the floor. Why do you think he needs to mop the floor? Who made the mess on the floor? Yes, the frog that was hopping made the mess. The frog tracked mud into the house.

Can you see from where the frog escaped? Who do you think had put him in the jar? Yes, probably the boy had caught the frog and put him in the jar.

Next, I will write three of the lines you just read from the poem on index cards.

(Have the child watch as you write each word with a pen. Label the first card with the lesson number for future use.)

| The | cOld | wind |

| was | blOwing, |

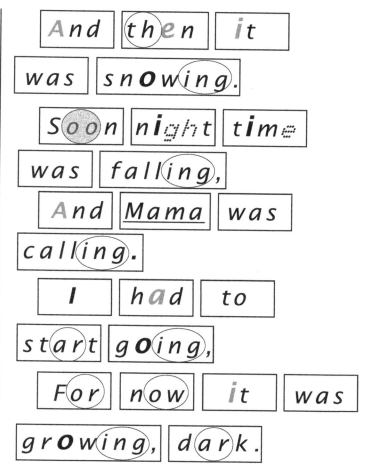

(**Note**: You may eliminate some of the print clues from the index cards with which your child is familiar. Be sure to include the print clues for sounds that have been recently introduced.)

I will underline the sight word *Mama* with a black crayon. I will trace over the *iii* sounds (as in *pig*), the *aaa* sounds (as in *cat*), and the *eee* sound (as in *wet*) with a gray crayon.

I will trace over the bold *o* sounds (as in *hope* and *show*) and the bold *i* sounds (as in *night* and *bike*) with a black crayon.

I will make dotted lines over the letters *g* and *h* in the word *night*. I will make dotted lines over the letter *e* in the word *time*. Can you tell me why I dotted these letters? That's right, they are silent. They make no sound.

I will draw a gray ring around the *ing* sound (as in *sing*) in the words *blowing, snowing, falling, calling, going,* and *growing.* I will also draw a gray ring around the *th* sound (as in *thick* or *this*) in the word *then.* I will draw a shaded gray ring around the *oo* sound (as in *boot*) in the word *soon.*

I will draw a gray ring around the *ar* sound (as in *car*) in the word *start* and in the word *dark.* I will draw a gray ring around the *or* sound (as in *corn*) in the word *for.* I will also draw a gray ring around the *ow* sound (as in *cow*) in the word *now.*

Read the lines from the poem. Good! Can you tell me which words in this part of the poem rhyme? Which words rhyme with *blowing?* Which word rhymes with *falling?*

Look at the index cards from the first line of the poem. Find the index card with the comma. Very good! What does the comma tell us? That's right. It tells us to pause before reading the next line of the poem. Commas are often used in poems. Can you find the other commas on the rest of the index cards?

Now I will mix the cards, and you can put them in the proper order to make the sentences again.

(Assist the child with putting the cards in proper order. Keep the cards from each sentence separate. Remind him, if necessary, a sentence begins with an uppercase letter and ends with a period or some other form of punctuation.)

Now read the sentences.

(**Note**: We are no longer using clues to assist the child with reading the copy work. It is important for the child to read the text located in this segment of the lesson even if he does not copy the sentences. This will give him an opportunity to practice reading text printed in a regular type.)

Copy Work: (The copy work is optional for children who have difficulty with writing.) (You may now encourage the child to copy the sentences directly from the model below. If this is too difficult, continue as directed.)

I will write the lines from the poem you just read on a piece of paper.

(Neatly write the sentences with a pen, paying close attention to letter spacing and formation.)

Now you can copy what I wrote.

The cold wind was blowing,
And then it was snowing.
Soon night time was falling,
And Mama was calling.
I had to start going,
For now it was growing, dark.

I would like for you to read the sentences once more. Very good! I would like for you to draw a picture to go

318

with your sentences. Here is a picture of some clouds and the moon you can draw.

(Assist the child with drawing the picture if necessary. The picture has been drawn with bold lines so the child may trace it if he likes.)

(**Note:** You may choose to encourage the child to dictate a short story to you about the picture he drew instead of only one sentence.)

Make up a story about the clouds and the moon you drew. Tell me the story, and I will write it on a piece of paper. Now you can copy one sentence from your story at the bottom of your picture.

(Draw lines if necessary for the child to write his sentence at the bottom of his picture.)

Read the story you dictated to me.

(Assist the child by reading any difficult words for him. If the story is long, have him read part of it and you read part of it.)

Now let's read a book together.

(Review material between lessons.)

Lesson 80

Materials: reading manual, index cards, pen, gray crayon, black crayon, and one construction paper circle.

Instructions: In today's lesson, the child will review the following sight words: *there, where, your, would, could, should, with, water, people, who, that,* and *two*. The child will be introduced to the new sight word *once*. Prepare one construction paper circle with the new sight word written on it.

He will be introduced to the *er* sound as in *her*. He will read the following words containing the *er* sound: *her, berg, fern, jerk, perk, serve, term, verse,* and *swerve*. He will also be introduced to the use of the *er* sound when it is added to the end of a word such as *taller*. He will read the following words with the *er* sound as in *taller*: *bigger, smaller, taller, shorter, faster, slower, lighter, darker, louder, softer, colder,* and *hotter*.

The child will read the following story and complete a variety of exercises based on the story.

Title: *"The Small Horse"*

Story: *Once there was a small horse who was sad. Her name was Rose.*

She said to the big horse, "I am sad. I am so small. I want to big big like you. You are bigger than all of the horses in the barn."

The big horse said, "Do not be sad. Once I was smaller than you. I was slower than all of the horses in the barn. Now I am bigger and faster than all of the horses in the barn."

The small horse said, "How did you get to be so big and fast?"

The big horse said, "Each day I ate all of my food. Soon I was growing and growing."

The two horses saw a man. It was the farmer.

The big horse said, "Here comes the farmer now. He has some hay for us. Eat all of your hay and soon you will be bigger and faster too."

Dialogue: Read the sight words below.

there	*where*
your	*would*
could	*should*

with   _water_

people   _who_

that   _two_

Look at the word below. It is the new sight word _once_. (Point to the word as you read it.)

once

Say _once_ as I point to the word.

Very good! Let's add the new sight word to your _Sight Word Worm_.

Now read the sentences below. You will find several sight words in these sentences.

(We are no longer underlining the following sight words as the child should be acquainted with them: _I, the, was, is, to, said,_ and _you_.)

Once there was **a**

fat pig who had

two bo**a**ts.

H**e** was pl**a**ying in

the water with his

bo**a**ts.

Look at the letters below. These letters make the _er_ sound (as in _her_). You will notice these letters have a gray ring around them to help you see them more easily. (Point to the letters as you make the sound.)

(er)

Say _er_ as I point to the letters. Very good!

Now look at the word below. This word has the _er_ sound (as in _her_). It is the word _her_.

h(er)

Read the words below that have the _er_ sound.

h(er)   b(er)g

f(er)n   j(er)k

p(er)k   s(er)ve

t(er)m   v(er)se

sw(er)ve

Read the word below.

t(all)

Very good! It is the word _tall_.

We can add the _er_ sound (as in _her_) to the end of the word _tall_ to make a new word. Look at the word below. It is the word _taller_. (Point to the word as you read it.)

tall(er)

Read the words below that have the _er_ sound (as in _her_) added to the end of the word.

bigg(er)   small(er)

tall(er)   sh(or)t(er)

faster   slower

lighter   darker

louder   softer

colder   hotter

Read the story below, and then I will show you a picture to go with the story.

(**Note**: We are no longer underlining the following sight words: *I, the, is, to, said, was, has,* and *you.* We are no longer dotting the letter *k* in the blend *ck.* We are no longer dotting the letter *y* as in *way* or the letter *w* as in *crow.* We are no longer drawing a ring around several beginning blends.)

"The Small Horse"

Once there was a small horse

who was sad. Her name was Rose.

She said to the big horse,

"I am sad. I am so small.

I want to be big like you.

You are bigger than all

of the horses in the barn."

The big horse said, "Do not be sad.

Once I was smaller than you.

I was slower than all of

the horses in the barn.

Now I am bigger and faster than

all of the horses in the barn."

The small horse said, "How did you get to be so big and fast?"

The big horse said,

"Each day I ate all of my food. Soon I was growing and growing."

The two horses saw a man. It was the farmer.

The big horse said, "Here comes the farmer now. He has some hay for us. Eat all of your hay and soon you will be bigger and faster too."

Now I will show you a picture of the small horse and the big horse.

Look at the picture. Why is the small horse sad? That's right. She is sad, because she wants to be big. See how little she is next to the big horse.

What did the big horse tell the small horse to do to help her to grow big? Yes, she told her to eat all of her food. What kind of food does she eat? In the story she is eating hay. Do you know what other kinds of food horses eat? They like oats. Do people eat hay? No, people do not eat hay, but people eat oats. Sometimes people cook the oats and make oatmeal.

Next, I will write three of the sentences you just read on index cards.

(Have the child watch as you write each word with a pen. Label the first card with the lesson number for future use.)

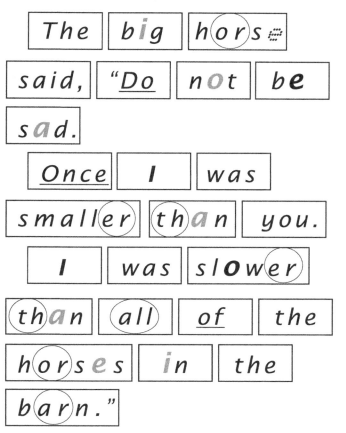

(**Note**: You may eliminate some of the print clues from the index cards with which your child is familiar. Be sure to include the print clues for sounds that have been recently introduced.)

I will underline the sight words *do, once,* and *of* with a black crayon. Next, I will trace over the *iii* sounds (as in *pig*), the *ooo* sound (as in *hot*), the *aaa* sounds (as in *cat*), and the *eee* sound (as in *wet*) with a gray crayon.

I will trace over the bold *e* sound (as in *heat*) and the bold *o* sound (as in *show*) with a black crayon.

I will make dotted lines over the letter *e* in the word *horse*. I will draw a

gray ring around the *or* sound (as in *corn*) in the word *horse* and in the word *horses*.

I will draw a gray ring around the *er* sound (as in *her*) in the word *smaller* and in the word *slower*. I will draw a gray ring around the *th* sound (as in *thick* or *this*) in the word *than*. I will also draw a gray ring around the *all* sound (as in *ball*) in the word *all* and around the *ar* sound (as in *car*) in the word *barn*.

Read the sentences. Great! Can you find the index cards that have the quotation marks on them? Good, the index cards with the words *Do* and *barn* have the quotation marks on them. (Point to the quotation marks on the index cards.)

The big horse said, "Do not be sad. Once I was smaller than you. I was slower than all of the horses in the barn." Remember, the words spoken by a character go inside the quotation marks.

Look at the index cards from the first sentence. Find the index card with the comma. Very good! What does the comma tell us? That's right. It tells us to pause before reading the next part of the sentence. A comma is used before quotation marks. (Point to the beginning quotation mark on the index card with the word *Do*.)

Now I will mix the cards, and you can put them in the proper order to make the sentences again.

(Assist the child with putting the cards in proper order. Keep the cards from each sentence separate. Remind him, if necessary, a sentence begins with an uppercase letter and ends with a period or some other form of punctuation.)

Now read the sentences.

Copy Work: (The copy work is optional for children who have difficulty with writing.) (You may now encourage the child to copy the sentences directly from the model below. If this is too difficult, continue as directed.)

I will write the sentences you just read on a piece of paper.

(Neatly write the sentences with a pen, paying close attention to letter spacing and formation.)

Now you can copy what I wrote.

The big horse said, "Do not be sad. Once I was smaller than you. I was slower than all of the horses in the barn."

I would like for you to read the sentences once more. Very good! I would like for you to draw a picture to go with your sentences. Here is a picture of a barn you can draw.

(Assist the child with drawing the picture if necessary. The picture has been drawn with bold lines so the child may trace it if he likes.)

(**Note:** You may choose to encourage the child to dictate a short story to you about the picture he drew instead of only one sentence.)

Make up a story about the barn you drew. Tell me the story, and I will write it on a piece of paper. Now you can copy one sentence from your story at the bottom of your picture.

(Draw lines if necessary for the child to write his sentence at the bottom of his picture.)

Read the story you dictated to me.

(Assist the child by reading any difficult words for him. If the story is long, have him read part of it and you read part of it.)

Now let's read a book together.

(Review material between lessons.)

Lesson 81

Materials: reading manual, index cards, pen, gray crayon, and black crayon.

Instructions: In today's lesson, the child will review the following sight words: *once, does, want, are, two, put, Mama, Papa, with, water, people, who,* and *that.*

He will review the *aw* sound as in *saw* by reading the following words: *saw, paw, claw, flaw, draw,* and *raw.*

The child will review the *er* sound as in *her* by reading the following words: *her, serve, term,* and *verse.* He will review the *er* sound when it is added to the end of a word such as *taller* by reading the following words: *bigger, taller, faster, lighter, louder,* and *colder.*

The child will be introduced to the *ir* sound as in *bird.* He will read the following words containing the *ir* sound: *bird, third, skirt, shirt, dirt, girl, swirl, sir, stir,* and *firm.*

The child will read the following story and complete a variety of exercises based on the story.

Title: *"The Girl in the Park"*

Story: *Once there was a kind girl. She rode her bike to the park. She put her bike by the swing. She could hear a sound. The sound was near the tree. She saw a small bird on the ground. The bird could not fly.*

The girl said to the small bird, "Did you break your wing? I will help you. My papa can fix your wing. Come home with me."

The girl put the bird in the box on her bike.

The bird said, "Cheep, cheep."

The bird was sad.

The girl said, "Do not be sad. Soon you will be well. I will feed you seeds. I will give you water too. I will take good care of you."

Dialogue: Read the sight words below.

once   does

want   are

two   put

Mama   Papa

with   water

people   who

that

Look at the letters below. What sound do these letters make? (*aw* as in *saw.*)

a w

Very good! These letters make the *aw* sound.

Read the words below that have the *aw* sound (as in *saw*).

saw   paw

claw   flaw

draw   raw

Look at the letters below. What sound do these letters make? (*er* as in *her.*)

er

Very good! These letters make the *er* sound.

Read the words below that have the *er* sound (as in *her*).

her   serve

term   verse

Read the word below.

cold

That's right. It is the word *cold*. Now read the word *cold* with the *er* sound added to the end.

c **o** ld(er)

Good! It is the word *colder*. Now read the words below with the *er* sound added to the end.

b **i** gg(er)   ta ll(er)

f **a** st(er)   l **i** gh t(er)

l(ou)d(er)   c **o** ld(er)

Look at the letters below. These letters also make the *ir* sound (as in *bird*). (Point to the letters as you make the sound.)

(i r)

Say *ir* (as in *bird*) as I point to the letters. You will notice these letters have a gray ring around them to help you see them more easily.

Read the words below that have the *ir* sound. I will read the first word for you. It is *bird*.

b(i r)d   t h(i r)d

s k(i r)t   s h(i r)t

d(i r)t   g(i r)l

s w(i r)l   s(i r)

s t(i r)   f(i r)m

Read the words below. These words will appear in today's story.

(Assist the child with reading any difficult words.)

k **i** nd   w(i n)g

br **e a** k   h e **a** r

f **i** x   s w(i n)g

(c h) **e e** p   s(o u)n d

c **a** re   fly

g r(o u)n d

Read the story below, and then I will show you a picture to go with the story.

(**Note**: We are no longer underlining the following sight words: *I, the, is, to, said, was, has,* and *you*. We are no longer dotting the letter *k* in the blend *ck*. We are no longer dotting the letter *y* as in *way* or the letter *w* as in *crow*. We are no longer drawing a ring around several beginning blends.)

"The G(i r)l **i** n the P(a r)k"

Once there was **a** k **i** nd g(i r)l.

She rode her bike to the park.

She put her bike by the swing.

She could hear a sound.

The sound was near the tree.

She saw a small bird on the ground.

The bird could not fly.

The girl said to the small bird,

"Did you break your wing?

I will help you.

My papa can fix your wing.

Come home with me."

The girl put the bird in

the box on her bike.

The bird said, "Cheep, cheep."

The bird was sad.

The girl said, "Do not be sad.

Soon you will be well.

I will feed you seeds.

I will give you water too.

I will take good care of you."

Now I will show you a picture of the girl and the bird.

Look at the picture. How do you think the bird got hurt? What do you see lying on the ground? That's right, you can see the bird's nest lying on the ground. Somehow, the nest fell from the tree. What do you think may have made the nest fall? Does the weather give you a clue? That's right. It is a very windy day. How can you tell it is a windy day?

Next, I will write four of the sentences from the story you just read on index cards.

(Have the child watch as you write each word with a pen. Label the first card with the lesson number for future use.)

The girl said to the small bird, "Did you break your wing? I will help you. My papa can fix your wing. Come home with me."

(**Note**: You may eliminate some of the print clues from the index cards with which your child is familiar. Be sure to include the print clues for sounds that have been recently introduced.)

I am going to underline four different sight words today with a black crayon. Can you read the sight words I have underlined?

Next, I will trace over the *iii* sounds (as in *pig*), the *eee* sound (as in *wet*), and the *aaa* sound (as in *cat*) with a gray crayon.

I will trace over the bold *a* sound (as in *cake*), the bold *o* sound (as in *hope*), and the bold *e* sound (as in *heat*) with a black crayon.

I will make dotted lines over the letter *e* in the word *break*. I will also make dotted lines over the letter *e* in the word *home*. Can you tell me why I dotted these letters? That's right, I dotted them, because they are silent. They make no sound.

I will draw a gray ring around the *ir* sound (as in *bird*) in the word *girl* and in the word *bird*. I will draw a gray ring around the *all* sound (as in *ball*) in the word *small*. I will also draw a gray ring around the *ing* sound (as in *sing*) in the word *wing*.

I will put a gray dot over the letter *y* in the word *my*. Can you tell me why I put a gray dot over this letter? What sound does this letter make? That's right, it makes the bold *i* sound (as in *fly*).

Read the sentences. Great! Find the index cards that have the quotation marks on them. Why do we use quotation marks? That's right, we use quotation marks when a character is speaking. Who is speaking in these sentences? To whom is the girl talking?

Now I will mix the cards, and you can put them in the proper order to make the sentences again.

(Assist the child with putting the cards in proper order. Keep the cards from each sentence separate. Remind him, if necessary, a sentence begins with an uppercase letter and ends with a period or some other form of punctuation.)

Now read the sentences.

Copy Work: (The copy work is optional for children who have difficulty with writing.) (You may now encourage the child to copy the sentences directly from the model below. If this is too difficult, continue as directed.)

I will write the sentences you just read on a piece of paper.

(Neatly write the sentences with a pen, paying close attention to letter spacing and formation.)

Now you can copy what I wrote.

The girl said to the small bird, "Did you break your wing? I will help you. My papa can fix your wing. Come home with me."

I would like for you to read the sentences once more.

Very good! I would like for you to draw a picture to go with your sentences. Here is a picture of a bird you can draw.

(Assist the child with drawing the picture if necessary. The picture has been drawn with bold lines so the child may trace it if he likes.)

329

(**Note:** You may choose to encourage the child to dictate a short story to you about the picture he drew instead of only one sentence.)

Make up a story about the bird you drew. Tell me the story, and I will write it on a piece of paper. Now you can copy one sentence from your story at the bottom of your picture.

(Draw lines if necessary for the child to write his sentence at the bottom of his picture.)

Read the story you dictated to me.

(Assist the child by reading any difficult words for him. If the story is long, have him read part of it and you read part of it.)

Now let's read a book together.

(Review material between lessons.)

Lesson 82

Materials: reading manual, index cards, pen, gray crayon, and black crayon.

Instructions: In today's lesson, the child will review the following sight words: *one, many, with, water, people, who, want, that, two,* and *once.*

He will review the *er* sound as in *taller* by reading the following words: *smaller, taller, brighter, lighter, older,* and *colder.*

The child will review the *ir* sound as in *bird* by reading the following words: *bird, skirt, shirt, dirt, girl, sir, stir,* and *firm.*

The child will read the following story and complete a variety of exercises based on the story.

Title: *"The Cub in the Woods"*

Story: *Once there was a cub. He was smaller than all the cubs in the woods.*

His Mama said, "You must stay on the path. You must not go too far."

The cub said, "I will go for a walk. I will not go far. I will stay on the path."

Then the cub saw a mouse.

He said, "I will chase the mouse."

The cub ran and ran. He could not catch the mouse. The mouse ran off the path. The cub did not stay on the path. The cub could not catch the mouse. He got a thorn in his paw. The mouse could hear the cub crying. He quit running. The mouse saw the thorn in the cub's paw.

He said, "I have sharp teeth. I can take out the thorn."

"Thank you," said the cub. "Mama was right. I should stay on the path. I should not go too far."

Dialogue: Read the sight words below.

<u>one</u>	<u>many</u>
<u>with</u>	<u>water</u>
<u>people</u>	<u>who</u>
<u>want</u>	<u>that</u>
<u>two</u>	<u>once</u>

Read the words below with the *er* sound (as in *taller*).

smaller   taller

brighter   lighter

older   colder

Look at the letters below. What sound do these letters make? (*ir* as in *bird*.)

ir

Very good! These letters make the *ir* sound.

Read the words below that have the *ir* sound (as in *bird*).

bird   skirt

shirt   dirt

girl   sir

stir   firm

Read the words below. These words will appear in today's story.

(Assist the child with reading any difficult words.)

smaller   chase

quit   running

thorn   crying

paw   sharp

walk   path

Read the story below, and then I will show you a picture to go with the story.

(**Note**: We are no longer underlining the following sight words: *I, the, is, to, said, was, has,* and *you*. We are no longer dotting the letter *k* in the blend *ck*. We are no longer dotting the letter *y* as in *way* or the letter *w* as in *crow*. We are no longer drawing a ring around several beginning blends.)

"The Cub in the Woods"

Once there was **a** cub.

He was smaller than all the

cubs in the woods.

His Mama said,

"You must stay on the path.

You must not go too far."

331

The cub said, "I will go for a walk.

I will not go far.

I will stay on the path."

Then the cub saw a mouse.

He said, "I will chase the mouse."

The cub ran and ran.

He could not catch the mouse.

The mouse ran off the path.

The cub did not stay on the path.

The cub could not catch the mouse.

He got a thorn in his paw.

The mouse could hear the cub crying.

He quit running.

The mouse saw the thorn

in the cub's paw.

He said, "I have sharp teeth.

I can take out the thorn."

"Thank you," said the cub.

"Mama was right.

I should stay on the path.

I should not go too far."

Now I will show you a picture of the cub.

Look at the picture. What happened to the cub? How did he get hurt? That's right. He got a thorn in his paw. Who helped the cub? Yes, the mouse helped the cub. The mouse showed kindness even to an enemy. Do you think the cub would have gotten hurt if he had obeyed his mother? No, he probably would not have gotten hurt if he had stayed on the path.

Next, I will write four of the sentences from the story you just read on index cards.

(Have the child watch as you write each word with a pen. Label the first card with the lesson number for future use.)

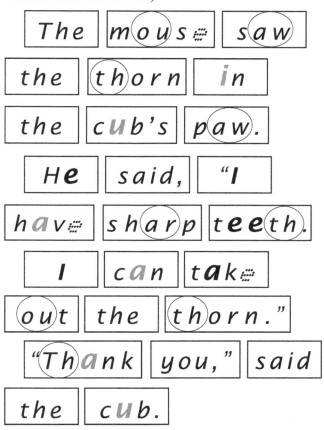

(**Note**: You may eliminate some of the print clues from the index cards with which your child is familiar. Be sure to include the print clues for sounds that have been recently introduced.)

(No sight words will be underlined today, as the child should be familiar with the sight words used in this portion of the lesson.)

Next, I will trace over the *iii* sound (as in *pig*), the *uuu* sounds (as in *cub*), and the *aaa* sounds (as in *cat*) with a gray crayon.

I will trace over the bold *e* sounds (as in *heat*) and the bold *a* sound (as in *cake*) with a black crayon.

I will make dotted lines over the letter *e* in the following words: *mouse, have,* and *take.* Can you tell me why I dotted these letters? That's right, I dotted them, because they are silent. They make no sound.

I will draw a gray ring around the *ou* sound (as in *house*) in the word *mouse* and in the word *out.* I will draw a gray ring around the *aw* sound (as in *saw*) in the word *saw* and in the word *paw.* I will draw a gray ring around the *th* sound (as in *thick* or *this*) in the following words: *thorn, teeth,* and *thank.* I will also draw a gray ring around the *ar* sound (as in *car*) in the word *sharp.*

Read the sentences. Very good! Find the index cards that have the quotation marks on them. Why do we use quotation marks? That's right, we use quotation marks when a character is speaking. Who is speaking in these sentences?

Now I will mix the cards, and you can put them in the proper order to make the sentences again.

(Assist the child with putting the cards in proper order. Keep the cards from each sentence separate. Remind him, if necessary, a sentence begins with an uppercase letter and ends with a period or some other form of punctuation.)

Now read the sentences.

(**Note**: We are no longer using clues to assist the child with reading the copy work. It is important for the child to read the text located in this segment of the lesson even if he does not copy the sentences.)

This will give him an opportunity to practice reading text printed in a regular type.)

Copy Work: (The copy work is optional for children who have difficulty with writing.) (You may now encourage the child to copy the sentences directly from the model below. If this is too difficult, continue as directed.)

I will write the sentences you just read on a piece of paper.

(Neatly write the sentences with a pen, paying close attention to letter spacing and formation.)

Now you can copy what I wrote.

The mouse saw the thorn in the cub's paw.

He said, "I have sharp teeth. I can take out the thorn."

"Thank you," said the cub.

I would like for you to read the sentences once more. Very good! I would like for you to draw a picture to go with your sentences. Here is a picture of a cub you can draw.

(Assist the child with drawing the picture if necessary. The picture has been drawn with bold lines so the child may trace it if he likes.)

(**Note:** You may choose to encourage the child to dictate a short story to you about the picture he drew instead of only one sentence.)

Make up a story about the cub you drew. Tell me the story, and I will write it on a piece of paper. Now you can copy one sentence from your story at the bottom of your picture.

(Draw lines if necessary for the child to write his sentence at the bottom of his picture.)

Read the story you dictated to me.

(Assist the child by reading any difficult words for him. If the story is long, have him read part of it and you read part of it.)

Now let's read a book together.

(Review material between lessons.)

Lesson 83

Materials: reading manual, index cards, pen, gray crayon, black crayon, and two construction paper circles.

Instructions: In today's lesson, the child will review the following sight words: *from, many, what, once, two, with, water, people, who,* and *that.* He will be introduced to two new sight words: *caught* and *taught.* Prepare two construction paper circles with the new sight words written on them.

The child will review the *er* sound as in *her* by reading the following words: *her, verse, smaller, older, slower, darker,* and *hotter.* He will review the *ir* sound as in *bird* by reading the following words: *bird, skirt, dirt, girl, sir,* and *stir.*

The child will be introduced to the *ur* sound as in *turn.* He will read the following words containing the *ur* sound: *turn, burn, burp, curb, curl, fur, hurt,* and *curve.*

The child will read the following story and complete a variety of exercises based on the story.

Title: *"The Small Red Car"*

Story: *Once there was a small red car. This car was an odd car. This car could drive by itself.*

One day the car said, "I think I will go for a drive. I will drive to the farm."

The car drove down the road. It came to a curve in the road. It did not turn. It hit the curb.

The small red car said, "Ouch! I hurt my wheels."

It drove on and on. Soon it came to a stop light. The light was red. It did not stop. A girl saw the small red car. She was in a green car.

She said, "Stop. You will get hurt."

The small red car said, "It is not safe for me to drive. I will turn and go back home."

Dialogue: Read the sight words below.

from   many

what   once

two   with

water   people

who   that

Look at the word below. It is a new sight word. It is the word *caught*. (Point to the word as you read it.)

caught

Say *caught* as I point to the word. Very good!

Now look at the next new sight word below. It is the word *taught*. (Point to the word as you read it.)

taught

Say *taught* as I point to the word. Very good!

Did you notice these two words rhyme? Look at the two new sight words below. Which word is *caught*? Which word is *taught*?

taught   caught

Read the sentences below that have the new sight words.

Dad taught me how to fish.

I caught a big fish in the lake.

Let's add the new sight words to your *Sight Word Worm*.

Look at the letters below. What sound do these letters make? (*er* as in *her*.)

er

Very good! These letters make the *er* sound.

Read the words below that have the *er* sound (as in *her*).

her   **verse**

smaller   **older**

slower   **darker**

hotter

Look at the letters below. What sound do these letters make? (*ir* as in *bird*.)

ir

Very good! These letters make the *ir* sound.

Read the words below that have the *ir* sound (as in *bird*).

bird   **skirt**

dirt   **girl**

sir   **stir**

Look at the letters below. These letters also make the *ur* sound (as in *turn*). (Point to the letters as you make the sound.)

ur

Say *ur* as I point to the letters above.

Very good!

Now read the words below that have the *ur* sound (as in *turn*). I will read the first word for you. It is *turn*.

turn   **burn**

b(u)rp   c(u)rb
c(u)rl   f(u)r
h(u)rt   c(u)rve

Read the words below.

it   s(e)lf

Now put the two words together and read the new word.

itself

Very good! Read the word again as I point to it.

Read the following words. These words will appear in the story.

(Assist the child with reading any difficult words.)

c(ar)   odd

drive   its(e)lf

dr(o)ve   wh(ee)ls

li(gh)t   gr(ee)n

ou(ch)

Read the story below, and then I will show you a picture to go with the story.

(**Note**: We are no longer underlining the following sight words: *I, the, is, to, said, was, has,* and *you*. We are no longer dotting the letter *k* in the blend *ck*. We are no longer dotting the letter *y* as in *way* or the letter *w* as in *crow*. We are no longer drawing a ring around several beginning blends.)

"The Sm(all) R(e)d C(ar)"

<u>Once</u> <u>there</u> was **a** sm(all) red c(ar).

(Th)is c(ar) was (a)n odd c(ar).

(Th)is c(ar) <u>could</u> drive by its(e)lf.

<u>One</u> d**a**y the c(ar) said,

"I (th)ink I will g**o** f(or) **a** dr**i**ve.

I will drive to the f(ar)m."

The c(ar) dr(o)ve d(ow)n the r(o)ad.

It c**a**me to **a** c(ur)ve in the r(o)ad.

It did not turn. It hit the curb.

The small red car said,

"Ouch! I hurt my wheels."

It drove on and on.

Soon it came to a stop light.

The light was red. It did not stop.

A girl saw the small red car.

She was in a green car.

She said, "Stop. You will get hurt."

The small red car said,

"It is not safe for me to drive.

I will turn and go back home."

Now I will show you a picture of the small car.

338

Look at the picture. Does the small car look happy? No, he does not look very happy. Why do you think he is unhappy? Yes, he is probably unhappy, because he hit the curb.

Is anyone in the small car? No, there is no one in the car. Do you think the car would be happier if someone was driving it? Why do you think this?

Next, I will write four sentences from the story you just read on index cards.

(Have the child watch as you write each word with a pen. Label the first card with the lesson number for future use.)

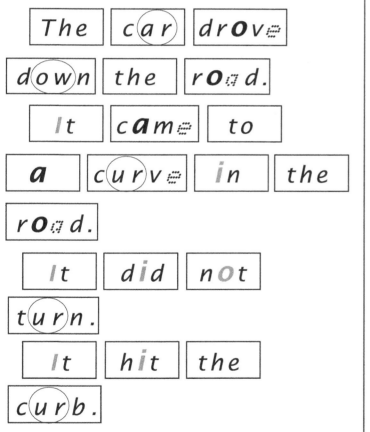

(**Note**: You may eliminate some of the print clues from the index cards with which your child is familiar. Be sure to include the print clues for sounds that have been recently introduced.)

(No sight words will be underlined today, as the child should be familiar with the sight words used in this portion of the lesson.)

I will trace over the *iii* sounds (as in *pig*) and the *ooo* sound (as in *hot*) with a gray crayon.

I will trace over the bold *o* sounds (as in *hope*) and the bold *a* sounds (as in *cake*) with a black crayon.

I will make dotted lines over the letter *e* in the words *drove, came,* and *curve*. I will also make dotted lines over the letter *a* in the word *road*. Can you tell me why I dotted these letters? That's right, I dotted them, because they are silent. They make no sound.

I will draw a gray ring around the *ar* sound (as in *car*) in the word *car*. I will draw a gray ring around the *ow* sound (as in *cow*) in the word *down*. I will also draw a gray ring around the *ur* sound (as in *turn*) in the words *curve, turn,* and *curb*.

Read the sentences. Very good! Now I will mix the cards, and you can put them in the proper order to make the sentences again.

(Assist the child with putting the cards in proper order. Keep the cards from each sentence separate. Remind him, if necessary, a sentence begins with an uppercase letter and ends with a period or some other form of punctuation.)

Now read the sentences.

(**Note**: We are no longer using clues to assist the child with reading the copy work. It is important for the child to read the text located in this segment of the lesson even if he does not copy the sentences. This will give him an opportunity to practice reading text printed in a regular type.)

Copy Work: (The copy work is optional for children who have difficulty with writing.) (You may now encourage the child to copy the sentences directly from the model below. If this is too difficult, continue as directed.)

I will write the sentences you just read on a piece of paper.

(Neatly write the sentences with a pen, paying close attention to letter spacing and formation.)

Now you can copy what I wrote.

The car drove down the road. It came to a curve in the road. It did not turn. It hit the curb.

I would like for you to read the sentences once more. Very good! I would like for you to draw a picture to go with your sentences. Here is a picture of a car you can draw.

(Assist the child with drawing the picture if necessary. The picture has been drawn with bold lines so the child may trace it if he likes.)

(**Note:** You may choose to encourage the child to dictate a short story to you about the picture he drew instead of only one sentence.)

Make up a story about the car you drew. Tell me the story, and I will write it on a piece of paper. Now you can copy one sentence from your story at the bottom of your picture.

(Draw lines if necessary for the child to write his sentence at the bottom of his picture.)

Read the story you dictated to me.

(Assist the child by reading any difficult words for him. If the story is long, have him read part of it and you read part of it.)

Now let's read a book together.

(Review material between lessons.)

Lesson 84

Materials: reading manual, index cards, pen, gray crayon, black crayon, and one construction paper circle.

Instructions: In today's lesson, the child will review the following sight words: *caught, taught, some, want, from, many, once, two, water, Mama, Papa,* and *that*. The child will be introduced to the new sight word *new*. Prepare one construction paper circle with the new sight word written on it.

The child will review the *er* sound as in *her* by reading the following words: *her, supper, bigger,* and *winner*. He will review the *ir* sound as in *bird* by reading the following words: *bird, shirt, dirt,* and *girl*. The child will review the *ur* sound as in *turn* by reading the following words: *turn, burn, fur,* and *hurt*.

The child will be introduced to the *ed* ending as in *played* and *looked*. He will read the following words containing the *ed* ending: *played, prayed, spilled, filled, mailed, nailed, looked, cooked, fixed,* and *mixed*.

The child will be introduced to the *ed* ending as in *landed*. He will read the following words containing the *ed* ending: *landed, sanded, fainted, painted, dusted, rusted, baited, waited,* and *wanted*.

The child will read the following story and complete a variety of exercises based on the story.

Title: *"The Old Bike"*

Story: *Tom had an old bike. He played with the bike for many years. The bike looked bad. The chain had rusted.*

Tom said, "I will fix my bike."

So, one day Tom sanded the old bike. He mixed some paint in a pail. Then he painted the old bike. It looked as good as new. A small boy saw the bike.

He said to Tom, "Will you paint my bike? I will pay you to fix my bike."

Tom fixed the small boy's bike. He painted it with bright red paint. The boy looked at the bike. He liked the bright red paint.

He said, "Thank you for fixing my bike. It looks like new."

Dialogue: Read the sight words below.

caught   taught

some   want

from   many

once   two

water   Mama

Papa   that

Look at the word below. It is the sight word *new*. (Point to the word as you read it.)

new

Say *new* as I point to the word. Very good!

Now read the sentence with the sight word in it.

The new girl sat in the hall.

Let's add the new sight word to your *Sight Word Worm*.

Look at the letters below. What sound do these letters make? (*er* as in *her*.)

er

Very good! They make the *er* sound.

Read the words below that contain the *er* sound (as in *her*).

her   supper

bigger   winner

Look at the letters below. What sound do these letters make? (*ir* as in *bird*.)

ir

Very good! They make the *ir* sound. Read the words below that contain the *ir* sound (as in *bird*).

b**ir**d   sh**ir**t

d**ir**t   g**ir**l

Look at the letters below. What sound do these letters make? (*ur* as in *turn*.)

ur

Very good! They make the *ur* sound. Read the words below that have the *ur* sound (as in *turn*).

t**ur**n   b**ur**n

f**ur**   h**ur**t

Read the word below.

play

We can add a *d* sound (say the letter sound, not the letter name) to the end of the word *play*. The new word is *played*. (Point to the word below as you read it.) Remember, the dotted letter is silent. It makes no sound.

play*e*d

Read the words below that have the *d* sound (say the letter sound, not the letter name) at the end.

play*e*d   pray*e*d

sp**i**ll*e*d   f**i**ll*e*d

m**ai**l*e*d   n**ai**l*e*d

l**oo**k*e*d   c**oo**k*e*d

f**i**x*e*d   m**i**x*e*d

Read the word below.

land

Now we will add the *eeed* sound (as in *landed*) to the end of this word to make a new word. The word is *landed*. (Point to the word below as you read it.)

l**a**nd*e*d

Read the words below that have the *eeed* sound (as in *landed*) at the end.

l**a**nd*e*d   s**a**nd*e*d

f**ai**nt*e*d   p**ai**nt*e*d

d**u**st*e*d   r**u**st*e*d

b**ai**t*e*d   w**ai**t*e*d

Read the sight word below.

<u>want</u>

Very good! Now we can add the *eeed* sound to the sight word *want* and get a new word. Read the new word below.

want*e*d

Great!
Read the words below. These words will appear in the story.
(Assist the child with reading any difficult words.)

br**i**g*h*t   c*h***ai**n

good   new

as   years

saw   thank

fixing

Read the story below, and then I will show you a picture to go with the story.

(**Note**: We are no longer underlining the following sight words: *I, the, is, to, said, was, has,* and *you.* We are no longer dotting the letter *k* in the blend *ck.* We are no longer dotting the letter *y* as in *way* or the letter *w* as in *crow.* We are no longer drawing a ring around several beginning blends.)

"The Old Bike"

Tom had an old bike.

He played with the bike for many years.

The bike looked bad.

The chain had rusted.

Tom said, "I will fix my bike."

So, one day Tom sanded the old bike.

He mixed some paint in a pail.

Then he painted the old bike.

It looked as good as new.

A small boy saw the bike.

He said to Tom,

"Will you paint my bike?

I will pay you to fix my bike."

Tom fixed the small boy's bike.

He painted it with bright red paint.

The boy looked at the bike.

He liked the bright red paint.

He said, "Thank you for fixing

my bike. It looks like new."

Now I will show you a picture of Tom and his bike.

Look at the picture. What is Tom doing? Yes, he is painting his bike. Do you think he did a good job painting his bike? What makes you think this? Do you think the small boy would have asked Tom to paint his bike if Tom had not done a good job on his own bike?

Next, I will write four sentences from the story you just read on index cards.

(Have the child watch as you write each word with a pen. Label the first card with the lesson number for future use.)

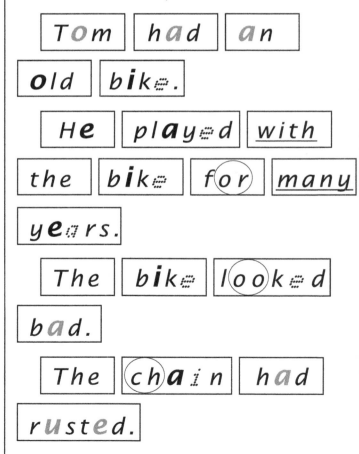

(**Note**: You may eliminate some of the print clues from the index cards with which your child is familiar. Be sure to include the print clues for sounds that have been recently introduced.)

I will underline two of the sight words with a black crayon. Can you read these sight words? I will trace over the *ooo* sound (as in *hot*) and the *aaa* sounds (as in *cat*) with a gray crayon. I will also trace over the *uuu* sound (as in *cub*) and the *eee* sound (as in *wet*) with a gray crayon.

I will trace over the bold *o* sound (as in *hope*) and the bold *i* sounds (as in *bike*) with a black crayon. I will also trace over the bold *e* sounds (as in *heat*) and the bold *a* sounds (as in *cake*) with a black crayon.

I will draw a gray ring around the *or* sound (as in *corn*) in the word *for*. I will draw a gray ring around the *oo* sound (as in *cook*) in the word *looked*. I will also draw a gray ring around the *ch* sound (as in *chip* and *patch*) in the word *chain*.

Read the sentences. Great! Now I will mix the cards from each sentence, and you can put them in the proper order to make the sentences again.

(Assist the child with putting the cards in proper order. Keep the cards from each sentence separate. Remind him, if necessary, a sentence begins with an uppercase letter and ends with a period or some other form of punctuation.)

Now read the sentences.

(**Note**: We are no longer using clues to assist the child with reading the copy work. It is important for the child to read the text located in this segment of the lesson even if he does not copy the sentences. This will give him an opportunity to practice reading text printed in a regular type.)

Copy Work: (The copy work is optional for children who have difficulty with writing.) (You may now encourage the child to copy the sentences directly from the model below. If this is too difficult, continue as directed.)

I will write the sentences you just read on a piece of paper.

(Neatly write the sentences with a pen, paying close attention to letter spacing and formation.)

Now you can copy what I wrote.

Tom had an old bike. He played with the bike for many years. The bike looked bad. The chain had rusted.

I would like for you to read the sentences once more. Very good! I would like for you to draw a picture to go with your sentences. Here is a picture of a bike you can draw.

(Assist the child with drawing the picture if necessary. The picture has been drawn with bold lines so the child may trace it if he likes.)

(**Note:** You may choose to encourage the child to dictate a short story to you about the picture he drew instead of only one sentence.)

Make up a story about the bike you drew. Tell me the story, and I will write it on a piece of paper. Now you can copy one sentence from your story at the bottom of your picture.

(Draw lines if necessary for the child to write his sentence at the bottom of his picture.)

Read the story you dictated to me.

(Assist the child by reading any difficult words for him. If the story is long, have him read part of it and you read part of it.)

Now let's read a book together.

(Review material between lessons.)

Lesson 85

Materials: reading manual, index cards, pen, gray crayon, and black crayon.

Instructions: In today's lesson, the child will review the following sight words: *new, caught, taught, water, where, there, with, people, who, want, what,* and *does.*

He will review the *ed* ending as in *played* and *looked* by reading the following words: *dropped, hopped, spilled, filled, smelled, yelled, looked, hooked, rained,* and *stained.* He will also review the *ed* ending as in *landed* by reading the following words: *needed, heeded, sounded, pounded, landed, handed, carted, started,* and *wanted.*

The child will be introduced to the long vowel sound for the letter *u* as in *cute.* This letter will be referred to as the bold *u* sound and will be represented with a bold letter as shown below.

u

Sometimes the bold letter *u* makes a slightly different sound. This is the *oo* sound as in *tune.* As the child reads words with the bold letter *u*, assist him in determining if the letter says *u* as in *cute* or *oo* as in *tune.* He will read the following words containing the bold *u* sound: *cute, mute, cube, tube, dune, tune, mule, rule, Luke, duke, fuse,* and *use.*

The child will read the following story and complete a variety of exercises based on the story.

Title: *"The Glad Mule"*

Story: *Once there was a mule. A man was riding the mule to town. The mule wanted to eat. He could not stop to eat. He had to take some bags on his back. Soon they saw a girl. The girl had a sack of corn on her head. The girl dropped the sack. Some of the corn spilled on the ground. The mule smelled the corn. The mule looked at the girl.*

The girl said, "You can eat the corn. It has dirt in it. I can not use it now."

The man said to the girl, "I will pay you for the corn."

He hopped down from the mule. He gave some coins to the girl. The girl was glad. The mule was glad too.

Dialogue: Read the sight words below.

<u>new</u> <u>caught</u>

<u>taught</u> <u>water</u>

<u>where</u> <u>there</u>

<u>with</u> <u>people</u>

<u>who</u> <u>want</u>

<u>what</u> <u>does</u>

Read the words below.

dropped hopped

spilled filled

smelled yelled

looked hooked

rained stained

Read the words below.

needed heeded

sounded pounded

landed handed

carted started

wanted

Look at the letter below. This letter makes the bold **u** sound (as in *cute*). (Point to the letter as you make the sound.)

u

Say **u** (as in *cute*) as I point to the letter. Very good!

Look at the word below. This word has the bold **u** sound (as in *cute*). It is the word *cute*. (Point to the word as you read it.)

c**u**te

Read the words below that have the bold **u** sound (as in *cute*).

c**u**te m**u**te

c**u**be t**u**be

d**u**ne t**u**ne

m**u**le r**u**le

L**u**ke d**u**ke

f**u**se **u**se

Read the words below. These words will appear in the story.

(Assist the child with reading any difficult words.)

r**i**ding wanted

bags soon

head ground

smelled dirt

coins girl

glad m**u**le

Read the story, and then I will show you a picture to go with the story.

(**Note**: We are no longer underlining the following sight words: *I, the, is, to, said, was, has,* and *you.* We are no longer dotting the letter *k* in the blend *ck.* We are no longer dotting the letter *y* as in *way* or the letter *w* as in *crow.* We are no longer drawing a ring around several beginning blends.)

"The Glad Mule"

Once there was a mule.

A man was riding the mule to town.

The mule wanted to eat.

He could not stop to eat.

He had to take some bags on his back.

Soon they saw a girl.

The girl had a sack of

corn on her head.

The girl dropped the sack.

Some of the corn spilled on the ground.

The mule smelled the corn.

The mule looked at the girl.

The girl said, "You can eat the corn.

It has dirt in it.

348

I can not use it now."

The man said to the girl,

"I will pay you for the corn."

He hopped down from the mule.

He gave some coins to the girl.

The girl was glad.

The mule was glad too.

Now I will show you a picture of the mule and the girl.

Look at the picture. What is the mule eating? That's right, he's eating the corn the girl spilled. Do you think the mule is happy? Why? Do you think the girl is happy? Why?

Now I will write four of the sentences you just read on index cards.

(Have the child watch as you write each word with a pen. Label the first card with the lesson number for future use.)

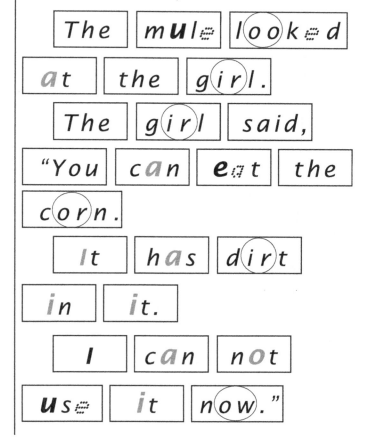

349

(**Note**: You may eliminate some of the print clues from the index cards with which your child is familiar. Be sure to include the print clues for sounds that have been recently introduced.)

(Today we will not underline any of the sight words, as the child should be familiar with the sight words in this passage.)

I will trace over the *aaa* sounds (as in *cat*), the *iii* sounds (as in *pig*), and the *ooo* sound (as in *hot*) with a gray crayon. I will trace over the bold *u* sounds (as in *cute*) and the bold *e* sound (as in *heat*) with a black crayon.

I will make dotted lines over the letter *e* in the word *mule, looked,* and *use*. I will also make dotted lines over the letter *a* in the word *eat*. Can you tell me why I dotted these letters? That's right. They are silent. They make no sound.

I will draw a gray ring around the *oo* sound (as in *cook*) in the word *looked*. I will draw a gray ring around the *ir* sound (as in *bird*) in the word *girl* and in the word *dirt*. I will also draw a gray ring around the *or* sound (as in *corn*) in the word *corn* and around the *ow* sound (as in *cow*) in the word *now*.

Read the sentences. Very good! Can you find the index cards that have the quotation marks on them? Why do we use these special marks? That's right, we use these marks when a character is speaking. Who is speaking? That's right, the girl is speaking.

Now I will mix the cards, and you can put them in the proper order to make the sentences again.

(Assist the child with putting the cards in proper order. Keep the cards from each sentence separate. Remind him, if necessary, a sentence begins with an uppercase letter and ends with a period or some other form of punctuation.)

Now read the sentences.

(**Note**: We are no longer using clues to assist the child with reading the copy work. It is important for the child to read the text located in this segment of the lesson even if he does not copy the sentences. This will give him an opportunity to practice reading text printed in a regular type.)

Copy Work: (The copy work is optional for children who have difficulty with writing.) (You may now encourage the child to copy the sentences directly from the model below. If this is too difficult, continue as directed.)

I will write the sentences you just read on a piece of paper.

(Neatly write the sentences with a pen, paying close attention to letter spacing and formation.)

Now you can copy what I wrote.

The mule looked at the girl. The girl said, "You can eat the corn. It has dirt in it. I can not use it now."

I would like for you to read the sentences once more. Very good! I would like for you to draw a picture to go with your sentences. Here is a picture of a mule you can draw.

(Assist the child with drawing the picture if necessary. The picture has been drawn with bold lines so the child may trace it if he likes.)

(**Note:** You may choose to encourage the child to dictate a short story to you about the picture he drew instead of only one sentence.)

Make up a story about the mule you drew. Tell me the story, and I will write it on a piece of paper. Now you can copy one sentence from your story at the bottom of your picture.

(Draw lines if necessary for the child to write his sentence at the bottom of his picture.)

Read the story you dictated to me.

(Assist the child by reading any difficult words for him. If the story is long, have him read part of it and you read part of it.)

Now let's read a book together.

(Review material between lessons.)

Lesson 86

Materials: reading manual, index cards, pen, gray crayon, and black crayon.

Instructions: In today's lesson, the child will review the following sight words: *new, caught, taught, water, people, Mama, Papa,* and *put.*

He will review the *ed* ending as in *played* and *looked* by reading the following words: *skipped, ripped, wagged,* and *dragged.* He will also review the *ed* ending as in *landed* by reading the following words: *skated, rated, tested,* and *rested.*

The child will review the bold *u* sound as in *cute* by reading the following words: *cute, mute, cube, tube, fuse,* and *use.*

The child will be introduced to the bold *e* sound made by the letter *y* at the end of words such as *baby.* He will read the following words containing the bold *e* sound as in *baby*: *baby, lady, happy, puppy, sunny, funny, dirty, mommy, daddy,* and *sleepy.* The letter *y* will be printed as a bold letter when it makes the bold *e* sound as shown below.

baby

The child will review the bold *i* sound as in *cry* by reading the following words: *cry, try, fry, sky, my, fly, sly, by,* and *why.*

He will read the following story and complete a variety of exercises based on the story.

Title: *"The Happy Baby"*

Story: *Once there was a baby girl. She was a happy baby. She was a cute baby. Her mommy and daddy were happy too. When she was sleepy she would cry for a bit. Then she would take a nap and be happy. One day the daddy got a puppy for the baby. The baby liked the puppy. The puppy licked the baby on the foot. It felt funny. The baby did not cry. She gave the puppy a big hug. Then the puppy licked the baby on the nose. The baby did not like this. She did not think that it was funny.*

She said to the puppy, "No, no!" The puppy looked at the baby. The puppy wagged his tail. The baby liked to see the puppy wag his tail.

Dialogue: Read the sight words below.

new   caught

taught   water

people   Mama

Papa   put

Read the words below.

skipped   ripped

wagged   dragged

skated   rated

tested   rested

Look at the letter below. What sound does this bold letter make? (*u* as in *cute*.)

u

Very good! This letter makes the bold *u* sound.

Read the words below that have the bold *u* sound (as in *cute*).

cute   mute

cube   tube

fuse   use

Look at the word below. (Point to the word as you read it.) It is the word *baby*.

baby

We have printed the letter *y* in a bold print. (Point to the letter *y*.) This bold *y* makes the bold *e* sound when it comes at the end of a word.

Read the word again as I point to it.

Very good! The word is *baby*. (Point to the word and emphasize the bold *e* sound.)

Read the words below that have the bold *e* sound at the end.

baby   lady

happy   puppy

sunny   funny

dirty   mommy

daddy   sleepy

Look at the word below. It is the word *cry*. Remember, the letter *y* makes the bold *i* sound when it has a gray dot over it.

cry

Read the words below.

cry   try   fry

sky   my   fly

sly   by   why

Read the words below. These words will appear in the story.

(Assist the child with reading any difficult words.)

were   liked

when   cry

think

Read the story below, and then I will show you a picture to go with the story.

(**Note**: We are no longer underlining the following sight words: *I, the, is, to, said, was, has,* and *you.* We are no longer dotting the letter *k* in the blend *ck.* We are no longer dotting the letter *y* as in *way* or the letter *w* as in *crow.* We are no longer drawing a ring around several beginning blends.)

"The Happy Baby"

Once there was a baby girl.

She was a happy baby.

She was a cute baby.

Her mommy and daddy

were happy too.

When she was sleepy

she would cry for a bit.

Then she would take a

nap and be happy.

One day the daddy got a

puppy for the baby.

The baby liked the puppy.

The puppy licked the baby on the foot.

It felt funny. The baby did not cry.

She gave the puppy a big hug.
Then the puppy licked the
baby on the nose.
The baby did not like this.
She did not think that it was funny.
She said to the puppy, "No, no!"
The puppy looked at the baby.
The puppy wagged his tail.
The baby liked to see the
puppy wag his tail.

Now I will show you a picture of the baby and the puppy.

Look at the picture. What is the puppy doing? That's right, he is licking the baby on the nose. Does the baby like this? What did the baby say to the puppy when he licked her on the nose? That's right, the baby said, "No, no!" What did the puppy do next? Yes, the puppy wagged his tail. Did the baby like this? Yes, she did.

Next I will write four sentences from the story you just read on index cards.

(Have the child watch as you write each word with a pen. Label the first card with the lesson number for future use.)

| The | puppy | licked |

354

the baby on the foot. It felt funny. The baby did not cry. She gave the puppy a big hug.

(**Note**: You may eliminate some of the print clues from the index cards with which your child is familiar. Be sure to include the print clues for new sounds that have been recently introduced.)

I will trace over the *uuu* sounds (as in *cub*) and the *iii* sounds (as in *pig*) with a gray crayon. I will trace over the *ooo* sounds (as in *hot*) and the *eee* sound (as in *wet*) with a gray crayon.

I will trace over the bold *e* sounds (as in *baby*) made by the letter *y* in the words *puppy, baby,* and *funny* with a black crayon. I will trace over the bold *a* sounds (as in *cake*) with a black crayon. I will also trace over the bold *e* sound (as in *heat*) in the word *she*.

I will put a gray dot over the bold *i* sound (as in *cry*) made by the letter *y* in the word *cry*. I will make dotted lines over the letter *e* in the word *licked* and in the word *gave*. Can you tell me why

I dotted these letters? That's right. They are silent. They make no sound.

I will draw a gray ring around the *oo* sound (as in *cook*) in the word *foot*.

Read the sentences. Great! Now I will mix the cards, and you can put them in the proper order to make the sentences again.

(Assist the child with putting the cards in proper order. Keep the cards from each sentence separate. Remind him, if necessary, a sentence begins with an uppercase letter and ends with a period or some other form of punctuation.)

Now read the sentences.

(**Note**: We are no longer using clues to assist the child with reading the copy work. It is important for the child to read the text located in this segment of the lesson even if he does not copy the sentences. This will give him an opportunity to practice reading text printed in a regular type.)

Copy Work: (The copy work is optional for children who have difficulty with writing.) (You may now encourage the child to copy the sentence directly from the model below. If this is too difficult, continue as directed.)

I will write the sentences you just read on a piece of paper.

(Neatly write the sentences with a pen, paying close attention to letter spacing and formation.)

Now you can copy what I wrote.

The puppy licked the baby on the foot. It felt funny. The baby did not cry. She gave the puppy a big hug.

I would like for you to read the sentences once more. Very good! I would like for you to draw a picture to go with your sentences. Here is a picture of a puppy you can draw.

(Assist the child with drawing the picture if necessary. The picture has been drawn with bold lines so the child may trace it if he likes.)

(**Note:** You may choose to encourage the child to dictate a short story to you about the picture he drew instead of only one sentence.)

Make up a story about the puppy you drew. Tell me the story, and I will write it on a piece of paper. Now you can copy one sentence from your story at the bottom of your picture.

(Draw lines if necessary for the child to write his sentence at the bottom of his picture.)

Read the story you dictated to me.

(Assist the child by reading any difficult words for him. If the story is long, have him read part of it and you read part of it.)

Now let's read a book together.

(Review material between lessons.)

Lesson 87

Materials: reading manual, index cards, pen, gray crayon, black crayon, and one construction paper circle.

Instructions: In today's lesson, the child will review the following sight words: *where, there, taught, caught, your, two,* and *new*. He will be introduced to the new sight word *learn*. Prepare one construction paper circle with the new sight word written on it.

The child will review the bold *u* sound as in *cute* by reading the following words: *cute, flute, June, tune, Luke,* and *duke*.

He will also review the bold *e* sound as in *baby* by reading the following words: *baby, rainy, silly, fuzzy, gloomy,* and *chilly*.

The child will be introduced to the *sss* sound made by the letter *c* in words such as *face*. He will read the following words containing the *sss* sound as in *face*: *face, race, lace, space, mice, rice, nice, slice, fence, hence, cell,* and *cent*. The *sss* sound made by the letter *c* will be represented as shown below with a gray ring around the letter *c*.

$$f\,a\,ⓒ e$$

The child will read the following story and complete a variety of exercises based on the story.

Title: *"The Silly Mice"*

Story: *Once there were five silly mice. They wanted to have a race. One of the mice was named June.*

June said, "Let us race to the fence."

All of the mice said, "That sounds good. We will race to the fence."

The mouse named Luke fell in the mud. He was not happy.

He said, "I have mud on my face. I do not like mud."

The mouse named June said, "I will help you."

She got a clean rag. She wiped his face.

Luke said, "Thank you. I do not want to race."

A mouse named Gus said, "I see a bag of rice in the grass."

The mice ran to the bag of rice.

A mouse named Russ said, "I will bite a hole in the bag. Then we can eat the rice."

All of the mice said, "Rice is nice."

Dialogue: Read the sight words below.

<u>where</u>   <u>there</u>

<u>taught</u>   <u>caught</u>

<u>your</u>   <u>two</u>

<u>new</u>

Look at the new sight word below. It is the word *learn.* (Point to the word as you read it.)

<u>learn</u>

Say *learn* as I point to the word.

Let's add the new sight word to your *Sight Word Worm.*

Very good! Now read the sentences below. The first sentence has the new sight word in it.

I can <u>learn</u> how

to read.

I will study

hard.

Look at the letter below. What sound does this bold letter make? (**u** as in *cute.*)

u

Very good! It makes the bold **u** sound (as in *cute*).

Read the words below that have the bold **u** sound (as in *cute*).

c**u**te   fl**u**te

J**u**ne   t**u**ne

L**u**ke   d**u**ke

Look at the word below. It is the word *baby.* (Point to the word as you read it.)

baby

Read the words below that have the bold *e* sound at the end of the word as in *baby.*

b a b**y**   r a i n**y**

s i l l**y**   f u z z**y**

g l o o m**y**   ch i l l**y**

Look at the word below. The letter c has a gray ring around it. That is because this letter makes a special sound. It makes the *sss* sound (as in *face*). (Point to the letter *c* as you make the *sss* sound.)

f a c e

The word is *face.* (Point to the word as you read it. Emphasize the *sss* sound.)

Read the words below that have the *sss* sound. Remember, the letter c with the gray ring around it makes the *sss* sound.

f a c e   r a c e

l a c e   s p a c e

mice   rice

nice   slice

fence   hence

cell   cent

Read the story below, and then I will show you a picture to go with the story.

(**Note**: We are no longer underlining the following sight words: *I, the, is, to, said, was, has,* and *you.* We are no longer dotting the letter *k* in the blend *ck.* We are no longer dotting the letter *y* as in *way* or the letter *w* as in *crow.* We are no longer drawing a ring around several beginning blends.)

"The Silly Mice"

Once there were five silly mice.

They wanted to have a race.

One of the mice was named June.

June said, "Let us race to the fence."

All of the mice said,

"That sounds good.

We will race to the fence."

The mouse named Luke fell in the mud.

He was not happy.

He said, "I have mud on my face.

I do not like mud."

The mouse named June said,

"I will help you."

358

She got a clean rag.

She wiped his face.

Luke said, "Thank you.

I do not want to race."

A mouse named Gus said,

"I see a bag of rice in the grass."

The mice ran to the bag of rice.

A mouse named Russ said,

"I will bite a hole in the bag.

Then we can eat the rice."

All of the mice said, "Rice is nice."

Now I will show you a picture of Luke and June.

Look at the picture. What happened to the little mouse named Luke? Yes, he fell in the mud. Who is helping him? That's right, it is a little mouse named June. How did she help Luke? Yes, she wiped his face with a clean rag. She was very kind.

Next, I will write four sentences from the story you just read on index cards.

(Have the child watch as you write each word with a pen. Label the first card with the lesson number for future use.)

The | mice | ran

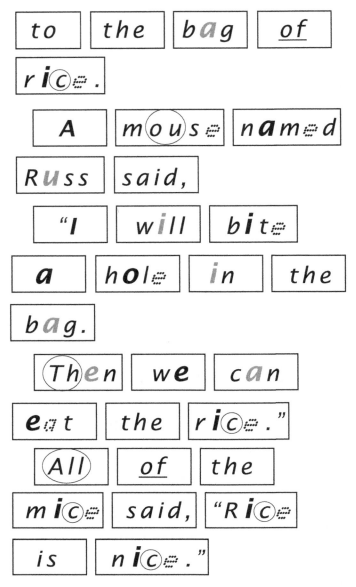

to the bag of

rice.

A mouse named

Russ said,

"I will bite

a hole in the

bag.

Then we can

eat the rice."

All of the

mice said, "Rice

is nice."

(**Note**: You may eliminate some of the print clues from the index cards with which your child is familiar. Be sure to include the print clues for sounds that have been recently introduced.)

Today, I will only underline one sight word. Can you read it as I underline it. This word appears two times in this exercise.

Next, I will trace over the *aaa* sounds (as in *cat*) and the *uuu* sound (as in *cub*) with a gray crayon. I will also trace over the *iii* sounds (as in *pig*) and the *eee* sound (as in *wet*) with a gray crayon.

I will trace over the bold *i* sounds (as in *bike*) and the bold *a* sounds (as in *cake*) with a black crayon. I will also trace over the bold *o* sound (as in *hope*) and the bold *e* sounds (as in *heat*) with a black crayon.

I will make dotted lines over the letter *e* in the words *mice, rice, mouse, named, bite, hole,* and *nice.* I will also make dotted lines over the letter *a* in the word *eat.* Can you tell me why I dotted all of these letters? Yes, that's right. I dotted them, because they are silent. They make no sound. We certainly had a lot of silent letters today!

Next, I will draw a gray ring around the *ou* sound (as in *house*) in the word *mouse.* I will draw a gray ring around the *th* sound (as in *thick* or *this*) in the word *Then.* I will draw a gray ring around the *all* sound (as in *ball*) in the word *all.* I will also draw a gray ring around the letter *c* in the words *mice, rice,* and *nice.* Why did I do this? What sound does the letter *c* make in these words? That's right. It makes the *sss* sound.

Read the sentences. Very good! Find the index cards that have the quotation marks on them. Why do we use these special marks? That's right. We use them when a character is speaking. Who is speaking in this passage?

Now I will mix the cards, and you can put them in the proper order to make the sentences again.

(Assist the child with putting the cards in proper order. Keep the cards from each sentence separate. Remind him, if necessary, a sentence begins with an uppercase letter and ends with a period or some other form of punctuation.)

Now read the sentences.

(**Note**: We are no longer using clues to assist the child with reading the copy work. It is important for the child to read the text located in this segment of the lesson even if he does not copy the sentences. This will give him an opportunity to practice reading text printed in a regular type.)

Copy Work: (The copy work is optional for children who have difficulty with writing.) (You may now encourage the child to copy the sentence directly from the model below. If this is too difficult, continue as directed.)

I will write the sentences you just read on a piece of paper.

(Neatly write the sentences with a pen, paying close attention to letter spacing and formation.)

Now you can copy what I wrote.

The mice ran to the bag of rice.

A mouse named Russ said, "I will bite a hole in the bag. Then we can eat the rice."

All of the mice said, "Rice is nice."

I would like for you to read the sentences once more.

Very good! I would like for you to draw a picture to go with your

sentences. Here is a picture of a mouse you can draw.

(Assist the child with drawing the picture if necessary. The picture has been drawn with bold lines so the child may trace it if he likes.)

(**Note:** You may choose to encourage the child to dictate a short story to you about the picture he drew instead of only one sentence.)

Make up a story about the mouse you drew. Tell me the story, and I will write it on a piece of paper. Now you can copy one sentence from your story at the bottom of your picture.

(Draw lines if necessary for the child to write his sentence at the bottom of his picture.)

Read the story you dictated to me.

(Assist the child by reading any difficult words for him. If the story is long, have him read part of it and you read part of it.)

Now let's read a book together.

(Review material between lessons.)

Lesson 88

Materials: reading manual, index cards, pen, gray crayon, and black crayon.

Instructions: In today's lesson, the child will review the following sight words: *learn, new, caught, taught, that, who, water, want, two, once, many*, and *what*.

The child will review the bold *u* sound as in *cute* by reading the following words: *use, fuse, mute, lute, rule*, and *mule*.

He will also review the bold *e* sound as *baby* by reading the following words: *happy, puppy, funny, hobby, Billy*, and *penny*.

The child will review the *sss* sound as in *face* by reading the following words: *space, lace, place, brace, mice, rice, nice*, and *spice*.

The child will read the following story and complete a variety of exercises based on the story. This is part one of a three-part story.

Title: *"Will Baby Bird Learn to Fly?"*

Story: *Mama Bird said, "Today you will learn to fly."*

Baby Bird said, "I do not want to learn to fly. I want to sit and eat."

Mama Bird said, "You must learn to fly. You can not sit and eat all day."

Baby Bird said, "Flying is too hard. It is too hard for me. I want to sit and eat."

Daddy Bird was flying in the sky. He landed in the nest.

Daddy Bird said, "Are you ready to learn to fly?"

Baby Bird said, "It is too hard for me. I want to sit and eat."

Daddy Bird said, "What do you want to eat?"

Baby Bird said, "I want a fat bug."

Daddy Bird said, "I can not get a fat bug. I need to rest."

Daddy Bird went to sleep.

Baby Bird said, "Mama, I want a fat bug."

Mama Bird said, "I can not get a fat bug. I must fix the nest. I must get some new sticks."

Dialogue: Read the sight words below.

learn   new

caught   taught

that   who

water   want

two   once

many   what

Look at the letter below. What sound does this bold letter make? (*u* as in *cute*.)

u

Very good! It makes the bold *u* sound.

Read the words below that have the bold *u* sound (as in *cute*).

use   fuse

mute   lute

rule   mule

Look at the word below. It is the word *baby*. (Point to the word as you read it.)

baby

Read the words below that have the bold *e* sound at the end of the word as in *baby*.

happy   puppy

funny   hobby

Billy   penny

Look at the next word. The letter c has a gray ring around it. That is because this letter makes a special sound. It makes the sss sound (as in *face*). (Point to the letter *c* as you make the *sss* sound.)

f **a** (c) ≋

The word is *face*. (Point to the word as you read it. Emphasize the *sss* sound.)

Read the words below that have the *sss* sound. Remember, the letter *c* with the gray ring around it makes the *sss* sound.

s p **a** (c) ≋   l **a** (c) ≋

p l **a** (c) ≋   b r **a** (c) ≋

m i (c) ≋   r i (c) ≋

n i (c) ≋   s p i (c) ≋

Read the story below, and then I will show you a picture to go with the story. This is the first part of a three-part story.

(**Note**: We are no longer underlining the following sight words: *I, the, is, to, said, was, has,* and *you*. We are no longer dotting the letter *k* in the blend *ck*. We are no longer dotting the letter *y* as in *way* or the letter *w* as in *crow*. We are no longer drawing a ring around several beginning blends.)

"Will **B a** b y B (ir) d Learn to Fly?"

Mama B (ir) d said,

"To d **a** y you will learn to fly."

B a b y B (ir) d said,

"I do n **o** t want to learn to fly.

I want to sit **a** nd **e** ⍾ t."

Mama B (ir) d said, "You m **u** st learn to fly.

You c **a** n n **o** t sit **a** nd **e** ⍾ t (all) d **a** y."

B a b y B (ir) d said, "Fl y (ing) is t (oo) h **a** (r) d.

It is t (oo) h **a** (r) d f (or) m **e**.

I want to sit **a** nd **e** ⍾ t."

363

Daddy Bird was flying in the sky.

He landed in the nest.

Daddy Bird said,

"Are you ready to learn to fly?"

Baby Bird said, "It is too hard for me.

I want to sit and eat."

Daddy Bird said,

"What do you want to eat?"

Baby Bird said, "I want a fat bug."

Daddy Bird said,

"I can not get a fat bug.

I need to rest."

Daddy Bird went to sleep.

Baby Bird said,

"Mama, I want a fat bug."

Mama Bird said,

"I can not get a fat bug.

I must fix the nest.

I must get some new sticks."

Now I will show you a picture of Baby Bird and Mama Bird.

Look at the picture. What is Mama Bird doing? Yes, she is gathering sticks. Why is she gathering sticks? That's right, she is gathering sticks to fix the nest. Often birds will use sticks, moss, and leaves to build their nests. They will even use manmade materials such as yarn, string, or bits of cloth they find on the ground.

Next I will write four sentences from the story you just read on index cards.

(Have the child watch as you write each word with a pen. Label the first card with the lesson number for future use.)

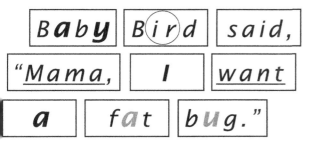

(**Note**: You may eliminate some of the print clues from the index cards with which your child is familiar. Be sure to include the print clues for sounds that have been recently introduced.)

Today, I will underline four different sight words. Can you read the sight words as I underline them?

I will trace over the *aaa* sounds (as in *cat*) and the *uuu* sounds (as in *cub*) with a gray crayon. I will also trace over the *ooo* sound (as in *hot*), the *iii* sounds (as in *pig*), and the *eee* sounds (as in *wet*) with a gray crayon.

I will trace over the bold *a* sounds (as in *cake*) with a black crayon. I will trace over the bold *e* sound (as in *baby*) made by the letter *y* in the word *baby* with a black crayon.

Next, I will draw a gray ring around the *ir* sound (as in *girl*) in the word *bird*.

Read the sentences. Great! Find the index cards that have the quotation marks on them. Why do we use these special marks? That's right. We use them when a character is speaking. Which characters are speaking in this passage?

Now I will mix the cards, and you can put them in the proper order to make the sentences again.

(Assist the child with putting the cards in proper order. Keep the cards from each sentence separate. Remind him, if necessary, a sentence begins with an uppercase letter and ends with a period or some other form of punctuation.)

Now read the sentences.

(**Note**: We are no longer using clues to assist the child with reading the copy work. It is important for the child to read the text located in this segment of the lesson even if he does not copy the sentences. This will give him an opportunity to practice reading text printed in a regular type.)

Copy Work: (The copy work is optional for children who have difficulty with writing.) (You may now encourage the child to copy the sentence directly from the model below. If this is too difficult, continue as directed.)

I will write the sentences you just read on a piece of paper.

(Neatly write the sentences with a pen, paying close attention to letter spacing and formation.)

Now you can copy what I wrote.

Baby Bird said, "Mama, I want a fat bug."

Mama Bird said, "I can not get a fat bug. I must fix the nest. I

must get some new sticks."

I would like for you to read the sentences once more. Very good! I would like for you to draw a picture to go with your sentences. Here is a picture of a nest you can draw.

(Assist the child with drawing the picture if necessary. The picture has been drawn with bold lines so the child may trace it if he likes.)

(**Note:** You may choose to encourage the child to dictate a short story to you about the picture he drew instead of only one sentence.)

Make up a story about the nest you drew. Tell me the story, and I will write it on a piece of paper. Now you can copy one sentence from your story at the bottom of your picture.

(Draw lines if necessary for the child to write his sentence at the bottom of his picture.)

Read the story you dictated to me. Now let's read a book together.

(Review material between lessons.)

Lesson 89

Materials: reading manual, index cards, pen, gray crayon, and black crayon.

Instructions: In today's lesson, the child will review the following sight words: *new, taught, caught, where, there, water, people, two,* and *that.*

The child will review various sounds learned so far by reading the following words: *cow, town, clown, chow, snow, blow, grow, flow, boil, foil, noise, coin, toy, joy, boy,* and *Troy.*

The child will read the following story and complete a variety of exercises based on the story. This is part two of a three-part story.

Title: *"Will Baby Bird Get a Bug?"*

Story: *Baby Bird was sad. Daddy Bird was sleeping. Mama Bird was looking for new sticks.*

Baby Bird said, "I want to eat a fat bug."

Baby Bird looked down at the grass. He saw a fat bug.

"I can not get that fat bug," he said. "I can not fly down to the grass. It is too hard for me."

Then Baby Bird saw a flash in the sky. He saw a bird fly down to the grass. The bird ate the fat bug. The bird was a baby bird too.

Baby Bird said, "How did that baby bird learn to fly? I am bigger than that baby bird."

Mama Bird landed in the nest. She had a stick in her beak. A fat bug was on the stick. Baby Bird saw the fat bug. Mama Bird did not see the fat bug.

Mama Bird said, "I need to rest. That stick is big."

Mama Bird went to sleep. Baby Bird said, "Now I can sit and eat. I can eat the fat bug."

The fat bug fell from the nest. It fell in the grass!

Dialogue: Read the sight words below.

new   taught

caught   where

there   water

people   two

that

Read the words below that have the *ow* sound (as in *cow*).

c(ow)   t(ow)n

cl(ow)n   ch(ow)

Read the words below that have the bold *o* sound (as in *snow*).

sn**o**w   bl**o**w

gr**o**w   fl**o**w

Read the words below that have the *oi* sound (as in *boil.*).

b(o i)l   f(o i)l

n(o)is☐   c(o)in

Read the words below that have the *oy* sound (as in *boy*).

t(o y)   j(o y)

b(o y)   Tr(o y)

Read the words below. These words will appear in the story.

(Assist the child with reading any difficult words.)

sl**ee**p(ing)   d(o)wn

learn   st**i**ck

sky   be☐k

l(oo)k☐d   fl**a**sh

Read the story below, and then I will show you a picture to go with the story. Today you will read more about Baby Bird.

"Will Baby Bird Get a Bug?"

Baby Bird was sad.

Daddy Bird was sleeping.

Mama Bird was looking for new sticks.

Baby Bird said,

"I want to eat a fat bug."

Baby Bird looked down at the grass.

He saw a fat bug.

"I can not get that fat bug," he said.

"I can not fly down to the grass.

It is too hard for me."

Then Baby Bird saw a

flash in the sky.

He saw a bird fly down to the grass.

The bird ate the fat bug.

The bird was a baby bird too.

Baby Bird said,

"How did that baby bird learn to fly?

I am bigger than that baby bird."

Mama Bird landed in the nest.

She had a stick in her beak.

A fat bug was on the stick.

Baby Bird saw the fat bug.

Mama Bird did not see the fat bug.

Mama Bird said, "I need to rest.

That stick is big."

Mama Bird went to sleep.

Baby Bird said,

"Now I can sit and eat.

I can eat the fat bug."

The fat bug fell from the nest.

It fell in the grass!

Now I will show you a picture of
Baby Bird.

Look at the picture. Baby Bird is looking at the bug that fell from the nest. Do you think Baby Bird is sad the bug fell? Yes, he is probably very sad.

Why doesn't Baby Bird fly down and get the bug? That's right, he is afraid to try to fly. Have you ever been afraid to try something new? Maybe you were afraid to try to skate or ride a bike.

Next, I will write four sentences from the story you just read on index cards.

(Have the child watch as you write each word with a pen. Label the first card with the lesson number for future use.)

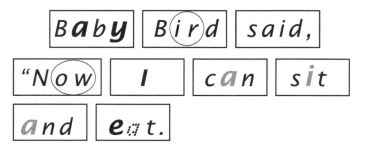

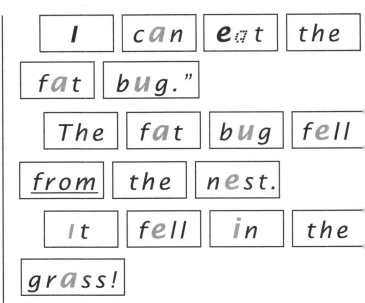

(**Note**: You may eliminate some of the print clues from the index cards with which your child is familiar. Be sure to include the print clues for sounds that have been recently introduced.)

Today, I will underline one sight word. Read the sight word as I underline it.

I will trace over the *aaa* sounds (as in *cat*) and the *iii* sounds (as in *pig*) with a gray crayon. I will also trace over the *uuu* sounds (as in *cub*) and the *eee* sounds (as in *wet*) with a gray crayon.

I will trace over the bold *a* sound (as in *cake*) and the bold *e* sounds (as in *heat*) with a black crayon.

I will make dotted lines over the letter a in the word *eat*. This word appears two times. Can you tell me why I dotted these letters? That's right, I dotted them, because they are silent. They make no sound.

I will trace over the bold *e* sound (as in *baby*) made by the letter y in the word *baby* with a black crayon.

370

Next, I will draw a gray ring around the *ir* sound (as in *girl*) in the word *Bird*. I will also draw a gray ring around the *ow* sound (as in *cow*) in the word *Now*.

Read the sentences. Very good! Find the index cards that have the quotation marks on them. Why do we use these special marks? That's right. We use them when a character is speaking. Which character is speaking in this passage?

Find the index card with the comma. Very good! What does the comma tell us to do? That's right. It tells us to pause before reading the next part of the sentence. A comma is used before quotation marks. (Point to the beginning quotation mark on the index card with the word *Now*.)

Find the index card with the exclamation point. Why do we use this special mark? That's right. We use it when we want to show surprise or excitement. Do you think Baby Bird was surprised when the bug fell in the grass?

Now I will mix the cards, and you can put them in the proper order to make the sentences again.

(Assist the child with putting the cards in proper order. Keep the cards from each sentence separate. Remind him, if necessary, a sentence begins with an uppercase letter and ends with a period or some other form of punctuation.)

Now read the sentences.

(**Note**: We are no longer using clues to assist the child with reading the copy work. It is important for the child to read the text located in this segment of the lesson even if he does not copy the sentences. This will give him an opportunity to practice reading text printed in a regular type.)

Copy Work: (The copy work is optional for children who have difficulty with writing.) (You may now encourage the child to copy the sentence directly from the model below. If this is too difficult, continue as directed.)

I will write the sentences you just read on a piece of paper.

(Neatly write the sentences with a pen, paying close attention to letter spacing and formation.)

Now you can copy what I wrote.

Baby Bird said, "Now I can sit and eat. I can eat the fat bug." The fat bug fell from the nest. It fell in the grass!

I would like for you to read the sentences once more. Very good! I would like for you to draw a picture to go with your sentences. Here is a picture of a bug you can draw.

(Assist the child with drawing the picture if necessary. The picture has been drawn with bold lines so the child may trace it if he likes.)

(**Note:** You may choose to encourage the child to dictate a short story to you about the picture he drew instead of only one sentence.)

Make up a story about the bug you drew. Tell me the story, and I will write it on a piece of paper. Now you can copy one sentence from your story at the bottom of your picture.

(Draw lines if necessary for the child to write his sentence at the bottom of his picture.)

Read the story you dictated to me.

(Assist the child by reading any difficult words for him. If the story is long, have him read part of it and you read part of it.)

Now let's read a book together.

(Review material between lessons.)

Lesson 90

Materials: reading manual, index cards, pen, gray crayon, and black crayon.

Instructions: In today's lesson, the child will review the following sight words: *from, come, some, one, once, learn,* and *who.*

The child will review various sounds learned so far by reading the following words: *shirt, girl, bird, skirt, burn, turn, burp, curve, her, verse, perk, term, bigger, faster, slower,* and *harder.*

The child will read the following story and complete a variety of exercises based on the story. This is part three of a three-part story.

Title: *"Baby Bird Gets a Bug"*

Story: *Baby Bird looked down at the fat bug. The fat bug was in the grass.*

Baby Bird said, "I will not cry. I will be brave. I will learn to fly."

Baby Bird climbed up on the side of the nest. He flapped his wings. He could not fly.

Baby Bird said once more, "I will not cry. I will be brave. I will learn to fly."

This time he flapped his wings. He hopped up and down. Still he could not fly.

Baby Bird said once more, "I will not cry. I will be brave. I will learn to fly."

This time he flapped his wings. He hopped up and down. Then he jumped in to the air. Now he could fly. Mama Bird woke up. Daddy Bird woke up. They saw a flash in the sky. They saw a bird fly down to the grass. The bird ate the fat bug. The bird was a baby. It was Baby Bird!

Dialogue: Read the sight words below.

from   come

some   one

once   learn

who

Read the words below that have the *ir* sound (as in *bird*).

s h (i r) t   g (i r) l

b(ir)d   sk(ir)t

Read the words below that have the ur sound (as in *turn*).

b(ur)n   t(ur)n

b(ur)p   cu(r)ve

Read the words below that have the er sound (as in *her*).

h(er)   v(er)se

p(er)k   t(er)m

Read the words below that have the er sound at the end of the word (as in *bigger*).

bigg(er)   fast(er)

slow(er)   hard(er)

Read the words at the top of the page. These words will appear in the story.

(Assist the child with reading any difficult words.)

brave   l(oo)ked

climbed   flapped

flash   sky

hopped   m(o)re

jumped   woke

air   ate

Read the story below, and then I will show you a picture to go with the story. This is the last part of the story about Baby Bird.

(**Note**: We are no longer underlining the following sight words: *I, the, is, to, said, was, has, you, Papa,* and *Mama.* We are no longer dotting the letter *k* in the blend *ck.* We are no longer dotting the letter *y* as in *way* or the letter *w* as in *crow.* We are no longer drawing a ring around several beginning blends.)

"Baby B(ir)d gets a Bug"

Baby B(ir)d l(oo)ked d(ow)n

at the fat bug.

The fat bug was in the grass.

Baby B(ir)d said, "I will not cry.

I will be brave. I will <u>learn</u> to fly."

373

Baby Bird climbed up on
the side of the nest.
He flapped his wings. He could not fly.
Baby Bird said once more,
"I will not cry. I will be brave.
I will learn to fly."
This time he flapped his wings.
He hopped up and down.
Still he could not fly.
Baby Bird said once more,
"I will not cry. I will be brave.
I will learn to fly."
This time he flapped his wings.
He hopped up and down.
Then he jumped in to the air.
Now he could fly.
Mama Bird woke up.
Daddy Bird woke up.

They saw a flash in the sky.

They saw a bird fly down to the grass.

The bird ate the fat bug.

The bird was a baby.

It was Baby Bird!

Now I will show you a picture of Baby Bird.

Look at the picture. Baby Bird is flying down to the grass. What will Baby Bird do? That's right, he will eat the fat bug. Do you think Baby Bird is happy now? Why is he happy? What did he learn to do? How did this help him? Do you think his mama and daddy are happy?

Next, I will write four sentences from the story you just read on index cards.

(Have the child watch as you write each word with a pen. Label the first card with the lesson number for future use.)

(**Note**: You may eliminate some of the print clues from the index cards with which your child is familiar. Be sure to include the print clues for sounds that have been recently introduced.)

(We will not underline any of the sight words today, as the child should be familiar with the sight words used in the passage.)

I will trace over the *aaa* sounds (as in *cat*) and the *uuu* sound (as in *cub*) with a gray crayon. I will also trace over the *iii* sound (as in *pig*) with a gray crayon.

I will trace over the bold *a* sounds (as in *cake*) with a black crayon. I will make dotted lines over the letter *e* in the word *ate*. Can you tell me why I dotted this letter? That's right. I dotted it, because it is silent. It makes no sound.

I will trace over the bold *e* sound (as in *baby*) made by the letter *y* in the word *baby* with a black crayon. Next, I will draw a gray ring around the *aw* sound (as in *paw*) in the word *saw*. I will draw a gray ring around the *ir* sound (as in *girl*) in the word *bird*. I will also draw a gray ring around the *ow* sound (as in *cow*) in the word *down*.

Next, I will place a gray dot over the letter *y* in the word *fly*. Can you tell me why I did this? That's right. I placed the gray dot over the letter *y*, because it makes the bold *i* sound.

Read the sentences. Great! Find the index card with the exclamation point. Why do we use this special mark? That's right. We use it when we want to show surprise or excitement. Do you think Mama Bird and Daddy Bird were surprised when they saw Baby Bird fly down to the grass and eat the bug?

Now I will mix the cards, and you can put them in the proper order to make the sentences again.

Now read the sentences.

Copy Work: (The copy work is optional for children who have difficulty with writing.) (You may now encourage the child to copy the sentence directly from the model below. If this is too difficult, continue as directed.)

I will write the sentences you just read on a piece of paper.

(Neatly write the sentences with a pen, paying close attention to letter spacing and formation.)

Now you can copy what I wrote.

They saw a bird fly down to the grass. The bird ate the fat bug. The bird was a baby. It was Baby Bird!

I would like for you to read the sentences once more. Very good! I would like for you to draw a picture to go with your sentences. Here is a picture of a baby bird you can draw.

(Assist the child with drawing the picture if necessary. The picture has been drawn with bold lines so the child may trace it if he likes.)

(**Note:** You may choose to encourage the child to dictate a short story to you about the picture he drew instead of only one sentence.)

Make up a story about the bird you drew. Tell me the story, and I will write it on a piece of paper. Now you can copy one sentence from your story at the bottom of your picture.

(Draw lines if necessary for the child to write his sentence at the bottom of his picture.)

Read the story you dictated to me.

(Assist the child by reading any difficult words for him. If the story is long, have him read part of it and you read part of it.)

Now let's read a book together.

(Review material between lessons.)

Lesson 91

Materials: reading manual, index cards, pen, gray crayon, and black crayon.

Instructions: In today's lesson, the child will review the following sight words: *of, want, what, who, water, that, caught, taught, where,* and *there.*

The child will review various sounds learned so far by reading the following words: *cook, brook, hood, stood, boot, shoot, broom, zoom, paw, saw, claw, draw, drink, pink, think,* and *link.*

The child will read the following story and complete a variety of exercises based on the story. This is part one of a three-part story.

Title: "*Eggs in a Nest*"

Story: *Once Papa Duck and Mama Duck lived by a pond. Mama Duck had six eggs in her nest. She sat on the eggs so that they would not get cold.*

Papa Duck said, "Go swim in the water. I will keep the eggs safe."

Mama Duck went down to the pond. She walked out in to the water.

"The water is nice," she said. "It is nice to swim and play."

She sang a song.

She sang, "Flap the wings, swish the feet. I will catch a fish to eat."

Then she caught a fish and ate it.

"Yum, yum," she said.

She walked up the bank. She went to her nest. She sat on the eggs. Papa Duck looked at Mama Duck.

Papa Duck said, "I am glad we will have six baby ducks. We will have fun."

Just then Mama Duck said, "I hear a crack. I hear a sound!"

Dialogue: Read the sight words below.

of	want
what	who
water	that
caught	taught

where   there

Read the words below that have the oo sound (as in *cook*).

c o o k   b r o o k

h o o d   s t o o d

Read the words below that have the oo sound (as in *boot*).

b o o t   s h o o t

b r o o m   z o o m

Read the words below that have the aw sound (as in *paw*).

p a w   s a w

c l a w   d r a w

Read the words below that have the ink sound (as in *drink*).

d r i n k   p i n k

t h i n k   l i n k

Read the words below. These words will appear in the story.

(Assist the child with reading any difficult words.)

would   p o n d

s a f e   w a l k e d

n i c e   s a n g

s o n g   s w i s h

f i s h   y u m

b a n k   c r a c k

s o u n d   h e a r

d u c k s   c a t c h

Read the story below, and then I will show a picture to go with the story. This is the first part of a story about ducks.

(**Note**: We are no longer underlining the following sight words: *I, the, is, to, said, was, has, you, Papa,* and *Mama.* We are no longer dotting the letter *k* in the blend *ck.* We are no longer dotting the letter *y* as in *way* or the letter *w* as in *crow.* We are no longer drawing a ring around several beginning blends.)

"Eggs in a Nest"

Once Papa Duck and Mama Duck lived by a pond.

Mama Duck had six eggs in her nest.

She sat on the eggs so

that they would not get cold.

Papa Duck said, "Go swim in the water.

I will keep the eggs safe."

Mama Duck went down to the pond.

She walked out in to the water.

"The water is nice," she said.

"It is nice to swim and play."

She sang a song.

She sang, "Flap the wings,

swish the feet.

I will catch a fish to eat."

Then she caught a fish and ate it.

"Yum, yum," she said.

She walked up the bank.

She went to her nest.

She sat on the eggs.

Papa Duck looked at Mama Duck.

Papa Duck said, "I am glad we will

have six baby ducks. We will have fun."

Just then Mama Duck said,

"I hear a crack. I hear a sound!"

Now I will show you a picture of Mama Duck.

Look at the picture. What is Mama duck doing? That's right she is sitting on her nest of eggs. What sound did the Mama duck hear? That's right. She said she heard a *crack?* What do you think is happening? Yes, the eggs are probably starting to hatch.

Next I will write four sentences from the story you just read on index cards.

(Have the child watch as you write each word with a pen. Label the first card with the lesson number for future use.)

(**Note**: You may eliminate some of the print clues from the index cards with which your child is familiar. Be sure to include the print clues for new sounds that have been recently introduced.)

I will trace over the *uuu* sounds (as in *cub*) and the *aaa* sounds (as in *cat*) with a gray crayon. I will also trace over the *iii* sounds (as in *pig*) and the *eee* sound (as in *wet*) with a gray crayon.

I will trace over the bold *e* sounds (as in *heat*) and the bold *a* sounds (as in *cake*) with a black crayon.

I will make dotted lines over the letter *e* in the word *have*. This word appears two times. I will also make dotted lines over the letter *a* in the word *hear*. This word also appears two times. Can you tell me why I dotted these letters? That's right. I dotted them, because they are silent. They make no sound.

I will trace over the bold *e* sound (as in *baby*) made by the letter *y* in the word *baby* with a black crayon.

I will draw a gray ring around the *th* sound (as in *thick* or *this*) in the word *then*. I will also draw a gray ring around the *ou* sound (as in *house*) in the word *sound*.

Read the sentences. Great! Look at the index card with the word *sound* written on it. What is the special mark called at the end of this word? Yes, it is called an exclamation point. Why do we use this special mark? That's right. We use it when we want to show surprise or excitement. Do you think Papa Duck and Mama Duck were surprised when they heard the sound?

Now I will mix the cards, and you can put them in the proper order to make the sentences again.

Now read the sentences.

(**Note**: We are no longer using clues to assist the child with reading the copy work. It is important for the child to read the text located in this segment of the lesson even if he does not copy the sentences. This will give him an opportunity to practice reading text printed in a regular type.)

Copy Work: (The copy work is optional for children who have difficulty with writing.) (You may now encourage the child to copy the sentence directly from the model below. If this is too difficult, continue as directed.)

I will write the sentences you just read on a piece of paper.

(Neatly write the sentences with a pen, paying close attention to letter spacing and formation.)

Now you can copy what I wrote.

Papa Duck said, "I am glad we will have six baby ducks. We will have fun."

Just then Mama Duck said, "I hear a crack. I hear a sound!"

I would like for you to read the sentences once more. Very good! I would like for you to draw a picture to go with your sentences. Here is a picture of a nest with eggs you can draw.

(Assist the child with drawing the picture if necessary. The picture has been drawn with bold lines so the child may trace it if he likes.)

Make up a story about the nest and eggs you drew. Tell me the story, and I will write it on a piece of paper. Now you can copy one sentence from your story at the bottom of your picture.

(Draw lines if necessary for the child to write his sentence at the bottom of his picture.)

Read the story you dictated to me.

(Assist the child by reading any difficult words for him. If the story is long, have him read part of it and you read part of it.)

Now let's read a book together.

Lesson 92

Materials: reading manual, index cards, pen, gray crayon, and black crayon.

Instructions: In today's lesson, the child will review the following sight words: *people, your, they, does, from, two, new,* and *learn.*

The child will review various sounds learned so far by reading the following words: *bank, thank, drank, sank, long, song, wrong, dong, ball, fall, stall, wall, talk, walk, chalk,* and *stalk.*

The child will read the following story and complete a variety of exercises based on the story. This is part two of a three-part story.

Title: *"Five Baby Ducks"*

Story: *Mama Duck said to Papa Duck, "Come and hear the sound. It is the eggs."*

Papa Duck sat by the nest.

He said, "I hear the sound."

The eggs went, "Crack, crack, crack, crack, crack!"

"I hear five cracks," said Mama Duck.

"I see five baby ducks," said Papa Duck.

Mama and Papa Duck were happy. They gave each baby duck a kiss on the head. Mama Duck looked in the nest.

She said, "There is one more egg in the nest. It has not cracked."

Mama Duck started to cry.

Papa Duck said, "Do not be sad. We have five baby ducks."

Mama Duck said, "I will sit on this egg in the nest. I will wait and I will rest."

Papa Duck said, "I will take the baby ducks for a walk. I will catch a fish to eat."

Dialogue: Read the sight words below.

people	_your_
they	_does_
from	_two_
new	_learn_

Read the words below that have the *ank* sound (as in *bank*).

b a n k   (th)a n k

dr a n k   s a n k

Read the words below that have the *ong* sound (as in *long*).

l o n g   s o n g

wr o n g   d o n g

Read the words below that have the *all* sound (as in *ball*).

b(a l l)   f(a l l)

st(a l l)   w(a l l)

Read the words below that have the *alk* sound (as in *talk*).

t(a l k)   w(a l k)

ch(a l k)   st(a l k)

Read the words below. These words will appear in the story.

(Assist the child with reading any difficult words.)

h a p p y   f i v e

k i s s   s t(a r)t e d

w a i t   s(o u)n d

w(e r e)   h e a d

Read the story below, and then I will show you a picture to go with the story. This is the second part of the story about the eggs in the nest.

(**Note**: We are no longer underlining the following sight words: *I, the, is, to, said, was, has, you, Papa,* and *Mama.* We are no longer dotting the letter *k* in the blend *ck*. We are no longer dotting the letter *y* as in *way* or the letter *w* as in *crow*. We are no longer drawing a ring around several beginning blends.)

"Five Baby Ducks"

Mama Duck said to Papa Duck, "<u>Come</u> and hear the s(o u)nd. It is the eggs."

Papa Duck sat by the nest.

He said, "I hear the s(o u)nd."

The eggs went, "Crack, crack, crack, crack, crack!"

"I hear five cracks," said Mama Duck.

"I see five baby ducks,"

said Papa Duck.

Mama and Papa Duck were happy.

They gave each baby duck

a kiss on the head.

Mama Duck looked in the nest.

She said, "There is one more egg

in the nest. It has not cracked."

Mama Duck started to cry.

Papa Duck said, "Do not be sad.

We have five baby ducks."

Mama Duck said, "I will sit on this egg

in the nest. I will wait and I will rest."

Papa Duck said, "I will take the

baby ducks for a walk.

I will catch a fish to eat."

384

Now I will show you a picture of Mama Duck, Papa Duck, and the baby ducks.

Look at the picture. What is Papa Duck doing? That's right, he is taking the baby ducks for a walk. What are baby ducks called? That's right, they are called *ducklings*.

What is Mama Duck doing? Yes, she is sitting on the nest. Why is she sitting on the nest? What is in the nest? That's right, an egg is in the nest. Mama Duck is trying to hatch the egg.

Next, I will write four sentences from the story you just read on index cards.

(Have the child watch as you write each word with a pen. Label the first card with the lesson number for future use.)

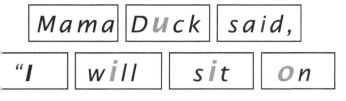

Mama	Duck	said,

"I	will	sit	on

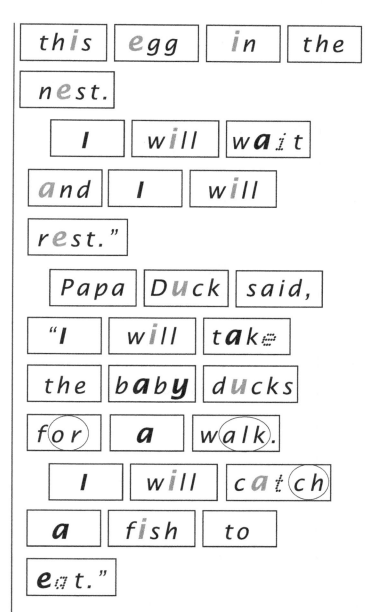

this	egg	in	the

nest.

I	will	wait

and	I	will

rest."

Papa	Duck	said,

"I	will	take

the	baby	ducks

for	a	walk.

I	will	catch

a	fish	to

eat."

(**Note**: You may eliminate some of the print clues from the index cards with which your child is familiar. Be sure to include the print clues for new sounds that have been recently introduced.)

I will trace over the *uuu* sounds (as in *cub*) and the *iii* sounds (as in *pig*) with a gray crayon. I will also trace over the *ooo* sound (as in *hot*), the *eee* sounds (as in *wet*), and the *aaa* sounds (as in *cat*) with a gray crayon.

I will trace over the bold *a* sounds (as in *cake*) with a black crayon. I will make dotted lines over the letter *i* in the word *wait*. I will also make dotted lines over the letter *e* in the word *take*, and I will make dotted lines over the letter *t* in the word *catch*. Next, I will also make dotted lines over the letter *a* in the word *eat*. Can you tell me why I dotted these letters? That's right. I dotted them, because they are silent. They make no sound.

I will trace over the bold *e* sound (as in *baby*) made by the letter *y* in the word *baby* with a black crayon.

Next, I will draw a gray ring around the *or* sound (as in *corn*) in the word *for*. I will draw a gray ring around the *alk* sound (as in *walk*) in the word *walk*. I will also draw a gray ring around the *ch* sound (as in *chip* and *patch*) in the word *catch*.

Read the sentences. Very good! Find the index cards with the quotation marks. Why do we use these special marks? That's right. We use them when a character is speaking. Which characters are speaking in this passage? Yes, Mama Duck and Papa Duck are speaking.

Find the index cards with the commas. What does a comma tell us? That's right, it tells us to pause before reading the next part of the sentence. A comma is used before quotation marks. (Point to the beginning quotation marks on the index cards.)

Now I will mix the cards, and you can put them in the proper order to make the sentences again.

Now read the sentences.

Copy Work: (The copy work is optional for children who have difficulty with writing.) (You may now encourage the child to copy the sentence directly from the model below. If this is too difficult, continue as directed.)

I will write the sentences you just read on a piece of paper.

(Neatly write the sentences with a pen, paying close attention to letter spacing and formation.)

Now you can copy what I wrote.

Mama Duck said, "I will sit on this egg in the nest. I will wait and I will rest."

Papa Duck said, "I will take the baby ducks for a walk. I will catch a fish to eat."

I would like for you to read the sentences once more. Very good! I would like for you to draw a picture to go with your sentences. Here is a picture of a duckling you can draw.

(Assist the child with drawing the picture if necessary. The picture has been drawn with bold lines so the child may trace it if he likes.)

(**Note:** You may choose to encourage the child to dictate a short story to you about the picture he drew instead of only one sentence.)

Make up a story about the duckling you drew. Tell me the story, and I will write it on a piece of paper. Now you can copy one sentence from your story at the bottom of your picture.

(Draw lines if necessary for the child to write his sentence at the bottom of his picture.)

Read the story you dictated to me.

(Assist the child by reading any difficult words for him. If the story is long, have him read part of it and you read part of it.)

Now let's read a book together.

(Review material between lessons.)

Lesson 93

Materials: reading manual, index cards, pen, gray crayon, black crayon, and one construction paper circle.

Instructions: In today's lesson, the child will review the following sight words: *many, who, with, come, put, some, are,* and *new*. He will be introduced to the new sight word *watch*. Prepare one construction paper circle with the new sight word written on it.

The child will review various sounds learned so far by reading the following words: *fly, sky, fry, sty, ring, bring, cling, zing, hopping, looking, baking, walking, cart, smart, chart,* and *far*.

The child will read the following story and complete a variety of exercises based on the story. This is part three of a three-part story.

Title: *"Wake up Baby Duck!"*

Story: *Mama Duck sat and sat and sat. Papa Duck took the baby ducks for a walk. Soon they came back to the nest.*

Papa Duck said to Mama Duck, "Go for a swim. I will watch the nest. I will watch the baby ducks."

Mama Duck went for a swim. She sang a song.

She sang, "Flap the wings, swish the feet, I will catch a fish to eat."

Mama Duck went back to the nest. She saw the baby ducks. They were in the nest. The baby ducks were talking to the egg.

They said, "Wake up, wake up. It is time to come out."

"Wake up, wake up!" they said with a shout.

Papa Duck said, "I hear a crack. I hear a sound."

Then the baby duck came out of his shell. All of the ducks were happy.

Papa Duck said, "Let's go for a swim."

Mama Duck led the way. She sang, "Flap the wings, swish the feet. We will catch a fish to eat."

Dialogue: Read the sight words below.

many   who

with

put

are

come

some

new

Today you will learn a new sight word. Look at the word below. It is the word *watch*. (Point to the word as you read it.)

watch

Say *watch* as I point to the word. Very good! Now read the sentence below that contains the new sight word.

I like to watch

the baby ducks.

Let's add the new sight word to your *Sight Word Worm*.

Read the words below that have the bold *i* sound (as in *fly*).

fly

fry

sky

sty

Read the words below that have the *ing* sound (as in *sing*).

ring

cling

bring

zing

Read some more words that have the *ing* sound (as in *hopping*).

hopping

baking

looking

walking

Read the words below that have the ar sound (as in *car*).

cart

chart

smart

far

Read the words below. These words will appear in the story.

(Assist the child with reading any difficult words.)

shout

watch

sound

happy

catch

swish

were

talking

Read the story, and then I will show you a picture to go with the story. This is the last part of the story about the baby ducks.

(**Note**: We are no longer underlining the following sight words: *I, the, is, to, said, was, has, you, Papa, Mama, do, of,* and *they*. We are no longer dotting the letter *k* in the blend *ck*. We are no longer dotting the letter *y* as in *way* or the letter *w* as in *crow*. We are no longer drawing a ring around several beginning blends.)

"Wake up Baby Duck!"

Mama Duck sat and sat and sat.

Papa Duck took the baby

ducks for a walk.

Soon they came back to the nest.

Papa Duck said to Mama Duck,

"Go for a swim. I will watch the nest.

I will watch the baby ducks."

Mama Duck went for a swim.

She sang a song.

She sang, "Flap the wings, swish the

feet, I will catch a fish to eat."

Mama Duck went back to the nest.

She saw the baby ducks.

They were in the nest.

The baby ducks were

talking to the egg.

They said, "Wake up, wake up.

It is time to come out."

"Wake up, wake up!"

they said with a shout.

Papa Duck said, "I hear a crack.

I hear a sound."

Then the baby duck

came out of his shell.

All of the ducks were happy.

Papa Duck said, "Let's go for a swim."

Mama Duck led the way.

She sang, "Flap the wings,

swish the feet.

We will catch a fish to eat."

Now I will show you a picture of
the duck family.

Look at the picture. Mama Duck is leading the way to the pond. Papa Duck is watching over the duck family as he walks behind the last baby duck.

How many baby ducks can you count? That's right. Now there are six baby ducks. Does the mother duck look pleased? Yes, she is holding her head up very high. She is proud of her baby ducks.

Next, I will write four sentences from the story you just read on index cards.

(Have the child watch as you write each word with a pen. Label the first card with the lesson number for future use.)

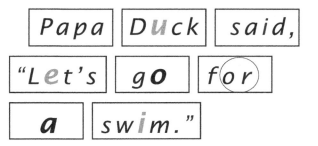

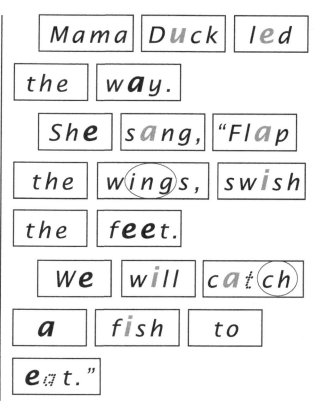

(**Note**: You may eliminate some of the print clues from the index cards with which your child is familiar. Be sure to include the print clues for new sounds that have been recently introduced.)

I will trace over the *uuu* sounds (as in *cub*) and the *eee* sounds (as in *wet*) with a gray crayon. I will also trace over the *iii* sounds (as in *pig*) and the *aaa* sounds (as in *cat*) with a gray crayon.

I will trace over the bold *o* sound (as in *hope*), the bold *a* sounds (as in *cake*), and the bold *e* sounds (as in *heat*) with a black crayon.

I will make dotted lines over the letter *t* in the word *catch*. I will also make dotted lines over the letter a in the word eat. Can you tell me why I dotted these letters? That's right. I dotted them, because they are silent. They make no sound.

Next, I will draw a gray ring around the *or* sound (as in *corn*) in the word *for*. I will draw a gray ring around the *ing* sound (as in *sing*) in the word *wings*. I will also draw a gray ring around the *ch* sound (as in *patch*) in the word *catch*.

Read the sentences. Great! Find the index cards with the quotation marks on them. Why do we use these special marks? That's right. We use them when a character is speaking. Which characters are speaking in this passage? Yes, Mama and Papa Duck are speaking.

Now I will mix the cards, and you can put them in the proper order to make the sentences again.

Now read the sentences.

(**Note**: We are no longer using clues to assist the child with reading the copy work. It is important for the child to read the text located in this segment of the lesson even if he does not copy the sentences. This will give him an opportunity to practice reading text printed in a regular type.)

Copy Work: (The copy work is optional for children who have difficulty with writing.) (You may now encourage the child to copy the sentences directly from the model below. If this is too difficult, continue as directed.)

I will write the sentences you just read on a piece of paper.

(Neatly write the sentences with a pen, paying close attention to letter spacing and formation.)

Now you can copy what I wrote.

Papa Duck said, "Let's go for a swim."

Mama Duck led the way.

She sang, "Flap the wings, swish the feet. We will catch a fish to eat."

I would like for you to read the sentences once more. Very good! I would like for you to draw a picture to go with your sentences. Here is a picture of a fish you can draw.

(Assist the child with drawing the picture if necessary. The picture has been drawn with bold lines so the child may trace it if he likes.)

(**Note:** You may choose to encourage the child to dictate a short story to you about the picture he drew instead of only one sentence.)

Make up a story about the fish you drew. Tell me the story, and I will write it on a piece of paper. Now you can copy one sentence from your story at the bottom of your picture.

(Draw lines if necessary for the child to write his sentence at the bottom of his picture.)

Read the story you dictated to me.

(Assist the child by reading any difficult words for him. If the story is long, have him read part of it and you read part of it.)

Now let's read a book together.

(Review material between lessons.)

(An interesting book to read about ducks is *Make Way for Ducklings* by Robert McCloskey. This book is available at your public library.)

Lesson 94

Materials: reading manual, index cards, pen, gray crayon, and black crayon.

Instructions: In today's lesson, the child will review the following sight words: *watch, they, one, of, water, there, caught, with,* and *from.*

The child will review various sounds learned so far by reading the following words: *fort, short, born, horn, house, mouse, cloud, shout, face, race, dance, fence, cute, duke, mule,* and *glue.*

The child will read the following poem and complete a variety of exercises based on the poem.

Title: *"I Caught"*

Poem: *I caught a fish, he was too small,*
Back into the water, I let him fall.
I caught a frog, and he did hop,
Back into the water, with a loud plop.
I caught a crab, and he did pinch,
Back into the water, he tried to inch.
I caught a snail, and he did creep,
Back into the water, with out a peep.
I caught a tad pole, he was so fast,
Back into the water, he went at last.
I caught a boot, and it did stink,
Back into the water, I let it sink.
I caught a shell, and it was white,
Back into the water, it fell from sight.
I caught a gold fish, and it was shiny,
Back into the water, it was too tiny.
I caught a jelly fish, and it did jiggle,
Back into the water, it did wiggle.
I caught a big one, it was a whale,
And this is the end, of my tall tale!

Dialogue: Read the sight words below.

watch	they
one	of
water	there
caught	with

from

Read the words below that have the or sound (as in *corn*).

f(o r)t   sh(o r)t

b(o r)n   h(o r)n

Read the words below that have the ou sound (as in *house*).

h(ou)se   m(ou)se

cl(ou)d   sh(ou)t

Read the words below. Remember, the letter c with a gray ring around it makes the sss sound (as in *face*).

fa(c)e   ra(c)e

dan(c)e   fen(c)e

Read the words below that have the bold *u* sound (as in *cute*).

c**u**te   d**u**ke

m**u**le   gl**u**e

Read the following words. These words will appear in the poem.

(Assist the child with reading any difficult words.)

pi(nch)   i(nch)

tad   pole

snail   sti(nk)

gold   shiny

jelly   jiggle

wiggle   whale

Read the words below.

in   to

If we put these words together we have a new word. It is the word *into*. Say the new word as I point it.

into

Read the poem, and then I will show you a picture to go with the poem.

(**Note**: We are no longer underlining the following sight words: *I, the, is, to, said, was, has, you, Papa, Mama, do, of,* and *they.* We are no longer dotting the letter *k* in the blend *ck.* We are no longer dotting the letter *y* as in *way* or the letter *w* as in *crow.* We are no longer drawing a ring around several beginning blends.)

"I Caught"

I caught **a** fish,

He was t(oo) sm(all),

Back into the water,

394

I let him f(all).

I caught **a** frog,

And h**e** did hop,

Back into the water,

With **a** l(ou)d plop.

I caught **a** crab,

And h**e** did pin(ch),

Back into the water,

He tried to in(ch).

I caught **a** snail,

And h**e** did cr**ee**p,

Back into the water,

With (out) **a** p**ee**p.

I caught **a** tad pole,

He was s**o** fast,

Back into the water,

He went at last.

I caught **a** b(oo)t,

395

And it did st(ink),
Back into the water,
I let it s(ink).
I caught a shell,
And it was white,
Back into the water,
It fell from sight.
I caught a gold fish,
And it was shiny,
Back into the water,
It was t(oo) tiny.
I caught a jelly fish,
And it did jiggle,
Back into the water,
It did wiggle.
I caught a big one,
It was a whale,
And (th)is is the end,

Of my tall tale!

Now I will show you a picture of the child with the jellyfish.

Look at the picture. The child said he caught a jellyfish. How did he catch the jellyfish? That's right. He caught it in a net. You do not want to touch a jellyfish, because it will sting you.

Have you ever seen a real jellyfish? Did you know a jellyfish has long tentacles? These arm-like parts trail behind the jellyfish. The tentacles of some jellyfish grow to be over thirty feet long!

Next, I will write eight lines from the poem you just read on index cards.

(Have the child watch as you write each word with a pen. Label the first card with the lesson number for future use.)

(**Note**: You may eliminate some of the print clues from the index cards with which your child is familiar. Be sure to include the print clues for new sounds that have been recently introduced.)

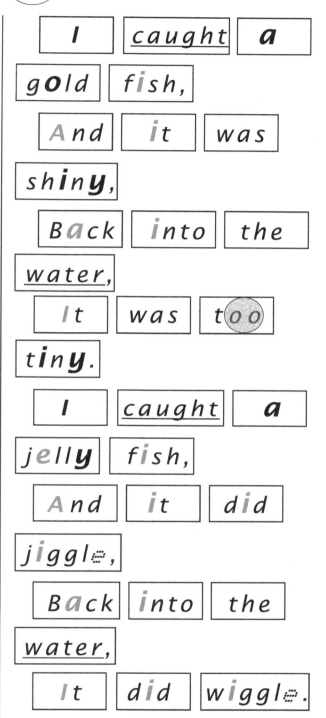

I caught a
gold fish,
And it was
shiny,
Back into the
water,
It was too
tiny.
I caught a
jelly fish,
And it did
jiggle,
Back into the
water,
It did wiggle.

Today I will underline two different sight words. Read the sight words as I underline them. I will trace over the *iii* sounds (as in *pig*), the *aaa* sounds (as in

397

cat), and the *eee* sound (as in *wet*) with a gray crayon.

I will trace over the bold *a* sounds (as in *cake*), the bold *o* sound (as in *hope*), and the bold *i* sounds (as in *bike*) with a black crayon. I will trace over the bold *e* sound (as in *baby*) made by the letter *y* in the words *shiny*, *tiny*, and *jelly* with a black crayon.

I will make dotted lines over the letter *e* in the word *jiggle* and in the word *wiggle*. Can you tell me why I dotted these letters? That's right. I dotted them, because they are silent. They make no sound.

Next, I will draw a shaded gray ring around the *oo* sound (as in *boot*) in the word *too*.

Read the lines from the poem. Very good! Find the index card with the word *shiny* and the card with the word *tiny*. These words rhyme. Can you find two other words in this passage that rhyme? Yes, the words *jiggle* and *wiggle* rhyme.

Find the index cards with the commas. Very good! There are six commas in these lines from the poem. What does a comma tell us? That's right, it tells us to pause before reading the next part of the poem. Commas are often used in poems.

Now I will mix the cards, and you can put them in the proper order to make the sentences again.

Now read the sentences.

(**Note**: We are no longer using clues to assist the child with reading the copy work. It is important for the child to read the text located in this segment of the lesson even if he does not copy the sentences. This will give him an opportunity to practice reading text printed in a regular type.)

Copy Work: (The copy work is optional for children who have difficulty with writing.) (You may now encourage the child to copy the sentences directly from the model below. If this is too difficult, continue as directed.)

I will write the lines from the poem you just read on a piece of paper.

(Neatly write the sentences with a pen, paying close attention to letter spacing and formation.)

Now you can copy what I wrote.

I caught a gold fish,
And it was shiny,
Back into the water,
It was too tiny.
I caught a jelly fish,
And it did jiggle,
Back into the water,
It did wiggle.

I would like for you to read the sentences once more. Very good! I would

398

like for you to draw a picture to go with your sentences. Here is a picture of a jellyfish you can draw.

(Assist the child with drawing the picture if necessary. The picture has been drawn with bold lines so the child may trace it if he likes.)

Make up a story about the jellyfish you drew. Tell me the story, and I will write it on a piece of paper. Now you can copy one sentence from your story at the bottom of your picture.

(Draw lines if necessary for the child to write his sentence at the bottom of his picture.)

Read the story you dictated to me.

(Assist the child by reading any difficult words for him. If the story is long, have him read part of it and you read part of it.)

Now let's read a book together.

(Review material between lessons.)

Lesson 95

Materials: reading manual, index cards, pen, gray crayon, and black crayon.

Instructions: In today's lesson, the child will review the following sight words: *taught, watch, put, who, that,* and *from.*

The child will review various sounds learned so far by reading the following words: *lady, mommy, daddy, happy, chip, cheese, chin, chop, patch, latch, pitch, hitch, phone, photo, graph,* and *phase.*

The child will read the following poem and complete a variety of exercises based on the poem.

Title: *"Who?"*

Poem: *Who taught the quail how to fly?*
Who taught the baby how to cry?
Who taught the wind how to blow?
Who taught the flower how to grow?
Who taught the lion how to roar?
Who taught the hawk how to soar?
Who taught the dog how to howl?
Who taught the bear how to growl?
Who taught the bug how to creep?
Who taught the frog how to leap?
Who taught the rose how to bloom?
Who taught the thunder how to boom?
Who taught the snow how to fall?
Who taught the ant how to crawl?
Who taught the bee how to sting?
Who taught the lark how to sing?
Who taught the brook how to flow?
Who taught the bird how to crow?
Who taught the pig how to grunt?
Who taught the tiger how to hunt?
Who taught the puppy how to play?
Who taught the mule how to bray?

Dialogue: Read the sight words below.

<u>taught</u>   <u>watch</u>

<u>put</u>   <u>who</u>

<u>that</u>   <u>from</u>

399

Read the words below that have the bold e sound made by the letter y (as in *baby*.)

l a d y   **m o m m y**

d a d d y   **h a p p y**

Read the words below that have the ch sound at the beginning of the word (as in *chip*).

c h i p   c h e e s e

c h i n   c h o p

Read the words below that have the ch sound at the end of the word (as in *patch*).

p a t c h   l a t c h

p i t c h   h i t c h

Read the words below that have the *fff* sound (as in *phone*).

p h o n e   p h o t o

g r a p h   p h a s e

Read the words below. These words will appear in the poem.

(Assist the child with reading any difficult words.)

q u a i l   f l o w e r

l i o n   h a w k

s o a r   r o a r

h o w l   g r o w l

t h u n d e r   c r a w l

g r u n t   t i g e r

b e a r   s a w

Read the poem below, and then I will show a picture to go with the poem.

(**Note**: We are no longer underlining the following sight words: *I, the, is, to, said, was, has, you, Papa, Mama, do, of* and *they*. We are no longer dotting the letter *k* in the blend *ck*. We are no longer dotting the letter *y* as in *way* or the letter *w* as in *crow*. We are no longer drawing a ring around several beginning blends.)

"Who?"

Who taught the quail how to fly?

Who taught the baby how to cry?

Who taught the wind how to blow?

Who taught the flower how to grow?

400

Who taught the lion how to roar?

Who taught the hawk how to soar?

Who taught the dog how to howl?

Who taught the bear how to growl?

Who taught the bug how to creep?

Who taught the frog how to leap?

Who taught the rose how to bloom?

Who taught the thunder how to boom?

Who taught the snow how to fall?

Who taught the ant how to crawl?

Who taught the bee how to sting?

Who taught the lark how to sing?

Who taught the brook how to flow?

Who taught the bird how to crow?

Who taught the pig how to grunt?

Who taught the tiger how to hunt?

Who taught the puppy how to play?

Who taught the mule how to bray?

Now I will show you a picture of an ant colony.

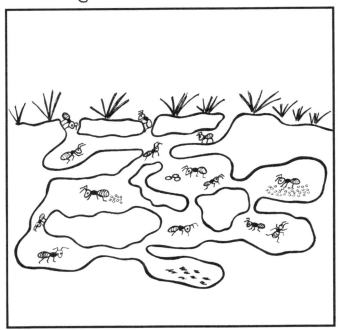

Look at the picture. Ants live in underground in colonies. Did you know ants are able to lift many times their own weight? There are over 15,000 kinds of ants. We have an awseome Creator!

Next I will write four lines from the poem you just read on index cards.

(Have the child watch as you write each word with a pen. Label the first card with the lesson number for future use.)

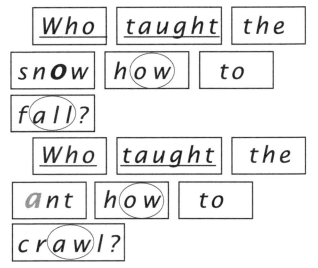

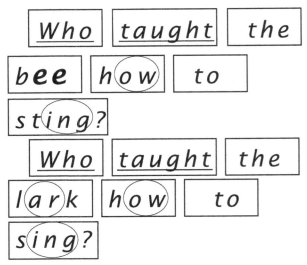

(**Note**: You may eliminate some of the print clues from the index cards with which your child is familiar. Be sure to include the print clues for new sounds that have been recently introduced.)

Today I will underline two different sight words. Read the sight words as I underline them.

I will trace over the *aaa* sound (as in *cat*) with a gray crayon. I will trace over the bold *o* sound (as in *snow*) and the bold *e* sound (as in *heat*) with a black crayon.

Next, I will draw a gray ring around the *ow* sound (as in *cow*) in the word *how*. I will draw a gray ring around the *all* sound (as in *ball*) in the word *fall*. I will draw a gray ring around the *aw* sound (as in *paw*) in the word *crawl*.

I will draw a gray ring around the *ing* sound (as in *sing*) in the word *sting* and in the word *sing*. I will also draw a gray ring around the *ar* sound (as in *car*) in the word *lark*.

Read the lines from the poem. Great! Find the index card with the word *fall* and the card with the word *crawl*. These words rhyme. Can you find two other words in these lines that rhyme? Yes, the words *sting* and *sing* rhyme.

Find the index cards with the question marks. Great! Why do we use question marks? That's right, we use them when we want to ask a question. This poem has a lot of question marks! Can you answer the questions being asked in the poem?

Now I will mix the cards, and you can put them in the proper order to make the sentences again.

Now read the sentences.

(**Note**: We are no longer using clues to assist the child with reading the copy work. It is important for the child to read the text located in this segment of the lesson even if he does not copy the sentences. This will give him an opportunity to practice reading text printed in a regular type.)

Copy Work: (The copy work is optional for children who have difficulty with writing.) (You may now encourage the child to copy the sentences directly from the model below. If this is too difficult, continue as directed.)

I will write the lines from the poem you just read on a piece of paper.

(Neatly write the sentences with a pen, paying close attention to letter spacing and formation.)

Now you can copy what I wrote.

Who taught the
snow how to fall?
Who taught the
ant how to crawl?
Who taught the
bee how to sting?

Who taught the
lark how to sing?

I would like for you to read the sentences once more. Very good! I would like for you to draw a picture to go with your sentences. Here is a picture of an ant on a blade of grass you can draw.

(Assist the child with drawing the picture if necessary. The picture has been drawn with bold lines so the child may trace it if he likes.)

Make up a story about the ant you drew. Tell me the story, and I will write it on a piece of paper. Now you can copy one sentence from your story at the bottom of your picture.

(Draw lines if necessary for the child to write his sentence at the bottom of his picture.)

Read the story you dictated to me.

Now let's read a book together.

(Review material between lessons.)

(An interesting story to read about ants is *Two Bad Ants* by Chris Van Allsburg. This is available at your public library.)

403

Lesson 96

Materials: reading manual, index cards, pen, gray crayon, and black crayon.

Instructions: In today's lesson, the child will review the following sight words: *caught, watch, people, there, your,* and *they.*

The child will review various sounds learned so far by reading the following words: *thick, think, thorn, this, landed, wanted, needed, counted, knock, knee, knit, know, night, might, bright,* and *high.*

The child will read the following poem and complete a variety of exercises based on the poem.

Title: *"The Funny Bunny"*

Poem: *Once there was a bunny named Fred,*
He wore his socks upon his head.
And you might think that this is silly,
But Fred did not like his ears to get chilly.
Now Fred is kind and Fred is nice,
He some times stops to help the mice.
One snowy day when Fred was out,
He could hear a mouse child shout.
Fred ran to see what was the matter,
For he could hear a noisy clatter.
He saw six mice upon the cliff,
And they were cold and they were stiff.
He wrapped them in his funny socks,
And helped them climb down from the rocks.
They said, "We used to think that you were silly
But you have made us not so chilly."
Fred took the mice right to the house,
Where they were met by Mama Mouse.
She said, "Thanks for bringing back my mice,
You are kind and you are nice."

Dialogue: Read the sight words below.

<u>caught</u>   <u>watch</u>

<u>people</u>   <u>there</u>

<u>your</u>   <u>they</u>

Read the words below that have the *th* sound (as in *thick* or *this*).

(th)ick   (th)ink

(th)orn   (th)is

Read the words below that have the *eeed* sound at the end of the word (as in *landed*).

land**ed**   want**ed**

n**ee**d**ed**   c(ou)nt**ed**

Read the words below that have the *nnn* sound (as in *knee*).

k n**o**ck   k n**ee**

k n**i**t   k n**ow**

Read the words below that have the bold *i* sound (as in *night*).

n**i**ght   m**i**ght

br**i**ght   h**i**gh

Read the words below. These words will appear in the poem.

(Assist the child with reading any difficult words.)

u**p**on   e**a**rs

(ch)ill**y**   n**i**(c)e

b**u**nn**y**   sn**o**w**y**

m**a**t(ter)   n(o)i s**y**

404

clatter　　wrapped

greeted　bringing

thanks

Read the poem, and then I will show you a picture to go with the poem.

(**Note**: We are no longer underlining the following sight words: *I, the, is, to, said, was, has, you, Papa, Mama, do, of,* and *they.* We are no longer dotting the letter *k* in the blend *ck.* We are no longer dotting the letter *y* as in *way* or the letter *w* as in *crow.* We are no longer drawing a ring around several beginning blends.)

"The Funny Bunny"

Once there was a bunny named Fred,

He wore his socks upon his head.

And you might think that this is silly,

But Fred did not like his

ears to get chilly.

Now Fred is kind and Fred is nice,

He some times stops to help the mice.

One snowy day when Fred was out,

He could hear a mouse child shout.

Fred ran to see what was the matter,

For he could hear a noisy clatter.

He saw six mice upon the cliff,

And they were cold and

405

they were stiff.

He wrapped them in his funny socks,

And helped them climb

down from the rocks.

They said, "We used to think

that you were silly,

But you have made us not so chilly."

Fred took the mice

right to the house,

Where they were met by Mama Mouse.

She said, "Thanks for

bringing back my mice,

You are kind and you are nice."

Now I will show you a picture of
the bunny.

406

Look at the picture. What does Fred have on his ears? Yes, he has a pair of socks on his ears. Why does Fred wear socks on his ears? That's right. He wears socks on his ears to keep them warm.

What did Fred use to help the cold mice? That's right. He used his funny socks. Do you think the mice will laugh at his funny socks anymore? No, they are probably glad Fred wears those funny socks.

Next, I will write four lines from the poem you just read on index cards.

(Have the child watch as you write each word with a pen. Label the first card with the lesson number for future use.)

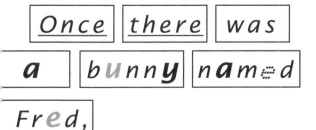

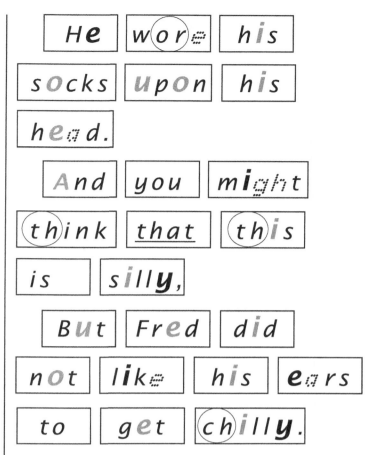

(**Note**: You may eliminate some of the print clues from the index cards with which your child is familiar. Be sure to include the print clues for new sounds that have been recently introduced.)

Today I will underline three different sight words. Read the sight words as I underline them.

I will trace over the *uuu* sounds (as in *cup*), the *eee* sounds (as in *wet*), and the *iii* sounds (as in *pig*) with a gray crayon. I will also trace over the *ooo* sounds (as in *hot*) and the *aaa* sound (as in *cat*) with a gray crayon.

I will trace over the bold *a* sounds (as in *cake*), the bold *e* sounds (as in *heat*), and the bold *i* sounds (as in *bike*) with a black crayon. I will trace over the bold *e* sound (as in *baby*) made by the letter *y* in the words *bunny, silly,* and *chilly.*

I will make dotted lines over the letter *e* in the words *named*, *wore*, and *like*. I will make dotted lines over the letter *a* in the word *head* and in the word *ears*. I will also make dotted lines over the letter *g* and the letter *h* in the word *might*. Can you tell me why I dotted these letters? That's right. I dotted them, because they are silent. They make no sound.

Next, I will draw a gray ring around the *or* sound (as in *corn*) in the word *wore*. I will draw a gray ring around the *th* sound (as in *thick* or *this*) in the word *think* and in the word *this*. I will also draw a gray ring around the *ch* sound (as in *chip* and *patch*) in the word *chilly*.

Read the lines from the poem. Find the card with the word *Fred* and the card with the word *head*. These words rhyme. Can you find two other words in these lines that rhyme? Yes, the words *silly* and *chilly* rhyme.

Now I will mix the cards, and you can put them in the proper order to make the sentences again.

Now read the sentences.

Copy Work: (The copy work is optional for children who have difficulty with writing.) (You may now encourage the child to copy the sentences directly from the model below. If this is too difficult, continue as directed.)

I will write the lines from the poem you just read on a piece of paper.

(Neatly write the sentences with a pen, paying close attention to letter spacing and formation.)

Now you can copy what I wrote.

Once there was a bunny named Fred,

He wore his socks upon his head.

And you might think that this is silly,

But Fred did not like his ears to get chilly.

I would like for you to read the sentences once more. Very good! I would like for you to draw a picture to go with your sentences. Here is a picture of a rabbit you can draw.

(Assist the child with drawing the picture if necessary. The picture has been drawn with bold lines so the child may trace it if he likes.)

408

(**Note:** You may choose to encourage the child to dictate a short story to you about the picture he drew instead of only one sentence.)

Make up a story about the rabbit you drew. Tell me the story, and I will write it on a piece of paper. Now you can copy one sentence from your story at the bottom of your picture.

(Draw lines if necessary for the child to write his sentence at the bottom of his picture.)

Read the story you dictated to me.

(Assist the child by reading any difficult words for him. If the story is long, have him read part of it and you read part of it.)

Now let's read a book together.

(Review material between lessons.)

(Beatrix Potter wrote a number of wonderful books about rabbits and mice. Two of my favorites are *The Tale of the Flopsy Bunnies* and *Two Bad Mice*. These are available at your public library.)

Lesson 97

Materials: reading manual, index cards, pen, gray crayon, black crayon, and three construction paper circles.

Instructions: In today's lesson, the child will review the following sight words: *learn, taught, caught, two,* and *new*. He will be introduced to three new sight words. Prepare three construction paper circles with the new sight words written on them. These new sight words are proper names that will be used in today's story. The names are *Gideon, Hannah,* and *Sarah*. We realize these names may prove difficult at first, so you may need to prompt the child with the correct names as he reads the story.

This lesson begins with chapter one of a twelve-chapter story entitled *Gideon's Gift*. You will read one chapter from this story to the child during each lesson. (The chapter to be read is included in each lesson.)

The child will then read a simple adaptation of the chapter to you. This adaptation has been written with the print clues we have been using in the previous lessons. In this manner, the child can participate in reading a story of higher literary quality.

After completing these twelve lessons, you will be encouraged to read a chapter book to the child and devise sentences pertaining to each chapter that he can read aloud to you. In essence, you will be creating an adaptation of the story. Naturally, letter combinations will occur to which he has not yet been introduced. You can use this opportunity to teach new letter combinations and the sounds they make.

A list additional phonics rules can be found in the Appendix. A list of suggested books to use to formulate these new reading exercises can also be found in the Appendix.

Eventually the child will be able to read more lengthy books on his own or with little guidance from you. The goal of reading is to enable the child to read material that is truly valuable to his life. This includes fiction as well as non-fiction material.

Next, you will read aloud chapter one from the story *Gideon's Gift*. Then the child will read the following adaptation from the chapter and complete a variety of exercises based on this adaptation.

Chapter title: *"Gideon Wants to Read"*

Story: *Gideon wanted Josh to read a book to him.*

Josh said, "I read that book to you two times."

"I know," said Gideon.

Gideon wanted to learn to read.

Gideon said, "I want to learn to read all by my self."

Hannah said, "Ask Mama to teach you to read."

"Mama taught us all to read," said Sarah.

Yes, Gideon would ask Mama. He would ask Mama to teach him to read. But, could he learn how to read?

Gideon stood by Mama's bed room door.

Mama said, "Come in Gideon. I want to talk to you."

Gideon stepped into the room.

Dialogue: Read the sight words below.

learn   taught

caught   two

new

Look at the new sight word below. This word is a person's name. The name is *Gideon*. (Point to the name as you read it.) Today we are going to begin reading a story about a boy named *Gideon*.

Gideon

Say *Gideon* as I point to the name. Very good! Next, I will show you another new sight word. This sight word is also a person's name. The name is *Hannah*. (Point to the name as you read it.)

Hannah is one of Gideon's sisters. He has three sisters. Hannah is the oldest sister.

Hannah

Say *Hannah* as I point to the name. Very good! Guess what? I have another new sight word for you. This sight word is also a person's name. The name is *Sarah*. (Point to the name as you read it.) Sarah is one of Gideon's three sisters too. She is the middle sister.

Sarah

Say *Sarah* as I point to the name. Great! Now you have learned three new names. Let's look at the names again and see if you can remember what they are. Try to read the names below. I will help you if you need it.

Hannah

Gideon

Sarah

Let's add the new sight words to your *Sight Word Worm*.

Read the sight word below.

want

If we add the letter s to this word we get the word *wants*. Read the word below as I point to it.

wants

If we add the letters *ed* to the word *want* we get the word *wanted*. Read the word below as I point to it.

wanted

Very good!

Now read the words below. They will appear in today's story.

(Assist the child with reading any difficult words.)

<u>taught</u>   *learn*

st(oo)d   <u>Mama</u>

re(a)d   r(oo)m

J(o)sh   <u>would</u>

<u>could</u>   (all)

my   s(e)lf

by   (i)nto

want(e)d

Now, I am going to read a story to you about a boy named Gideon. This story takes place in America in the early 1900s. I am going to read chapter one today. After I read chapter one, you will read some sentences about the chapter to me.

(Read the following story aloud to the child.)

Chapter One
"Gideon Wants to Read"

"Josh, read this book to me. Will you please?" asked Gideon.

"I read that book to you already two times today!" exclaimed Josh.

"I know," said Gideon as he hung his head, "I wish I could read *all by myself*."

"Ask Mama to teach you," said Hannah as she gently touched Gideon's shoulder.

"You know she taught us all to read when we were about your age," Sarah added kindly.

Gideon knew Mama had taught them all to read. She taught Josh first. He was the oldest. Mama was determined all of her children would get an education, even if they couldn't go to school.

Mama and Papa had bought an apple orchard when they were first married. They knew they would be far away from any schools. But Mama always said, "First you learn to read. Then you read to learn."

Yes, she taught Josh to read first, then Hannah, then Sarah, then Rachel, and then Benjamin. Now, Gideon wanted to learn to read too. He loved looking through the special birthday books that belonged to his brothers and sisters. He knew about how Josh had learned to read, before Gideon was even born, and about how Mama and Papa had let him choose a special book for his birthday.

Then they did the same for Hannah when she learned to read. Well, after that, it became a family tradition. Gideon thought each book was beautiful. He carefully examined them nearly every day. His brothers and sisters had read their books to him many, many, times, but he never grew tired of listening to the stories. Mama teased that he would wear out the pages and cause the print to fade.

Gideon was much younger than the other children. He could always find someone who was willing to read to him, but now that wasn't enough. Sure, he loved it when Mama read aloud to the family each day. That was special, but Gideon wanted to read all by himself too. He wanted to feel grown up like his brothers and sisters.

Yes, that's what he would do. He would ask Mama to teach him to read, but could he really learn how? All those letters in the books looked jumbled together. Gideon thought about it some more. "Maybe Mama hasn't taught me to read yet, because she thinks I can't do it."

He stood at her bedroom door and hesitated to enter. Suddenly a voice came from inside the room.

"Gideon, is that you?" Mama asked. "Come on in. I've been meaning to talk to you about something."

Gideon slowly opened the door and stepped inside the bedroom.

That ends chapter one of our story. Now I want you to read some sentences that tell us a little bit about chapter one. Then I will show you a picture to go with the story.

(**Note**: We are no longer underlining the following sight words: *I, the, is, to, said, was, has, you, Papa, Mama, do, of, they,* and *want*. We are no longer dotting the letter *k* in the blend *ck*. We are no longer dotting the letter *y* as in *way* or the letter *w* as in *crow*. We are no longer drawing a ring around several beginning blends.)

"Gideon Wants to Read"

Gideon wanted Josh to read a book to him.

Josh said, "I read that book to you two times."

"I know," said Gideon.

Gideon wanted to learn to read.

Gideon said, "I want to learn to read all by my self."

Hannah said, "Ask Mama to teach you to read."

"Mama taught us all to read," said Sarah.

Yes, Gideon would ask Mama. He would ask her to teach him to read.

412

But, could he learn how to read?
Gideon stood by Mama's bed room door.

Mama said, "Come in Gideon. I want to talk to you."

Gideon stepped into the room.

Now I will show you a picture of Gideon and his big brother, Josh.

Look at the picture. What is Gideon holding? Yes, he is holding a book. He is asking his big brother, Josh, to read the book to him. Can Gideon read yet? No, he cannot. Does he want to learn to read? Yes, he wants to learn to read. The story tells us Gideon likes to look at the special books that belong to his brothers and sisters. Why are these books special? That's right. Each child received a special book for his birthday when he learned to read.

Who taught each of the children to read? Yes, their mother taught them to read. Were the children able to go to school? No, they were not able to go to school. Why were they not able to go to school? That's right. They lived too far from any school. Where did they live? Yes, they lived on a farm that had an apple orchard.

Next, I will write four of the sentences from the story you just read on index cards.

(Have the child watch as you write each word with a pen. Label the first card with the lesson number for future use.)

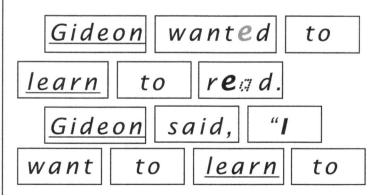

Gideon	wanted	to
learn	to	read.
Gideon	said,	"I
want	to	learn	to

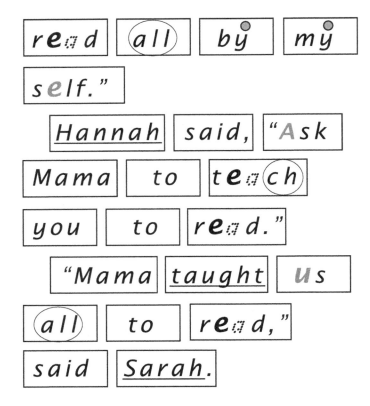

re_dd | (all) | by | mÿ

s**e**lf."

Hannah | said, | "Ask

Mama | to | te**a**(ch)

you | to | re_dd."

"Mama | taught | us

(all) | to | re_dd,"

said | Sarah.

(**Note**: You may eliminate some of the print clues from the index cards with which your child is familiar. Be sure to include the print clues for new sounds that have been recently introduced.)

We have a lot of sight words to underline today. Read the sight words as I underline them.

I will trace over the *eee* sounds (as in *wet*), the *aaa* sound (as in *cat*), and the *uuu* sound (as in *cub*) with a gray crayon.

I will trace over the bold *e* sounds (as in *heat*) with a black crayon. I will make dotted lines over the a in the words *read* and *teach*. Can you tell me why I dotted these letters? That's right. I dotted them, because they are silent. They make no sound.

I will draw a gray ring around the *all* sound (as in *ball*) in the word *all*. I will also draw a gray ring around the *ch* sound (as in *chip* and *patch*) in the word *teach*.

I will place a gray dot over the letter y in the word *by* and in the word *my*. Can you tell me why I put a gray dot over these letters? That's right. I put a gray dot over them, because the letter y makes the bold *i* sound in these words.

Read the sentences. Great! Now find the index cards with the quotation marks on them. Why do we use these special marks? That's right. We use them when a character is speaking. You will find these special marks are used twice in this passage. Who is speaking here? That's right. Gideon is speaking first, and then Hannah is speaking.

Now I will mix the cards, and you can put them in the proper order to make the sentences again.

Now read the sentences.

(**Note**: We are no longer using clues to assist the child with reading the copy work. It is important for the child to read the text located in this segment of the lesson even if he does not copy the sentences. This will give him an opportunity to practice reading text printed in a regular type.)

Copy Work: (The copy work is optional for children who have difficulty with writing.) (You may now encourage the child to copy the sentence directly from the model below. If this is too difficult, continue as directed.)

I will write the sentences you just read on a piece of paper.

(Neatly write the sentences with a pen, paying close attention to letter spacing and formation.)

Now you can copy what I wrote.

Gideon wanted to learn to read.

Gideon said, "I want to learn to read all by my self."

Hannah said, "Ask Mama to teach you to read."

"Mama taught us all to read," said Sarah.

I would like for you to read the sentences once more. Very good!

Make up a few sentences describing Gideon. Tell me the sentences, and I will write them on a piece of paper. You may draw a picture to go with your sentences if you like.

Now you can copy one of your sentences at the bottom of your picture.

(Draw lines if necessary for the child to write his sentence at the bottom of his picture.)

Read the sentences you dictated to me.

Now let's read a book together.

(Review material between lessons.)

Lesson 98

Materials: reading manual, index cards, pen, gray crayon, black crayon, and two construction paper circles.

Instructions: In today's lesson, the child will review the following sight words: *learn, where, there, taught, caught, people, new, Gideon, Hannah,* and *Sarah.* He will be introduced to two new sight words: *brother* and *mother.* Prepare two construction paper circles with the new sight words written on them. If you find your *Sight Word Worm* growing too large, begin a new one.

He will review the *aw* sound as in *saw* by reading the following words: *saw, paw, flaw, draw, thaw,* and *claw.*

He will review the *ing* sound as in *taking* and *hopping* by reading the following words: *kneeling, mixing, mopping, raking, running, reading, spelling,* and *batting.*

He will review the *th* sound as in *thick* or *this* by reading the following words: *thick, thing, thank, this, these, than,* and *those.*

He will review the *er* sound as in *her* when it is added to the end of a word such as *sister* by reading the following words: *sister, supper, dinner, rubber, gutter, after, rafter,* and *bigger.*

You will read chapter two from the story *Gideon's Gift.* Then the child will read the following adaptation from the chapter and complete a variety of exercises based on this adaptation.

Chapter title: *"Lessons for Gideon"*

Story: *Gideon saw his Mama. She was kneeling on the floor. She was kneeling by the old trunk. She took some things out of the trunk. She took out some books.*

Mama said, "Do you know what these are? These are books for reading and spelling. My big sister taught me to read and spell with these books. I taught your sisters to read and spell with these books. I taught your brothers to read and spell with these books. I will teach you to read and spell too."

"Do you really think I can learn to read?" asked Gideon.

"Yes," said Mama. "We will start after supper."

Dialogue: Read the sight words below.

learn   where

there   taught

caught   people

new   Gideon

Hannah   Sarah

Today you will learn two new sight words. Look at the word below. It is the word *brother*. (Point to the word as you read it.)

brother

Say *brother* as I point to the word. Very good!

Now look at the next sight word. It sounds like *brother*, but it begins with the letter *m*. Can you guess what the word is? (Point to the word.)

mother

Very good! It is the word *mother*. Read the sentence below that has the two new sight words.

My mother and my brother went f(or) **a** w(al)k.

Let's add the new sight words to your *Sight Word Worm*.

Look at the letters below. What sound do these letters make? (*aw* as in *saw*.)

(aw)

That's right. The letters make the *aw* sound.

Read the words below that have the *aw* sound (as in *saw*).

s(aw)   p(aw)

fl(aw)   dr(aw)

th(aw)   cl(aw)

Read the words below that have the *ing* sound (as in *sing*).

k n **ee** l(ing)   m i x(ing)

m **o** pp(ing)   r **a** k(ing)

r **u** n n(ing)   r **e** a d(ing)

s p e ll(ing)   b **a** t t(ing)

Look at the letters below. What sound do these letters make? (*th* as in *thick* or *this*.)

(th)

That's right. The letters make the *th* sound.

Read the words below that have the *th* sound (as in *thick* or *this*).

(th)i c k   (th)i n g

(th)**a** n k   (th)i s

(th)**e** s e   (th)**a** n

(th)**o** s e

416

Read the words below that have the er sound (as in *sister*).

sist(er)   supp(er)

dinn(er)   rubb(er)

gutt(er)   aft(er)

raft(er)   bigg(er)

Read the words below. They will appear in the story.

(Assist the child with reading any difficult words.)

aft(er)   trunk

know   taught

supp(er)   sist(er)

fl(o)or   st(a)rt

really   lessons

Now I am going to read chapter two from *Gideon's Gift*. After I read chapter two, you will read some sentences about the chapter to me.

(Read the following chapter from the story aloud to the child.)

Chapter Two
"Lessons for Gideon"

Mama was kneeling beside the old leather trunk at the foot of her bed. She was carefully taking out her treasures. First, the old quilt made by her great-grandmother, Pearl, and then the little stuffed calico dog she had made as a child. Merely a few strands of yarn held the dog's head in place.

Then she took out a package, neatly wrapped in brown paper and tied firmly with string. She smoothed her hands over the paper. It crinkled under her touch. She deftly untied the strings, and then she sat quietly for a moment.

"Do you know what's in here?" she asked Gideon.

"It looks like a box, or maybe books," he said as he edged closer to the slim figure kneeling on the floor.

"That's right," Mama said. "These are books. They are special books. Three of the books are readers and one is a speller. My big sister, Loraine, taught me to read and spell with these books. When I was a little mite, I would sit and watch her like a hawk as she studied her lessons. I kept asking her what all the letters meant. I was so persistent she taught me to read. She said I had a knack for reading. It came easy for me. God gives special gifts and abilities to each person. It is up to us to use our gifts wisely."

Gideon wondered what his special gift could be, but he was too afraid to ask Mama, for fear he didn't have one.

"Now, Gideon," continued Mama, "I taught all the other children to read and spell with these books. We live too far from town for you children to go to school. If you apply yourself, you can learn anything you desire. I will teach you to read and spell. First, you learn to read, and then you read to learn. Do you understand what that means?"

Gideon had heard Mama say that many times before.

"It means you can educate yourself," Mama said. "I told you I learned to read when I was very little, and you may think that is special. And it is. But, your papa didn't learn to read until he was thirteen. And that was special too. Do you know why that was special?"

"No," answered Gideon. "Wasn't that a little old for him to be learning to read?"

"Well, ordinarily so," replied his mother, "but Papa never had anyone teach him to read. You see, his pa died when he was six years old. He couldn't go to school, because his ma needed him to help around the farm. He had three younger brothers and two older sisters. The older children helped their ma with all the chores. There was so much to do that schooling was put aside."

"Papa's ma didn't neglect her duty as a mother. She knew the Lord commanded her to bring up her children to be good Christians. She felt the best way to do this was to memorize passages from the Bible. Each night his ma would read aloud from the gospels. She encouraged the children to learn key verses, but your papa has an incredible memory. Did you know he memorized the Sermon on the Mount by the time he was nine years old?"

"Goodness," said Gideon, "that's chapter's five, six, and seven of the Gospel according to Matthew."

Gideon knew Papa had memorized many passages from the Bible. Gideon remembered Papa reciting Scripture as they worked in the orchard ever since he was a small boy.

"But how did Papa teach himself to read?" Gideon wondered aloud.

"Well," began Mama, "one day your papa's ma sent him to town to buy something. Everyone in town was in an uproar. Papa asked, 'What's going on?' Someone handed him a newspaper and said, 'Just read this!'"

"Your papa did not want to admit he couldn't read. He purposed in his mind right then and there that he would learn to read. When he got home that evening, he took down the big family Bible and turned to the Sermon on the Mount. Since he had memorized it years before, he could make out the words. It was not easy, but after working diligently every evening, he learned to read in only one month. Why, he is even a better speller than I am!"

"Wow," said Gideon. "Mama, do you think I really can learn to read too?"

"Of course you can," Mama replied quickly, "And we will begin after supper."

That ends chapter two of our story. Now I want you to read some sentences that tell us a little bit about chapter two. Then I will show you a picture to go with the story.

(**Note**: We are no longer underlining the following sight words: *I, the, is, to, said, was, has, you, Papa, Mama, do, of, they,* and *want*. We are no longer dotting the letter *k* in the blend *ck*. We are no longer dotting the letter *y* as in *way* or the letter *w* as in *crow*. We are no longer drawing a ring around several beginning blends.)

"Lessons for Gideon"

Gideon saw his Mama. She was kneeling on the floor. She was kneeling by the old trunk. She took some things out of the trunk. She took out some books.

Mama said, "Do you know what these are? These are books for reading and spelling. My big sister taught me to read and spell with these books. I taught your sisters to read and spell with these books. I taught your brothers to read and spell with these books. I will teach you to read and spell too."

"Do you really think I can learn to read?" asked Gideon.

"Yes," said Mama. "We will start after supper."

Now I will show you a picture of Mama.

Look at the picture. What is Mama doing? Yes, she is kneeling on the floor. What is she holding in her hands? Yes, she is holding some books. What kind of books are these? That's right. Three of the books are readers, and one is a speller.

What is Mama going to do with these books? Yes, she is going to teach Gideon to read and spell. Do you think Gideon wants to learn to read?

Next, I will write four of the sentences from the story you just read on index cards.

(Have the child watch as you write each word with a pen. Label the first card with the lesson number for future use.)

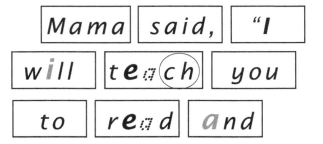

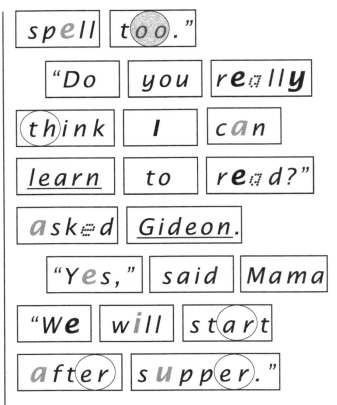

(**Note**: You may eliminate some of the print clues from the index cards with which your child is familiar. Be sure to include the print clues for new sounds that have been recently introduced.)

We are only underlining two sight words today. Read the sight words as I underline them.

I will trace over the *iii* sounds (as in *pig*) and the *aaa* sounds (as in *cat*) with a gray crayon. I will also trace over the *eee* sounds (as in *wet*) and the *uuu* sound (as in *cub*) with a gray crayon.

I will trace over the bold *e* sounds (as in *heat*) with a black crayon. I will trace over the bold *e* sound (as in *baby*) made by the letter *y* in the word *really*.

I will make dotted lines over the letter *a* in the words *teach*, *read*, and *really*. I will also make dotted lines over the letter *e* in the word *asked*. Can you tell me why I dotted these letters?

420

That's right. I dotted them, because they are silent. They make no sound.

I will draw a gray ring around the *ch* sound (as in *chip* and *patch*) in the word *teach*. I will draw a shaded gray ring around the *oo* sound (as in *boot*) in the word *too*. I will draw a gray ring around the *th* sound (as in *thick* or *this*) in the word *think*.

I will draw a gray ring around the *ar* sound (as in *car*) in the word *start*. I will also draw a gray ring around the *er* sound (as in *her*) in the word *after* and in the word *supper*.

Read the sentences. Great! Find the index cards with the quotation marks on them. Why do we use these special marks? That's right. We use them when a character is speaking. You will find these special marks are used four times in this passage. Who are the characaters speaking here?

Now I will mix the cards, and you can put them in the proper order to make the sentences again.

Now read the sentences.

(**Note**: We are no longer using clues to assist the child with reading the copy work. It is important for the child to read the text located in this segment of the lesson even if he does not copy the sentences. This will give him an opportunity to practice reading text printed in a regular type.)

Copy Work: (The copy work is optional for children who have difficulty with writing.) (You may now encourage the child to copy the sentence directly from the model below. If this is too difficult, continue as directed.)

I will write the sentences you just read on a piece of paper.

(Neatly write the sentences with a pen, paying close attention to letter spacing and formation.)

Now you can copy what I wrote.

Mama said, "I will teach you to read and spell too."

"Do you really think I can learn to read?" asked Gideon.

"Yes," said Mama. "We will start after supper."

I would like for you to read the sentences once more. Very good!

Make up a few sentences about Mama. Tell me the sentences, and I will write them on a piece of paper. You may draw a picture to go with your sentences if you like.

Now you can copy one of your sentences at the bottom of your picture.

(Draw lines if necessary for the child to write his sentence at the bottom of his picture.)

Read the sentences you dictated to me.

Now let's read a book together.

(Review material between lessons.)

421

Lesson 99

Materials: reading manual, index cards, pen, gray crayon, black crayon, and two construction paper circles.

Instructions: In today's lesson, the child will review the following sight words: *brother, mother, new, Gideon, Hannah,* and *Sarah.* He will be introduced to two new sight words. They are the names: *Benjamin* and *Rachel.* Prepare two construction paper circles with the new sight words written on them.

He will review the *or* sound as in *corn* by reading the following words: *corn, chores, more, porch, fork,* and *sore.*

He will review the *sss* sound as in *face* by reading the following words: *face, lace, dance, prance, rice,* and *mice.*

He will review the bold *e* sound as in *baby* by reading the following words: *baby, city, funny, bunny, sleepy,* and *dirty.*

You will read aloud chapter three from the story *Gideon's Gift.* The child will read the following adaptation from the story and complete a variety of exercises based on this adaptation.

Chapter title: *"The First Lesson"*

Story: *Gideon ran to the barn to do his chores. Benjamin came in the barn.*

Benjamin said, "Why are you so happy?"

Gideon said, "Mama is going to teach me how to read tonight."

Benjamin said, "You can not learn to read in one night."

"I know that," said Gideon. "We will start tonight."

Rachel stood on the porch.

She said, "Come and eat. It is time for supper."

The boys ran into the house.

After supper, Mama said, "Come here Gideon. Look and see what I have for you."

She handed Gideon a slate.

Mama said, "Papa got it for you when he was in town."

Dialogue: Read the sight words below.

brother   mother

new   Gideon

Hannah   Sarah

Look at the new sight words below. Both of these words are names of people in the story. The first name is Benjamin. (Point to the name as you read it.) The second name is Rachel. (Point to the name as you read it.)

Benjamin   Rachel

Let's add the new sight words to your *Sight Word Worm.*

Read the words below that have the or sound (as in *corn*).

c(or)n   ch(or)es

m(o)(r)e   p(o)(r)ch

f(o)(r)k   s(o)(r)e

Read the words below in which the letter c makes the sss sound. I will read the first word for you. It is *face.*

fa(c)e   la(c)e

dan(c)e   pran(c)e

ri(c)e   mi(c)e

Read the following words in which the letter y makes the bold e sound. I will read the first word for you. It is baby.

b**a**b**y**   ⓒ**i**t**y**

f**u**nn**y**   b**u**nn**y**

sl**ee**p**y**   d**ir**t**y**

Read the words below.

t o   n **i** *gh* t

That's right. The words are *to* and *night*. If we join the words together we have a new word. It is the word *tonight*. Look at the word below and read the new word.

t o n **i** *gh* t

Very good!

Now read the words below that will appear in the story.

(Assist the child with reading any difficult words.)

b ⓐ **r** n   h **a** p p **y**

w *h* **y**   l e a r n

t ⓞ ⓦ n   s t ⓐ **r** t

s t ⓞⓞ d   s u p p ⓔ **r**

b ⓞ **y** s   h ⓞⓤ s e

s l **a** t e   t o n **i** *gh* t

Now I am going to read chapter three from *Gideon's Gift*. After I read the chapter, you will read some sentences to me about the chapter.

(Read the following chapter from the story aloud to the child.)

Chapter Three

"The First Lesson"

Gideon practically flew to the barn to do his chores. He wanted to be sure to finish by suppertime. As he cleaned the stalls and fed the few animals his family owned, his mind soared with thoughts of learning to read. He purposed he would study very hard everyday and make Mama and Papa proud. He hoped through his lessons God would reveal his gift to him.

Benjamin arrived several minutes later to help with the chores. Gideon's excitement was obvious.

"What's gotten into you, Gideon?" Benjamin asked as he put his barn frock over his clothes.

"Tonight, Mama's going to teach me how to read," said Gideon breathlessly.

"You can't learn to read in just one night," Benjamin quipped.

"I know that," said Gideon, "but she's going to start teaching me to read tonight, and soon I'll be able to read all by myself."

Gideon was determined not to allow Benjamin's quick remark to dampen his spirits. Soon Gideon and Benjamin heard the clanging of the dinner bell. As they came from the barn, they saw Rachel standing on the porch.

"I've made a special dessert from Mama's cookbook, so hurry up and get washed," she ordered.

The boys did not need to be told twice to get ready for supper. Within a couple of minutes they were sitting in their places at the table. Papa blessed the food, and then a clatter of plates and spoons was heard as Mama filled each plate with good things to eat.

"Well," said Josh, "What's this special dessert you've cooked up, Rachel?"

"I bet it has chocolate in it," piped Benjamin as he sniffed the air and pretended to collapse in his seat.

"You have a keen nose," commented Rachel. "I have made chocolate cream puffs, and I must say, they even look delicious."

Everyone was talking about how they loved chocolate and about how long it had been since they had eaten anything made with chocolate. Mrs. Anderson, their nearest neighbor, had been to town the day before and she bought some chocolate. Mama traded a tub of her fresh butter for a pound of the chocolate.

Gideon sat silently and ate. He was too busy thinking about his first reading lesson to be bothered with thoughts of chocolate. Of course, he decided it would be a good idea to have some of the dessert. After all, he did not want to hurt Rachel's feelings.

After everyone had their fill of dessert, and the dishes were cleared away, Mama called Gideon into the kitchen.

"You will have your lessons at the kitchen table. Papa bought you a slate and a slate pencil while he was in town last month."

So Mama really had been planning to teach me how to read, Gideon thought to himself.

Mama opened the reading book to the first lesson. Gideon strained to sit properly and pay close attention. He wanted to be certain he didn't miss a thing. Gideon was so absorbed in the lesson that the hour passed quickly.

"You did a fine job with the first lesson, Gideon," praised Mama. "Keep that up and you'll be reading by yourself by the end of the summer."

"By the end of summer!" thought Gideon happily.

Gideon's birthday was at the beginning of autumn. He loved autumn, for the woods were clothed in marvelous colors: brown, yellow, orange, and all sorts of colors in between. Yes, autumn was a wonderful time of year, and this birthday would be extra special. If he worked hard all summer, he would learn to read. Then he would get his own birthday book. With that happy thought, Gideon kissed his mother goodnight and went upstairs to bed.

That ends chapter three of our story. Now I want you to read some sentences that tell us a little bit about this chapter. Then I will show you a picture to go with the story.

(**Note**: We are no longer underlining the following sight words: *I, the, is, to, said, was, has, you, Papa, Mama, do, of, they, want,* and *that.* We are no longer dotting the letter *k* in the blend *ck.* We are no longer dotting the letter *y* as in *way* or the letter *w* as in *crow.* We are no longer drawing a gray ring around several beginning blends.)

"The First Lesson"

Gideon ran to the barn to do his chores. Benjamin came in the barn. Benjamin said, "Why are you so happy?"

Gideon said, "Mama is going to teach me how to read tonight."

Benjamin said, "You can not learn to read in one night."

"I know that," said Gideon. "We will start tonight."

Rachel stood on the porch.

She said, "Come and eat. It is time for supper."

The boys ran into the house.

After supper Mama said, "Come here Gideon. Look and see what I have for you."

She handed Gideon a slate.

Mama said, "Papa got it for you when he was in town."

Now I will show you a picture of Gideon and Mama.

Look at the picture. What did Mama give Gideon? That's right. She gave him a slate. A slate is another word for a chalkboard.

Why do you think Gideon needs a slate? Yes, he needs a slate to write his lessons. Children used slates to do a lot of their schoolwork, because paper was expensive.

Do you know what a slate pencil is? That's right. It is a piece of chalk. Long ago people called it a slate pencil. Children had to take good care of their slates and slate pencils. Sometimes two children in a family would have to share a slate in school.

It is fun to write on a chalkboard or slate. If you have a chalkboard, you may want to do your copying exercises on it today.

Next, I will write four of the sentences from the story you just read on index cards.

(Have the child watch as you write each word with a pen. Label the first card with the lesson number for future use.)

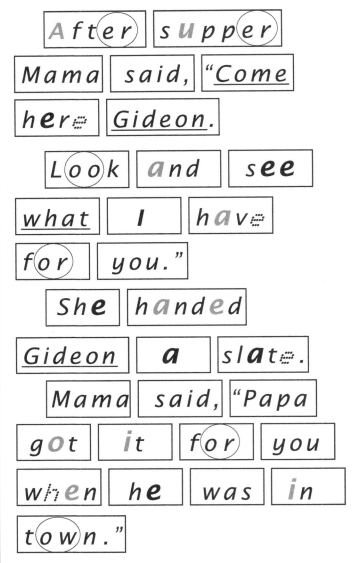

(**Note**: You may eliminate some of the print clues from the index cards with which your child is familiar. Be sure to include the print clues for new sounds that have been recently introduced.)

Today I will underline three different sight words. Read the sight words as I underline them with a black crayon.

I will trace over the *aaa* sounds (as in *cat*), the *uuu* sound (as in *cub*), and the *eee* sounds (as in *wet*) with a gray crayon. I will also trace over the *ooo* sound (as in *hot*) and the *iii* sounds (as in *pig*) with a gray crayon.

I will trace over the bold *e* sounds (as in *heat*) and the bold *a* sounds (as in *cake*) with a black crayon.

I will make dotted lines over the letter *e* in the words *here, have,* and *slate*. I will also make dotted lines over the letter *h* in the word *when*. Can you tell me why I dotted these letters? That's right. I dotted them, because they are silent. They make no sound.

I will draw a gray ring around the *er* sound (as in *her*) in the words *after* and *supper*. I will draw a gray ring around the *oo* sound (as in *cook*) in the word *look*.

I will draw a gray ring around the *or* sound (as in *corn*) in the word *for*. I will also draw a gray ring around the *ow* sound (as in *cow*) in the word *town*.

Read the sentences. Very good! Find the index cards that have quotation marks on them. Why do we use these special marks? That's right. We use them when a character is speaking. Who is speaking in this passage? That's right. Both times the quotation marks are used it is Mama who is speaking.

Now I will mix the cards, and you can put them in proper order to make the sentences again.

Now read the sentences.

(**Note**: We are no longer using clues to assist the child with reading the copy work. It is important for the child to read the text located in this segment of the lesson even if he does not copy the sentences.

This will give him an opportunity to practice reading text printed in a regular type.)

Copy Work: (The copy work is optional for children who have difficulty with writing.) (You may now encourage the child to copy the sentences directly from the model below. If this is too difficult, continue as directed.)

I will write the sentences you just read on a piece of paper.

(Neatly write the sentences with a pen, paying close attention to letter spacing and formation.)

Now you can copy what I wrote.

After supper Mama said, "Come here Gideon. Look and see what I have for you."

She handed Gideon a slate.

Mama said, "Papa got it for you when he was in town."

I would like for you to read the sentences once again. Very good!

Make up a few sentences about Gideon's slate.

Tell me the sentences, and I will write them on a piece of paper. You may draw a picture to go with your sentences if you like. Now you can copy

427

one of your sentences at the bottom of your picture.

(Draw lines if necessary for the child to write his sentence at the bottom of his picture.)

Read the sentences you dictated to me.

Now let's read a book together.

(Review material between lessons.)

Lesson 100

Materials: reading manual, index cards, pen, gray crayon, and black crayon.

Instructions: In today's lesson, the child will review the following sight words: *would, could, should, Benjamin, Rachel, brother, mother, Gideon, Hannah,* and *Sarah.*

He will be introduced to the meaning of syllables, and he will practice reading words with two syllables. Although the child has read other two-syllable words in earlier lessons, for example, *baking* and *bigger*, we have not introduced the idea of syllables until this lesson. He will read the following two-syllable words: *wagon, dragon, button, basket, market, rocket, winter, summer, letter, cracker, sister, rooster, open, sharpen,* and *rotten.*

You will read aloud chapter four from *Gideon's Gift*. The child will read the following adaptation from the story and complete a variety of exercises based on this adaptation.

Chapter title: *"Going to Town"*

Story: *The next day Papa said, "Who would like to go to town?"*

Mama said, "Rachel and I will stay at home. We will bake the bread."

Papa took his hat from the rack. Papa and Josh hitched the horses to the wagon.

Hannah said, "Where is Gideon?"

"I will go and see," said Sarah.

Sarah went into the house. She took Gideon by the hand. They walked to the wagon.

Gideon said, "I want to be a writer some day."

They rode to town in the wagon. Papa and the big boys went to the feed store. Gideon and the girls went to the post office. Sarah mailed a letter to Mama's sister.

The clerk said, "I have a letter for your mother."

Hannah said, "We must go to the hat shop now."

Later they met Papa and the big boys at the store.

Dialogue: Read the sight words below.

would   could

should   Benjamin

Rachel   brother

mother   Gideon

Hannah   Sarah

Read the words below that will appear in the story.

(Assist the child with reading any difficult words.)

bread   hitched

horses   walked

writer   store

post   office

mailed

Look at the word below. The word is wagon. (Point to the word as you read it.) Listen as I say the word again slowly.

wag/on

Do you notice this word has two parts? We have put a gray line between the two parts. The first part of the word is waaag and the second part of the word is ooon. When we put the two parts together we say wagon. We call each part of the word a syllable. The word wagon has two syllables or two parts.

(We will use a line to divide syllables in selected words in the remaining lessons. We will not use this aid in the stories.)

Read the words below. These words each have two syllables.

wag/on   drag/on

but/ton   bas/ket

mar/ket   rock/et

win/ter   sum/mer

let/ter   crack/er

sis/ter   roos/ter

o/pen   shar/pen

rot/ten

Now I am going to read chapter four from *Gideon's Gift*. After I read the chapter, you will read some sentences about the chapter to me.

(Read the following story aloud to the child.)

Chapter Four

"Going to Town"

The next morning at breakfast Papa announced, "I'm going to town today to do some trading. Would anyone like to come along?"

Mama and Rachel decided to stay home and do the baking for the week.

"We've extra baking to do this week," said Mama. "The church picnic is tomorrow, and I agreed to make all the bread."

"Well," Papa chimed in, "if you didn't bake such delicious bread, you wouldn't get yourself into such a fix!"

Mama smiled as Papa took his hat from the rack and headed out the door.

"Try to be home by supper time," Mama added as she handed Hannah the basket lunch she had prepared.

"We'll do our best," Papa said, "but the roads are in poor shape since the river flooded and washed away the good hard dirt. It will be slow going with all the holes. But, we'll hurry as best we can."

The children climbed into the wagon, eager for the trip to town.

Just as Papa and Josh hitched the horses to the wagon, Hannah asked, "Isn't Gideon going with us?"

"I'll run into the house and see," said Sarah.

As Sarah opened the kitchen door, she heard Mama say, "Now Gideon, you run along to town with Papa. You'll have your next reading lesson after supper. There's no need to rush things."

"Okay," sighed Gideon, "I just thought maybe I could have two lessons a day instead of one."

Sarah laughed and took Gideon by the hand.

As they walked to the wagon she asked, "Why are you in such a hurry to learn to read?"

"Because, once I learn to read, then I can learn to write," said Gideon in a serious tone.

"Well," asked Sarah, "why do you want to learn to write?"

"Because, I've got lots and lots of stories locked up in my head, and I need to put them down on paper. You see, I want to be a writer someday."

"With determination like yours, Gideon, I bet you *will* be a writer one day. I bet you will be a fine writer," Sarah added as she stroked Gideon's blond hair.

The two jumped into the wagon, and with a jolt they were on their way to town.

"I'm glad for such a nice dry day," said Papa. "We've not been to town since the river flooded, and our supplies are getting low. Josh and Benjamin and I will stop at the feed store and load the wagon.

Sarah, you and Hannah and Gideon get the things we need at the general store. We'll come by after we finish our errands."

"Papa," asked Hannah, "may we stop in at the millinery shop? I would like to look at the new hats. Mama said she would help me make a hat if I can find a style I like."

"That would be fine," Papa answered. "Oh, I almost forgot," he said, "Mama gave me this letter to mail to her sister in Hagerstown. Please stop by the post office first. Check to see if any mail is waiting there for us too."

The girls and Gideon climbed down from the wagon and headed for the post office. Gideon bounded up the post office steps in a single leap.

"You are full of energy today, Gideon," Hannah exclaimed.

Sarah handed the clerk the letter to be mailed and paid for the postage.

"I've got a letter for your mother," said the clerk as he read the name on the back of the envelope Sarah had given him. "The letter is from Hagerstown," he said, "It's a very busy place, you know."

Sarah thanked the clerk and the three children looked at the letter with interest.

"We must wait and let Mama open it," remarked Sarah. "It's addressed to her. It's from Aunt Loraine."

"She always has such interesting news. It must be exciting to live in such a big city," said Hannah with a longing sigh. "Someday I'm going to live in New York City."

"I prefer the country," said Sarah. "Even this small town makes me feel crowded and hemmed in."

"I like all kinds of places," Gideon added. "I want to travel to lots of fascinating places when I grow up."

"We had better hurry and go to the millinery shop. We will only be able to browse about for a short while. Papa will expect us to have everything ordered by the time he gets to the general store. We don't want to keep him waiting. Mama doesn't want us to be late, and we've got a long ride ahead of us," Hannah reminded them.

That ends chapter four of our story. Now I want you to read some sentences that tell us a little bit about this chapter. Then I will show you a picture to go with the story.

(Note: We are no longer underlining the following sight words: *I, the, is, to, said, was, has, you, Papa, Mama, do, of, they, want,* and *that.* We are no longer dotting the letter *k* in the blend *ck.* We are no longer dotting the letter *y* as in *way* or the letter *w* as in *crow.* We are no longer drawing a gray ring around several beginning blends.)

"Going to Town"

The next day Papa said, "Who would like to go to town?"

Mama said, "Rachel and I will stay at home. We will bake the bread."

Papa took his hat from the rack. Papa and Josh hitched the horses to the wagon.

Hannah said, "Where is Gideon?"

"I will go and see," said Sarah.

Sarah went into the house. She took Gideon by the hand. They walked to the wagon.

Gideon said, "I want to be a writer some day."

They rode to town in the wagon.

Papa and the big boys went to the feed store. Gideon and the girls went to the post office. Sarah mailed a letter to Mama's sister.

The clerk said, "I have a letter for your mother."

Hannah said, "We must go to the hat shop now."

Later they met Papa and the big boys at the store.

Now I will show you a picture of Gideon and his sisters at the post office.

Look at the picture. What is the postal clerk giving to Sarah? That's right. He is giving her a letter. Who is the letter from? That's right. It is from their Aunt Loraine.

Where are Gideon and Hannah and Sarah going after they leave the post office? Yes, they are going to go to the millinery shop. A millinery shop is a hat shop. Long ago, women and girls wore hats or bonnets whenever they went out of the house.

Next, I will write four of the sentences from the story you just read on index cards.

(Have the child watch as you write each word with a pen. Label the first card with the lesson number for future use.)

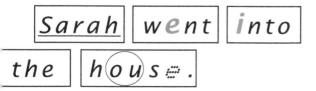

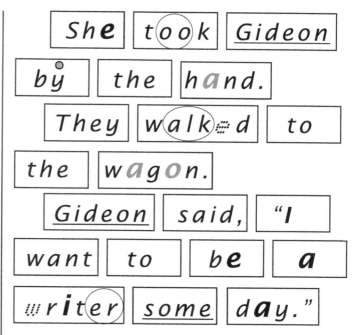

(**Note**: You may eliminate some of the print clues from the index cards with which your child is familiar. Be sure to include the print clues for new sounds that have been recently introduced.)

I will underline several sight words with a gray crayon. Read the sight words as I underline them.

I will trace over the *eee* sound (as in *wet*) and the *iii* sound (as in *pig*) with a gray crayon. I will also trace over the *aaa* sounds (as in *cat*) and the *ooo* sound (as in *hot*) with a gray crayon.

I will trace over the bold *e* sounds (as in *heat*), the bold *a* sounds (as in *cake*), and the bold *i* sound (as in *bike*) with a black crayon.

I will make dotted lines over the letter *e* in the word *house* and in the word *walked*. I will also make dotted lines over the letter *w* in the word *writer*. Why did I dot these letters? That's right. I dotted them, because they are silent. They make no sound.

433

I will draw a gray ring around the ou sound (as in *house*) in the word *house*. I will draw a gray ring around the oo sound (as in *cook*) in the word *took*. I will draw a gray ring around the alk sound (as in *talk*) in the word *walked*. I will also draw a gray ring around the er sound (as in *her*) in the word *writer*.

I will place a gray dot over the letter y in the word *by*. Can you tell me why I did this? That's right, I did this because the letter y makes a bold *i* sound (as in *fly*) in the word *by*.

Read the sentences. Great! Find the index cards with the quotation marks. Why do we use these special marks? That's right, we use them when a character speaks. Who is speaking in this passage? That's right. Gideon is speaking.

Now I will mix the cards, and you can put them in proper order to make the sentences again.

Now read the sentences.

(**Note**: We are no longer using clues to assist the child with reading the copy work. It is important for the child to read the text located in this segment of the lesson even if he does not copy the sentences. This will give him an opportunity to practice reading text printed in a regular type.)

Copy Work: (The copy work is optional for children who have difficulty with writing.) (You may now encourage the child to copy the sentences directly from the model below. If this is too difficult, continue as directed.)

I will write the sentences you just read on a piece of paper.

(Neatly write the sentences with a pen, paying close attention to letter spacing and formation.)

Now you can copy what I wrote.

Sarah went into the house. She took Gideon by the hand. They walked to the wagon.

Gideon said, "I want to be a writer some day."

I would like for you to read the sentences once again. Very good!

Make up a few sentences about the chapter, "Going to Town."

Tell me the sentences, and I will write them on a piece of paper. You may draw a picture to go with your sentences if you like. Now you can copy one of your sentences at the bottom of your picture.

(Draw lines if necessary for the child to write his sentence at the bottom of his picture.)

Read the sentences you dictated to me.

Now let's read a book together.

(Review material between lessons.)

Lesson 101

Materials: reading manual, index cards, pen, gray crayon, and black crayon.

Instructions: In today's lesson, the child will review the following sight words: *many, new, learn, caught, taught, Benjamin, Rachel, brother, mother, Gideon, Hannah,* and *Sarah.*

He will practice reading the following words printed with conventional type: *cat, fat, mad, sad, wet, vet, bed, fed, pup, cup, club, sub, hot, pot, mop, drop, pig, wig, fix,* and *mix.*

He will read the following words ending in the letters *le*: *bottle, rattle, fiddle, puddle, giggle, gobble, juggle,* and *battle.*

You will read aloud chapter five from *Gideon's Gift*. The child will read the following adaptation from the story and complete a variety of exercises based on this adaptation.

Chapter title: *"News from Town"*

Story: *Rachel looked out the window. She saw the clouds of dust. The wagon was coming home from town. Gideon ran into the house. He had a letter in his hand. Mama was making bread. She wiped her hands. She took a pin from her hair and slit open the letter. Mama read the letter. It was from her sister. The letter said that a book wagon would be coming soon. The wagon has shelves to hold the books. Gideon was too happy to speak.*

Papa said, "The book wagon will be coming in two weeks!"

Mama said, "Supper is getting cold. Come and eat."

Gideon dreamed of the books going from town to town in the wagon.

Dialogue: Read the sight words below.

<u>many</u>　　　　<u>new</u>

<u>learn</u>　　　　<u>caught</u>

<u>taught</u>　　　　<u>Benjamin</u>

<u>Rachel</u>　　　　<u>brother</u>

<u>mother</u>　　　　<u>Gideon</u>

<u>Hannah</u>　　　　<u>Sarah</u>

Read the words below. These words are printed with regular type like you will find in most books. We have not used gray letters or bold black letters. We have not drawn gray rings around any of the letters either. Soon all of the words you will read will be printed with regular type.

cat　　　　fat

mad　　　　sad

wet　　　　vet

bed　　　　fed

pup　　　　cup

club　　　　sub

hot　　　　pot

mop　　　　drop

pig　　　　wig

fix　　　　mix

Look at the word below. It is the word *bottle*. (Point to the word as you read it.) Which letter in this word is silent? That's right. The letter *e* is silent. It makes no sound. The word *bottle* ends in the /l/ sound.

bottle

Read the following words that end in the /l/ sound like the word *bottle*.

435

bottle   rattle

fiddle   puddle

giggle   gobble

juggle   battle

Read the word below.

come

Very good! It is the sight word come.

We can add the *ing* sound (as in *sing*) to make a new word. Look at the new word below. The new word is *coming*.

com(ing)

Read the word below.

new

Very good! It is the sight word *new*. We can add the letter *s* to make another word. Look at the word below. The word is *news*.

news

Read the words below that will appear in the story.

(Assist the child with reading any difficult words.)

window   cl(ou)ds

le(tt)(er)   slit

open   shelves

com(ing)   su(pp)(er)

two   dreamed

news   hair

Now I am going to read chapter five from *Gideon's Gift*. After I read the chapter, you will read some sentences about the chapter to me. (Read the following chapter aloud to the child.)

Chapter Five

"News from Town"

Clouds of dust rose in the distance signaling the return of Papa and the children from town. Rachel was the first to spot them from the kitchen window where she and Mama were still busy baking the last loaves of bread.

"Thank goodness they're home on time," remarked Mama, "Supper's on the table and we're almost done with the baking."

Gideon was the first one in the house. He was waving the letter from Aunt Loraine and shouting, "It's for you Mama, a letter from Hagerstown!"

Mama turned the lump of dough once more on the floured board and patted it into a loaf. Then she wiped her hands on the dishcloth. Gideon handed her the letter. Using a hairpin from her hair, she slit open the end of the envelope.

"It's from Aunt Loraine," she said merrily.

The rest of the family clambered into the hot kitchen to hear the news. The letter read:

June 15th, 1905

Dear Opal, William, and Children,

I am doing very well. I love my new job at the Washington County Free Library. It is a pleasure to work with everyone here. We are like one big family.

Marvelous things are happening around the state for our free public libraries. I am writing to tell you of a wonderful new program developed by our head librarian that will allow you to borrow books from the Washington County Free Library. A wagon has been purchased which has been fitted with shelves for holding and carrying books.

The book wagon will visit the town of Elmerton just twelve miles northeast of you. It will be stationed at the Woodbury stables where it can be sheltered in the event of rain. The book wagon will begin service to your area on July 27. It will come on the first Tuesday of each month. It is expected in town at approximately noon. To borrow books, you must register with the attendant. The books are to be returned the following month. A small fee will be charged if the books are not returned at this time.

I feel this will be a tremendous resource for your lovely family. I have enclosed a map showing the exact route the book wagon will make, with each stopping post clearly marked.

Affectionately Yours,

Loraine

The children all hollered at the thought of being able to borrow books from the book wagon. They talked about the kind of books they wanted to read, but Gideon was so deep in thought he didn't utter a sound.

"What's on your mind, Son," asked Papa as he sat next to Gideon in the noisy kitchen.

"I'm just too happy to speak," Gideon managed to say. "It seems too good to be true."

"Just think," said Papa, "the book wagon will be coming our way in only two short weeks!"

Mama hurried everyone to the table.

"Supper is getting cold," she said. "Don't forget Gideon, we'll have your second reading lesson after supper."

Gideon ate silently as he dreamed about all those wonderful books being carted from town to town in a wagon.

"What will they think of next?" he wondered.

That ends chapter five of our story. Now I want you to read some sentences that tell us a little bit about this chapter. Then I will show you a picture to go with the story.

(**Note**: We are no longer underlining the following sight words: *I, the, is, to, said, was, has, you, Papa, Mama, do, of, they, want,* and *that*. We are no longer dotting the letter *k* in the blend *ck*. We are no longer dotting the letter *y* as in *way* or the letter *w* as in *crow*. We are no longer drawing a gray ring around several beginning blends.)

"News from Town"

Rachel looked out the window. She saw the clouds of dust. The wagon was coming home from town.

Gideon ran into the house. He had a letter in his hand. Mama was making bread. She wiped her hands.

She took a pin from her hair and slit open the letter. Mama read the letter. It was from her sister.

The letter said that a book wagon would be coming soon. The wagon has shelves to hold the books. Gideon was too happy to speak.

Papa said, "The book wagon will be coming in two weeks!"

Mama said, "Supper is getting cold. Come and eat."

Gideon dreamed of the books going from town to town in the wagon.

Now I will show you a picture of Mama in the kitchen.

Look at the picture. What is Mama opening? That's right. She is opening a letter. Who is the letter from? Yes, it is from her sister. Do you remember what her sister's name is? That's right. Her name is Lorraine. She is the children's aunt.

Where does Aunt Loraine work? Yes, she works at the library. What news does Aunt Lorraine send in her letter? That's right. She sends news of the new book wagon that will come to a town near Gideon's home.

Do you think Gideon is excited about visiting the book wagon? It is interesting to know the first book wagon really came from the Washington County Free Library in Hagerstown, Maryland.

(See page 495 in the Appendix for a short history of the first book wagon operated by a public library.)

Today we have bookmobiles instead of book wagons. Have you ever visited a bookmobile? A bookmobile is a motorized vehicle that carries books to people in areas where there is no public library.

Next, I will write five of the sentences from the story you just read on index cards.

(Have the child watch as you write each word with a pen. Label the first card with the lesson number for future use.)

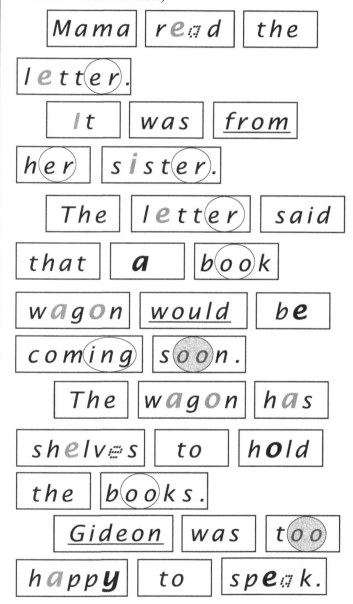

(**Note**: You may eliminate some of the print clues from the index cards with which your child is familiar. Be sure to include the print clues for sounds that have been recently introduced.)

I will underline several sight words with a black crayon. Read the sight words as I underline them.

Next, I will trace over the *eee* sounds (as in *wet*) and the *iii* sounds (as in *pig*) with a gray crayon. I will also trace over the *aaa* sounds (as in *cat*) and the *ooo* sounds (as in *hot*) with a gray crayon.

I will trace over the bold *a* sound (as in *cake*), the bold *e* sounds (as in *heat*), and the bold *o* sound (as in *hope*) with a black crayon.

I will also trace over the letter *y* in the word *happy* with a black crayon. The letter *y* makes the bold *e* sound in the word *happy*.

I will make dotted lines over the letter *a* in the words *read* and *speak*. I will also make dotted lines over the letter *e* in the word *shelves*. Can you tell me why I dotted these letters? Yes, they are silent, and they make no sound.

I will draw a gray ring around the *er* sound (as in *her*) in the words *letter, her,* and *sister.* I will draw a gray ring around the *ing* sound (as in *sing*) in the word *coming.* I will draw a gray ring around the *oo* sound (as in *boot*) in the word *soon* and in the word *too.* I will also draw a gray ring around the *oo* sound (as in *cook*) in the word *book* and in the word *books.*

Read the sentences. Very good! Now I will mix the cards, and you can put them in proper order to make the sentences again.

Now read the sentences again.

Copy Work: (The copy work is optional for children who have difficulty with writing.) (You may now encourage the child to copy the sentences directly from the model below. If this is too difficult, continue as directed.)

I will write the sentences you just read on a piece of paper.

(Neatly write the sentences with a pen, paying close attention to letter spacing and letter formation.)

Now you can copy what I wrote.

Mama read the letter. It was from her sister. The letter said that a book wagon would be coming soon. The wagon has shelves to hold the books. Gideon was too happy to speak.

I would like for you to read the sentences once again. Very good!

Make up a few sentences about the chapter, "News from Town."

440

Tell me the sentences, and I will write them on a piece of paper. You may draw a picture to go with your sentences if you like. Now you can copy one of your sentences at the bottom of your picture.

(Draw lines if necessary for the child to write his sentence at the bottom of his picture.)

Read the sentences you dictated to me.

Now let's read a book together.

(Review material between lessons.)

Lesson 102

Materials: reading manual, index cards, pen, gray crayon, black crayon, and three construction paper circles.

Instructions: In today's lesson, the child will review the following sight words: *learn, water, there, where, Benjamin, Rachel, Hannah,* and *Sarah.* He will be introduced to a new sight word. It is the name *Anna.* The child will also be introduced to the sight words *work* and *cover.* Prepare three construction paper circles with the new sight words written on them.

He will practice reading the following words printed with conventional type: *feed, seed, meat, seat, soap, goat, rope, note, cute, flute, cube, tube, cake, make, tail, sail, pile, file, bite,* and *kite.*

You will read aloud chapter six from *Gideon's Gift.* The child will read the following adaptation from the story and complete a variety of exercises based on this adaptation.

Chapter title: *"A Trip to the Book Wagon"*

Story: *Gideon woke up. Today they would go to see the book wagon. Gideon could not wait. He got his slate and did his writing. He must work hard on his writing. Soon they were all up.*

Papa said to the boys, "Come to the barn. We will put the cover on the wagon. It looks like it will rain."

"Do not forget to pick up Anna," said Mama.

Gideon was glad that Anna was coming too.

The children took off in the wagon. Anna ran to meet the wagon. Soon it started to rain. They tied the wagon cover shut.

"Can you read, Gideon?" asked Anna.

"I am learning to read," said Gideon.

"I can not read," said Anna.

"I will teach you," said Gideon.

Soon they could see the town.

Dialogue: Read the sight words below.

learn	*water*
there	*where*
Benjamin	*Rachel*

Hannah   Sarah

Today you will read about a new person in our story. Her name is *Anna*. (Point to the name below.)

Anna

Say *Anna* as I point to the name.
Very good!
Now I have two more new sight words for you to learn. The first sight word is *work*. (Point to the word below as you read it.)

work

Say *work* as I point to the word.
Very good!
Now look at the next sight word below. It is the word *cover*. (Point to the word as you read it.)

cover

Say *cover* as I point to the word.
Great!
Let's add the new sight words to your *Sight Word Worm*.
Read the words below. These words are printed with regular type like you will find in most books. We have not used gray letters or bold black letters. We have not drawn gray rings around any of the letters either. Soon all of the words you will read will be printed with regular type.

feed   seed

meat   seat

soap   goat

rope   note

cute   flute

cube   tube

cake   make

tail   sail

pile   file

bite   kite

Read the words below.

f(o r)   g e t

If we put the two words together we make a new word. It is the word *forget*. Say the word as I point to it.

f(o r)g e t

Great!
Read the sight word below.

learn

Now if we add the *ing* sound (as in *sing*) we will make a new word. It is the word *learning*. Say *learning* as I point to the word below.

learn(ing)

Very good!
Read the words below.

to   d**a**y

If we put the two words together we make a new word. It is the word *today*. Say the word as I point to it.

442

*to/d**a**y*

Great!
Read the words below that will appear in today's story.

(Assist the child with reading any difficult words.)

w̶r i t (i n g)   *s t **a**̤ i r s*

c o v e r   *f (o r/g e t*

*t i **̈** d*   *s t (a r/t e d*

*s h **u** t*   *(c h) i/d r e n*

*to/d**a**y*   *l e a r n (i n g)*

Now I am going to read chapter six from *Gideon's Gift*. After I read the chapter, you will read some sentences about the chapter to me.

(Read the following story aloud to the child.)

Chapter Six

"A Trip to the Book Wagon"

Gideon was the first one to awaken that special morning. After all, the day to visit the book wagon had finally arrived. Gideon dressed and washed quickly. He practiced writing his sentences on his slate.

His reading lessons were coming along fine. Mama said if he worked on his sentences each morning, then he could show them to her after supper when it was time for his reading lesson. Gideon was pleased he could do some writing by himself. He knew he must work hard if he was going to be a writer someday.

Soon Gideon heard the scramble of feet overhead. Sarah was the first to come downstairs.

"What are you doing up so early?" she asked Gideon.

I'm practicing my sentences and getting ready for the trip to Elmerton!" said Gideon in an excited tone.

"I almost forgot about the book wagon," said Sarah. "I hope to find a book about plants. I want to be able to identify the plants and herbs in the woods behind our place. I'm going to make a notebook with drawings and descriptions," she added.

Benjamin came into the kitchen and dropped into his chair. His head banged on the table in front of him.

"What's wrong with you," asked Sarah and Gideon both at once.

"I hardly slept all night," he remarked, "I kept dreaming I was on a ship in a bad storm. I was tossed back and forth all night," he said. "I guess I was thinking too hard about borrowing a book about ships from the book wagon."

"I think it also has to do with the fact that you had three pieces of pie for dessert last night," Sarah broke in.

Gideon and Sarah laughed. Mama had admonished Benjamin for being so foolish when she found him in the pantry sneaking another piece of pie.

"Now I know why Mama said my punishment would catch up with me sometime in the middle of the night," Benjamin managed to say.

In a few minutes the family assembled in the kitchen to eat a quick breakfast of fruit and bread. Hannah and Rachel packed sandwiches and lemonade in the wicker hamper.

Papa said, "Josh and Benjamin, it looks like you might run into some rain later today. Come to the barn and we'll put the cover on the wagon."

Mama and Gideon and the girls hurried out to meet Papa and the older boys at the wagon.

"Now remember to drop by and pick up Anna Anderson. Her ma asked if she might ride with you to visit the book wagon," said Mama.

Gideon was glad Anna was coming along. She was just a little bit younger than he was. It was nice to have a friend along from time to time, and Anna could tell the funniest stories Gideon had ever heard. Her family moved to America from Norway, and Anna was an only child. She was good at inventing stories and games and such to entertain herself.

As the wagon turned into the Anderson's farm, Anna came running down the drive to meet them. In one hand she held her hat, and in the other she held a big basket.

"My, you've brought a huge lunch!" said Rachel.

"Oh, it's not all for me," said Anna with a smile. "Ma baked cookies and cinnamon rolls for everyone. She said we needed something to help make the time go by more quickly."

The children all agreed that Mrs. Anderson was very kind and thoughtful to think of them. They decided to celebrate the big occasion by each having a cinnamon roll and a cookie.

After traveling for several miles, a musty smell suddenly rose from the ground. The sky began to darken.

"It looks like Papa was right about the weather," Josh commented. "I better put on my raincoat and hat, and I had better do it fast!" he said as a terrific boom sounded in the distance.

Benjamin and Sarah strained to tie the wagon cover shut as the wind fought against them. It seemed as if Josh had driven straight into a sheet of rain. The wagon lurched as it hit a hole in the road. Gideon and Anna managed to peek out of a tiny hole in the back of the canvas cover.

"You sure are going to a lot of trouble just to borrow some books," Anna shouted so as to be heard over the din of the storm.

"Oh, you just wait and see," said Gideon with reverence in his voice. "Books are like good friends," he said, "they keep you company, and they reveal to you the secrets of the world!"

The other children laughed at Gideon's serious tone.

Anna sat quietly for a moment. Then she whispered to Gideon, "Can you read?"

"I'm learning to read," he said proudly. "Mama has been teaching me for several weeks now. I can read all of the lessons in the first reading book. Mama says that by the end of summer, I'll be able to read most anything by myself."

"How about you?" asked Gideon.

"Well, I can't read yet," Anna said rather shyly. "But maybe once I borrow a book I'll learn how."

"Oh," said Gideon, "is your ma or your pa going to teach you?"

"Well, no, you see they have trouble with English. At least they can't read it too well. Ma says one day the government will build a school close by. Then I'll learn how to read."

"I could teach you," said Gideon with delight. "I'll just recite the lessons Mama taught me."

"Do you think I could learn," she asked hesitantly.

"Of course," he said with authority. "First you learn to read, and then you read to learn. We'll begin tomorrow afternoon. I'll meet you at your place. I'll bring my slate and slate pencil and my reading book."

At that moment the wagon swerved to miss a tree branch that had fallen in the roadway.

Benjamin poked his head out the front of the wagon cover. "Josh," he asked, "do you think the book wagon will be waiting in Elmerton?"

"According to Aunt Loraine it will be sheltered in the Woodbury stables in the event of rain. As a matter of fact, I do believe it will stay all night. A heavy wagon like that would get bogged down on these muddy roads."

The rain began to lessen as Josh saw the town of Elmerton in the distance.

"We're almost there," he shouted from the driver's seat.

Benjamin drew back the wagon cover and six pairs of eyes strained to see signs of the town. The sun broke through the clouds as they passed the first building in Elmerton.

"I see the Woodbury stables ahead on the left!" Josh said triumphantly.

Gideon sat up on his heels so he could get a better look.

That ends chapter six of our story. Now I want you to read some sentences that tell us a little bit about this chapter. Then I will show you a picture to go with the story.

(**Note**: We are no longer underlining the following sight words: *I, the, is, to, said, was, has, you, Papa, Mama, do, of, they, want,* and *that.* We are no longer dotting the letter *k* in the blend *ck.* We are no longer dotting the letter *y* as in *way* or the letter *w* as in *crow.* We are no longer drawing a gray ring around several beginning blends.)

"A Trip to the Book Wagon"

Gideon woke up. Today they would go to see the book wagon. Gideon could not wait. He got his slate and did his writing. He must work hard on his writing. Soon they were all up.

Papa said to the boys, "Come to the barn. We will put the cover on the wagon. It looks like it will rain."

"Do not forget to pick up Anna," said Mama.

Gideon was glad that Anna was coming too. The children took off in the wagon. Anna ran to meet the wagon. Soon it started to rain. They tied the wagon cover shut.

"Can you read, Gideon?" asked Anna.

"I am learning to read," said Gideon.

"I can not read," said Anna.

"I will teach you," said Gideon.

Soon they could see the town.

Now I will show you a picture of Gideon and Anna in the wagon.

Look at the picture. What are Gideon and Anna doing? That's right. They are peeking out of the tiny hole in the back of the wagon cover. Why is the cover on the wagon? Yes, it is raining.

Do you think Gideon is excited? Why? Where are they going?

Next, I will write five of the sentences from the story you just read on index cards.

(Have the child watch as you write each word with a pen. Label the first card with the lesson number for future use.)

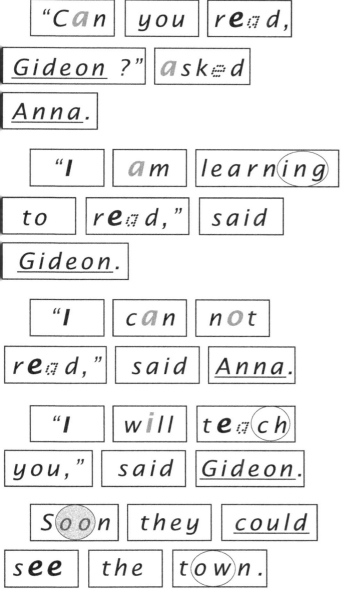

"Can you read, Gideon?" asked Anna.

"I am learning to read," said Gideon.

"I can not read," said Anna.

"I will teach you," said Gideon.

Soon they could see the town.

(**Note**: You may eliminate some of the print clues from the index cards with which your child is familiar. Be sure to include the print clues for sounds that have been recently introduced.)

I am going to underline several sight words with a black crayon. Read the words as I underline them.

Next, I will trace over the *aaa* sounds (as in *cat*) and the *ooo* sound (as in *hot*) with a gray crayon. I will also trace over the *iii* sound (as in *pig*) with a gray crayon.

I will trace over the bold *e* sounds (as in *heat*) with a black crayon. I will make dotted lines over the letter *a* in the words *read* and *teach*. I will also make dotted lines over the letter *e* in the word *asked*. Can you tell me why I dotted these letters? That's right, I dotted them, because they are silent. They make no sound.

I will draw a gray ring around the *ing* sound (as in *sing*) in the word *learning*. I will draw a gray ring around the *ch* sound (as in *chip* and *patch*) in the word *teach*. I will draw a shaded gray ring around the *oo* sound (as in *boot*) in the word *soon*. I will also draw a gray ring around the *ow* sound (as in *cow*) in the word *town*.

Read the sentences. Great! Now find the index cards that have the quotation marks on them. Who is speaking in this passage? Yes, Anna and Gideon are speaking.

Now I will mix the cards, and you can put them in proper order to make the sentences again.

Now read the sentences.

(**Note**: We are no longer using clues to assist the child with reading the copy work. It is important for the child to read the text located in this segment of the lesson even if he does not copy the sentences. This will give him an opportunity to practice reading text printed in a regular type.)

Copy Work: (The copy work is optional for children who have difficulty with writing.) (You may now encourage the child to copy the sentences directly from the model below. If this is too difficult, continue as directed.)

I will write the sentences you just read on a piece of paper.

(Neatly write the sentences with a pen, paying close attention to letter spacing and formation.)

Now you can copy what I wrote.

"Can you read, Gideon?" asked Anna.

"I am learning to read," said Gideon.

"I can not read," said Anna.

"I will teach you," said Gideon.

Soon they could see the town.

I would like for you to read the sentences once again. Very good!

Make up a few sentences about the chapter, "A Trip to the Book Wagon."

Tell me the sentences, and I will write them on a piece of paper. You may draw a picture to go with your sentences if you like. Now you can copy one of your sentences at the bottom of your picture.

(Draw lines if necessary for the child to write his sentence at the bottom of his picture.)

Read the sentences you dictated to me.

Now let's read a book together.

Lesson 103

Materials: reading manual, index cards, pen, gray crayon, black crayon, and one construction paper circle.

Instructions: In today's lesson, the child will review the following sight words: *put, work, cover, Anna, many, does, people, Benjamin, Rachel, Hannah,* and *Sarah.* He will be introduced to the new sight word *four.* Prepare one construction paper circle with the new sight word written on it.

He will practice reading the following words printed with conventional type: *park, car, farm, barn, cook, book, shook, took, boot, food, broom,* and *zoom.*

You will read aloud chapter seven from *Gideon's Gift.* The child will read the following adaptation from the chapter and complete a variety of exercises based on this adaptation.

Chapter title: *"The Book Wagon at Last"*

Story: *The wagon creaked as it drove into town. Many people had come to see the book wagon. The wagon was shiny and black.*

Benjamin said, "Let's look at the books."

A man stood up on a crate. He said, "You may each choose one book. Bring the book back in four weeks."

Each child got a book.

Josh said, "We need to go soon. The roads are muddy. We have a long way to go."

They all climbed into the wagon. The children looked at the books.

Gideon said, "I cannot wait to show the books to Mama and Papa."

Rachel read to the children. She read a chapter from her book. Soon the wagon turned into Anna's farm. Josh turned the horses to go home. As they came close to home Josh saw Mama. Mama was running to meet them.

Dialogue: Read the sight words below.

put   *work*

cover   *Anna*

many   *does*

448

<u>people</u>   <u>Benjamin</u>

<u>Rachel</u>   <u>Hannah</u>

<u>Sarah</u>

Look at the new sight word below. It is the word *four*. (Point to the word as you read it.)

<u>four</u>

Say *four* as I point to the word. Very good!

Now read the sentence below that has the new sight word in it.

The sm(all) b(oy)

h(a)d <u>four</u> b(all)s.

Let's add the new sight word to your *Sight Word Worm*.

Read the words below. These words are printed with regular type like you will find in most books. We have not used gray letters or bold black letters. We have not drawn gray rings around any of the letters either. Soon all of the words you will read will be printed with regular type.

park	car
farm	barn
cook	book
shook	took
boot	food
broom	zoom

Read the words below.

c a n   n o t

Great!

If we put the two words together we make a new word. It is the word *cannot*. Say the word as I point to it.

c a n/n o t

Very good!

Read the words below that will appear in the story.

(Assist the child with reading any difficult words.)

cre(a)ked	cr(a)te
t(ur)ned	long
ch(oo)se	cl(o)se
ch(i)ldren	ch(i)ld
ch(a)p/ter	mu(d/dy)
r(u)n/(ning)	cl(i)mbed

c a n/n o t

Now I am going to read chapter seven from *Gideon's Gift*. After I read the chapter, you will read some sentences about the chapter to me.

(Read the following story aloud to the child.)

Chapter Seven

"The Book Wagon at Last"

The wagon wheels creaked and moaned as they continued down Main Street. Josh pulled the wagon alongside of the Woodbury stables. Everyone jumped out of the wagon, carefully avoiding the mud puddles. A crowd of people had gathered inside the stables. Old and young alike were marveling over the wagon and the books.

Sarah said, "Hannah and I will register our family. There's a line of people standing in front of a small table. That must be the place."

The girls made their way across the stable to wait in line. Meanwhile, Benjamin said, "Let's have a look at the books."

Benjamin and the other children edged closer to the book wagon.

"Isn't it marvelous!" exclaimed Gideon.

Painted on the side of the wagon were the words *Washington County Free Library*. The wagon's black exterior gleamed like a piece of polished glass. Shelves mounted in cabinets stood inside. The shelves held rows and rows of fascinating books.

A man stood up on a crate and said, "May I have everyone's attention please? My name is Mr. Thomas. I will be bringing the library wagon to town on the first Tuesday of each month. If you have not registered with the library clerk, please stand in line at the far end of the stable. Due to the big crowd, we will only be able to loan one book per person. All books are to be returned to this same location, four weeks from today."

Sarah and Rachel joined the others and soon each had selected a book.

After the children had spent some time browsing, Josh urged, "We had better leave right away. The roads are muddy, and we've still got a long ride ahead of us."

The children eagerly climbed into the wagon. By now, they were hungry again. Hannah handed out the sandwiches.

Anna said, "We've still got cookies and cinnamon rolls too."

They quickly ate their sandwiches and the rest of the lunch. Excitedly the children began to look at their books. They admired each one, carefully examining the book jackets and spines.

"Mama and Papa will be pleased when they see our beautiful books," said Gideon. "I can't wait to show them."

The wagon traveled slowly over the bumpy roads and creaked and groaned at each turn. Josh was a good driver and made certain to avoid the ruts and holes. As Josh urged the horses on, he sang a song his papa had taught him as a little boy. His thoughts turned toward home as he wondered how Papa had fared working alone in the orchard. A recent illness had left him rather weak, and Josh and Benjamin had been doing most of the work. Josh could hear the happy chatter of the children inside the wagon.

Rachel said, "How would you like for me to read a chapter from my book to help pass the time?"

All the children agreed this was a good idea. Rachel had a pleasant reading voice and all the children enjoyed listening to her read. She had a way of making the characters seem real.

"What's the name of your book," asked Anna.

"The book is called *Heidi*," said Rachel. "It's a favorite story of mine. Heidi is a little girl about your age, Anna. She lives in the country of Switzerland."

"That's in Europe, near Germany," added Benjamin.

"That's right," said Rachel. "And Heidi lives way up in the mountains, in the Swiss Alps. She lives with her grandfather, whom she loves very much. Heidi has a friend named Peter, and he is just a little older than you, Gideon. Peter is a goatherd, and he and Heidi have great times together on the mountain. But one day, something happens, and Heidi's life is changed," said Rachel in a dramatic voice.

"Oh, what happens? You must tell us," Anna pleaded.

"I will get to that later," said Rachel, "but we must begin at the beginning."

Slowly Rachel opened the beautifully bound book and turned to the first chapter.

"Chapter one," she said with a flourish. "Up the Mountain to Alm-Uncle."

The children listened attentively as Rachel read the story in her special manner. Before they knew it, the wagon turned into the Anderson's farm.

"Oh, I want to hear more," begged Anna.

"Have your pa bring you tomorrow evening, and I'll read another chapter," promised Rachel.

Benjamin lifted the small figure to the ground as her mother came down the drive to greet them.

"Thank you for taking my Anna," called Mrs. Anderson in her broken English.

Josh turned the horses toward home. As they drew nearer to the orchard, Josh noticed someone in the distance. It was Mama running toward them.

"Something dreadful must have happened," said Hannah in a worried tone.

Josh pressed the horses to pick up the pace. Within a couple of minutes, they reached Mama who was trying to catch her breath.

That ends chapter seven of our story. Now I want you to read some sentences that tell us a little bit about this chapter. Then I will show you a picture to go with the story.

(**Note**: We are no longer underlining the following sight words: *I, the, is, to, said, was, has, you, Papa, Mama, do, of, they, that, are, want,* and *from.* We are no longer dotting the letter *k* in the blend *ck.* We are no longer dotting the letter *y* as in *way* or the letter *w* as in *crow.* We are no longer drawing a gray ring around several beginning blends.)

"The Book Wagon at Last"

The wagon creaked as it drove into town. Many people had come to see the book wagon. The wagon was shiny and black.

Benjamin said, "Let's look at the books."

A man stood up on a crate.

451

He said, "You may each choose one book. Bring the book back in four weeks."

Each child got a book.

Josh said, "We need to go soon. The roads are muddy. We have a long way to go."

They all climbed into the wagon. The children looked at the books.

Gideon said, "I cannot wait to show the books to Mama and Papa."

Rachel read to the children. She read a chapter from her book. Soon the wagon turned into Anna's farm. Josh turned the horses to go home. As they came close to home Josh saw Mama. Mama was running to meet them.

Now I will show you a picture of the book wagon.

Look at the picture. The book wagon is parked at the Woodbury Stables. How is it able to carry so many books? That's right. It has shelves mounted in cabinets. The shelves hold rows and rows of books.

How does the book wagon travel from place to place? Yes, horses pull it.

(Turn to page 494 in the Appendix to see a picture of the first real book wagon operated by a public library.)

Next, I will write four of the sentences from the story you just read on index cards.

(Have the child watch as you write each word with a pen. Label the first card with the lesson number for future use.)

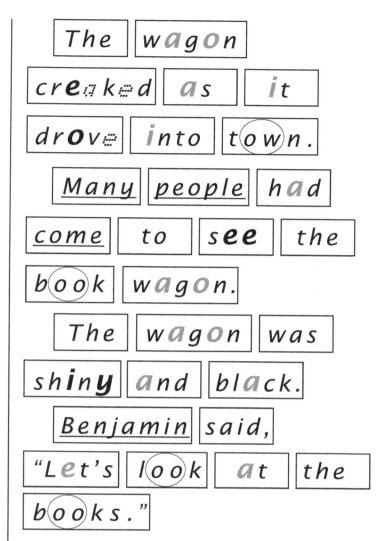

(**Note**: You may eliminate some of the print clues from the index cards with which your child is familiar. Be sure to include the print clues for sounds that have been recently introduced.)

I will underline several sight words. Read the sight words as I underline them.

I will trace over the *aaa* sounds (as in *cat*) and the *ooo* sounds (as in *hot*) with a gray crayon. I will also trace over the *iii* sounds (as in *pig*) and the *eee* sound (as in *wet*) with a gray crayon.

I will trace over the bold *e* sounds (as in *heat*), the bold *o* sound (as in *hope*), and the bold *i* sound (as in *bike*) with a black crayon.

453

I will trace over the letter y in the word shiny with a black crayon. The letter y in the word shiny makes the bold e sound (as in baby). I will draw a gray ring around the ow sound (as in cow) in the word town. I will draw a gray ring around the oo sound (as in cook) in the words book, look, and books.

I will make dotted lines over the letter a and the letter e in the word creaked. I will also make dotted lines over the letter e in the word drove. Can you tell me why I dotted these letters? That's right. I dotted them, because they are silent. They make no sound.

Read the sentences. Great! Look at the index cards that have quotation marks on them. Who is speaking in this passage? That's right. Benjamin is speaking.

Now I will mix the cards, and you can put them in proper order to make the sentences again.

Now read the sentences.

(**Note**: We are no longer using clues to assist the child with reading the copy work. It is important for the child to read the text located in this segment of the lesson even if he does not copy the sentences. This will give him an opportunity to practice reading text printed in a regular type.)

Copy Work: (The copy work is optional for children who have difficulty with writing.) (You may now encourage the child to copy the sentences directly from the model below. If this is too difficult, continue as directed.)

I will write the sentences you just read on a piece of paper.

(Neatly write the sentences with a pen, paying close attention to letter spacing and formation.)

Now you can copy what I wrote.

The wagon creaked as it drove into town. Many people had come to see the book wagon. The wagon was shiny and black.

Benjamin said, "Let's look at the books."

I would like for you to read the sentences once again. Very good!

Make up a few sentences about the chapter, "The Book Wagon at Last."

Tell me the sentences, and I will write them on a piece of paper. You may draw a picture to go with your sentences if you like. Now you can copy one of your sentences at the bottom of your picture.

(Draw lines if necessary for the child to write his sentence at the bottom of his picture.)

Read the sentences you dictated to me.

Now let's read a book together.

Lesson 104

Materials: reading manual, index cards, pen, gray crayon, black crayon, and one construction paper circle.

Instructions: In today's lesson, the child will review the following sight words: *put, work, cover, Anna, many, four, people, taught, caught, new,* and *Sarah.* He will be introduced to the new sight word *money.* Prepare one construction paper circle with the new sight word written on it.

He will practice reading the following words printed with conventional type: *cow, plow, now, town, snow, blow, grow, know, pork, fork, torn,* and *horn.*

You will read chapter eight from *Gideon's Gift* aloud to the child. The child will read the following adaptation from the chapter and complete a variety of exercises based on this adaptation.

Chapter title: *"Mama's Story"*

Story: *Mama said, "Papa fell. He is hurt."*

Josh helped Mama into the wagon.

"We had a bad storm," Mama said. "A tree caught on fire. We could see the smoke from the house. Papa climbed up the ladder to put out the flames. Then he fell."

They found Papa on the ground.

"Are you hurt?" asked Josh.

"Yes, it is a bad break," said Papa.

The big boys put Papa in the wagon. Soon Papa was resting in bed.

Mama said, "You boys will have to take Papa to the doctor. You can go in the morning." Mama gave some money to Josh. "Use this money to pay the doctor," Mama said. "I was saving it to get a book for Gideon."

Mama walked to the barn. She said to Gideon, "You are doing well with your reading. I wanted to get you a book for your birthday."

Gideon said, "We need the money to fix Papa's leg. I do not need a book."

Mama said, "You are a good and kind boy. I know that one day you will be like Gideon in the Bible."

"Tell me the story of Gideon," he said. "I like that story."

Dialogue: Read the sight words below.

put	work
cover	Anna
many	four
people	taught
caught	new

Sarah

Today you will learn a new sight word. It is the word *money*. (Point to the word below as you read it.)

money

Say *money* as I point to the word. Let's add the new sight word to your *Sight Word Worm*.

Read the words below. These words are printed with regular type like you will find in most books. We have not used gray letters or bold black letters. We have not drawn gray rings around any of the letters either. Soon all of the words you will read will be printed with regular type.

cow	plow
now	town
snow	blow
grow	know
pork	fork
torn	horn

Read the words below.

b(ir)t h   d**a** y

Very good!
If we put the two words together we make a new word. It is the word birthday. Say the word as I point to it.

b(i)r t h / d **a** y

Great!
Read the words below that will appear in the story.

(Assist the child with reading any difficult words.)

m o n e y   s m **o** k e

l **a** d / d(e)r   g r(ou)n d

f **i** r e   m(o)r(n)i n g

d **o** c / t(o)r   B **i** b l e

s t(o r)**y**   r e s t(in)g

f l **a** m e s   w a n t(e)d

b(i)r t h / d **a** y   d(o)(in)g

Now I am going to read chapter eight from *Gideon's Gift*. Then after I read the chapter, you will read some sentences about the chapter to me.

(Read the following story aloud to the child.)

Chapter Eight

"Mama's Story"

Mama drew a deep breath and said in a worried tone, "It's Papa, he's in the orchard and he has fallen from the ladder."

Josh helped his mother into the wagon and they headed for the orchard.

"We had a bad storm while you were gone," Mama began, "and lightning struck one of the trees in the orchard. It caught on fire. We could see the smoke from the front porch. I told Papa the rain would probably put out the flames, but he wanted to see for himself."

The children's eyes were moist as they listened to Mama's frightening story.

Mama continued, "After a few minutes the rain stopped, but the smoke continued to rise. We hitched the cow to the cart and hauled the ladder, grain sacks, and shovels to the orchard. The branches were burning on one tree, but Papa was afraid the flames would spread from tree to tree. He steadied the ladder on a secure branch and climbed up with his long pruning shears."

The horses felt tired from the long day's journey, but Josh urged them toward home.

"At that moment," Mama said, "a gust of wind caused the flames to spread, and the ladder caught on fire. Papa lost his balance and fell. The burning branches fell beside him. I took the shovel and covered the branches with dirt. Soon after, I caught a glimpse of the wagon across the field and started running toward you."

They pulled into the orchard where Papa lay on the ground.

"Are you badly hurt, Papa?" asked Josh as he hurried to his side.

"I'm afraid it's a serious break," said Papa as he labored to speak.

Benjamin and Josh lifted Papa carefully into the wagon as the other children spread a blanket on the wagon bed.

Benjamin spoke up, "Doc Pritchard has gone to Washington to visit his sick mother. He won't be back for several weeks."

"Well then, you boys will have to take Papa to the doctor in Hagerstown. I understand from my sister there is a bone specialist in town," said Mama. "It's already getting dark, so you had better not leave until morning."

Josh slowly drove the wagon to the house so as not to disturb his father.

After settling Papa comfortably in bed, Mama spoke to Josh, "Doc Prichard would have taken his pay in apple cider come this winter, but the doctors in the city want cash."

Mama walked quietly over to the kitchen cupboard. She opened the door and took an old sugar bowl down from the top shelf. She opened the lid and inside lay several crisp dollar bills.

"I've been saving this money for Gideon's birthday book. He's doing a fine job with his reading. He will be awfully disappointed if he doesn't get that book. His birthday is only six weeks away. Maybe we will be able to raise the money somehow," said Mama sadly as she placed the bills in Papa's billfold.

"Do you think we will need all of the money to pay the doctor's fee?" asked Josh.

"You will need some money for a hotel. Papa will be exhausted from the trip to town and you will have to stay overnight. The important thing now is to take care of Papa. You know his health has not been good this year. Gideon is growing up into a fine young man. He will understand about the book."

"Benjamin and I are going to bed now so we can get an early start tomorrow," said Josh as he started up the stairs. "Good night, Mama."

"Good night, Josh," she said.

Mama walked to the barn where Gideon was putting the animals in their stalls for the night.

"Gideon," said Mama. "I need to have a talk with you."

"Yes, Mama."

"You know your birthday is in just six weeks. You have been learning to read very well. As a matter of fact, you've almost finished the third reader. I've been saving money to buy your birthday book, but..."

Gideon interrupted, "Oh, Mama, don't worry about that. I know we need the money to pay the doctor to fix Papa's leg. That's more important than a book. And besides, now that the book wagon comes every month, I can read tons of books!"

"You are not only a smart boy Gideon, but you are a good and thoughtful boy. One day, I am certain you will be a great leader like Gideon in the Bible."

"Tell me the story of Gideon again, Mama" begged the young boy. "You make it sound so exciting."

"Gideon," began Mama, "was a special individual chosen by the Lord to save his people from the Midianites."

"What were the Midianites doing?" asked Gideon.

"They were attacking the Lord's people, the people of Israel. They burned their wheat and killed their animals. But there was something happening even worse than that," she said.

"What was that?" asked Gideon.

"Well," she said, "the people of Israel had begun to worship other gods, idols. So the Lord sent an angel to Gideon and told him to destroy the altar of Baal. Gideon did this and placed an altar to the Lord in its place."

"But how did Gideon save his people from the Midianites?" Gideon asked.

"He gathered together an army by the spring of Harod. Then he told the men to go home if they were afraid. 22,000 men went home. Then the Lord told him to take the 10,000 men who were left down to the spring to drink. The Lord said to Gideon, 'Watch how the men drink. Those who cup their hands, have them stay; but those who put their faces into the water, send them away.' Finally Gideon was left with only three hundred men."

"That doesn't seem like very many men for an army," Gideon remarked.

"You are right," said Mama, "but the Lord is mighty. He doesn't need great numbers of people. He would rather have a few people with great faith than a great number of people with little faith."

"What happened next," asked Gideon who always looked forward to this part of the story.

"Gideon and his men looked down on the Midianite army where they were camped in the valley below. When it became dark, Gideon gave each man a trumpet made of ram's horn and a flaming torch. They put clay jars over the torches to hide the light. The Israelite army silently surrounded the enemy's camp. When Gideon signaled, they sounded a loud blast on their trumpets and smashed the jars to let the light shine from the torches. Then they shouted as loud as they could. The Midianite army became terrified and confused. They began fighting with each other as they fled into the darkness. Gideon won the victory without a battle."

"I like that story," said Gideon. "Do you think soon I'll be able to read it for myself in the Bible?" he asked.

"You are doing very well with your reading, and, yes, soon you will even be able to read the Bible by yourself. The story of Gideon is in the book of Judges. But now you must have another reading lesson, for it is nearly bedtime."

Gideon ran into the house and took down the reader and his slate from the kitchen shelf. He hurried to the kitchen table as Mama came in the back door.

"You are very enthusiastic about your reading," she said, "and soon we will need to work on your spelling. It is atrocious!" Mama laughed and stroked Gideon's head as she said this. She knew he tried, but somehow he couldn't manage to spell correctly.

"Maybe now that Papa will be in the house recovering from his broken leg," said Gideon, "he will be able to help me with my spelling."

"That's an excellent idea," said Mama, "and I'm sure he will enjoy your company. It will be hard for your Papa to stay down for so long."

That ends chapter eight of our story. Now I want you to read some sentences that tell us a little bit about this chapter. Then I will show you a picture to go with the story.

(**Note**: We are no longer underlining the following sight words: *I, the, is, to, said, was, has, you, Papa, Mama, do, of, they, that, are, from, with, what, put, does, some, come, from, want, could, should, would, there, where, your, one, many, who,* and *water.* We are no longer dotting the letter *k* in the blend *ck.* We are no longer dotting the letter *y* as in *way* or the letter *w* as in *crow.* We are no longer drawing a gray ring around several beginning blends. We are no longer drawing a gray ring around several phonetic combinations such as *oo* as in *cook, oo* as in *room, ing, or, ow,* or *all.*)

"Mama's Story"

Mama said, "Papa fell. He is hurt."

Josh helped Mama into the wagon.

"We had a bad storm," Mama said. "A tree caught on fire. We could see the smoke from the house. Papa climbed up the ladder to put out the flames. Then he fell."

They found Papa on the ground.

"Are you hurt?" asked Josh.

"Yes, it is a bad break," said Papa.

The big boys put Papa in the wagon. Soon Papa was resting in bed.

Mama said, "You boys will have to take Papa to the doctor. You can go in the morning."

Mama gave some money to Josh.

"Use this money to pay the doctor," Mama said. "I was saving it to get a book for Gideon."

Mama walked to the barn.

She said to Gideon, "You are doing well with your reading. I wanted to get you a book for your birthday."

Gideon said, "We need the money to fix Papa's leg. I do not need a book."

Mama said, "You are a good and kind boy. I know that one day you will be like Gideon in the Bible."

"Tell me the story of Gideon," he said. "I like that story."

Now I will show you a picture of Gideon.

Look at the picture. Gideon is in the barn. What is he doing? That's right, he's putting down fresh hay for the horses.

Why does Mama come out to the barn to talk to Gideon? What does she say about the book for his birthday? That's right. She tells him the money she had saved to buy his book had to go to pay the doctor bill. What does Gideon say about this? Yes, he said Papa's leg was more important than a book.

What Bible story does Mama tell Gideon? That's right, she tells him the story of Gideon in the Bible. How did the Lord tell Gideon to choose the men for his army? Yes, the Lord told him to choose the men who cup the water in their hands when they drink.

Next, I will write four of the sentences from the story you just read on index cards.

(Have the child watch as you write each word with a pen. Label the first card with the lesson number for future use.)

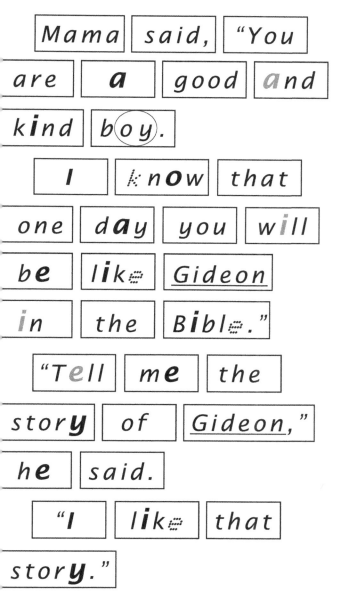

(**Note**: You may eliminate some of the print clues from the index cards with which your child is

familiar. Be sure to include the print clues for sounds that have been recently introduced.)

I will underline one sight word. This sight word appears two times in this passage. Read the sight word as I underline it.

I will trace over the *aaa* sound (as in *cat*), the *iii* sounds (as in *pig*), and the *eee* sound (as in *wet*) with a gray crayon.

I will trace over the bold *a* sounds (as in *cake*), the bold *i* sounds (as in *bike*), and the bold *e* sounds (as in *heat*) with a black crayon.

I will trace over the letter *y* in the word *story* with a black crayon. The letter *y* in the word *story* makes a bold *e* sound (as in *baby*).

I will make dotted lines over the letter *k* in the word *know*. I will also make dotted lines over the letter *e* in the word *like* and in the word *Bible*. Can you tell me why I dotted these letters? That's right. I dotted them, because they are silent. They make no sound.

I will draw a gray ring around the *oy* sound (as in *toy*) in the word *boy*.

Read the sentences. Very good! Can you find the index cards that have the quotation marks on them? Who is speaking in this passage? Yes, Mama is speaking first, and then Gideon speaks.

Now I will mix the cards, and you can put them in proper order to make the sentences again.

Now read the sentences.

(**Note**: We are no longer using clues to assist the child with reading the copy work. It is important for the child to read the text located in this segment of the lesson even if he does not copy the sentences. This will give him an opportunity to practice reading text printed in a regular type.)

Copy Work: (The copy work is optional for children who have difficulty with writing.) (You may now encourage the child to copy the sentences directly from the model below. If this is too difficult, continue as directed.)

I will write the sentences you just read on a piece of paper.

(Neatly write the sentences with a pen, paying close attention to letter spacing and formation.)

Now you can copy what I wrote.

Mama said, "You are a good and kind boy. I know that one day you will be like Gideon in the Bible."

"Tell me the story of Gideon," he said. "I like that story."

I would like for you to read the sentences once again. Very good!

Make up a few sentences about the chapter, "Mama's Story."

Tell me the sentences, and I will write them on a piece of paper. You may draw a picture to go with your sentences if you like. Now you can copy one of your sentences at the bottom of your picture.

(Draw lines if necessary for the child to write his sentence at the bottom of his picture.)

Read the sentences you dictated to me.

Now let's read a book together.

(Review material between lessons.)

462

Lesson 105

Materials: reading manual, index cards, pen, gray crayon, black crayon, and two construction paper circles.

Instructions: In today's lesson, the child will review the following sight words: *water, work, cover, should, four, there, where, taught, new,* and *money*. He will be introduced to two new sight words: *aunt* and *about*. Prepare two construction paper circles with the new sight words written on them.

He will practice reading the following words printed with conventional type: *night, fight, sight, right, might, bright, by, fly, try, my, sly,* and *cry*.

You will read aloud chapter nine from *Gideon's Gift*. The child will read the following adaptation from the chapter and complete a variety of exercises based on this adaptation.

Chapter title: *"Going to See the Doctor"*

Story: *Benjamin and Josh got the wagon ready to go to town. Sarah and Hannah packed food in a big hamper. Mama gave a note to Benjamin.*

"This note tells where my sister lives," Mama said. "She lives close to the doctor."

Benjamin and Josh put Papa in the wagon. They headed down the dusty road. Soon Papa went to sleep.

Josh said to Benjamin, "You can read out loud while I drive.

Benjamin said, "I got a book about the sea."

Benjamin began to read the book. They liked the story. The trip to town seemed short. Benjamin and Josh took Papa to see the doctor. Benjamin went to find his aunt. She was working at the library. He told his aunt about Papa's leg.

She said, "I will come and see you tonight. I will bring a cake."

The doctor told Papa to stay off his leg for six weeks. That night Aunt Loraine came to see them. She told them about a writing contest.

She said, "The winner will get a book and a Bible."

Dialogue: Read the sight words below.

water   work

cover   should
four   there
where   taught
new   money

Look at the new sight word below. It is the word *aunt*. (Point to the word as you read it.)

aunt

Say *aunt* as I point to the word. Very good!
Now look at the next new sight word. It is the word *about*. (Point to the word as you read it.)

about

Say *about* as I point to the word. Very good!
Let's add the new sight words to your *Sight Word Worm*.
Read the words below. These words are printed with regular type like you will find in most books. We have not used gray letters or bold black letters. We have not drawn gray rings around any of the letters either. Soon all of the words you will read will be printed with regular type.

night   fight
sight   right
might   bright
by   fly
try   my

463

sly   cry

Read the two words below.

to   night

Very good!
If we put the two words together we make a new word. It is the word tonight. Say the word as I point to it.

tonight

Great!
Read the words below that will appear in the story.
(Assist the child with reading any difficult words.)

ready	hamper
contest	winner
headed	dusty
Bible	shorter
story	working
library	Loraine

Now I am going to read chapter nine from Gideon's Gift. After I read the chapter, you will read some sentences about the chapter to me.
(Read the following story aloud to the child.)

Chapter Nine
"Going to See the Doctor"

The next morning Benjamin and Josh were up early getting the wagon and horses ready for the trip to Hagerstown. They wanted to make the wagon as comfortable as possible for Papa. Mama was making breakfast for the travelers. Sarah and Hannah packed a large hamper with sandwiches, muffins, and fruit.

"Be sure to make a jug of lemonade," said Mama thoughtfully. "Your papa loves lemonade."

Mama took breakfast to Papa in bed. He had slept well through the night in spite of his discomfort.

"The herb pack you placed on my leg has kept the swelling down," said Papa as he tried to prop himself up on the bed pillows.

"My mother taught me how to make that," Mama said. "She was always good at doctoring. She had a special knack for helping folks get well."

Papa ate his breakfast and Mama helped him to dress.

"The boys said to stay in bed," said Mama, "They've made a special chair to carry you to the wagon."

Soon Papa was settled comfortably in the wagon and Mama gave the boys the last instructions before they headed to town. She handed Benjamin a slip of paper.

"Here's my sister's address. She lives at the boarding house only a few blocks from the doctor's office. Be sure to stop in and pay her a visit. She will want to check in on Papa while you are at the hotel. Here's a letter that I've written to her too."

Mama and the children kissed Papa good-bye, and the wagon headed down the dusty road. After a short time, the motion and creaking of the wagon lulled Papa to sleep.

"It is good he can rest," said Benjamin, "It will make the trip seem shorter to him."

"And to make the trip seem shorter to us," said Josh, "you can read aloud while I drive."

Benjamin climbed onto the wagon seat next to Josh and opened his library book.

"By the way, Benjamin, what book did you get?" asked Josh. "I bet it has something to do with boats and the sea."

Josh laughed as he said this, for Benjamin was determined to be a sailor, even though he had never seen the sea.

"It's not that funny," said Benjamin, "but I did get a book about the sea. It's called *Twenty Thousand Leagues Under the Sea.*"

"Oh, yes," said Josh. "It was written by Jules Verne. He has written several fantastical books. Did you know he even wrote a book called *From the Earth to the Moon?* I read about it in a magazine that Aunt Loraine sent us a while ago. Can you imagine anyone traveling to the moon! What a crazy idea."

"Well, I for one would like to travel over the entire ocean, and then I would like to go to the moon too!" said Benjamin indignantly.

"Oh, just read the book," said Josh. "No man will ever go to the moon!"

Benjamin and Josh became so interested in the story that the trip to Hagerstown seemed only a short jaunt.

"We are here in plenty of time to see the doctor," said Josh. "You deliver the letter to Aunt Loraine and find us a room for the night. I will stay with Papa."

Benjamin helped Josh carry Papa into the small doctor's office. Then Benjamin hurried off to complete his errands.

"Hello, I'm Dr. Johnson. What seems to be the problem?"

Papa related the story about the accident and the doctor examined his leg. Meanwhile, Benjamin went to find Aunt Loraine. After checking at the boarding house, he found she had already gone to work at the library. The landlady gave Benjamin directions to the library.

"Thank you very much," replied Benjamin.

Benjamin jumped onto the wagon seat and drove toward the library. He was amazed at the beautiful library building. He put the horses and wagon under a large tree where the horses could rest in the shade. After watering and feeding the horses, he walked across the lawn. Quietly he entered through the massive doors of the library. The silence penetrated every corner of the library, and Benjamin felt as if he was inside a great cathedral. Everywhere he looked, he saw shelves and shelves of books.

"Wow," he thought. "Gideon would love to see this place."

He remembered how thrilled Gideon was about the book wagon. The book wagon had only a small number of books in comparison to the library.

After taking in the new sight, Benjamin walked over to a large desk where a neatly dressed woman was busy filing cards.

"Excuse me," he said, "I'm looking for my aunt. Her name is Loraine Wilkinson."

"One moment, please," said the clerk, "I will get her."

Soon Aunt Loraine came walking quickly from behind several rows of bookshelves.

"What brings you here?" she exclaimed. "Is everything all right?"

"Papa broke his leg, and he and Josh are at the doctor's office now. Doc Pritchard is out of town, so we had to come into Hagerstown to see Dr. Johnson. We will be staying overnight. It's too late now to start back home, especially with Papa so weak. Mama asked me to deliver this letter to you," he added.

"Thank you," she said. "Have you found a room yet?"

"No," said Benjamin.

She quickly wrote down the address of a nearby hotel and said, "Take this. You will be able to get a nice room at the Pinewood Hotel for a reasonable price. Meals are included. I will come by to see you this evening. I'll bring a chocolate cake too."

Benjamin hurried to the hotel and rented a room for the night. Then he went to the doctor's office to check on Josh and Papa.

"Now I want you to stay off that leg for six weeks," Dr. Johnson said to Papa. "If it gives you any trouble after that, come back and see me."

Benjamin entered the office as the doctor was giving Papa the final instructions.

"Young man," said Dr. Johnson to Benjamin, "Go two blocks west to Jefferson Street to the mercantile store and buy your father a pair of crutches. That will allow him to get around by himself."

In a short time Benjamin returned with the new wooden crutches. Papa paid the doctor and they went on their way.

"I've rented a room at the Pinewood Hotel," said Benjamin. "Meals are included and it's almost suppertime."

"Let's go then," said Josh, "I feel as if I haven't eaten all day!"

They climbed into the wagon and headed for the hotel.

"Aunt Loraine will meet us here this evening. She said she will bring a chocolate cake," said Benjamin patting his stomach.

"Aunt Loraine makes the best chocolate cakes," said Papa.

After they had eaten their fill at the hotel, Josh said, "Supper was good, but it can't compete with Mama's cooking."

"That's for sure," said Papa.

Aunt Loraine came shortly after dinner, and they all enjoyed the cake and conversation.

"I've got a magazine for you to take to your Mama," she said. "The *Weekly* magazine is

sponsoring a writing contest for children. There will be prizes awarded for three age groups. The theme of the contest is *What Reading Means to Me*. I thought surely one of you children could win," she said to Josh and Benjamin. "After all, your Mama has done an excellent job in teaching you all to read."

"What kind of prizes are they giving?" asked Benjamin.

"The winner in each age category will receive the book of his choice and a gold edged Bible. The free public library in the county closest to where the child resides also receives $500 for buying new books.

Josh turned to Papa, "Maybe if one of us children wins the contest, Gideon will get his birthday book after all!"

Papa nodded, "It's certainly worth a try!"

That ends chapter nine of our story. Now I want you to read some sentences that tell us a little bit about this chapter. Then I will show you a picture to go with the story.

(**Note**: We are no longer underlining the following sight words: *I, the, is, to, said, was, has, you, Papa, Mama, do, of, they, that, are, from, with, what, put, does, some, come, from, want, could, should, would, there, where, your, one, many, who,* and *water.* We are no longer dotting the letter *k* in the blend *ck.* We are no longer dotting the letter *y* as in *way* or the letter *w* as in *crow.* We are no longer drawing a gray ring around several beginning blends. We are no longer drawing a gray ring around several phonetic combinations such as *oo* as in *cook, oo* as in *room, ing, or, ow,* or *all.*)

"Going to See the Doctor"

Benjamin and Josh got the wagon ready to go to town. Sarah and Hannah packed food in a big hamper. Mama gave a note to Benjamin.

"This note tells where my sister lives," Mama said. "She lives close to the doctor."

Benjamin and Josh put Papa in the wagon. They headed down the dusty road. Soon Papa went to sleep.

Josh said to Benjamin, "You can read out loud while I drive.

Benjamin said, "I got a book about the sea."

Benjamin began to read the book. They liked the story. The trip to town seemed short. Benjamin and Josh took Papa to see the doctor.

Benjamin went to find his aunt. She was working at the library. He told his aunt about Papa's leg.

She said, "I will come and see you tonight. I will bring a cake."

The doctor told Papa to stay off his leg for six weeks. That night Aunt Loraine came to see them. She told them about a writing contest.

She said, "The winner will get a book and a Bible."

Now I will show you a picture of Josh and Benjamin in the wagon.

Look at the picture. Josh and Benjamin are sitting on the wagon seat. Where are they going? That's right. They are driving Papa to town to see the doctor.

What does Benjamin have in his hands? What is he doing? Yes, he has a book in his hands, and he is reading out loud. Why do you think he is reading out loud? That's right. Josh wanted him to read to help pass the time. The trip to town was long.

Can you remember what book Benjamin was reading? Yes, it was called *Twenty Thousand Leagues Under the Sea.*

Next, I will write four of the sentences from the story you just read on index cards.

(Have the child watch as you write each word with a pen. Label the first card with the lesson number for future use.)

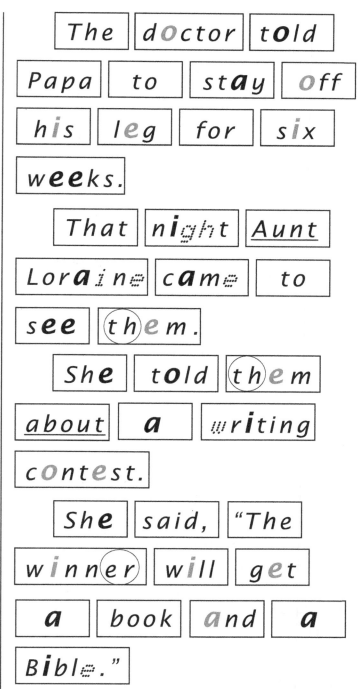

(**Note**: You may eliminate some of the print clues from the index cards with which your child is familiar. Be sure to include the print clues for sounds that have been recently introduced.)

I will underline two sight words in this passage. Read the sight words as I underline each one.

I will trace over the *ooo* sounds (as in *hot*) and the *iii* sounds (as in *pig*) with a gray crayon. I will also trace over the *eee* sounds (as in *wet*) and the *aaa* sound (as in *cat*) with a gray crayon.

I will trace over the bold *o* sounds (as in *hope*), the bold *a* sounds (as in *cake*), the bold *e* sounds (as in *heat*), and the bold *i* sounds (as in *bike*) with a black crayon.

I will make dotted lines over the letters *g* and *h* in the word *night*. I will make dotted lines over the letters *i* and *e* in the word *Loraine*. I will make dotted lines over the letter *e* at the end of the words *came* and *Bible*. I will also make dotted lines over the letter *w* in the word *writing*. Can you tell me why I dotted these letters? That's right they are silent. They make no sound.

I will draw a gray ring around the *th* sound (as in *this* or *thick*) in the word *them*. I will also draw a gray ring around the *er* sound (as in *her*) in the word *winner*.

Read the sentences. Great! Find the index cards that have quotation marks on them. Who is speaking in this passage? Yes, Aunt Loraine is speaking.

Now I will mix the cards, and you can put them in proper order to make the sentences again.

Now read the sentences.

(**Note**: We are no longer using clues to assist the child with reading the copy work. It is important for the child to read the text located in this segment of the lesson even if he does not copy the sentences. This will give him an opportunity to practice reading text printed in a regular type.)

Copy Work: (The copy work is optional for children who have difficulty with writing.) (You may now encourage the child to copy the sentences

directly from the model below. If this is too difficult, continue as directed.)

I will write the sentences you just read on a piece of paper.

(Neatly write the sentences with a pen, paying close attention to letter spacing and formation.)

Now you can copy what I wrote.

The doctor told Papa to stay off his leg for six weeks. That night Aunt Loraine came to see them. She told them about a writing contest.

She said, "The winner will get a book and a Bible."

I would like for you to read the sentences once again. Very good!

Make up a few sentences about the chapter, "Going to See the Doctor."

Tell me the sentences, and I will write them on a piece of paper. You may draw a picture to go with your sentences if you like. Now you can copy one of your sentences at the bottom of your picture.

(Draw lines if necessary for the child to write his sentence at the bottom of his picture.)

Read the sentences you dictated to me.

Now let's read a book together.

(Review material between lessons.)

Lesson 106

Materials: reading manual, index cards, and pen.

Instructions: In today's lesson, the child will review the following sight words: *work, cover, four, where, new, money, aunt,* and *about.*

He will practice reading the following words printed with conventional type: *house, mouse, ground, sound, loud, proud, bigger, fatter, smaller, older, wetter,* and *hotter.*

You will read aloud chapter ten from *Gideon's Gift.* The child will read the following adaptation from the chapter and complete a variety of exercises based on this adaptation.

Chapter title: *"Gideon Gives a Lesson"*

Story: *Gideon was slicing a piece of bread. Mama said, "Why are you up so soon?"*

"I am going to give Anna a reading lesson," said Gideon. "First I will do my chores."

Mama said, "Helping Anna to read will help you to read better too."

Gideon ran to the barn to do his chores. Soon he walked to Anna's farm. He had his slate under his arm. He had his reading book under his arm too.

Anna waved when she saw Gideon. Gideon and Anna sat in the hay. Gideon gave Anna her first lesson.

Soon it was time for Gideon to go home. As he walked home he saw Papa's wagon. Gideon ran to meet the wagon.

Gideon said, "How is your leg, Papa?"

"It is better," said Papa. "I must not use it for six weeks." Papa was sad. He said, "We had to pay the doctor. There is no money left for your birthday."

Gideon was not sad. He said, "Papa, will you help me with my spelling? I want to be a writer some day."

Papa said, "I will be glad to help."

Benjamin told Gideon about the writing contest.

Dialogue: Read the sight words below.

work   cover

four   *where*

new   *money*

aunt   *about*

Read the words below. These words are printed with regular type like you will find in most books. We have not used gray letters or bold black letters. We have not drawn gray rings around any of the letters either. Soon all of the words you will read will be printed with regular type.

house   *mouse*

ground   *sound*

loud   *proud*

bigger   *fatter*

smaller   *older*

wetter   *hotter*

Read the words below that will appear in the story.

(Assist the child with reading any difficult words.)

slicing   piece

chores   writing

better   contest

first   lesson

under   walked

birthday

Now I am going to read chapter ten from *Gideon's Gift*. After I read chapter ten, you will read some sentences about the chapter to me.

(Read the following story aloud to the child.)

Chapter Ten

"Gideon Gives a Lesson"

The next morning, Gideon was up and dressed before the rest of the household. Mama came into the kitchen as Gideon was slicing a piece of bread.

"What inspires you to rise so early?" she asked.

"I'm giving Anna a reading lesson as soon as I finish my chores," he said.

"That's very kind of you, Gideon," she remarked.

"Anna's mother doesn't speak much English," replied Gideon, "so it's hard for her to teach Anna to read."

"Well, Gideon," added Mama, "as you teach Anna to read, you will find that your own reading skills will improve too."

Gideon rushed to the barn filled with excitement. He had not realized that helping Anna would improve his own reading.

Soon Gideon was walking the dusty path to the Anderson farm. He carried the reading book and slate under his arm, whistling as he went along. Anna spotted him from the front porch. She waved and hurried to the gate to meet him.

"I've got the perfect spot for learning," she said excitedly. "It's where I go when I want to think."

Anna ushered Gideon into the barn, past the stalls, and up the ladder to the hayloft.

"This is a great place," he said.

"I told Mama you are going to teach me how to read," said Anna. "She's very glad about that."

"Tell me Anna," questioned Gideon, "How is it that you can speak such plain English when your folks are from Norway, and you don't go to school?"

"Oh, that's because Jake, Pa's hired man, teaches me. Ma and Pa have learned much English from Jake too, but he says children naturally pick up a new language. He says it's much harder when you are older," Anna replied.

Gideon settled himself in the hay and turned to the first lesson in the book.

"Sometimes Jake brings his daughter, Rebecca, when he comes to work. We like to play house under the big oak tree," added Anna.

Gideon laid the slate across his knees and took the slate pencil from his shirt pocket.

"We'll begin with the letters of the alphabet," said Gideon. "Let's begin with the letter *A*."

The sweet smell of hay made Anna's nose twitch as she tried to concentrate on the lesson. The children studied together until at last Anna's mother called from the barnyard, "Anna, time to eat dinner. It is noon time."

"I'd better run home," replied Gideon, "I'll be back tomorrow about the same time."

"Learning to read sure does make a person hungry," said Anna as the two children clambered down the ladder.

Gideon waved good-bye to Anna from the gate. Then he began the walk to his home. As he came around the bend in the road, he spotted Papa's wagon up ahead. Running with all his might, he managed to come within shouting distance. Josh stopped the wagon as he heard Gideon's call from behind.

"Papa, Papa," cried Gideon as he ran to meet the wagon. "How is your leg?"

"It's doing pretty well," Papa answered, "but the doctor says I must take it easy for about six weeks. By then it should be completely healed."

"That's good because your leg will be all better by my birthday," said Gideon.

Gideon climbed in the back of the wagon and Josh headed for home.

"I'm sorry I fell off the ladder, Gideon. Now all your birthday money has gone to pay the doctor bills."

"I've been thinking, Papa, since you need lots of rest, maybe you could listen to me practice my reading and help me with my spelling," Gideon said. "Mama says my reading is coming along great, but my spelling is terrible. She says if I want to be a writer some day, I need to improve myself. Mama says you are a better speller than she is."

Papa and the older boys laughed, for Gideon was so serious when he talked about being a writer.

"I'll be glad to help," said Papa enthusiastically.

Benjamin joined the conversation. "Gideon, if you really want to write, there's an opportunity for you."

"What do you mean?" he asked impatiently. "Tell me, tell me."

"Aunt Loraine gave me a copy of *Weekly* magazine. The editors of the magazine are sponsoring a writing contest," Benjamin said as he waved the magazine in the air.

"What kind of writing contest?" Gideon asked quickly.

"Oh, it's something called, *What Reading Means to Me*. Let me see if I can find the article," said Benjamin as he thumbed through the pages.

As Benjamin found the article, Josh pulled the wagon up to the front porch.

"Here, take the magazine in the house, Gideon. I'll help Papa inside while Josh tends to the horses," said Benjamin.

Gideon scurried inside the house. The aroma of fresh baked bread greeted his nose and he almost forgot about the magazine article. Mama and the three girls huddled around Papa, anxious to hear the news about his leg.

"Give Papa some breathing room," urged Mama. "And for goodness' sake, let him sit down!"

With the aid of the crutches, Papa swung himself across the living room floor. Hannah steadied the rocking chair as he lowered himself into the seat.

"We've prepared a special supper for your return, Papa," said Hannah.

In the center of the kitchen table sat a beautiful flower arrangement.

"See the flowers that Sarah so prettily arranged," said Mama, "and Rachel prepared your favorite dish -- chicken pot pie."

"Yes," said Rachel, "but we can all thank Hannah for making strawberry ice cream."

"Yahoo!" screamed Gideon in delight, for ice cream was a rare treat.

"I almost forgot," Benjamin remarked, "We visited with Aunt Loraine. She's doing fine and sends her love. She also sent a copy of *Weekly* magazine. The editors are sponsoring a contest for children in the Eastern United States. Aunt Loraine says she thinks that one of us children should give it a try."

Gideon's mind began to whirl as he thought about the contest. He handed Mama the magazine.

"Am I old enough to enter the contest, Mama?" Gideon asked hopefully.

"Let's see," said Mama as she searched through the article. She glanced over the article and said, "Why, yes, Gideon, it says here there are three age categories. Your age falls into the first category."

Mama proceeded to read the entire article aloud to the family.

"I see the contest winners will be announced just a week before your birthday, Gideon," Mama added. "Gideon, I think you should enter the contest," Mama said earnestly.

"Yes, yes" the other children chorused.

"I do think I will give it a try," said Gideon.

Mama thought to herself, *This could be the answer to my prayers. If Gideon wins, he will get his birthday book and his very own Bible.*

That ends chapter ten of our story. Now I want you to read some sentences that tell us a little bit about this chapter. Then I will show you a picture to go with the story.

(**Note**: We are no longer underlining the following sight words: *I, the, is, to, said, was, has, you, Papa, Mama, do, of, they, that, are, from, with, what, put, does, some, come, from, want, could, should, would, there, where, your, one, many, who,* and *water.* We are no longer dotting the letter *k* in the blend *ck.* We are no longer dotting the letter *y* as in *way* or the letter *w* as in *crow* or the letter *w* as in *write.* We are no longer drawing a gray ring around several beginning blends. We are no longer drawing a gray ring around several phonetic combinations such as *oo* as in *cook, oo* as in *room, ing, or, ow,* or *all.*)

"Gideon Gives a Lesson"

Gideon was slicing a piece of bread.

Mama said, "Why are you up so soon?"

"I am going to give Anna a reading lesson," said Gideon. "First I will do my chores."

Mama said, "Helping Anna to read will help you to read better too."

Gideon ran to the barn to do his chores. Soon he walked to Anna's farm. He had his slate under his arm. He had his reading book under his arm too.

Anna waved when she saw Gideon. Gideon and Anna sat in the hay. Gideon gave Anna her first lesson.

Soon it was time for Gideon to go home. As he walked home he saw Papa's wagon. Gideon ran to meet the wagon.

Gideon said, "How is your leg, Papa?"

"It is better," said Papa. "I must not use it for six weeks."

Papa was sad.

He said, "We had to pay the doctor. There is no money left for your birthday."

Gideon was not sad.

He said, "Papa, will you help me with my spelling? I want to be a writer some day."

Papa said, "I will be glad to help."

Benjamin told Gideon about the writing contest.

Now I will show you a picture of Gideon and Anna.

He had his slate under his arm.

He had his reading book under his arm too.

Anna waved when she saw Gideon.

Look at the picture. Where are Gideon and Anna sitting? That's right. They are sitting in the hayloft. What are they doing? Yes, Gideon is giving Anna a reading lesson.

Why doesn't Anna's mother or father teach her how to read? That's right. They are from another country and do not speak English very well. What did Gideon's mama say when he told her he was going to teach Anna how to read? Yes, she said Gideon's reading skills will improve as he helps Anna learn to read.

Next, I will write four of the sentences from the story you just read on index cards.

(Have the child watch as you write each word with a pen. Label the first card with the lesson number for future use.)

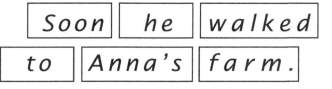

(We are no longer tracing over the letters of the words on the index cards with gray or black crayons, nor are we underlining the sight words or drawing gray rings around the letters. By using conventional text in these exercises, we hope to wean the child from the clues we have been using.)

Read the sentences. Very good! Now I will mix the cards, and you can put them in proper order to make the sentences again.

Now read the sentences.

(**Note**: <u>We are no longer using clues to assist the child with reading the copy work. It is important for the child to read the text located in this segment of the lesson even if he does not copy the sentences. This will give him an opportunity to practice reading text printed in a regular type.</u>)

Copy Work: (The copy work is optional for children who have difficulty with writing.) (You may now encourage the child to copy the sentences directly from the model below. If this is too difficult, continue as directed.)

I will write the sentences you just read on a piece of paper.

(Neatly write the sentences with a pen, paying close attention to letter spacing and formation.)

Now you can copy what I wrote.

Soon he walked to Anna's farm.

He had his slate under his arm. He had his reading book under his arm too.

Anna waved when she saw Gideon.

I would like for you to read the sentences once again. Very good!

Make up a few sentences about the chapter, "Gideon Gives a Lesson."

Tell me the sentences, and I will write them on a piece of paper. You may draw a picture to go with your sentences if you like. Now you can copy one of your sentences at the bottom of your picture.

(Draw lines if necessary for the child to write his sentence at the bottom of his picture.)

Read the sentences you dictated to me.

Now let's read a book together.

Lesson 107

Materials: reading manual, index cards, pen, and one construction paper circle.

Instructions: In today's lesson, the child will review the following sight words: *four, new, money, aunt, could, people, water,* and *about*. He will be introduced to the new sight word *very*. Prepare one construction paper circle with the new sight word written on it.

He will practice reading the following words printed with conventional type: *raining, draining, raking, baking, paving, waving, flapping, tapping, flagging, tagging, backing,* and *packing*.

You will read aloud chapter eleven from *Gideon's Gift*. The child will read the following adaptation from the chapter and complete a variety of exercises based on this adaptation.

Chapter title: *"Gideon's Essay"*

Story: *Gideon got up and did his chores. He went to Anna's house to give her a reading lesson.*

Anna said, "You seem happy today. What is up?"

"I am thinking about what I am going to write," said Gideon. "I am going to write an essay. I am going to enter it in a contest."

"I hope you win," said Anna.

Gideon helped Anna with her reading lesson. Then Gideon went home and had dinner. After dinner Papa helped Gideon with his spelling lesson.

Then Gideon got some paper from the desk. He got the pen and ink too. He put them all in a box.

Mama said, "What are you doing?"

Gideon said, "I am going to the barn to write."

After two hours Sarah went to find Gideon. Sarah found Gideon in the hay loft. Sarah read his essay.

Sarah said, "That is very good. Go and show it to Mama and Papa."

Mama and Papa read Gideon's essay. "This is very good," they said.

Mama said, "Josh will take us to town. You can mail the essay at the post office."

Dialogue: Read the sight words below.

four   *new*

money   aunt

could   people

water   about

Look at the word below. It is the word *very*. (Point to the word as you read it.)

very

Say *very* as I point to the word. Very good! Now read the sentence below that has the new sight word in it.

My aunt has a

very nice cat.

Let's add the new sight word to your *Sight Word Worm*.

Read the words below. These words are printed with regular type like you will find in most books. We have not used gray letters or bold black letters. We have not drawn gray rings around any of the letters either. Soon all of the words you will read will be printed with regular type.

raining	draining
raking	baking
paving	waving
flapping	tapping
flagging	tagging
backing	packing

Read the words below that will appear in the story.

(Assist the child with reading any difficult words.)

happy	write
essay	thinking
ink	paper
hours	enter
very	loft
office	contest
after	

Now I am going to read chapter eleven from *Gideon's Gift*. After I read the chapter, you will read some sentences about the chapter to me.

(Read the following story aloud to the child.)

Chapter Eleven

"Gideon's Essay"

The next day Gideon rose early to do his chores. After breakfast he headed to Anna's house to give her another reading lesson.

"You seem awfully cheerful today," exclaimed Anna, "What's up?"

"I'm just thinking," said Gideon.

"Thinking about what?" she asked.

"I'm thinking about *What Reading Means to Me*," he said.

"Why?" she questioned.

"Well, because I'm going to write an essay on *What Reading Means to Me.* Then I'm going to enter the essay in a contest."

"Oh," said Anna, "That does sound exciting. I hope you win the contest."

"I hope I win the contest too, but most of all, I want to be a writer. This is my first chance to write something really special."

Anna listened eagerly as her friend told of his plans for the future.

"I've written short pieces for Mama before, but I've never written something for other folks to read."

"I'm certain you will do well," said Anna, "You explain things so clearly. You are even able to teach me how to read."

"Speaking of that," said Gideon, "we had better begin the reading lesson. Papa says he will help me with my spelling when I get home. Then I'm going to work on my essay."

The two children worked diligently until at last it was time for Gideon to go home.

"I'll see you at church Sunday," Gideon called to Anna as he opened the gate to leave.

"Good bye," Anna called.

Soon Gideon was at home enjoying a pleasant dinner.

"After dinner I'll help you with your spelling, Gideon," said Papa.

"Okay, Papa," said Gideon with a bite of apple in his mouth.

After the dishes were cleared, Gideon brought the spelling book to the kitchen table. Papa helped him with his lessons for nearly an hour.

Papa asked, "How is that essay of yours coming along?"

"I've been thinking about it quite a bit," answered Gideon, "I'm going to begin writing this afternoon."

"It needs to arrive at the magazine office within ten days," said Papa. "First they have to read all of

the entries, judge them, and print the winning essays in the magazine. It takes some time to do all that."

"I didn't realize how much is involved," said Gideon. "I'll go work on it right away!"

Gideon collected his book and slate and returned them to the shelf. Then he carefully took several sheets of crisp, white paper from the writing desk. He gathered the pen and the ink bottle and placed them in a small box.

"What are you doing with all those things?" questioned Mama.

"I'm going to the barn to do my writing," he said, "I need to be alone where I can think."

Mama laughed to herself as he headed out the kitchen door.

"The boy is serious about his writing," Papa said to Mama, "I hope he won't be disappointed if he doesn't win the contest."

"Gideon and I have already talked about that," said Mama, "He knows that all he can do is try to do his best."

A couple of hours went by and still there was no sign of Gideon.

"I think you had better check on Gideon and take him a snack," Mama said to Sarah. "He's been in the barn working on his essay for some time."

Sarah grabbed an apple and a left over cinnamon roll from the breadbox. She went into the barn, but she couldn't find Gideon.

"Gideon," she shouted, "Where are you?"

"I'm up here," he said, "In the hayloft."

"In the hayloft!" she exclaimed, "Why on earth are you up there?"

"I'm writing my essay. I can be alone and think up here."

"Well, you've been alone for quite awhile. Would you like to have a snack?" asked Sarah.

"That sounds great!" said Gideon, "I didn't realize I'd been up here for so long."

Sarah climbed the ladder to the hayloft.

"Here's an apple and a cinnamon roll."

"Thanks, " said Gideon. I didn't realize it, but I'm hungry!"

"How's the essay coming along?" Sarah asked.

"Well, I'm afraid it's not very long, but I've written it over five times now."

"Do you mind if I read it?" she asked.

"Well, my spelling isn't too good, but go ahead."

Sarah read the essay and a smile lighted up her face.

"Gideon, this is wonderful. You are right, it isn't long, but it doesn't have to be long to be good. You have managed to say a lot with a few words."

Gideon beamed as he munched on his apple.

"You should take your paper to Mama and Papa and let them read it."

Gideon and Sarah made their way down the ladder. As they crossed the yard, Sarah said, "You really have done a fine job. Mama and Papa will be proud."

Gideon felt a warmth inside of him. Perhaps he did have a gift. Perhaps his gift was writing. His heart beat heavily as he followed Sarah into the kitchen.

"Show Mama and Papa what you've been up to for the past couple of hours," said Sarah.

"Yes, let's see, Gideon," said Mama.

"Well, I must tell you I need to copy it over, and I need help with my spelling," Gideon said quickly.

"That's okay, Son," said Papa, "those things are to be expected. Anyone who writes must carefully go over his paper and make corrections. That's a process we call *editing*."

Mama took the paper from Gideon and began to read it aloud.

What Reading Means to Me

An essay by Gideon David Harrison

It is a blessing to be able to read. Reading allows me to travel in another man's boots. I can feel his sorrow and his joy. I can feel his fear and his courage. I can feel his defeat and his victory. Reading allows me to visit far away places and times long ago. Reading takes me to the highest mountain or the lowest valley or the deepest sea. Reading helps me to know about God and His ways. As my mother says, "First you learn to read, and then you read to learn."

Mama breathed a sigh, "That's beautiful, Gideon, just beautiful. You have a special way with words."

"You've done a fine job, Gideon," Papa said encouragingly.

"Tomorrow I will give you some special embossed paper for you to copy your essay," said Mama. "Then Josh can take us into town to mail your letter at the post office."

Benjamin and the other children were listening at the doorway and said, "Oh, can we come too?"

"Yes," said Papa, "We can all go if you would like us to, Gideon."

"I would like that very much," said Gideon who was still blushing from all the praise.

"Well, let's hurry and have supper so we can get to bed early," said Mama. "Tomorrow will be a long day, and it's best to get an early start."

Gideon remarked, "That sounds like a good idea. I'm famished!"

That ends chapter eleven of our story. Now I want you to read some sentences that tell us a little bit about this chapter. Then I will show you a picture to go with the story.

"Gideon's Essay"

Gideon got up and did his chores.

He went to Anna's house to give her

a reading lesson.

Anna said, "You seem happy today.

What is up?"

"I am thinking about what I am

going to write," said Gideon. "I am

going to write an essay. I am going

to enter it in a contest."

"I hope you win," said Anna.

Gideon helped Anna with her

reading lesson. Then Gideon went

home and had dinner. After dinner

Papa helped Gideon with his spelling

lesson.

Then Gideon got some paper from the desk. He got the pen and ink too. He put them all in a box.

Mama said, "What are you doing?"

Gideon said, "I am going to the barn to write."

After two hours Sarah went to find Gideon. Sarah found Gideon in the hay loft. Sarah read his essay.

Sarah said, "That is very good. Go and show it to Mama and Papa."

Mama and Papa read Gideon's essay.

"This is very good," they said.

Mama said, "Josh will take us to town. You can mail the essay at the post office."

Now I will show you a picture of Gideon in the barn.

Look at the picture. Where is Gideon? That's right. He is up in the loft of his barn. What is he doing up there? Yes, he's writing an essay.

Do you know what an essay is? It is a short piece of writing about a certain topic. (Read Gideon's essay again, on page 481, and discuss it with your child.)

Next, I will write four of the sentences from the story you just read on index cards.

(Have the child watch as you write each word with a pen. Label the first card with the lesson number for future use.)

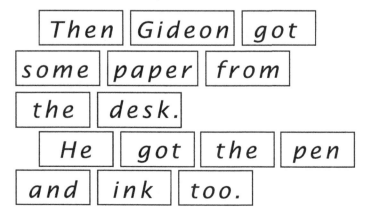

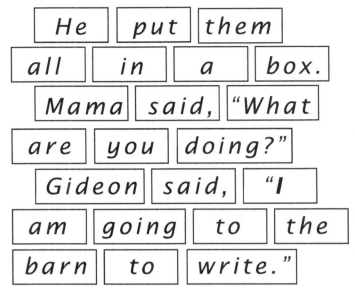

(We are no longer tracing over the letters of the words on the index cards with gray or black crayons, nor are we underlining the sight words or drawing gray rings around the letters. By using conventional text in these exercises, we hope to wean the child from the clues we have been using.)

Read the sentences. Great! Now I will mix the cards, and you can put them in proper order to make the sentences again.

Now read the sentences again.

(**Note**: We are no longer using clues to assist the child with reading the copy work. It is important for the child to read the text located in this segment of the lesson even if he does not copy the sentences. This will give him an opportunity to practice reading text printed in a regular type.)

Copy Work: (The copy work is optional for children who have difficulty with writing.) (You may now encourage the child to copy the sentences directly from the model below. If this is too difficult, continue as directed.)

I will write the sentences you just read on a piece of paper.

(Neatly write the sentences with a pen, paying close attention to letter spacing and formation.)

Now you can copy what I wrote.

Then Gideon got some paper from the desk. He got the pen and ink too. He put them all in a box.

Mama said, "What are you doing?"

Gideon said, "I am going to the barn to write."

I would like for you to read the sentences once again. Very good!

Why do you like to read? Make up a few sentences about why you like to read.

Tell me the sentences, and I will write them on a piece of paper. You may draw a picture to go with the sentences if you like. Now you can copy one of your sentences at the bottom of your picture.

(Draw lines if necessary for the child to write his sentence at the bottom of his picture.)

Read the sentences you dictated to me.

Now let's read a book together.

Lesson 108

Materials: reading manual, index cards, pen, and one construction paper circle.

Instructions: In today's lesson, the child will review the following sight words: *learn, caught, taught, four, new, money, aunt, very,* and *about.* He will be introduced to the new sight word *shoe.* Prepare one construction paper circle with the new sight word written on it.

He will practice reading the following words printed with conventional type: *walked, talked, showed, mowed, mopped, dropped, added, padded, painted, fainted, pasted,* and *wasted.*

You will read aloud chapter twelve from *Gideon's Gift.* The child will read the following adaptation from the chapter and complete a variety of exercises based on this adaptation.

Chapter title: *"Gideon Gets a Letter"*

Story: *The next day Gideon wrote his essay on nice paper. Josh hitched the horses to the wagon. He drove up to the house. Mama and Papa got in the wagon. The children got in the wagon.*

They picked up Anna at her house. Anna was very happy. She showed Gideon her new slate. Her papa got it in town.

"Look," said Anna, "Papa carved my name on the frame."

"That is very nice," said Gideon.

Rachel said, "I will read some more from my book."

Soon they drove into town. Mama and Gideon went to the post office. Gideon mailed his essay.

Many weeks went by. Soon it would be Gideon's birthday.

Papa said to Mama, "One of the horses needs a new shoe. Gideon and Josh and I will go to town. We will stop at the post office."

"Good," said Mama. "I want to know about the contest."

The next day they went to town. Gideon and Papa went to the post office.

Gideon got a letter. He opened the letter. Gideon had won the contest. He would get a book and a Bible. Gideon was too happy to speak. Gideon had found his gift.

Dialogue: Read the sight words below.

learn   caught

taught   four

new   money

aunt   very

about

Look at the new sight word below. It is the word *shoe*. (Point to the word as you read it.)

shoe

Say *shoe* as I point to the word. Very good!

Let's add the new sight word to your *Sight Word Worm*.

Read the words below. These words are printed with regular type like you will find in most books. We have not used gray letters or bold black letters. We have not drawn gray rings around any of the letters either. Soon all of the words you will read will be printed with regular type.

walked   talked

showed   mowed

mopped   dropped

added   padded

painted   fainted

pasted   wasted

Read the words below that will appear in the story.

(Assist the child with reading any difficult words.)

essay   children

nice   carved

horses   shoe

office   mailed

hitched   opened

Bible   contest

Now I am going to read chapter twelve from *Gideon's Gift*. After I read the chapter, you will read some sentences about the chapter to me.

(Read the following story aloud to the child.)

Chapter Twelve

"Gideon Gets a Letter"

The entire household was up early the next morning preparing for the trip to town. Papa was helping Gideon to correct the spelling in his essay and make certain he copied it properly onto the beautifully embossed paper. When it was all finished, Mama and Hannah read it over carefully to check for mistakes.

"It looks fine to me," said Mama.

Hannah agreed it couldn't look better. The family enjoyed a quick breakfast before they headed for town. Josh hitched the horses to the wagon and drove up to the house to pick up everyone.

"Papa, you certainly handle those crutches well. When you first began using them, you walked like a circus clown on stilts," said Hannah who couldn't keep from laughing.

"Well," said Papa, "it just goes to show that you *can* teach an old dog new tricks."

All the children laughed as they scrambled into the wagon.

"I brought along my library book, *Heidi*, to read aloud while we ride," said Rachel. We will begin after we pick up Anna. I promised her ma we would take her with us to town today. Her ma is going to take care of her sick aunt. She lives several miles away, and her pa will be working in the fields all day."

Anna came racing through the gate to meet the wagon. She could hardly wait to see Gideon. She wanted to show him her new slate her pa had bought while he was in town the day before. When Gideon had taught Anna her reading lessons, he had brought his slate along for her to use. Now she had her own slate.

"See my new slate!" Anna said excitedly. "Pa even carved my name in the wooden frame! And he carved hearts and flowers on it too."

"That's a beautiful slate," said Gideon. "And I see you've already been practicing your writing. It says, 'Thank you, Gideon, for teaching me to read.'"

Below the sentence, Gideon neatly wrote with Anna's slate pencil, *You are welcome, Anna.*

The two children laughed and everyone admired Anna's new slate.

"If everyone is ready," said Rachel, "I will continue reading from *Heidi*."

"We're ready," chorused the children.

"We last left Heidi high on the mountain with Peter the goatherd and Clara. Let's read on and find out what happens next."

The wagon drove into town just as Rachel was finishing another chapter.

"Will you read some more on the way home," begged Anna.

"Oh, yes," said Rachel, "for we must find out what happens to Clara!"

The first stop was at the post office. Mama went in with Gideon to mail his special letter to the *Weekly* magazine.

"Don't be so nervous, Gideon. The postal clerk is not going to read your essay!" said Mama.

Gideon smiled, "I know. I guess I'm afraid I won't win the contest."

"This is your first essay. Most writers must write many essays, poems, or stories, before they get even one published. But you have done the best job you can, and we can't ask for more than that," said Mama thoughtfully.

The postal clerk stamped the letter with his big rubber stamp. Mama paid the clerk, and she and Gideon went back to the wagon. Next, they stopped at the general store and everyone climbed out of the wagon. The girls admired the lovely fabrics, while the boys had fun playing checkers and investigating the pocketknives. Mama and Papa purchased the food stores they needed, and then the family headed home.

Several weeks passed in which life went on as usual. Gideon continued his reading and spelling lessons with Mama and Papa. He also continued to teach Anna to read. She was making excellent progress and her folks were overjoyed.

The children made one more trip to visit the book wagon in Elmerton. They returned the books they had borrowed and found new ones to take home. Anna was thrilled because now she could read some of the books by herself.

In only one week it would be Gideon's birthday. Anna's ma had asked if she could bake the cake as a thank you to Gideon for teaching Anna to read. Everyone knew Mrs. Anderson was a wonderful cook. She had won several prizes for her baking at last year's county fair.

Mama was making all the arrangements for Gideon's special birthday supper. The children were planning games, and Papa had carved a bear for Gideon out of wood. Each year Papa had carved a wooden animal for Gideon's birthday. This year Gideon would have eight figures in his collection. He kept them on a shelf in his room with his rocks and other treasures.

One evening Papa said to Mama, "One of the horses needs a new shoe. Tomorrow, Josh and Gideon and I will go to town to get it fitted. We will stop at the post office to see if Gideon has received a letter from the magazine."

"Oh, I'm glad you are going," sighed Mama with relief, "I don't think I could bear to wait any longer!"

Papa walked to the kitchen where Gideon was writing sentences on his slate.

"Josh and I have to go to town tomorrow. One of the horses needs a new shoe. How would you like to come along? We could drop by the post office."

Gideon's brown eyes grew wide.

"Oh, yes, I've been wondering about the contest," said Gideon.

"Then hurry to bed," said Papa. "We'll need to get an early start."

Gideon got in bed right away, but it was a long time before he could fall asleep. He kept wondering about the essay contest.

The next morning Gideon felt like he had hardly slept. However, he quickly jumped out of bed when he remembered the plans for the day. When he came downstairs, Mama and the girls already had a hot breakfast waiting. Sarah was packing a cold dinner in the hamper.

When they were ready to leave, Mama said encouragingly to Gideon, "Remember, winning is not the most important thing. You have done your best. If you do win, the glory belongs to the Lord, for he made you as you are. Remember, God gives different gifts to different people."

She kissed Gideon on the forehead as he opened the kitchen door.

"We'll have a good supper waiting for you when you get home," Mama called to them.

As the wagon pulled into town, Papa said to Josh, "Drop Gideon and me at the post office. We will join you at the blacksmith's shop when we are done."

Josh stopped in front of the post office and helped Papa down from the wagon.

"Are you sure you want to walk all the way to the blacksmith's shop, Papa?" asked Josh.

"Yes," answered Papa, "the exercise and fresh air will do me good."

Papa and Gideon entered the post office. Gideon stood in line while Papa rested on a bench by the door. Gideon saw a young girl with her mother at the clerk's window.

"Here's your letter from the *Weekly* magazine," the girl's mother said excitedly to her daughter.

The girl opened the letter and quickly read it to herself. Then she began to cry, "Oh, Mama I didn't win the contest."

"Now, now," comforted he mother, "There will be other contests to enter in the future."

As the girl and her mother left the post office, Gideon's heart sank. Perhaps he would receive a disappointing letter too. But there was no longer time to worry about it, for he was next in line.

"Do you have any mail for Gideon Harrison?" he asked rather shyly.

"Why, yes," the clerk answered cheerily. "Another letter from the *Weekly* magazine. We've been getting quite a few of these lately."

Gideon thanked the clerk and slowly walked over to sit on the bench by Papa.

"Well, open it, Gideon. The news is the same whether you open the letter or not. You may as well find out now," said Papa.

Careful not to tear the postmark, Gideon slit the envelope with his pocketknife. He took out the letter and slowly unfolded it. His eyes quickly scanned the sentences. No, he must have misread the letter. Slowly he read the letter again to himself. Then with tears of joy in his eyes, he handed the letter to Papa.

Gideon won the contest. Now he would have a birthday book after all. He would also have a beautiful Bible with gold edges for his very own. Aunt Loraine would be pleased too, for the library would receive the sum of $500 to buy new books.

The book wagon would bring those books to families like Gideon's who live far from a library.

Gideon was too happy to speak as his papa gave him a hug. And Gideon remembered the words of his mother once again, "First you learn to read, and then you read to learn." But the words she spoke that impressed him most of all kept ringing in his mind, *The glory belongs to the Lord.*

Gideon had found his gift.

That ends chapter twelve of our story. Now I want you to read some sentences that tell us a little bit about this chapter. Then I will show you a picture to go with the story.

(Note: The story is printed in conventional type without any clues.)

"Gideon Gets a Letter"

The next day Gideon wrote his essay on nice paper. Josh hitched the horses to the wagon. He drove up to the house. Mama and Papa got in the wagon. The children got in the wagon.

They picked up Anna at her house. Anna was very happy. She showed Gideon her new slate. Her papa got it in town.

"Look," said Anna, "Papa carved my name on the frame."

"That is very nice," said Gideon .

Rachel said, "I will read some more from my book."

Soon they drove into town. Mama and Gideon went to the post office. Gideon mailed his essay.

Many weeks went by. Soon it would be Gideon's birthday.

Papa said to Mama, "One of the horses needs a new shoe. Gideon and Josh and I will go to town. We will stop at the post office."

"Good," said Mama. "I want to know about the contest."

The next day they went to town. Gideon and Papa went to the post office.

Gideon got a letter. He opened the letter. Gideon had won the contest. He would get a book and a Bible. Gideon was too happy to speak. Gideon had found his gift.

Now I will show you a picture of Gideon.

Look at the picture. Where is Gideon? That's right. He is at the post office. What does he have in his hand? Yes, he has a letter in his hand from the magazine. What does the letter say? Has Gideon won the contest? Yes, Gideon won the contest.

Can you remember what Gideon's mother told him about winning the contest? That's right. She said even if he won, the glory belongs to the Lord, for He made him as he is.

Sometimes if we do something very well, we are proud of ourselves. We must always remember the Lord gives us our special abilities, and we must thank Him for the gifts he has given us. We must also remember to use our gifts wisely, so we can help others and bring glory to His name.

Next, I will write five of the sentences from the story you just read on index cards.

(Have the child watch as you write each word with a pen. Label the first card with the lesson number for future use.)

He	opened	the

letter.

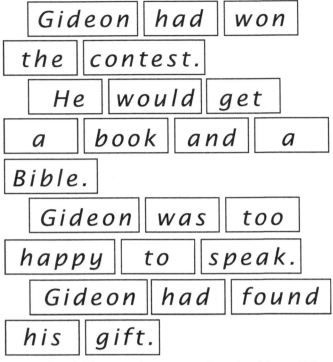

Gideon had won the contest. He would get a book and a Bible. Gideon was too happy to speak. Gideon had found his gift.

Read the sentences. Great! Now I will mix the cards, and you can put them in proper order to make the sentences again.

Now read the sentences again.

Copy Work: (The copy work is optional for children who have difficulty with writing.) (You may now encourage the child to copy the sentence directly from the model below. If this is too difficult, continue as directed.)

I will write the sentences you just read on a piece of paper.

(Neatly write the sentences with a pen, paying close attention to letter spacing and formation.)

Now you can copy what I wrote.

He opened the letter. Gideon had won the contest. He would get a book and a Bible.

Gideon was too happy to speak. Gideon had found his gift.

I would like for you to read the sentences once again. Very good!

Make up a few sentences about the chapter, "Gideon Gets a Letter."

Tell me the sentences, and I will write them on a piece of paper. You may draw a picture to go with your sentences if you like. Now you can copy one of your sentences at the bottom of your picture.

(Draw lines if necessary for the child to write his sentence at the bottom of his picture.)

Read the sentences you dictated to me.

Now let's read a book together.

(Please refer to the information located in the Appendix to assist you with developing further reading lessons. Visit our website at **www.ValerieBendt.com** for information concerning future publications.)

Appendix

The First Book Wagon in America

The First Book Wagon in America

Since homeschooling has become a popular means of educating children, the public libraries find themselves loaded with eager families making good use of their facilities. This fact spurred me to investigate the history of America's public libraries. The original story contained within this reading manual, entitled *Gideon's Gift*, was inspired by a bit of interesting information gained while I was conducting my research.

In 1905, Mary Lemist Titcomb, librarian of the Washington County Free Library in Hagerstown, Maryland, proposed a new idea to increase library service. It occurred to her that a delivery wagon could be outfitted with shelves mounted in cabinets on the sides of the wagon. These shelves could house a collection of books which would then be easily transported to patrons in rural areas. Thus the bookmobile was born.

In April of 1905, Mr. Joshua Thomas began driving the book wagon, pulled by two horses, on its well planned route and dispensing the books. He was of invaluable service to the Hagerstown Library in the early years of the book wagon. Unfortunately, the original book wagon was destroyed in August of 1910 while crossing a train track. The driver and both horses survived the accident.

You can read more about the first book wagon and about other interesting material relating to the public libraries in America by checking out the book at your local library entitled, *The Library in America, A Celebration in Words and Pictures.*

Additional Phonics Rules

As your child reads other stories and books aloud to you, use this opportunity to teach him new rules he will encounter. For example, if he comes across an unfamiliar word such as *nation,* use this word to teach the *tion* ending. On a piece of paper or index cards, write the word *nation* and several other words that also have the *tion* ending such as *vacation, creation, action* and so forth. Circle the *tion* ending in each word. Have the child copy the words for better retention.

You may find that although you have not taught your child a particular rule, he can read words containing this rule. As we mentioned in the introduction, part of learning to read is being able to predict what word will come next in a sentence. The child will make use of the rules he does know, coupled with the meaning derived from the text, to decode an unfamiliar word. If your child seems to glide effortlessly over new words, do not make a lesson out of the words. On the other hand, if he seems to be struggling with new words, take a few minutes to break these words into parts. You may also want to use the print clues that we used in the manual to assist him in reading unfamiliar words. The following is a listing of rules not covered in this manual. Use these rules as needed to teach new words that your child encounters.

tion: nation, creation

sion: vision, mission

tain: mountain, captain

ture: nature, rapture

eigh: eight, sleigh

y: gym, system

be: behold, belong

ful: joyful, playful

sch: school, schooner

ch: chorus, choir, ache

ou: touch, young

u: pull, full, bush, push

al: also, almost

ough: enough, rough

dge: fudge, badge

g: age, huge

w(ar): war, warm, ward

w(or): worm, world

ought: bought, fought

chr: Christ, chrome

ey: key, honey, monkey

ey: obey, prey

au: fault, haul

o: love, other

ew: flew, crew, drew

ear: earth, pearl, early, search

a: asleep, awake, apart, alone

wa: wash, wand, wad

gn: gnat, gnash, gnome

str: stream, stripe

thr: three, thrill

spr: spread, spray

scr: screen, scratch

squ: squish, squid, squash

spl: splatter, splash

tw: twist, twig

err: merry, berry, cherry

Books for Parents to Read Aloud to the Child

On the following pages you will find lists of books children delight in listening to as an adult reads them aloud. You may use these books as a springboard for further reading lessons. Read aloud a chapter or portion from a selected book. Then devise sentences for the child to read which simply convey the meaning of the portion read aloud. These sentences may be a retelling of one whole book or one chapter of a book (depending upon the length of the book and whether or not it has chapters). These simple sentences may be a retelling of only one small portion of what the parent has read aloud. A complete summary of the material read is not necessary or even desirable. The focus should be on the passages the child finds particularly interesting. The sentences formulated by the parent may be as few as five or as many as twenty-five. The reading ability and attention span of the child should be considered when devising reading lessons.

You may wish to use the print clues presented in this manual to assist the child in reading the sentences you create. If the child is able, have him read the sentences you write neatly on a piece of paper. If this still proves difficult for him, write the sentences with crayons as shown in the lessons. You may still find it helpful to write a few select sentences on index cards which the child can arrange in proper order. (Remember to keep index cards from each sentence separate.) This offers an opportunity to discuss punctuation and capitalization. Some children need to be physically involved in order to learn. Being able to manipulate the index cards helps to fill this need.

Please refer to *Honey for a Child's Heart,* by Gladys Hunt, and *Books Children Love,* by Elizabeth Wilson, for an extensive list of good reading material.

Books for Parents to Read Aloud

Books **without** chapters.
These are books that can be read in a single sitting:

Song and Dance Man
> Karen Ackerman

Madeline
Madeline's Rescue, and others
> Ludwig Bemelmans

The Ox-Cart Man
> Barbara Cooney

Corduroy
> Don Freeman

Bedtime for Frances
Baby Sister for Frances
Bread and Jam for Frances, and others
> Russel Hoban

Angelina
Angelina Ballerina
Angelina's Birthday Surprise, and others
> Katharine Holabird

Froggy Gets Dressed
Let's Go Froggy
Froggy Learns to Swim
Froggy Plays Soccer, and others
> Jonathan London

Make Way for Ducklings
    Robert McCloskey

The Tale of Custard the Dragon
Custard the Dragon and the Wicked Knight
    These stories are told in verse and are especially pleasing to hear.
    Ogden Nash

Buford the Little Bighorn
Cyrus the the Unsinkable Sea Serpent
How Droofus the Dragon Lost His Head, and others
    Bill Peet

The Tale of Peter Rabbit
The Tale of Benjamin Bunny
The Tale of Flopsy Bunnies
Johnny Town Mouse, and others
    Beatrix Potter

Curious George
Curious George Rides a Bike, and others
    Hans A. Rey

Brave Irene
    William Steig

Henry Explores the Jungle
Henry Explores the Mountain, and others
    Mark Taylor

The Popcorn Dragon
    Jane Thayer

Thy Friend Obadiah

Obadiah the Bold

Rachel and Obadiah, and others

    Brinton Turkle

The Biggest Bear

    Lynd Ward

County Fair

Dance at Grandpa's

Farmer Boy's Birthday

Going to Town

Winter Days in the Big Woods

Winter on the Farm, and others

These books are part of the *My First Little House Series*. They are beautiful picture books which simply retell an event from the original books by Laura Ingalls Wilder. Very well done.

    Laura Ingalls Wilder

Harry the Dirty Dog

No Roses for Harry, and others

    Gene Zion

Least of All

    Carol Purdy

Books for Parents to Read Aloud

Books **with** chapters.
Each chapter can be read in a single sitting:

The Courage of Sarah Noble
> Alice Dalgliesh

My Father's Dragon, and others
> Ruth Gannett

Betsy-Tacy
Betsy and Tacy go over the Big Hill
Betsy, Tacy, and Tib, and others
> Maud Hart Lovelace

Sarah Plain and Tall
Skylark
> Patricia MacLachlan

All-of-a-Kind Family
All-of-a-Kind Family Downtown, and others
> Sydney Taylor

The Boxcar Children
Surprise Island
The Yellow House Mystery, and others
> Gertrude Chandler Warner

Charlotte's Web
Stuart Little
The Trumpet of the Swan
> E.B. White

Little House in the Big Woods

Little House on the Prairie

Farmer Boy

On the Banks of Plum Creek

By the Shores of Silver Lake

The Long Winter

Little Town on the Prairie

These Happy Golden Years

The First Four Years

   Laura Ingalls Wilder

Easy Readers

Books written on an easy reading level for beginning readers:

HarperCollins publishes a series of books entitled *I Can Read.* There are four levels in this series of readers. The first and simplest is called, *My First I Can Read.* Next comes *I Can Read* levels 1, 2, and 3. The highest level books in this series are called *I Can Read Chapter Books.* I've included some titles in each category. There are over 200 titles in this series of books. Please visit their website at **www.harperchildrens.com** for more titles.

My First I Can Read:

Biscuit

Biscuit Finds a Friend

Bathtime for Biscuit

Biscuit's New Trick, and

Biscuit Wants to Play
   Alyssa Satin Capucilli

Go Away, Dog
   Joan L. Nodset

How Many Fish?
   Caron Lee Cohen

I See, You Saw
   Nurit Karlin

Sid and Sam
   Nola Buck

Splish, Splash!
   Sarah Weeks

Thump and Plunk
   Janice May Udry

Oh, Cats!
   Nola Buck

Mine's the Best
   Crosby Bonsall

I Can Read Level 1:

Silly Tilly's Valentine
   Lillian Hoban

Danny and the Dinosaur go to Camp
   Syd Hoff

Harry and the Lady Next Door
   Gene Zion

Albert the Albatross
   Syd Hoff

All of Our Noses Are Here and
Other Noodle Tales
   Alvin Schwartz

And I Mean It, Stanley
   Crosby Bonsall

Captain Cat
   Syd Hoff

Stuart at the Fun House
Stuart at the Library,
and others
   Susan Hill

Barkley
   Syd Hoff

Barney's Horse
   Syd Hoff

Cat and Dog
   Else Holmelund Minarik

The Fire Cat
   Esther Averill

Digby
   Barbara Shook Hazen

I Can Read Level 2:

Arthur's Honey Bear
Arthur's Great Big Valentine
Silly Tilly's Thanksgiving Dinner,
and others
   Lillian Hoban

A Bargain for Frances
   Russel Hoban

Mouse Soup
Frog and Toad are Friends, and
others
   Arnold Lobel

Buzby
   Julia Hoban

Amelia Bedelia
Come Back Amelia Bedelia, and
others
   Peggy Parish

Aunt Eater Loves a Mystery
Aunt Eater's Mystery Vacation
and others
   Doug Cushman

The Case of the Two Masked
Robbers
   Lillian Hoban

The Great Snake Escape
   Molly Coxe

I Can Read Level 3:

The Josephina Story Quilt
Eleanor Coerr

The Boston Coffee Party
Doreen Rappaport

The 18 Penny Goose
Sally M. Walker

The Big Balloon Race
Eleanor Coerr

Blast Off! Poems About Space
Lee Bennett Hopkins

Clipper Ship
Thomas P. Lewis

Daniel's Duck
Clyde Robert Bulla

Dust for Dinner
Ann Turner

Clara and the Bookwagon
Nancy Smiler Levinson

Weather
Lee Bennett Hopkins

I Can Read Chapter Books

The Animal Rescue Club
John Himmelman

First Flight: The Story of Tom Tate and the Wright Brothers
George Shea

Prairie School
Avi

Abigail Takes the Wheel
Avi

Little House Chapter Books

These stories have been adapted from the *Little House* books for young readers.

Animal Adventures
Christmas Stories
Hard Times on the Prairie
Laura and Nellie

Laura's Ma
Laura's Pa
Little House Farm Days
Little House Friends
Pioneer Sisters
School Days, and others.
Laura Ingalls Wilder

Encouraging Your Child to Write His Own Readers

In a number of lessons, the child was asked to write a sentence or a story about a picture he had drawn. In other lessons he was asked to write sentences about the story you read aloud. (These were the lessons centered around the story of *Gideon's Gift*.)

Now you may encourage your child to write his own story. This can serve as his personal reader. Allow the child to dictate a story to you. Print it neatly on large lined paper or blank paper. Assist him as needed with reading the story. Use gray and black crayons to trace over the letters in the words that he finds difficult. (For example, the long vowels are traced with a black crayon to make them bold, and the short vowels are traced with a gray crayon to make them soft.) Use this opportunity to teach new sounds, such as *tion* as in *nation*. (See list of additional phonics rules on page 496.)

If your child struggles with writing a story, have him retell a favorite Bible story or write about something he likes to do. It is helpful to explain to the child that a story has a beginning, middle, and end. In the beginning, one or more characters are introduced. Details about the characters are included here. In the middle, the main character or characters are faced with some problem or mystery. Details concerning this problem or mystery continue to be presented throughout the middle. The end concerns itself with solving the character's problem. "And they all lived happily ever after." Most stories written for children and by children end on a happy note. And that's basically all there is to writing a story.

Your child's own creativity and life experience will give his story personality. He may want to copy his story from your written model and/or illustrate it. It is exciting for a child to be able to read a story on his own, especially a story that he has written. For further ideas to make your child's story into a book, see my book *Creating Books With Children.* For additional ideas to encourage your child to love to read see my book *For the Love of Reading.* (Visit my website for a listing and description of all my books at **www.ValerieBendt.com**.)

May the Lord bless you as you seek His best for your family!

what	was	is
do	I	the
to	you	has

has	do	I
you	is	to
the	what	was

Sight Word Worm Pattern

Cut colored construction paper circles from these patterns. Use the small circle for the sight words and the large circle for the head.

You will need approximately 60 small circles and 4 large circles. You may want to cut ten small circles of six different colors. It is helpful to cut these in advance, although you will need only a few small circles at one time.

You will make four *Sight Word Worms* during the course of the program. These offer a fun and easy way to review the sight words. There are 56 sight words in all. Six of these are proper names. Each *Sight Word Worm* can be made up of 14 small circles and one large circle.

You will also need two sheets of poster board (22" x 28"). You will cut each of these in half, (14" x 22"), thereby giving you four sheets on which to make 4 *Sight Word Worms.* Initially you will only need 1/2 sheet of poster board, but it is good to have these materials in advance.

Practice placing one large head circle and 14 small body circles on 1/2 sheet of poster board to see how they will fit. You will need to slightly overlap the small circles. Your *Sight Word Worms* can be displayed in your "schoolroom."

Pattern for body. Sight words are written on these body parts. Glue circles on paper or poster board and use a marker to draw feet as shown in diagram below.

Pattern for head. Add eyes, nose, mouth, and antenna as shown in diagram below. (Antenna can be drawn with a marker or made from pipe cleaners.)

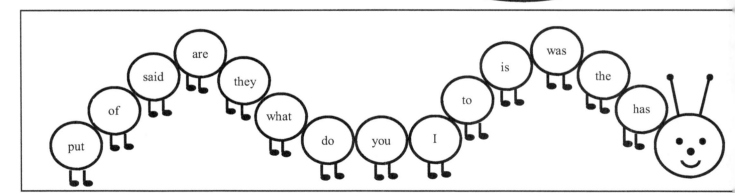

Photocopy or trace. Do not cut page out of book.

the	what	you	(free)
has	they	are	to
is	(free)	do	was
of	put	said	I

free	do	to	has
the	you	said	put
was	is	free	of
they	I	what	are

CPSIA information can be obtained at www.ICGtesting.com
Printed in the USA
LVOW02s1209190114

370043LV00001B/78/P